Women and Yugoslav Partisans

This book focuses on one of the most remarkable phenomena of World War II: the mass participation of women, including numerous female combatants, in the communist-led Yugoslav Partisan resistance. Drawing on an array of sources – archival documents of the Communist Party and Partisan army, wartime press, Partisan folklore, participant reminiscences, and Yugoslav literature and cinematography – this study explores the history and postwar memory of the phenomenon. More broadly, it is concerned with changes in gender norms caused by the war, revolution, and establishment of the communist regime that claimed to have abolished inequality between the sexes. The first archive-based study on the subject, *Women and Yugoslav Partisans* uncovers a complex gender system in which revolutionary egalitarianism and peasant tradition interwove in unexpected ways.

Jelena Batinić is currently a Fellow in the Thinking Matters Program at Stanford University. She is a historian specializing in modern Eastern Europe, World War II, and gender history. Her work has been published in edited volumes and journals including the *Journal of International Women's Studies* and *Journal of Women's History*. She has been a Mellon/ACLS Recent Doctoral Recipients Fellow and Postdoctoral Fellow in Stanford University's Introduction to the Humanities Program.

Women and Yugoslav Partisans

A History of World War II Resistance

JELENA BATINIĆ

Stanford University

CAMBRIDGE
UNIVERSITY PRESS

CAMBRIDGE
UNIVERSITY PRESS

University Printing House, Cambridge CB2 8BS, United Kingdom

One Liberty Plaza, 20th Floor, New York, NY 10006, USA

477 Williamstown Road, Port Melbourne, VIC 3207, Australia

4843/24, 2nd Floor, Ansari Road, Daryaganj, Delhi - 110002, India

79 Anson Road, #06-04/06, Singapore 079906

Cambridge University Press is part of the University of Cambridge.

It furthers the University's mission by disseminating knowledge in the pursuit of
education, learning and research at the highest international levels of excellence.

www.cambridge.org
Information on this title: www.cambridge.org/9781107463073

© Jelena Batinić 2015

First published 2015
First paperback edition 2017

A catalogue record for this publication is available from the British Library

Library of Congress Cataloging in Publication data
Batinić, Jelena.
Women and Yugoslav partisans : a history of World War II resistance /
Jelena Batinić (Stanford University).
pages   cm
Includes bibliographical references and index.
ISBN 978-1-107-09107-8 (hardback)
1. World War, 1939–1945 – Underground movements – Yugoslavia.
2. World War, 1939–1945 – Participation, Female.   3. Women guerrillas –
Yugoslavia – History.   4. Women soldiers – Yugoslavia – History.   5. World War,
1939–1945 – Women – Yugoslavia.   6. World War, 1939–1945 – Social aspects –
Yugoslavia.   7. Sex role – Yugoslavia – History.   8. Collective memory –
Yugoslavia – History.   9. War and society – Yugoslavia – History.
10. Yugoslavia – Social conditions.   I. Title.
D802.Y8B38   2015
940.53´497082–dc23   2015003331

ISBN 978-1-107-09107-8 Hardback
ISBN 978-1-107-46307-3 Paperback

Contents

List of Illustrations   *page* vi

Note on Translation   vii

Acknowledgments   ix

Introduction   1

1   "To the People, She Was a Character from Folk
    Poetry": The Party's Mobilizing Rhetoric   26

2   The "Organized Women": Developing the AFW   76

3   The Heroic and the Mundane: Women in the Units   124

4   The Personal as a Site of Party Intervention: Privacy
    and Sexuality   168

5   After the War Was Over: Legacy   213

    Conclusion   258

Selected Bibliography   271

Index   283

Illustrations

1 Map: The partition of Yugoslavia, 1941   *page* 19
2 Villagers of Glamoč (Bosnia and Herzegovina)
   attending a Partisan cultural event, 1942   46
3 Kata Pejnović, circa 1945   56
4 Women carrying food to Partisans, n.d.   99
5 A peasant woman speaking at an AFW conference, Croatia,
   May 1944   108
6 Fighters of the 2nd Batallion, the 4th Montenegrin
   Proletarian Brigade, with the party leader Ivan Milutinović,
   in Janj (Bosnia), 1942   131
7 A column of fighters, the 3rd Sandžak Proletarian
   Brigade, in the area of Prijepolje-Pljevlja-Bijelo Polje
   (Montenegro), 1943   141
8 Savka Bursać, nurse of the 6th Krajina Division, bandaging
   a wounded soldier, Vučja Gora near Travnik, Herzegovina,
   January 1945   145
9 A Partisan nurse tending a fighter of the 6th Lika Division
   at the Srem/Srijem (Syrmian) front, 1945   162
10 A Partisan girl from the mountain of Kozara (*Kozarčanka*),
   winter 1943/1944   227
11 Creating the icon: Slavica with Marin. *Slavica*, dir.
   Vjekoslav Afrić, 1947   233

Note on Translation

All translations from the South Slavic languages to English are mine unless otherwise indicated. In contrast to English, there are three grammatical genders in Bosnian/Croatian/Serbian. There are no satisfactory English equivalents for nouns that indicate a person's sex, such as *partizan* (Partisan, male) and *partizanka* (Partisan, female), or *drug* (comrade, male) and *drugarica* (comrade, female). I indicate a person's sex by adding woman/female or man/male to the noun, for example, Partisan women, male comrades, female fighters.

There are two terms, *komitet* and *odbor*, in Bosnian/Croatian/Serbian that correspond to the English word "committee." In World War II, the term *komitet(i)* was reserved for party committees, while *odbor(i)* was used for organs of the Antifascist Front of Women (AFW) and the people's government. To mark the distinction, I have decided to keep the English "committee" when referring to *komitet*, and to use "council" for *odbor*. The following text thus mentions "party committees," "AFW councils," and "national-liberation councils."

For translations of South Slavic national and geographic appellations, I have decided to adopt the system proposed by Ivo Banac.[1] For adjectives, Croat, Serb, and Slovene indicate one's ethnonational origin, for example, Croat leader, Serb woman, Slovene politician. By contrast, the adjectives Croatian, Serbian, and Slovenian refer to the *land*, the *language*, and other notions that assume a long history, for example, Serbian army,

---

[1] Ivo Banac, *The National Question in Yugoslavia: Origins, History, Politics* (Ithaca, NY: Cornell University Press, 1984), 17–18.

Croatian coast, Slovenian language. For nouns, I use Serb(s), Croat(s), and Slovene(s). Therefore, Croatian Serb refers to a person of Serb ethnonational extraction who lives in Croatia; Bosnian Croat refers to an ethnically Croat person who is from Bosnia, and so on.

Acknowledgments

This study has its origins in a seminar paper I wrote as a student more than a decade ago. Over the years, as the paper evolved into a book manuscript, I have incurred many debts. I have had the great fortune of working with exceptional scholars at Stanford University. My deepest gratitude goes to Norman Naimark, who encouraged me to pursue this project and provided guidance along the way. An outstanding mentor and exemplary historian, he has played an invaluable role in my intellectual development. I have learned a great deal about gender and war in Eastern Europe from Katherine Jolluck. I thank her for her careful reading of multiple drafts and many insightful suggestions, which have significantly improved this study. James J. Sheehan inspired rigor in my analysis and gave me valuable advice on the manuscript.

My thanks are due to the two anonymous readers for Cambridge University Press for their excellent comments; they encouraged me to situate this study in a broader comparative context than I had originally intended. A supportive community of graduate students and colleagues at Stanford helped me refine my ideas at various stages of this project. Daniela Blei, Jovana Knezevic, Yair Mintzker, Julia Sarreal, and Kari Zimmerman read chapter drafts and I thank them for their suggestions. I am grateful for the encouragement and constructive feedback I received at this work's inception, at the Ohio State University, from Leila Rupp, Katherine David-Fox, Nicholas Breyfogle, and Dorothy Noyes.

The research for this project was carried out in several archives and libraries in the Balkans and the United States, and I owe special gratitude to their respective staffs. I spent many months in the Military Archive (formerly known as the Archive of the Institute of Military History), the Archive of Yugoslavia, and the National Library in Belgrade. This book would not have been possible without the assistance of the archivists and librarians who work there. The staff of the Museum of Yugoslav History helped me search through thousands of wartime photos. At Jugoslovenska Kinoteka I received assistance with illustrations and permissions; I remember Marijana Cukućan's kindness with particular gratitude. In the United States, I conducted research in the Hoover Institution Archives and enjoyed access to the vast resources of the Hoover and Stanford libraries.

For generously supporting the writing of this study I am indebted to the American Council of Learned Societies and the Andrew Mellon Foundation, as well as the Humanities Center and Michelle R. Clayman Institute for Gender Research at Stanford University. Research for this project was made possible by grants and fellowships I received from Stanford University's History Department; Center for Russian, East European, and Eurasian Studies; Freeman Spogli Institute for International Studies; School of Humanities and Sciences; Vice Provost for Graduate Education; and the Thinking Matters Program.

Finally, and most of all, I thank my family members for their unconditional support. They went with me through all the frustrations of book writing without experiencing its many rewards. I am grateful to my parents, Branka and Željko Batinić, for their endless belief in me. Throughout the writing process, my sons, Konstantin and Filip, were a source of much-needed perspective. I thank them for their patience during the long hours I spent working on this book. My husband, Dušan, has been my greatest supporter and best critic. His understanding, encouragement, and sense of humor helped sustain me through this project.

Introduction

It was a strange yet most impressive sight when girls of eighteen and twenty went into battle with men.... Some of them had rifles slung across their shoulders, a few bore stretchers, and others carried first aid kit[s]. They were scattered throughout the ranks among the men, beautiful, healthy, strong girls, both dark and fair ... the reality seemed fantastic.

(Major William Jones, the first British officer to parachute to Tito's Partisans)[1]

Yesterday we had our second black day, we had to leave many dead and badly wounded on a bridge. And when you consider that we suffered these losses at the hands of a *female* Partisan company, it really makes you want to throw up.

(Lieutenant Peter Geissler of the Wehrmacht's 714th Infantry Division, in a 1942 letter from Bosnia)[2]

[Partisan] women showed extraordinary bravery in these struggles and they freely charged at our machine guns. Before the battle began, the women had been dressed in black, but after the first shots they threw away their black overcoats and all of a sudden they were in white overcoats. It has been noticed that many were pregnant among the killed women and girls, although, according to the seized acts of the Communist archive, it

---

[1] Major William Jones, *Twelve Months with Tito's Partisans* (Bedford: Bedford Books, 1946), 78.
[2] As quoted in Ben Shepherd, *Terror in the Balkans: German Armies and Partisan Warfare* (Cambridge, MA: Harvard University Press, 2012), 209. Italics in the original.

was strictly forbidden that women get pregnant in order to have as many
of them as possible participating in combat.

(Report to the Serbian Ministry of Interior, 17 November 1943)[3]

Who could've known last year, comrades,	*Oj drugovi, ko bi znao lani*
That girls would become Partisans.	*Da će cure biti Partizani.*

(Wartime folk song)

When, in 1943, William Jones saw Yugoslav Partisan women in action,
the sight struck him as strange, impressive, and fantastic. Such sights
were no less fantastic in the eyes of Partisans' adversaries, who sometimes
struggled to rationalize the presence of female warriors on the battlefield,
as the preceding quotes suggest. The unlikely scene of wardrobe change
at the beginning of the battle, after which the women, "many of them
pregnant," charged at machine guns, seems like a bizarre ritual. Nor were
male Partisans themselves always sure how to understand the appearance
of female soldiers in their units. Who, indeed, could have known that
women would become fighters?

The mass participation of women in the communist-led Yugoslav
Partisan resistance is one of the most remarkable phenomena of the
Second World War. According to official figures, by the end of the
war two million women had been involved in the Partisan movement.
Some 100,000 served in the Partisan army – a degree of female military involvement unprecedented and unrepeated in the region.[4] Why and
how did the Partisans recruit women? What made these women – the
majority of them peasants from underdeveloped areas with strong patriarchal traditions – decide to take up arms? More intriguing still: What
made their transformation into warriors acceptable to the peasant-filled

---

[3] Report on the struggle between the Partisans and the Serbian gendarmerie under the collaborationist puppet government of Milan Nedić, 18 October, 1943. In Bosa Cvetić et al.,
eds., *Žene Srbije u NOB* (Beograd: Nolit, 1975), 686.

[4] It is difficult to verify the preceding figures. In the past two decades, scholars have revised
some official estimates of the communist era concerning World War II in the region, but
not those on women's participation in the war. Extant historical records about women
in the Partisan movement are incomplete at best. However, they do suggest that it is
safe to talk about tens of thousands of female Partisans, an unprecedented mass mobilization of women in the rear support system, and a truly extraordinary wartime phenomenon. Official figures taken from Dušanka Kovačević, *Women of Yugoslavia in
the National Liberation War* (Belgrade: Jugoslovenski Pregled, 1977), 51; *Leksikon
Narodnooslobodilačkog rata i revolucije u Jugoslaviji 1941–1945* (Belgrade: Narodna
knjiga, 1980), vol. 2, p. 1251.

Partisan ranks? How were they integrated into the movement and how were their relations with men regulated? Last but not least, what was the legacy of women's mass military and political mobilization in the region? To try to answer these questions, this study explores the history and postwar memory of the phenomenon. It is, more broadly, concerned with changes in gender norms caused by the war, revolution, and the establishment of the communist regime, which claimed to have solved the "woman question" and instituted equality between the sexes.

The Yugoslav Partisans, led by Josip Broz Tito, were probably the most successful antifascist resistance movement in Europe. Championing a supraethnic patriotism in a region troubled by interethnic strife, they managed to win authentic popular support, seize power, and liberate a significant portion of the country on their own. Their values were to dominate Yugoslavia's official culture for decades afterward. Consequently, their wartime exploits have attracted some scholarly attention in the West. Yet gender has been paid scant attention in the existing literature, which tends to overlook its centrality for the Partisans' resistance strategy and nation-building practices.

The present work draws on the scholarship on gender and war. Scholars have noted, first, that total war of the twentieth century "acted as a clarifying moment, one that has revealed systems of gender in flux and thus highlighted their workings." War, in other words, is a good place to study gender. Second, emergency conditions of total war destabilized all social arrangements and opened up possibilities "to either alter or reinforce existing notions of gender, the nation, and the family."[5] This destabilization was perhaps nowhere more obvious than in Yugoslavia, which, occupied and dismembered, saw a war of resistance against the invaders together with an explosion of interethnic violence, a civil war, and a social revolution. Women's mass military engagement took place in such turmoil, posing a challenge to traditional gender norms. Accordingly, the definition of womanhood became one of the focal points of contestation among multiple rival factions. While anticommunist groups tried to discredit the Partisans by making the female fighter a favorite target of their propaganda, Partisan leaders took pride in proclaiming the birth of the "new woman" and, with her, the dawn of a new era of equality. The present study explores this flux of the gender system, the ways that the Communist Party attempted to stabilize and fix it, and the ways it was recast in the process.

---

[5] Margaret R. Higonnet et al., "Introduction," in *Behind the Lines: Gender and the Two World Wars*, ed. Margaret R. Higonnet et al. (New Haven, CT: Yale University Press, 1987), 5.

The reformulation of gender norms during the war could be registered on three levels, the level of political rhetoric, the level of institutions, and the level of daily practice, and this study addresses each. The three-level approach allows me to examine what the Partisan leadership said about gender, whether and how this language corresponded to party policy and the movement's institutional setup, and how these policies and institutions affected the daily lives of men and women in the movement. It also allows me to investigate the ways that ordinary men and women on the ground reacted to and shaped Partisan gender politics from below.

The study begins by analyzing the *rhetoric* that Partisan leaders devised to recruit women and justify their active participation in the movement. It shows how their strategy rested upon a skillful combination of traditional Balkan culture with a revolutionary idiom. In its appeals to women, the party consistently stressed its dedication to women's emancipation and gender equality. Parallel to such statements it also drew on patriarchal folk traditions. For modern purposes of mass mobilization, the communists consciously invoked the heroic imagery of freedom fighters from South Slavic folklore, which appealed to the patriotic sentiments of the population. References to the epic lore allowed the party's leaders to claim lineage with the legendary Balkan heroes and establish cultural authority among the peasantry. Most important for our discussion here, traditional culture provided acceptable models for women's participation in warfare. The communists evoked the images of epic heroines to attract women to the movement and legitimize the *partizanka* (female Partisan) in the eyes of the populace.[6]

Second, this work examines the *institutional* basis – in the form of the Antifascist Front of Women (AFW) – that the leadership developed for

---

[6] I have decided to use the term "rhetoric" here rather than the broader and more neutral term "language," as my analysis focuses primarily on the communists' addresses to the masses, including their own ranks, and examines what I see as persuasive strategies. It is important to note, however, that my use of "rhetoric" does not necessarily imply a dishonest motivation behind Partisan mobilizing strategies. Nor does it exclude the possibility of a genuine ideological belief on the part of the leadership; quite the contrary. For communists, political rhetoric – or, in their terminology, "agitation and propaganda" – had no negative connotations, but was considered a legitimate and necessary tool of the revolutionary struggle. Incidentally, Carol Lilly's recent study has shown that official rhetoric in revolutionary Yugoslavia tended to reflect the party's goals and intentions accurately. See Lilly, *Power and Persuasion: Ideology and Rhetoric in Communist Yugoslavia, 1944–1953* (Boulder, CO: Westview Press, 2001), 9.

women's mobilization. Focusing on the AFW's wartime history, it shows how in the Partisans' institutions, much as in their rhetoric, the revolutionary coexisted with the traditional. Females recruited by the AFW contributed to the Partisan war effort primarily through an extension of their customary tasks within the family and village communities: feeding, cleaning, nursing, and caring for others. The chief goal of the communist women's organization was to channel women's labor and help create a reliable support system for the Partisans; it did so largely by adapting local traditions to a new institutional framework. Through modern organizational devices, the communists put peasant women's age-old labor skills to use in a systematic fashion, transforming local customs of village women supporting their warrior men into instruments of mass participation in modern warfare.

Third, I focus on realities on the ground: on *daily practice* and, in particular, the problems of women's integration into the movement. A close look at everyday life allows me to explore, among other things, how ideology functioned in unscripted conditions. Without much guidance from Moscow and with no precedents in local history, the leaders in the units had to decide on the spot about such questions as what kind of relations between the sexes would be acceptable; whether Partisans would be allowed to marry and spouses to serve together in the same unit; who would do the laundry, cooking, and other chores. Delving into these mundane issues concerning the division of labor and regulations of sexual conduct, this study probes the dynamics between revolutionary agendas on the top and realities on the ground. It sheds light on the power of old patterns and the prevalence of a belief in "natural" and unchangeable gender features and duties in the movement. In daily life, too – and perhaps most obviously on this level – an accommodation of the traditional went hand in hand with revolutionary changes.

The party's mobilizing genius, this study argues, lay precisely in this rhetorical, institutional, and practical adaptation of peasant traditions in a distinctly modern way. It was largely thanks to their deft appropriation of traditional culture that the Partisans managed to enlist not only men but also the female masses, justify their active participation in the war, and build a powerful, relatively self-sustaining resistance movement. But this strategy also had a flipside, as it helped institutionalize old concepts of gender difference and the accompanying hierarchies.

The story of the phenomenon of women's participation in the Partisan struggle would not be complete without an examination of its postwar legacy. The fourth level of analysis, then, entails a study of memory. I look at the ways that the *partizanka* was memorialized in Yugoslavia's culture, tracing her journey from the revolutionary icon par excellence in the early postwar years to the oblivion of the present. The crumbling of the *partizanka*'s icon through growing sexualization and marginalization, this book shows, mirrored the gradual erosion of Yugoslav communism and, more generally, of the Yugoslav nation itself.

GENDER, REVOLUTION, AND WAR
IN SCHOLARLY LITERATURE

Scholars have documented the multiple roles that women played in the Partisan movement but have not asked questions about gender as an organizing criterion. For Yugoslav historians during the communist era, the victorious Partisan struggle – as the foundational myth of the ensuing communist regime – was in many respects the most privileged topic. In the first decades following the war, as Stevan Pavlowitch explains, historiography was intended to support the revolution and the building of socialism. "History was then made to begin when the Communist Party went over to the resistance in 1941. All the rest was prehistory leading to that event."[7] The state and the party encouraged, commissioned, and funded scholarship concentrating on the so-called National Liberation War. A result of these research incentives from above is a vast corpus of publications on the Partisan movement. Some focus on a particular region, district, or even village; others are more comprehensive. Almost every Partisan brigade has a historical study dedicated to it. Profuse as they are, though, these academic works constitute a small fraction of what may be termed a hyperproduction of texts on the war and revolution. There exists a plethora of published primary and secondary sources, including memoirs, collections of documents and data, compilations of Tito's and other leaders' speeches, reprints of wartime Partisan publications, and anthologies on war-related subjects.

Accordingly, there is also a considerable communist-era literature on women in the Partisan movement. It includes a volume on women of Yugoslavia as a whole,[8] several separate volumes on female participants

---

[7] Stevan Pavlowitch, *The Improbable Survivor: Yugoslavia and Its Problems, 1918–1988* (Columbus: Ohio State University Press, 1988), 129.

[8] Dušanka Kovačević, ed., *Borbeni put žena Jugoslavije* (Beograd: Leksikografski zavod "Sveznanje," 1972), provides introductory historical narratives on women from each of the Yugoslav republics.

from each of the republics of the Yugoslav federation,[9] innumerable contributions on women from specific localities,[10] books on the *partizanka*s from select units,[11] as well as biographies of the most prominent female leaders.[12] Conceptualized as communist memorials, these works typically feature a patchwork of veteran reminiscences, biographical sketches, select documentary records, and historical commentary. Although professional historians did contribute pieces, a good portion of this literature was written by former participants and intended for broad audiences. It is then not surprising that these contributions vary in scholarly rigor as much as they vary in scope. What they do have in common – besides glorifying the valor of female Partisans and emphasizing

[9] Bosnia-Herzegovina – for a collection of reminiscences see Rasim Hurem, ed., *Žene Bosne i Hercegovine u narodnooslobodilačkoj borbi 1941–1945. godine: sjećanja učesnika* (Sarajevo: Svjetlost, 1977). Croatia – for a collection of primary documents, biographical sketches, and reminiscences, see Marija Šoljan, ed., *Žene Hrvatske u narodnooslobodilačkoj borbi* (Zagreb: Savez Ženskih Društava Hrvatske, 1955). Macedonia – for a collection of documents, see Vera Veskovik-Vangeli and Marija Jovanovik, ed, *Ženite na Makedonija vo NOV: Zbornik na dokumenti za učestvoto na ženite od Makedonija vo narodnoosloboditelnata vojna i revolucijata 1941–1945* (Skopje: Institut za nacionalna istorija, 1976). For historical narrative, see Vera Veskovik-Vangeli, *Ženata vo osloboditelnite borbi na Makedoniia 1893–1945* (Skopje: Kultura, 1990), and idem., *Ženata vo revolucijata na Makedonija 1941–1945* (Skopje: Institut za nacionalna istorija, 1982). Montenegro – for an introductory historical narrative, see Jovan Bojović et al., *Žene Crne Gore u Revolucionarnom pokretu 1918–1945* (Titograd: Istorijski Institut u Titogradu, 1969). Serbia – for a combination of biographical sketches, documentary sources, and introductory historical narrative, see Bosa Cvetić et al., ed., *Žene Srbije u NOB.* For Vojvodina, see Danilo Kecić, ed., *Žene Vojvodine u ratu i revoluciji, 1941–1945* (Novi Sad: Institut za istoriju, 1984).Slovenia – for a collection of documents, memoirs, and articles see Stana Gerk, Ivka Križnar, and Štefanija Ravnikar-Podvebšek, eds., *Slovenke v Narodnoosvobodilnem boju: Zbornik dokumentov, člankov in spominov*, vols. 1–2 (Ljubljana: Zavod 'Borec', 1970).

[10] See, for example, Anka Brozičević-Rikica, ed., *Žene Vinodola u NOB-u: Zbornik radova* (Rijeka: Koordinacioni odbor za njegovanje i razvoj tradicije NOB-a, 1986); Radivoj Ačanski, *Žene kulske opštine u radničkom pokretu, NOR-u i socijalističkoj revoluciji* (Kula: Konferencija za društveni položaj i aktivnost žena, 1985); Ruža Gligović-Zeković, *San i vidici: žene nikšićkog kraja u NOB* (Nikšić: Organizacija žena i SUBNOR, 2000), and others.

[11] Desanka Stojić, *Prva ženska partizanska četa* (Karlovac: Historijski Arhiv u Karlovcu, 1987); Špiro Lagator and Milorad Čukić, *Partizanke Prve Proleterske* (Beograd: "Eksport-pres" i Konferencija za pitanja društvenog položaja žena u Jugoslaviji, 1978); Stana Džakula Nidžović, *Žene borci NOR-a Sedme banijske udarne divizije* (Čačak: Bajić, 1999); Ljiljana Bulatović, *Bila jednom četa devojačka* (Beograd: Nova knjiga, 1985), Obrad Egić, *Žene borci Druge Proleterske Dalmatinske narodnooslobodilačke udarne brigade* (Zadar: "Narodni List," 1983); and others.

[12] For biographies of individual women, see Stanko Mladenović, *Spasenija Cana Babović* (Belgrade: Rad 1980); Milenko Predragović, *Kata Pejnović: Životni put i revolucionarno delo* (Gornji Milanovac: Dečje novine, 1978), and others.

"the Communist Party's leading role" – is the dominant ideological interpretation, which greatly limits their analytical and explanatory powers,
reducing even the more sophisticated among them to fact-heavy, dull,
often propagandistic accounts.

With the fall of communism, this literature has lost much of its appeal
in the region, yet no new local scholarship has emerged to replace it.
Attempts to incorporate the insights of feminist scholarship or the rich
literature on gender and war have been extremely rare. A pioneer in this
respect was the sociologist Lydia Sklevicky, whose study of the Croatian
AFW provides the most balanced and thoroughly researched account of
women's organizational activity during the war and in the early postwar era
available. Unfortunately, because of her untimely death in 1990, Sklevicky's
work remains unfinished.[13] In the turbulent political climate following
the country's disintegration in the 1990s, the topic of women's mobilization was neglected, while scholars in the region tended to concentrate on
issues of communist violence or ethnonational aspects of the war; for more
than two decades, the *partizanka* seemed all but forgotten. Lately, there
have appeared sporadic signs of new scholarly interest in women and revolution.[14] All postcommunist studies, however, are regional in scope and
tend to focus on the women's organization or select female leaders; no
synthesis, thematic or geographic, and no extensive archival research on
the Yugoslav-wide phenomenon of women's mass mobilization have been
attempted.

In the Anglo-American scholarship on World War II in Yugoslavia,
works on British and American policy toward Tito's Partisans and Draža
Mihailović's Chetniks prevail.[15] Little has been done on other aspects of the

---

[13] See Lydia Sklevicky, *Organizirana djelatnost žena Hrvatske za vrijeme Narodnooslobodilačke borbe 1941–1945* (Zagreb: Institut za historiju radničkog pokreta Hrvatske, 1984). A collection of Sklevicky's works, which includes her unfin- ished dissertation, has been posthumously published in Zagreb. See Sklevicky, *Konji, Žene, Ratovi* (Zagreb: Ženska infoteka, 1996).

[14] Two recent works, one on the postwar position of leading Partisan women, another on the AFW in Vojvodina, follow in Sklevicky's steps. Ivana Pantelić, *Partizanke kao građanke: društvena emancipacija partizanki u Srbiji, 1945–1953* (Beograd: Institut za savremenu istoriju, 2011); Gordana Stojaković, "Skica za portret: Antifašistički Front Žena Vojvodine, 1942–1953," in *Partizanke – Žene u Narodnooslobodilačkoj borbi,* ed. Daško Milinović and Zoran Petakov (Novi Sad: CENZURA, 2010), 13–39.

[15] The standard reference work in this respect is Walter R. Roberts, *Tito, Mihailovic, and the Allies, 1941–1945* (New Brunswick, NJ: Rutgers University Press, 1973). See also Phyllis Auty and Richard Clogg eds., *British Policy towards Wartime Resistance in Yugoslavia and Greece* (New York: Barnes & Noble Books, 1975); Mark Wheeler, *Britain and the War for Yugoslavia* (Boulder, CO: East European Monographs, 1980); Thomas M. Barker, *Social Revolutionaries and Secret Agents: The Carinthian Slovene*

war, and very few studies attempt to combine political analyses with social or cultural ones. The memoirs and polemics written by the Allied operatives in wartime Yugoslavia, who often espoused the cause of either the Partisans or the Chetniks, have long been favorite sources of information on the Yugoslav resistance in the West.[16] Much of this literature was produced in the Cold War context, its chief question being why the Allies decided to shift their support from the royalist Chetnik movement to the communist Partisans. Only lately have different kinds of studies begun to emerge. The fall of communism and disintegration of Tito's Yugoslavia stimulated new approaches to the country's turbulent history. Newer studies seek to reexamine the war and Yugoslavia's past in general with an eye to nationality problems.[17] Yet most of this scholarship, much as the Cold War works that preceded it, remains largely gender-blind.

The minuscule body of works on women in the Partisan movement constitutes a separate and isolated subsection in Anglo-American scholarship on wartime Yugoslavia. This literature has explored women's roles and the influence of the revolutionary war on women, challenging the

---

Partisans and Britain's Special Operations Executive (Boulder, CO: East European Monographs, 1990); Kirk Ford, *OSS and the Yugoslav Resistance, 1943–1945* (College Station: Texas A&M University Press, 1992); Heather Williams, *Parachutes, Patriots, and Partisans: The Special Operations Executive and Yugoslavia, 1941–1945* (London: C. Hurst, 2003); and others.

16 On the Partisans see the writings of Fitzroy Maclean, Stephen Clissold, William Deakin, William Jones, Franklin A. Lindsay, and Basil Davidson. David Martin and Michael Lees are advocates of the Chetnik cause. The best and most comprehensive scholarly account in English on the Chetniks is Jozo Tomasevich, *War and Revolution in Yugoslavia, 1941–1945: The Chetniks* (Stanford, CA: Stanford University Press, 1975). To the best of my knowledge, there is no comparable work on the Partisans.

17 Much like the works in local languages, the English-language literature on interethnic relations during World War II has been preoccupied by the issues of culpability of individual nationalities for genocidal attacks, ethnic cleansing campaigns, and/or collaboration with the occupiers. Some of these works are not balanced and will not be cited here. Among the earliest studies to look at the issues of nationalism and interethnic strife during World War II and adhere to scholarly standards are Aleksa Djilas, *The Contested Country: Yugoslav Unity and Communist Revolution, 1919–1953* (Cambridge, MA: Harvard University Press, 1991) and Jill A. Irvine, *The Croat Question: Partisan Politics in the Formation of the Yugoslav Socialist State* (Boulder, CO: Westview Press, 1993). For a more recent look that stresses the significance of ideology in the Chetnik-Partisan conflict in Bosnia, see Marko A. Hoare, *Genocide and Resistance in Hitler's Bosnia: The Partisans and the Chetniks, 1941–1943* (New York: Published for the British Academy by Oxford University Press, 2006). Emily Greble's excellent study of wartime Sarajevo moves away from the conventional focus on ethnonational categories to shed light on the importance of civic loyalties and confessional bonds. See Greble, *Sarajevo 1941–1945: Muslims, Christians, and Jews in Hitler's Europe* (Ithaca, NY: Cornell University Press, 2011).

official Yugoslav interpretation, but has not examined the role of gender. The sole English-language monograph is the work of the political scientist Barbara Jancar-Webster, *Women & Revolution in Yugoslavia* (1990). This study is valuable for broaching the subject to Western audiences and providing important introductory information. As Jancar-Webster did not have an opportunity to consult archival sources, her analysis is based on a limited selection of published material and on interviews with Partisan women.[18]

Besides Yugoslav studies, the present book is involved in debates that belong to several historiographical contexts. The first one concerns the flourishing field of gender and war studies. Scholarship on the subject of women and the two great wars of the twentieth century was long dominated by the so-called watershed debate; the focus, as Joan W. Scott explains, was "on women's experience, on the impact of war upon them, with evidence being presented to affirm or deny that war was a turning point for them."[19] Emerging from the social history of war, the notion that the world wars had served as catalysts of emancipatory social changes captured scholarly imagination in the 1970s. As Scott explains, proponents of this notion list the many new opportunities in the labor force and the military that opened to women during the wars; they also emphasize the fact that females gained suffrage and other political and legal rights after World War I or II in a number of countries worldwide. Many feminist scholars disagree, pointing to the impermanence and incompleteness of these improvements in women's position. They argue that the power of traditional ideology hindered lasting change, stressing the facts that the wartime expansion of women's roles was "only for the duration," that there was a backlash pushing women back to domesticity shortly after the war, and that political rights had little meaning if not

[18] The English-language literature includes one monograph on Yugoslavia as a whole, one dissertation focusing on Croatia, and several articles by the same authors. See Barbara Jancar-Webster, *Women and Revolution in Yugoslavia, 1941–1945* (Denver: Arden Press, 1990); Mary E. Reed, "Croatian Women in the Yugoslav Partisan Resistance, 1941–1945" (Ph.D. Diss., University of California, Berkeley, 1980); idem., "The Anti-Fascist Front of Women and the Communist Party in Croatia: Conflicts within the Resistance," in *Women in Eastern Europe and the Soviet Union*, ed. Tova Yedlin (New York: Praeger, 1980), 129–39. Besides the Anglo-American works, there is a recent German-language monograph on Partisan women, Barbara Wiesinger's *Partisaninnen: Widerstand in Jugoslawien (1941–1945)* (Köln: Böhlau Verlag Köln, 2008). Wiesinger also had no opportunity to conduct archival research, and her monograph is based on interviews and a somewhat larger selection of published sources.

[19] Joan W. Scott, "Rewriting History," in Higonnet, *Behind the Lines*, 23.

accompanied with profound reforms in other domains.[20] This scholarship has done much to enrich our knowledge of women's wartime experiences, but such debates tend to block other important questions. What is more, as Scott argues and Penny Summerfield seconds, they are ultimately irresolvable. In her study, Summerfield puts to test three mutually opposed theses regarding the impact of World War II on British women. The first thesis is that the war had a *transformative* and positive effect; the second emphasizes *continuity* with the prewar era rather than change; and the third sees the war as a *polarizing* force that further deepened inequalities between the sexes instead of minimizing them. By analyzing statistical data and women's narratives, Summerfield shows that one can find evidence in support of each of the three.[21]

The second historiographical context involves the literature on women and communism. Here a debate akin to the one in gender and war studies had long dominated the field; it centered on whether the revolutionaries succeeded or not in their attempt to liberate women.[22] Whereas histories from the socialist bloc stressed successes, Western scholars typically emphasized communism's failure to solve the "woman question," often seeing the communists' dedication to gender equality as self-serving and instrumental rather than genuine.[23] However, they also had to acknowledge the many benefits of communist policies for women. In both of these contexts, newer scholarship has increasingly moved past the preceding preoccupations to studies of gender, offering new insights that have transformed our understanding of war and communism alike.[24]

[20] Ibid. The phrase "only for the duration" is from Leila Rupp, *Mobilizing Women for War: German and American Propaganda, 1939–1945* (Princeton, NJ: Princeton University Press, 1978).

[21] Scott, "Rewriting History," 23–5. Penny Summerfield, "British Women in Transition from War to Peace," in *When the War Was Over: Women, War and Peace in Europe, 1940–1956*, ed. Claire Duchen and Irene Bandhauer-Schoffman (New York: Leicester University Press, 2000), 13–27.

[22] This observation was made by Elizabeth Wood in reference to the Soviet historiography. It holds true for the literature on women and communism in general. Elizabeth Wood, *The Baba and the Comrade: Gender and Politics in Revolutionary Russia* (Bloomington: Indiana University Press, 2000), 3.

[23] Ibid. For contributions to the debate: on women and communism in general, see Barbara Jancar, *Women under Communism* (Baltimore: Johns Hopkins University Press, 1978); on Yugoslavia, see Jancar Webster, *Women and Revolution*; on Eastern Europe, Sharon L. Wolchik and Alfred Meyer, eds., *Women, State, and Party in Eastern Europe* (Durham, NC: Duke University Press, 1985); on the Soviets, Gail Lapidus, *Women in Soviet Society: Equality, Development, and Social Change* (Berkeley: University of California Press, 1978), etc.

[24] For successful models of a different approach to gender and war, see Miranda Pollard, *Reign of Virtue: Mobilizing Gender in Vichy France* (Chicago: University of Chicago

Following this trend, the present study shifts the focus to gender, examining how notions of gender difference informed party policy and effected a particular organization of the Partisan movement. It explores how the communist leadership both mobilized women and reformulated notions of womanhood in order to construct a strong, autonomous resistance network and reorder society. And it reveals how, for purposes of mass mobilization in the context of total war, traditional gender values were appropriated and adapted in a modern, revolutionary key. Despite the obvious expansion of women's roles and the party's egalitarianism, gender remained one of the central organizational principles and delineators of hierarchy in the Partisan movement and the nascent communist state alike. The umbrella topic of gender politics allows me to probe other interrelated problems, including Partisan culture, folklore, values and behavioral codes, sexual norms, and marriage and family policies.

The field of comparative communist studies constitutes the third larger historiographical context for this study. By shedding light on the complexities and accommodations that accompanied the building of the communist system in Yugoslavia, this book joins current discussions in East European history. Recent scholarship has moved away from a narrow focus on communist repression to investigate the strategies the regime adopted to establish legitimacy, and explore its interactions with the society under its rule. These studies have uncovered a surprising diversity among East European communist states, and shown how, in its attempts to consolidate power and create legitimacy, each regime adjusted its policies to accommodate national legacies, political culture, and local traditions.[25] Within its larger East European context, the Yugoslav case

Press, 1998); Susan Grayzel, *Women's Identities at War: Gender, Motherhood, and Politics in Britain and France during the First World War* (Chapel Hill: University of North Carolina Press, 1999); Katherine Jolluck, *Exile & Idenity: Polish Women in the Soviet Union during World War II* (Pittsburgh: University of Pittsburgh Press, 2002); Nancy M. Wingfield and Maria Bucur eds, *Gender and War in 20th Century Eastern Europe* (Bloomington: Indiana University Press, 2006); and others. For gender and communism, see Malgorzata Fidelis, *Women, Communism, and Industrialization in Postwar Poland* (New York: Cambridge University Press, 2010); Elizabeth Wood, *The Baba and the Comrade*; Wendy Goldman, *Women at the Gates: Gender and Industry in Stalin's Russia* (New York: Cambridge University Press, 2002); Shana Penn and Jill Massino, eds., *Gender Politics and Everyday Life in State Socialist Eastern and Central Europe* (New York: Palgrave Macmillan, 2009); and others.

[25] On postwar Poland, see Malgorzata Fidelis, *Women, Communism, and Industrialization in Postwar Poland* (New York: Cambridge University Press, 2010); for Hungary, see Mark Pittaway, *The Workers' State: Industrial Labor and the Making of Socialist Hungary, 1944–1958* (Pittsburgh: University of Pittsburgh Press, 2012); for a comparative study of East Germany, Czechoslovakia and Poland, which shows the importance

was distinct. In contrast to most of their East European peers, who owed their rule to the Soviet Red Army and never commanded a comparable mass following, Yugoslav communists rose to power largely on their own, having acquired considerable popular support as resistance leaders in World War II. Their main support base and main source of manpower during the war was the peasantry. It is due to this peculiar wartime partnership between a modern, revolutionary, urban-based party and the peasantry that the Partisans succeeded in surviving and winning the war. The present study elucidates key aspects of this partnership, showing how a conscious and active adaptation of Balkan peasant culture underpinned the consolidation of communist power in its formative years.

Finally, this book sheds light on the workings of the modern state, which could rest upon invoking and reinventing traditional practices and beliefs to a much greater degree than previously thought. As Eric Hobsbawm has shown, the invention and appropriation of traditions were common responses of the modern state in Europe to the rapid social transformation and the exigencies of mass politics at the turn of the century;[26] they remained so in the ensuing decades. To ensure popular support on the eve of World War II, various governments in Europe and around the world – fascist, socialist, authoritarian, and democratic alike – embraced the rallying power of traditional symbols and appeals.[27] The active use of Balkan peasant culture by the embryonic Yugoslav communist regime during the war constitutes a particular variant – and a prime example – of one of the modern state's most potent mobilizing strategies.

SOURCES AND ORGANIZATION

This work draws on an array of sources. First, records of the Communist Party of Yugoslavia (CPY), the Partisan army, and the Antifascist Front of Women, held in the Military Archive and the Archive of Yugoslavia in Belgrade, constitute the core of my source base. I was fortunate to have been granted access to the Military Archive, whose vast collections on

---

of local political culture, see John Connelly, *Captive University: The Sovietizaton of East German, Czech, and Polish Higher Education, 1945–1956* (Chapel Hill: University of North Carolina Press, 2000).

[26] Eric Hobsbawm, "Mass-Producing Traditions: Europe, 1870–1914," in Eric Hobsbawm and Terence Ranger, ed., *The Invention of Traditions* (New York: Cambridge University Press, 1992), 263–307.

[27] David Hoffmann, *Stalinist Values: The Cultural Norms of Soviet Modernity, 1917–1941* (Ithaca, NY: Cornell University Press, 2003) 9–10; 186.

the National Liberation War (group of fonds *Narodnooslobodilački Rat*, NOR) inform much of the following discussion.[28] In addition to original wartime sources of the Partisan army's core units, the Military Archive holds materials from numerous regional and local archives of former Yugoslavia, which were microfilmed and stored there in Tito's times, thus creating the most comprehensive collection of documents on the Partisan movement available. CPY and AFW sources held in the Archive of Yugoslavia have provided vital information on the Partisan leadership's decision making and gender ideology, as well as postwar activities of the women's organization. I have also drawn on published collections of primary documents, such as the voluminous series *Zbornik dokumenata*;[29] however, as some sources in the communist-era collections were altered prior to publication, I preferred to consult their archival originals whenever it was possible.

Second, I have studied the Partisan press in general and organs of the AFW in particular for their rhetorical calls to the masses. In 1942, AFW activists started editing and distributing publications that specifically addressed women. This unique set of resistance journals – by women, for women, and about women – includes more than two dozen different periodicals released during the war, the majority of which I was able to examine. Third, participant reminiscences, memoirs, diaries, and other personal narratives have offered valuable insights into the motivations, experiences, and memories of Partisan veterans. Finally, I have studied representations of the *partizanka* in major Yugoslav literary and cinematographic works.

The monograph is organized thematically. The first chapter focuses on political rhetoric, examining the gendered imagery in the party's appeals to the masses. The Partisan leaders invoked time-honored Balkan folk culture, the chapter shows, combining it deftly with the revolutionary rhetoric that stressed equality. In Partisan propaganda the *partizanka* appeared as the supreme successor of the great South Slavic epic heroines. At the same time, she was celebrated as the herald of a new, modern, socialist age: the "new woman" herself. The two visions, one traditional,

---

[28] At the time I began my research, the archive was known as the Archive of the Institute of Military history (Arhiv Vojnoistorijskog Instituta, AVII). It has since changed its name to the Military Archive (Vojni arhiv). I have kept the former name and acronym in the citations throughout the book.

[29] *Zbornik dokumenata i podataka o narodnooslobodilackom ratu jugoslovenskih naroda* (Beograd: Vojnoistorijski institut, 1949–86), 15 volumes, 173 books. Hereafter referred to as *Zbornik*, vol.#. book#.

another revolutionary, merged in her representation as a folk heroine who wins equality by proving worthy of it in battle, which was used to justify both women's participation in combat and the new egalitarian order. The party's strategy of "neotraditionalism" is shown to have been part of a larger international trend of invoking traditions for markedly modern purposes of mass mobilization.[30]

The second chapter traces the development of the women's organization, revealing how peasant customs and old gender divisions of labor came to be integrated into the Partisan institutional structure. Parallel to this institutionalization of the traditional, the chapter discusses the contradictions inherent to the communist project of emancipating women from above while denouncing feminism. Early in the war, realizing that men would be leaving for the front and that women would have to take over the rear, the party formed the AFW to facilitate women's mobilization. The AFW appealed to traditional women's concerns to recruit them into the movement and successfully put women's traditional labor skills to use, thus creating a rear support system largely relying on females. In addition to supporting the guerrilla army, the organization had a revolutionary goal: to become a medium for women's enlightenment, politicization, and integration into the new socialist society. Though the AFW was founded as a tool of the CPY, as it developed, it became progressively autonomous and focused on women's issues. Disapproving, the party leadership accused female activists of bourgeois "feminism," restructured the AFW, and ended the organization's independence once and for all.

Chapter 3 shifts attention to Partisan units, outlining the history of women's military mobilization. It traces how communist policy on women in combat developed and changed, from the hesitation of the first months, to Tito's approval of the recruitment and mass mobilizations of women in 1942–3, to the withdrawal of the *partizanka* from the front lines in the final phases of the war. In addition to the evolution of

---

[30] I borrow the term "neotraditionalism" from the Soviet historiography. Much has been made out of relatively recent debates between the so-called modernity and neotraditionalist schools among students of Stalinism. I join critics who see the two positions not as mutually exclusive but as reconcilable in that both consider modern phenomena. On the debate, see Michael David-Fox, "Multiple Modernities vs. Neo-Traditionalism: On Recent Debates in Russian and Soviet History," *Jahrbücher für Geschichtes Osteuropas* 54 (2006): 535–55. For a case on "neotradionalism" in Soviet nationality policy, which inspired my use of the term, see Terry Martin, "Modernization or Neo-Traditionalism: Ascribed Nationality and Soviet Primordialism," in David Hoffman and Yanni Kotsonis, ed., *Russian Modernity: Politics, Knowledge, Practices* (New York: St. Martin's Press, 2000), 161–82. The term itself originates in 1980s social science.

the policy at the top, the chapter examines difficulties of its implementation on the local level. At the same time, it looks at the motivations and experiences of female Partisans themselves. Their case exposes the perseverance of traditional values – including a sex-based hierarchy – in the movement and shows how gender served as a pillar of social organization even in a revolutionary guerrilla army. Veteran women, however, remember the war as the high point of their lives, when they acted as historical agents and political subjects in their own right, their narratives suggesting that the very experience of active participation in the struggle was liberating. The chapter places party policies and women's experiences in a larger international comparative context, without which, it shows, they cannot be fully understood.

Chapter 4 examines behavioral norms and values, sexual mores, and notions of privacy in the movement. Women's presence in the units, it shows, provided the Partisans' adversaries with exceptional propaganda material. To combat accusations of sexual debauchery and to resolve many actual problems in the movement, CPY leaders instituted a strict code of sexual behavior. Partisan discipline accommodated the patriarchal morality of the peasants who peopled the units, at the same time allowing the party to intervene in the most personal relationships of its members and followers. These regulations strengthened the party's control over the burgeoning movement and normalized its interventionism in the private sphere. Although the Partisan code in theory did not differentiate between the sexes, the chapter reveals, on the local level the party's policing measures disproportionally targeted women and double sexual standards persisted in the movement.

Postwar legacy of the *partizanka* forms the subject of the final chapter. After an overview of legal reforms and changes in women's position that the new regime instituted after the war, the chapter turns to the study of memory. It examines both the official memory featured in state-sponsored commemorations, historiography, and memorials, and the competing imagery that developed in Yugoslavia's literature and cinematography. In the early postwar years, the chapter shows, the *partizanka* found herself at the very center of the communist master narrative of the war. Her official image, which came to symbolize supranational Yugoslavism, was based on the notions of heroism and self-sacrifice for a noble cause. But in the following decades, her representations in Yugoslav culture gradually diverged from the official revolutionary icon. The *partizanka*'s subsequent downfall, political in nature, was, however, expressed in gender-specific terms. Once her heroic portrait underwent the first minor revisions in the 1960s, she started to slide toward the sidelines of the war iconography, where she appeared in more conventional and increasingly sexualized roles. Her gradual dethroning and ultimate demise in the last decades of the twentieth century paralleled the waning of Titoism and the disintegration of Yugoslavia.

The present study makes both empirical and conceptual contributions to existing scholarship on wartime Yugoslavia. It draws on archival sources unused by Western scholars and probes the hitherto unexplored issues of gender, sexuality, and memory, providing a new interpretation of women's mobilization and novel insights into the history of the Partisan movement. In addition, it places Yugoslav communist policies, typically studied within the confines of East European or national history, in a broader comparative international context, thus shedding new light on their origins and meaning. Most important, this study speaks to issues that transcend regional and disciplinary boundaries. By addressing cross-cultural and interdisciplinary questions about the triangular relationship involving gender, revolution, and war through a historical case study, this book contributes to recent debates in women's history, gender and war studies, studies of war and society, comparative communism, and the modern state and modernization.

WORLD WAR II IN THE WESTERN BALKANS:
THE BACKGROUND

The war began in Yugoslavia with Axis bombing and invasion in the spring of 1941.[31] Earlier that year, the Yugoslavs were put under intense pressure to join the Tripartite Pact, as Hitler turned to the Balkans to help the Italians, who were stuck in Greece. Politically disunited and beset by ethnonational antagonisms, the Yugoslav kingdom was no match for Hitler's Germany, either diplomatically or militarily. Besides, it was

[31] Reducing a topic as complex as World War II in the Balkans to a couple of pages is a challenge. My discussion here focuses only on major players and events in the Yugoslav theater. For a much more detailed, synthetic work, see Stevan Pavlowitch, *Hitler's New Disorder: The Second World War in Yugoslavia* (New York: Columbia University Press, 2008). The best short English-language introductions remain Jozo Tomasevich's "Yugoslavia during the Second World War," in *Contemporary Yugoslavia*, ed. Wayne S. Vucinich (Berkeley: University of California Press, 1969), 59–118; and Joseph Rothschild's in *Return to Diversity*, 3rd ed. (New York: Oxford University Press, 2000), 42–5, and my discussion draws on these works. On the Chetniks and the puppet regimes in Croatia and Serbia, see Tomasevich, *War and Revolution in Yugoslavia, 1941–1945: The Chetniks, and idem., War and Revolution in Yugoslavia, 1941–1945: Occupation and Collaboration* (Stanford, CA: Stanford University Press, 2001), respectively.

completely surrounded by the Axis partners and their satellites. The government finally signed the pact on 25 March 1941, which provoked a mutiny among pro-British Serbian factions in the military. On the night of 26–27 March in a bloodless coup, they overthrew the government and the prince regent, and proclaimed Peter II (heir to the throne, who was a minor) king. In some parts of the country, the coup was vastly popular, with masses gathering at anti-Axis demonstrations in several cities on March 27. Nazi retaliation for the coup was brutal – on April 6, heavy bombing of Belgrade and other cities started, followed by German, Hungarian, and Italian invasions. Disorganized, poorly led and poorly equipped, and experiencing internal dissension, the Yugoslav royal army was defeated in a little more than a week, leaving even the Germans surprised by the swiftness of their victory. The new government and the young king fled the country, remaining in exile (London and Cairo) for the duration of the war. Yugoslavia was occupied and dismembered, its territory partitioned by the Axis forces, their allies, and the newly formed Independent State of Croatia (see Figure 1).

1) Germany occupied the largest, northern, part of Slovenia, the Banat in Vojvodina, and Serbia proper. In northern Slovenia, the Germans immediately launched a program of linguistic and demographic Germanization and expelled large numbers of Slovenes from the region. Rump Serbia, approximately in its pre-1912 borders, was the only part of Yugoslavia in which an outright German military government was instituted; the Banat was nominally part of that system but actually the local Volksdeutsche had autonomous rule there. To help maintain law and order in Serbia, the Germans established a local collaborationist administration headed by General Milan Nedić. From January 1942 on, the Bulgarians too helped in the policing of rump Serbia. They extended their occupational zones well into Serbia proper to relieve some of the German troops needed on the Eastern front. Power, however, remained in German hands.

2) Italy annexed the southern part of Slovenia with Slovenia's capital of Ljubljana, a strip of land along the Adriatic coast, including the majority of islands (with the exceptions of Pag, Brač, and Hvar), and the whole region of the Bay of Kotor. Italy also occupied most of Montenegro. Albania, under Italian control, annexed Kosovo, a part of western Macedonia, and a small part of Montenegro.

3) Bulgaria annexed most of Macedonia, the southeastern part of Serbia, and a tiny portion of Kosovo, launching a harsh policy of Bulgarization of the local Slavic populace.

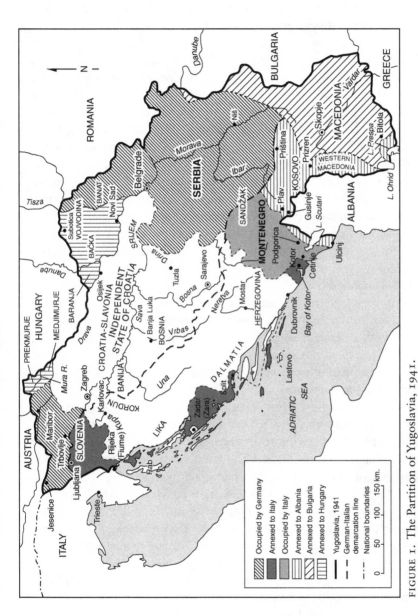

FIGURE 1. The Partition of Yugoslavia, 1941.

From *War and Revolution in Yugoslavia, 1941–1945: Occupation and Collaboration* by Jozo Tomasevich. Copyright © 2001 by the Board of Trustees of the Leland Stanford Jr. University. All rights reserved. Used with the permission of Stanford University Press, www.sup.org.

19

4) Hungary annexed Bačka (Vojvodina), Baranja in present-day Croatia, and the two neighboring areas of Prekomurje in Slovenia and Medjumurje in Croatia, reinstating its old, pre–World War I program of Magyarization in these regions.

5) The rest of the ex-Yugoslav spoils, including Croatia-Slavonia and parts of the Croatian/Dalmatian littoral (with islands Pag, Brač, and Hvar), all of Bosnia-Herzegovina, and Srem of today's Vojvodina, were incorporated into the Independent State of Croatia (NDH) under the fascist Ustasha regime headed by Ante Pavelić. Although nominally autonomous, the Independent State of Croatia de facto operated under German and Italian suzerainty. Its territory was divided roughly into two halves by a demarcation line that ran throughout Yugoslavia separating the German and Italian zones of occupation. Italian and German garrisons stationed in the country, though officially considered friendly troops, were actually parts of the occupational apparatus.

Yugoslavia's capitulation marked the beginning of a catastrophic period for its peoples. Not only did the occupiers in practically all South Slavic lands launch harsh programs of racial classification, political terror, and economic exploitation, but their presence and policies also added fuel to internecine struggles among the locals. During the four years of conflict on the Yugoslav soil, a war of resistance took place simultaneously with a series of genocidal attacks and civil wars. In addition, instead of pacifying the South Slavic lands, the complicated division of Balkan spoils became a source of tension among the Axis powers, their partners, and local satellites.

The decision to allow a fringe fascist group, the Ustashas, to establish and run a separate state in Croatia, now greatly enlarged by the addition of Bosnia-Herzegovina to its territory, "soon emerged as a major political blunder" for the Axis.[32] The Ustasha leaders instituted a dictatorship notorious for its brutality, their main fixation being the elimination of the Serb element from the Croatian lands. The Serb minority of the Independent State of Croatia counted about 1.9 million, constituting about 30 percent of the total population. Under attack, the country's Serb populace provided a steady pool of highly motivated and militant recruits for the guerrilla resistance troops in the hills. In addition to persecuting the Serbs, the Ustasha leadership went on to exterminate the Jews and the Roma people, and to alienate the majority of its Croat constituents, who were sickened by the atrocities and angered by the fact that

[32] Rothschild, 49.

Pavelić had handed Dalmatia over to Italy and remained humiliatingly subservient to Germany. The quisling Croatian regime had sizable armed forces (peaking at some 260,000 men), which functioned as a tool of the Wehrmacht; these forces consisted of the elite Ustasha militia (essentially the Ustasha party army), the regular Croatian army also known as the Domobrans (Home Guard), and gendarmerie. Yet the Germans could not rely on Croatia's military. The Home Guard was one of the most dispirited armies in wartime Europe and never a reliable fighting force. The Ustasha militia, "composed of fully indoctrinated volunteers devoted to Pavelić," by contrast, was fierce in combat, but rather unruly and frequently at odds with the regular army and the German commanders.[33]

The first resistance organization was Draža Mihailović's Chetnik guerrilla. Mihailović was a colonel of the supreme staff of the royal army, who, together with a group of Serb officers, refused to surrender when his army collapsed. In May 1941, Mihailović's Chetniks set up a resistance base on the Ravna Gora in southwestern Serbia. Ideologically, they stood for Serbian nationalism, conservatism, and devotion to the king, while their political goal was to restore the prewar Yugoslav monarchy dominated by the Serbs. Their loyalty and initial exploits led to the recognition of their movement by the Yugoslav government in exile and support by the British. Although physically remaining in the country, Mihailović was promoted to the rank of general and appointed the minister of the army, navy, and air force of the royal government in exile in January 1942; his guerrillas became officially known as the Yugoslav Army in the Homeland. Thanks largely to its parochial Serbocentric orientation, the Chetnik movement had a relatively narrow recruitment base, attracting mainly Serb peasants from Serbia proper, Montenegro, and the NDH. Mihailović's military strategy was to collect arms and prepare his adherents for a general uprising when the Allies were close to defeating Germany. As the war progressed, the Chetniks became less interested in harassing the occupiers than in protecting the Serbs from Ustasha atrocities, massacring Muslims and Croats in "reprisal" actions, and, most of all, fighting their communist-led rivals, Tito's Partisans.

The Communist Party leaders began organizing their insurgency after the Nazi attack on the Soviet Union on 22 June 1941. On 7 July following the party's call for a general uprising, fighting broke out in Serbia, marking the beginning of armed resistance. A series of uprisings followed in Montenegro, Slovenia, and the Independent State of Croatia.

[33] Tomasevich, *The Chetniks*, 107–8.

By the end of the summer, considerable Partisan forces had formed in
Serbia. Their initial success was the liberation of a region surrounding
the Serbian town of Užice – the so-called Užice Republic – where Tito
established his headquarters and began setting up socialist institutions.
The Partisans' undisguised revolutionary proclivities, however, alarmed
and alienated a significant portion of the local population together with
the Chetnik leadership. In spite of the existence of some early joint
Chetnik-Partisan actions against the German troops, attempts to create
unified resistance forces failed. Tito and Mihailović met twice in the fall
of 1941; ideological differences, as well as differences between their military strategies, proved irreconcilable and they reached no agreement.
In November 1941, the first armed clashes between the two movements
occurred, precipitating a long and bloody civil war.

These clashes also marked the beginning of a difficult period for the
Partisans. In what has been known in Yugoslav historiography as the first
of the seven enemy offensives, the Partisan main forces were expelled from
Serbia, their "Užice Republic" destroyed. The leadership, with the core of
hardened fighters, moved to Bosnia, where successive Axis offensives and
skirmishes with the Chetniks and Ustashas kept Partisan troops on the
move, interspersed with only short breaks, until mid-1943. Two sweeping Axis operations in the first half of 1943 almost spelled their doom.
After the British and American successes in North Africa, the Germans
began fearing a potential Allied landing in the Balkans and decided to
annihilate the guerrillas who might help the Allies' advance in the region.
The operations Weiss in January–March and Schwartz in May–June –
the fourth and fifth offensives – dealt significant blows to Tito's forces
but failed to eliminate them. Each time the Partisans faced an immensely
superior enemy in the form of combined German, Italian, and quisling
troops, and each time they managed to break the encirclement, though
with considerable losses. Since their main objective at the time was simple
survival, they emerged from these conflicts as victors.

It is a testament to the party leadership's ingenuity and perseverance that it succeeded during this trying period in consolidating and
strengthening the movement organizationally, militarily, and politically.
Militarily, the CPY initiated the formation of a regular army out of
Partisan guerrillas. Initial Partisan detachments were based on voluntary
territorial recruitment; they operated within a specific geographic area
and remained more or less bound to it. After their defeat in Serbia,
the Partisan leaders were forced to consider a different model. On 21
December 1941, the party formed the First Proletarian Brigade from the

dedicated Serbian fighters who had remained with Tito. It was the first regular mobile Partisan unit capable of leaving its territory and fighting wherever necessary. Other proletarian and shock brigades followed swiftly and, in November 1942, the party announced the creation of the National Liberation Army organized in divisions and corps. Recruitment for territorial detachments was never abandoned, though. These detachments were responsible for local actions and were particularly useful in involving the local populace in the Partisan movement. Tito's army, of course, was never a match for the Wehrmacht. But it was a determined and persistent challenge to the Nazi order in the Balkans, one that repeatedly put sizable liberated territories on the Balkan map and provoked several large-scale operations of German troops unlike any other European resistance movement.

Parallel to the consolidation of the Partisan army, the CPY started setting up civil administrations in Partisan-held areas. The so-called national-liberation councils (*narodnooslobodilački odbori*) emerged as communist-controlled yet participatory political organs of the new "people's government" on the local level. In late 1942, Tito felt confident enough for bolder political claims. In November, in the northwestern Bosnian town of Bihać, the Partisans convened an assembly of delegates from various parts of the country and established their Anti-Fascist Council of National Liberation of Yugoslavia (AVNOJ) to administer the liberated territories. Tito's political ambitions alarmed Stalin, and it was only thanks to the latter's moderation that AVNOJ refrained from declaring itself the sole representative of Yugoslav sovereignty and the country's interim government. That happened a year later, just as the Big Three were to meet in Tehran. At its second congress on 29 November 1943, in Jajce, AVNOJ proclaimed itself the country's supreme legislative and executive body, established the so-called National Committee as its executive organ (Tito being premier, defense minister, and marshal), and resolved that Yugoslavia would be founded upon a federal principle. The government in exile was deposed and the king forbidden to return to the country before a plebiscite on the form of the future regime had been organized.

Two major political developments in 1943 changed the situation on the ground in favor of the Partisans. As a result of the surrender of Italy in September that year, the Partisans were able to rearm and extend the areas under their control, which gradually spread over a good portion of the formerly Italian zones in the Independent State of Croatia, Montenegro, Dalmatia and the Adriatic islands, and southern Slovenia.

Meanwhile, the Western Allies began showing interest in Tito and decided to establish contact. The first British mission reached Tito in April. British operatives apparently sent back such favorable reports that the Western Allies decided to start sending aid. As the year neared its end, the Allies began shifting their support from the Chetniks, who were compromised by their collaboration with the Italians and Germans and their unwillingness to kill Axis personnel, to the Partisans, who had broader popular backing and were more effectively fighting against the occupiers. In late November, the Big Three in Tehran recognized the Partisans as an Allied force. All of this greatly raised the Partisans' morale and political standing in the country, drawing many new recruits into their ranks.

The war, to be sure, was not over yet. In their attempts to quell the insurgency, the Germans launched two additional large-scale operations against the Partisans in the winter of 1943–4 and the spring of 1944 (the sixth and seventh offensives). In May, a German airborne attack almost succeeded in destroying Tito's staff in the Bosnian town of Drvar. But although the fighting continued, after 1943 the Partisans saw a succession of victories on all fronts. In 1944, pressured by the British, the government in exile made a series of agreements with Tito and ultimately the king himself appealed to the Yugoslav peoples to join the Partisans. That summer and fall, Tito's shrewd move of granting amnesty to his local adversaries who deserted to join his forces further increased the influx of men, particularly those from the ranks of the Domobrans (Home Guard), to the Partisan units. His Partisans were now no longer a guerrilla but a large, regular military force, organized in four armies and preparing for frontal engagement. At the same time, Tito concluded an agreement with the Soviets allowing their forces temporary entry into Yugoslav territory in pursuit of the Germans. His troops joined the advancing Red Army to liberate Belgrade and the northeastern corner of Yugoslavia in October and November 1944. The Partisans cleared the rest of the country from the retreating German and quisling forces on their own, though with great losses, breaking through the German and Croatian defense lines on the Syrmian (Sremski/Srijemski) front in April and liberating Yugoslavia's western lands by mid-May 1945. The victors showed little mercy to their wartime opponents, and tens of thousands of Croatian and Slovenian troops, Serbian and Montenegrin Chetniks, and other local factions were summarily executed at the end of the war.

The Communist Party, a weak underground organization with relatively marginal political powers in the interwar period, ended up taking over the country at the end of the war. Historians have identified the major factors that helped the CPY rebuild, strengthen, and advance to the position of resistance leader and ultimate victor of the war on Yugoslav soil. First, the purge and "bolshevization" of the CPY once Tito became its general secretary in 1937 turned the party into an exceptionally disciplined and efficient political organization. Second, the communists' adoption of the "popular front" line helped end the party's political isolation, uniting many noncommunist patriots and antifascists behind the Partisan cause. Third, thanks to the CPY's interwar underground work and the participation of many of its members in the Spanish civil war, the Partisans had a leadership with formidable conspiratorial skills and military experience that proved invaluable during the war. Fourth, the Partisans made enormous political gains from their federalist approach to the national question and their supraethnic Yugoslav patriotism. Amid horrific interethnic violence, they claimed to protect the victims on all sides and presented themselves both as liberators from the invaders and as reconcilers of the Yugoslav peoples. As important, the chaos of total war and internecine struggle uprooted and awakened the previously marginalized and apathetic peasant masses, turning them into receptive audiences for the Partisans' message. The final – crucial but often overlooked – factor that distinguished the Partisans from all their opponents and contributed greatly to their success was their emphasis on women's mobilization and mass participation in the struggle. The party's unique gender politics, as Tomasevich notes, dramatically broadened the Partisan social base and gave the movement a genuinely popular character.[34] This gender politics forms the subject of the present study.

---

[34] Tomasevich, "Yugoslavia…," 97.

"To the People, She Was a Character from Folk Poetry"

The Party's Mobilizing Rhetoric

Above all of those women about whom the history of our peoples speaks and our folk poems sing, like the Serbian mother of the nine Jugovićs and the Croat Mother Margarita, the most radiant is the character of the Partisan woman…. When our today's man says to a woman: "Comrade!," it is not a conventional word, used customarily or out of courtesy – it is the word whereby the Partisan man admits that the Partisan woman is his equal in everything.

For us, the woman question has been solved.

And we can be proud that in these difficult but also great days, we gave to the world a new type of woman – the Partisan woman.

(Vladimir Nazor, in a speech presented in Otočac, Croatia)

When, in January 1944, the Croatian poet Vladimir Nazor announced the birth of a "new type of woman," he was referring to female Partisan fighters. According to his enthusiastic speech, it was the *partizanka* who brought about the resolution of the woman question in Yugoslavia and who stood as a distinctive Yugoslav wartime contribution to the world. Before declaring an end to gender inequality, Nazor reassured his audience that Partisan women's venture from the kitchen into what had appeared to be an exclusive male sphere was "not at all unnatural." Their forebears he found in the "glorious" female military and political tradition that, fusing myth and history, spanned several millennia and many cultures – from the ancient Amazons, through Joan of Arc and various female sovereigns, to the South Slavic epic heroines. The *partizanka*, in Nazor's view, represented the crown of this tradition. She was the Amazon's ultimate resurrection, enriched by the strength, wisdom, and knowledge women had accumulated in the past centuries of oppression. And, what a delight – of all places, she appeared "exactly in our lands [*baš kod nas*]!" Thus spoke Nazor to the peasants of a liberated territory in Croatia in 1944. Widely reported in the wartime Partisan press and quoted in the subsequent decades, his speech signaled the rise of the female Partisan to the status of a revolutionary icon in postwar Yugoslav culture.[1]

The *partizanka*'s entrance into Yugoslavia's political vocabulary is a phenomenon almost as remarkable as her debut at the military front. Having committed a major transgression in the traditional gender order, she became one of the main topics in the propaganda wars among the local warring factions. Focusing on her sexuality, the Chetniks and the Ustashas made her the "favored butt" of their anti-Partisan rhetoric.[2] In Partisan view, she was the "new woman," the harbinger of a new era of equality. At the same time, party leaders proclaimed her the greatest and "most radiant" of the South Slavic folk heroines.[3]

This chapter focuses on the gendered imagery in Partisan addresses to the populace. It begins with a discussion of the key features of the party's recruitment strategy, which set the Partisans apart from all other warring factions in Yugoslavia. It then turns to the rhetoric that the party devised to win women over to the Partisans and justify their new roles. Two motifs stand out in the CPY's rhetoric regarding women: the revolutionary promise of gender equality and the invocation of heroic imagery from South Slavic epic folklore. Scholars tend to ignore the latter, often

---

[1] As reported in "Nazor o Partizankama," *Žena u borbi*, March 1944, 17. Nazor's speech, in its full length, was reproduced after the war in Vladimir Nazor, "Od amazonke do partizanke," *Partizanska knjiga* (Zagreb: Nakladni zavod Hrvatske, 1949), 332–8. The speech was widely quoted in the Yugoslav literature of the communist era. See, for example, Dušanka Kovačević, ed., *Borbeni put žena Jugoslavije* (Beograd: Leksikografski zavod "Sveznanje," 1972), 25, and others.

[2] Quote from Jozo Tomasevich, *War and Revolution in Yugoslavia, 1941–1945: The Chetniks* (Stanford, CA: Stanford University Press, 1975), 189. For more on the *partizanka* in enemy propaganda, see Chapter 4.

[3] For texts that refer to the new woman, see Stanko Opačić Ćanica, "Narodnooslobodilačka borba stvorila je ženu novog tipa," *Žena u borbi*, June 1943, 5; Mira Morača, "Junačke žene Srijema," *Žena danas*, January 1943, 34; Mitra Mitrović, "O Antifašističkom frontu žena," *Žena danas*, September 1944, 8, and others. The wartime journal of the Partisan women's organization in Bosnia was itself entitled *Nova žena* (The New Woman). For texts that, similarly to Nazor's, proclaim the birth of the new woman and trace the history of women's heroism from the biblical times, through the South Slavic epic women, to the climax in the *partizanka*, see Jovan Popović's piece in *Žena danas* January 1943, 10, and Svetozar Rittig, "Viteštvo, posestrimstvo, i idealizam narodne borbene žene," *Žena u borbi*, December 1944/January 1945, 4–6. For a scholarly analysis of the notion of the "new woman," see Lydia Sklevicky, "Kulturnom mijenom do žene 'novog tipa'," in *Konji, Žene, Ratovi* (Zagreb: Ženska infoteka, 1996), esp. 50–5.

stressing communist egalitarianism as the decisive factor for women's mobilization into the Partisan movement. I will argue that the emphasis on equality of the sexes per se was not a particularly successful mobilizing tool. Rather, the party's genius lay in its ability to appropriate traditional Balkan culture and modify it in a revolutionary key. For mobilizational purposes, to appeal to peasant patriotism, the CPY systematically evoked the folk tradition. Through allusions to the epic lore, the Partisans tried to establish lineage with legendary "freedom fighters" and thus assert cultural authority among the masses. Most important for this discussion, the Partisans drew on traditional images and narrative structures to represent women's participation in warfare. Party ideologues portrayed the *partizanka* as the ultimate heiress of epic heroines. The revolutionary and the traditional were reconciled in her image as the heroic woman who earned equality by proving her valor on the battlefield. This new heroic icon served to legitimize the role of women as fighters and facilitate their acceptance by the larger populace.

THE PARTISAN RECRUITMENT STRATEGIES

The Communist Party was the leader of the only military faction in wartime Yugoslavia that championed the cause of gender equality. The Partisans were also the only ones successful in attracting and organizing women on a large scale. Their willingness to recruit women was as much a consequence of wartime necessity as it was of their egalitarian ideology – Partisan guerrillas needed a reliable rear support system, which would provide supplies such as food, shoes, and clothes; local accommodation of the units; and continued agricultural production, among other tasks. At the time when most men were drafted into local military forces or took to the hills, it was women's work that was vital for the maintenance of the rear.

Several factors distinguished the Partisans' recruitment strategy from that of their opponents and contributed to their unparalleled success in attracting women to their movement. First, the party leaders recognized early on in the war how essential women's support was for their war effort. In August 1941, communist activists prepared the first wartime women's conference in Drvar (Bosnian Krajina), at which they explained the need for an efficient rear system and asked women to help. The women responded with enthusiasm. The accomplishments of the Drvar conference encouraged party leaders to undertake similar actions elsewhere – already in September several such meetings took place in various villages of Bosnia and Lika (Croatia). This leads us to the second factor: The communist leadership developed an organizational basis for the mass mobilization of women in the rear support network. In order to involve as many women as possible and to orchestrate their volunteer activities, the CPY began founding women's councils. Soon such councils mushroomed throughout the liberated territories. At their first national conference in Bosnia in December 1942, they united on the national level into a centralized, mass-based women's organization, the Antifascist Front of Women (AFW). The organization's major goal was to organize women's material and moral support for the Partisan war effort. In addition, the organization strove to transform women into political subjects and ensure their integration, on an equal basis, into the future socialist society. The AFW was a unique institution in the war-torn Yugoslav lands. Although the adversaries of the Partisans similarly relied upon women's work, none managed to channel it in such an organized fashion. No other faction developed a women's organization that could rival – in terms of structural sophistication, scope, and membership – the Antifascist Front of Women. The third factor is that the Partisans were the only faction in wartime Yugoslavia that opened the doors of their combat units to a large number of women. Allowing women to enter the military opened new vistas for young females and at the same time substantiated the party's claim of egalitarianism.

Who were the typical female participants in the Partisan movement? In the initial Partisan units the female element was represented almost exclusively by prewar CPY and Communist Youth League members, but as the war progressed that changed. The experienced communist activists moved to leadership positions in the AFW and political functions in the units, while peasant women swelled the Partisan ranks. Barbara Jancar-Webster's analysis of the available biographical data on about 850 women involved in the Partisan movement in Croatia shows that most Partisan women were of peasant background, young (in their teens and twenties), and little – if at all – educated. The young female fighters usually came from occupied and war-ravaged villages. Similarly, most women in the rear were peasants.[4] My research confirms that the profile of the typical Partisan woman in most other Yugoslav lands corresponded with the Croatian one.[5] To understand how the Partisans managed to attract so many peasant women, one needs to look at another crucial factor of

---

[4] Jancar-Webster, *Women & Revolution*, 48–9, 60–1.
[5] For more detailed demographic information, see Chapters 2 and 3.

the Partisan mobilizing strategy: the rhetoric the party devised to appeal to peasant women and to justify their military and political participation in the eyes of the conservative peasant masses.

"BACKWARD" PEOPLES, "IGNORANT" WOMEN, AND "THE PROMISE OF GENDER EQUALITY"

In September 1941, the Valjevo (Serbia) Partisan detachment issued a proclamation to local women asking for their support for the fighters on the front. "Serb women, Serb mothers, wives, and sisters!" it read, "... help your brothers, sons and husbands who joined in the struggle for freedom." Women were invited to harden their hearts and hold back their tears before the horrors of the war "like the Mother of the nine Jugovićs" and to take an active part in the struggle themselves. The proclamation reminded the women that they could fight for freedom in a number of ways: by feeding, clothing, and encouraging the soldiers; by nursing the wounded, "like the Kosovo Maiden once did"; by sending their men to the units; and finally, by signing up themselves. (The Mother of the nine Jugovićs and the Kosovo Maiden are characters from the traditional oral epic poems about the medieval Battle of Kosovo, and the central epitomes of motherhood and womanhood in the Serbian folk imagery.) The proclamation concluded with a series of pledges: Even after the liberation from the occupiers, the struggle would not stop until women's equality with men was achieved. The Partisans promised to win women's suffrage; the right of all workers, peasants, and housewives to pensions; and free health care for mothers and children.[6]

This proclamation encompasses all the major characteristics of the early Partisan rhetoric regarding women. It asks women to participate through their traditional tasks and simultaneously invites them to break out of their traditional roles by joining the units as fighters. It also combines the two central motifs of the Partisan mobilizing rhetoric: one that invokes the images of the "heroic past" from the epic folk tradition and appeals to the patriotic, antiinvader, even ethnonationalist sentiments of the population; and another that offers a supranational revolutionary platform of social and gender equality. These motifs are based on two mutually opposed ideological premises: The former is past oriented, patriarchal, and nationalist, while the latter is future oriented, egalitarian, transnational, communist. Throughout the war, the two would continue

---

[6] *Zbornik* 1.2, doc. 37, p. 137-9.

to coexist uneasily, yet only the latter has been acknowledged in the existing literature.

The official explanation for women's mass participation in the Partisan movement is what may be termed the communist "promise of gender equality," which is well summed up in the following quotation from the Yugoslav literature of the communist era:

> Led by the Yugoslav Communist Party, the working class fought for all issues concerning the social status of women.... This led to the large-scale participation of women in actions undertaken by the working class and the Yugoslav Communist Party both in the prewar period and in the struggle for the country's liberation, participation unparalleled in the history of Yugoslav peoples.[7]

Some Western scholars seem to agree. "The banner of women's equality that flew beside others," writes Mary Reed, "attracted thousands of women by promising them an equal place in the new postwar Yugoslavia."[8] Women's emancipation was indeed an integral part of the communists' platform, which they did not hesitate to put into practice. At the onset of the uprising, the party gave women the right to vote and be elected in the people's committees it set up in the liberated areas. Already in July 1941, a directive of the temporary high command of Montenegro accorded that right to all citizens eighteen and older, "male and female, regardless of their religion, nationality, and race."[9] This had little practical effect since the Italians swiftly crushed the initial Montenegrin rising. However, the Supreme Staff's guidelines codified in Foča (Bosnia) were actually implemented in all Partisan-held territories. These guidelines for the organization of the national liberation councils, known as the Foča regulation, remained in effect until the end of the war. The regulation stated that "all peasants, male and female," could vote and be elected to the village councils.[10] This was in sharp contrast with interwar Yugoslavia, where females had no political rights. As Thomas Emmert reminds us, women in the Yugoslav kingdom were not only denied suffrage, but were also, by custom and law, among the most subjugated in Europe.[11] Particularly

---

[7] Cvetić, *Žene Srbije u NOB*, p. 937 (translation to English provided in the book).

[8] Mary E. Reed, "The Anti-Fascist Front of Women," 128.

[9] *Zbornik* 3. 4, doc 1, p. 10. Several Montenegrin party directives reiterated that women should be allowed to vote and be elected. See *Zbornik* 3.1, doc. 10, p. 34; ibid. doc. 73, p.189; or *Zbornik* 9. 1, doc. 7, pp. 18–20.

[10] *Zbornik* 2.2, doc. 198, p. 415.

[11] Thomas Emmert, "Ženski Pokret: The Feminist Movement in Serbia in the 1920s," in *Gender Politics in the Western Balkans: Women and Society in Yugoslavia and the Yugoslav Successor States*, ed. Sabrina P. Ramet (University Park: Pennsylvania State University Press, 1999), 37.

notorious for its discriminatory family and inheritance laws was the Serbian Civil Code, which was designed in 1844 to protect the traditional multigenerational peasant family (the *zadruga*). With regard to their legal ability to make decisions about their own property, the code placed married women in the same category with minors, the insane, those heavily in debt, and bums (*propalice*). This legal system was utterly out of date in the twentieth century.[12]

Granting political rights to females substantiated the communists' claim that their struggle would result in the creation of a new system, in which gender equality would be instituted in accordance with the Soviet model. It empowered women in the rear and was welcomed by female party members and the communist youth. However, one can find little evidence that the promise of gender equality was a successful mobilizing strategy that motivated peasant women to join the Partisan ranks, and much to the contrary.

Two larger issues are involved in the question of the party's appeal to peasant women: its appeal to women, on the one hand, and to the peasantry, on the other. The communist alliance with the latter, as Melissa Bokovoy shows, had been tenuous from the start. When the war began, the CPY declaratively adopted the Soviet-dictated popular front line, which called for the unification of all antifascist forces and for a stress on national liberation rather than revolution. Yet already in the initial stages of the uprising, the CPY ignored Soviet instructions. When the Partisans established a liberated territory in Serbia around the town of Užice in the fall of 1941, the CPY began setting up socialist institutions. Property confiscation and occasional executions of those thought to be traitors alienated the locals, leaving the Partisans with very few peasant followers.[13]

The situation only worsened in the winter of 1941–2, the period of what has been known as "left deviationism" in the CPY's history. After

---

[12] Ibid. The interwar kingdom inherited all the legal systems of its constituent lands; on its territory Austrian, Hungarian, Serbian, and Montenegrin laws coexisted. In addition, Muslim communities adhered to old Ottoman and sharia laws. Despite considerable regional variations, all these legal systems sanctioned women's subordination to their husbands, fathers, or brothers. See Neda Božinović, "Žene u modernizacijiskim procesima u Jugoslaviji i Srbiji," in Perović, ed, *Srbija u modernizacijskim procesima* vol. 2, 513. On the Serbian civil law, see Marija Draškić and Olga Popović-Obradović, "Pravni položaj žene prema srpskom građanskom zakoniku (1844–1946)," in the same volume, 11–25.

[13] Melissa K. Bokovoy, *Peasants and Communism: Politics and Ideology in the Yugoslav Countryside, 1941–1953* (Pittsburgh: University of Pittsburgh Press, 1998), 7–12.

the first confrontations with the Chetniks and the fall of the "Užice Republic," party leaders adopted hard-line communist rhetoric that defined the Partisan cause primarily in terms of class struggle. In addition, in early 1942, the party launched a large-scale purge to eliminate the "fifth column" from the local populace and the Partisan ranks. Communist excesses, particularly in Montenegro and Herzegovina, included summary trials and wanton executions of the so-called kulaks (rich peasants), "class enemies," and "ideologically unreliable elements." The "red terror" in these regions intimidated the peasantry as a whole, radically narrowing the Partisan support base. Even in other areas, where the purge did not match the Montenegrin and Herzegovinian terror, left deviationism alienated the peasant masses, creating a "rift" between the party and the local populace. Communist orthodoxy, in short, failed to generate rapport between the Partisans and the peasantry.[14]

That the party had been mainly urban based before the war did not help. CPY leaders had long been suspicious of the peasantry, seeing it in negative terms as a backward group needing special tutelage; their first wartime encounters and thorny experiences with the Balkan rural populations only reinforced that notion. East Bosnia's peasants – who peopled the volunteer detachments that revitalized the battered Partisans in retreat from Serbia in the winter of 1941–2 – were habitually labeled "backward," "raw," and "ignorant." Party reports abound in complaints about the lack of "political consciousness" among the villagers. A similar sense of frustration characterizes the Partisan Vladimir Dedijer's wartime diary entries. For example, he writes about the peasant fighters of eastern Bosnia early in 1942: "In the volunteer units ... 99 percent of the fighters are peasants. And these peasants politically are completely backward." And the peasants who attended Partisan conferences Dedijer describes as "a very raw element." "They are horribly backward people," he writes. "Someone must constantly work with them."[15] In his report to Tito, Gojko Nikoliš, head doctor of the Partisan medical corps, provided this description of the East Bosnian volunteers: "horrible cultural

---

[14] Ibid., 7–14. For more on "left deviationism" (sometimes translated as "left deviation" and "left errors") see also Jill Irvine, *The Croat Question* (Boulder, CO: Westview Press, 1993), 123–9; Marko A. Hoare, *Genocide and Resistance in Hitler's Bosnia: The Partisans and the Chetniks, 1941–1943* (Oxford, New York: Published for the British Academy by Oxford University Press, 2006), 196–233. On the adoption of the "class war" approach, see Milovan Djilas, *Wartime* (New York: Harcourt Brace Jovanovich, 1977), 118, 122.

[15] Vladimir Dedijer, *The War Diaries of Vladimir Dedijer* (Ann Arbor: University of Michigan Press, 1990), vol. 1, 87, 91.

backwardness (95% illiterate), overgrown hair and beards, scruffy and scabby."[16] The situation elsewhere was not much better. Even the rank and file soldiers, many of peasant origin themselves, sometimes deemed the peasantry in general, and peasant women in particular, backward and inferior. Partisan staff members in Bosnian Krajina complained that their soldiers were "vulgar and rude" toward "politically backward" village women.[17] About the villagers in Sandžak whom the Partisans retreating from Serbia encountered in December 1941, Djilas writes: "Our people were too advanced for such primitive conditions.... Our women could not accept the centuries-old backwardness of the Moslem housewives, whom they rounded-up and dragged to conferences," apparently to no avail.[18]

The communists saw the widespread illiteracy of the peasantry as a major hindrance in their work to generate cadres, and this was particularly the case with women. According to the 1931 census, in Yugoslavia there were some 1.5 million illiterate men and 2.8 million illiterate women – 32.3 percent of men and 56.4 percent of women older than age ten could not read or write. In the rural regions of Bosnia-Herzegovina and Kosovo, the illiteracy rate for women was as high as 83–93 percent.[19] It was a difficult task to present the party's program to this kind of audience, to adjust the Marxist-Leninist jargon to understandable concepts, and to win over the local people for the Partisan cause. A typical communist oration could communicate little to peasant women. Dedijer recounts how an "otherwise good" speech of a female communist at an AFW conference in eastern Bosnia in February 1942 turned "weak": "She babbled some foreign phrases to the peasant Muslim women: 'Tsarist absolutism, counterrevolutionary bands, chicanery, the Moscow metro, conductors, harassed women, state institutions, state institutions ...' and so forth."[20] There was nothing here that could be related to the peasant women's experience of the war. Speeches about class conflict and bourgeois treachery did not resonate with the picture of the enemy who had burned their

---

[16] *Zbornik* 2.2, doc. 172, 344.

[17] *Zbornik* 9.1, doc. 98, p. 354.

[18] Djilas, *Wartime*, 124.

[19] There was a considerable regional variation: The largest number of illiterate women in relation to the total number of illiterates was recorded in Kosovo (93.9%); it was followed by Bosnia-Herzegovina (83.9%), central Serbia (78.3%), Montenegro (77.3%), Croatia (39.5%), Vojvodina (23.6%), and Slovenia (5.8%). Neda Božinović, "Žene u modernizacijiskim procesima u Jugoslaviji i Srbiji," in Perović, *Srbija u modernizacijskim procesima 19. i 20. veka*, vol. 2, 509.

[20] Dedijer, *The War Diaries*, vol. 1, 93.

villages; this enemy was the foreign invader or one of the local warring factions, not infrequently the women's peasant neighbors. The notion of class war and references to the Soviet model thus often failed to produce the intended effect on the peasants.

So did the "promise of gender equality" on the peasant women. Internal party documents repeatedly complained that women lacked knowledge about their role in the national liberation struggle and especially stressed women's ignorance of the fact that this struggle was being fought for their own rights. This held true both for the still uninvolved women and for those "organized" in the AFW, even though the latter were exposed to communist indoctrination. A representative passage from an internal party report reads: "Along the AFW line, we have 13 organized women, among whom there is none aware of her role in today's struggle, which is also being fought for her rights."[21] Even the female Partisan fighters showed a striking lack of awareness of what exactly they were fighting for. "Our female comrades themselves are still not aware of the magnitude of goals for which women are fighting in our NOV [National Liberation Army]," noted a deputy political commissar of the 16th Slavonian Brigade; "They are not aware that our struggle will completely change the social position of women."[22]

The CPY invested effort in the "political education" of females to familiarize them with Partisan goals, one of which was their equality with men. Among others, "women's position in the USSR" was a frequent subject of discussions at women's conferences and Partisan meetings.[23] But the leadership's accomplishments in this regard often seemed limited. Judging by internal party correspondence, women's support for the Partisan war effort remained within the practical, material domain – they worked, cooked, sewed, and cleaned for the army – but their political literacy and motivation lagged behind.[24] The party committee of northern Herzegovina noted that women tended to support the Partisan units

---

[21] *Zbornik* 1.19, doc. 78, p. 373, my italics. See also *Zbornik*, 9.4, doc. 127, p. 609, and others.

[22] *Grada za historiju Narodnooslobodilačkog Pokreta u Slavoniji* (Slavonski Brod: Historijski Institut Slavonije, 1966), vol. 5, doc. 141, p. 314.

[23] See *Zbornik* 9. 1, doc. 29, p. 96; also doc. 121, p. 444; doc. 129, p. 482; *Zbornik* 9.2, doc. 30, p. 206; doc. 45, p. 269, and others.

[24] See, for instance, Arhiv Vojnoistorijskog Instituta (The Archive of the Institute for Military History; in the following text AVII), NOR, CK SK Hrvatske 16/5, December 1942; AVII, NOR, Muzej NR Split NOB 7/182–189, 188, Kotarski kom. KPH za Makarsku Okr. kom.u KPH za Makarsku, 3 November 1943; AVII, NOR, IRP BiH 3/428–431, 430, Okr. Kom. Za Bihać-Cazin Ob.Kom-u za B. Krajinu, 4 January 1945; and others.

but showed little interest in political matters. "Although we pointed at women's equality in the National Liberation Movement," stated the report, "they are mostly passive towards that issue."[25]

With the exception of prewar communists, many women in the Partisan movement not only knew or cared little about the forthcoming socialist world of gender equality, but also knew surprisingly little about the Partisan leadership. New recruits often harbored misconceptions about the party. For example, one young female courier thought that the party (*Partija* in Serbo-Croatian; the gender of the noun is feminine) was a "lovely woman from the Soviet Union." The prewar female communists, on the other hand, who also occupied the leading positions in the movement and the AFW, had a clearer vision of their goals and role. Yet they saw the issue of gender equality situated within the context of social and revolutionary changes that were to be brought about by the CPY and had no "feminist leanings" whatsoever. Jancar-Webster interviewed nineteen of those women, and none cited the woman question as the reason for joining the party or the Partisans.[26]

Apparently, even though the party put the solution to the woman question at the forefront, that did not seem to be a major motivator for female Partisans. Neither the peasant women in the rear, nor the female fighters, nor the leading female party activists had decided to join the Partisans for the sole purpose of gaining future equality. It is thus difficult to believe that the communist promise of equal rights was the most successful strategy in attracting peasant women, and it is even less likely that it was particularly appealing to peasant men.

The party leaders themselves recognized the limitations of their attempts to attract the masses through communist orthodoxy. Besides, their insistence on revolution infuriated their Soviet mentors. "Left deviationism" proved catastrophic for the Partisans, who found themselves battered and isolated. Recognizing its mistake, in the spring of 1942, the party began modifying its line by downplaying the revolutionary rhetoric in favor of a more inclusive patriotic one. Instead of insisting on the primacy of class struggle, the Partisan leadership finally decided to create a broad popular front that would unite all patriots and antifascists to drive the occupiers out of the country. In addition, the CPY took various

[25] AVII, NOR, IRP BiH 9/204–210, 208, Okr. Kom. za S. Herzegovinu Ob. Kom-u za Hercegovinu, 20 August 1944.

[26] Jancar-Webster, *Women & Revolution*, 50, 70. Other scholars who have collected oral histories report similar findings. See Pantelić, *Partizanke kao građanke*, 47; see also Wiesinger, *Partisaninnen*, 70–5.

measures to attempt to repair its relationship with the peasants and attract them to the Partisan ranks.[27]

This new approach proved a success. Thereupon the Partisans' major supporters would become precisely the "backward" peasants and "ignorant" peasant women. With respect to women, the moderation of the rhetoric was mirrored in the party's new approach to the issue of gender equality. But before discussing this new approach, it is necessary to introduce another element of party rhetoric, one curiously ignored by most local and Western scholars: the communist appropriation of the heroic imagery of the South Slavic folk heritage.[28] As we shall see, rhetorical uses of the epic imagery lay at the heart of the party's effort to establish cultural authority among the peasantry. Most important for our discussion, the traditional imagery was used to attract women to the movement and legitimize their admission to the most exclusive male role – that of a warrior.

INVOKING THE EPICS

It is difficult to overstate the importance of folk poetry in South Slav cultures. Besides being part of the peasant tradition, it played an invaluable role in the development of a premodern national consciousness. With the romantic national "awakeners" of the nineteenth century, the folk tradition entered the written cultural domain as the most profound expression of the "national spirit" and served as the basis for modern literary language. Oral epic poetry was also widely imitated in both form and content by local writers and was instrumental in the development of modern South Slavic literatures. One of the best known examples of a literary variant of traditional heroic verse is the work of the prince-bishop of Montenegro, Petar II Petrović Njegoš (1813–1851), whose *Gorski*

[27] These measures included the party's resolution to provide safe havens for peasant refugees, to confiscate land and property from the enemy and divide it among the peasants, to suspend "rents and debts that the peasants owed to former landowners, the banks and the state," etc. In addition, strict Partisan discipline and the party's federalist platform helped win over some peasants. See Bokovoy, *Peasants and Communists*, 15–19.

[28] A rare exception is Ivo Žanić's work. Žanić focuses on the wars of the 1990s in Yugoslavia. He shows how the epic tradition (especially the *hajduk* imagery) was invoked by nationalist ideologues in order to foster separation along ethnic lines and incite various groups to rally behind their nationalist leaders, although this tradition's moral codex transcended ethnic divisions. Even though World War II is not the subject of his work, Žanić does discuss the ways that the traditional epic imagery fit into the Partisan/communist rhetoric. See Ivo Žanić, *Prevarena povijest: Guslarska estrada, kult hajduka i rat u Hrvatskoj i Bosni i Hercegovini, 1990–1995. godine* (Zagreb: Durieux, 1998).

Vijenac (*The Mountain Wreath*) assumed the central place in the Serbian/ Montenegrin – and, more broadly, Yugoslav – literary canon. Another is the Illyrianist work of the Croatian *ban* and poet Ivan Mažuranić (1814–1890), *Smrt Smail-age Čengića* (*The Death of Smail-aga Čengić*). In the past two centuries, the influence of the folk heritage was pervasive on several levels – once taken from "the people," it was recorded, sometimes embellished, systematized, analyzed, imitated, idealized, and ideologized, and then reimposed onto the common folk. Well before the Partisans entered the historical stage, the oral folk tradition had been recognized as a Yugoslav cultural phenomenon. In the interwar period, it would have been hard to find any school textbook, literary anthology, or history book of which a significant portion would not be devoted to folk poetry.[29] Most important, in one form or another, it was well known and revered among all strata of Slavic society in the Yugoslav lands.

Systematic collection and publication of the South Slavic oral heritage began in the early nineteenth century, though records of individual epics could be found earlier.[30] The pioneer in this respect was the Serbian language reformer Vuk Karadžić (1787–1864). Karadžić started his work in exile after the crushing of the First Serbian Uprising (1804–13). In Vienna he wrote down the poems he remembered from his childhood and youth and transcribed others told by Serbian exiles and refugees, and, in 1814, his first collection of folk poetry appeared in print. In the following three decades, Karadžić traveled extensively, visiting Srem, Serbia, Montenegro, the Bay of Kotor, Lika, Herzegovina, Dubrovnik, and Dalmatia, where he recorded a vast array of oral poems. His final Viennese edition, entitled *Srpske narodne pjesme* (*Serbian Folk Poems*), contained one thousand and forty-five pieces.[31]

Thanks to its oral tradition, the simple South Slavic folk premiered on Europe's romantic scene as a sensation. Among international admirers of

---

[29] Andrew Wachtel, *Making a Nation, Breaking a Nation: Literature and Cultural Politics in Yugoslavia* (Stanford, CA: Stanford University Press, 1998), 101.

[30] Among earlier recordings, the most notable is that of the Italian explorer Alberto Fortis, whose travel books featured his translation of two South Slavic epics into Italian. Both epics, one in Goethe's translation, were included in Johann Gottfried Herder's *Folksongs* (1778). Koljević, *The Epic in the Making*, pp. 4–5.

[31] Vladan Nedić, "Pogovor," in *Srpske Narodne Pjesme*, ed. by Vladan Nedić (Belgrade: Prosveta, 1969), vol. 4, 385–92; Svetozar Koljević, *The Epic in the Making* (New York: Oxford University Press, 1980), 344–5. The Serbian provenance of the poems collected by Vuk has been contested, and compellingly so. The prevalence of similar motifs, the appearance of the same heroes in poems collected among different groups in various regions, and a mixture of diverse dialects in a single poem also suggest a shared South Slavic cultural heritage.

the South Slavic poetry one could find such figures as Johann Wolfgang von Goethe, Jakob Grimm, Johann Gottfried von Herder, Prosper Mérimée, Aleksandr Pushkin, and Walter Scott. Having earned such literary acclaim, the South Slavic epos began to attract academic as well as political attention abroad. Vuk's collection inspired many European revivalists – Hungarian, Russian, West Ukrainian, German, French, and others – and served as a model for collectors and publishers of oral literature for decades.[32] Since the oral epics were considered an accurate reflection of the South Slavic national character, interethnic relations, and historical aspirations, they came to be widely discussed each time a political crisis loomed in the region.[33] From a literary perspective as well, international scholarly interest in South Slavic folk poems continued unabated through much of the twentieth century, mostly as a result of their Homeric features and persistence as a living tradition.[34]

But Vuk's collection had its greatest impact in the South Slavic lands, where, following its international recognition, oral folk poetry became "the object of literary cult" and "sacred veneration."[35] This popularity among the region's elites the oral epos owes at least as much to its political potency as to its literary excellence. Romantic nationalists saw epic poetry as an expression of resistance that had survived centuries of foreign rule. As Margaret Beissinger writes, the folk epos was "a vehicle through which ideals of liberation and national identity were expounded and promoted"; it was "fully exploited" in the attempts to create a modern national consciousness and "manipulated for political purposes."[36] Local interest in the oral tradition, however, far outlived the

---

[32] V. Nedić, "Pogovor," 389–90.

[33] Koljević, *The Epic in the Making*, 6–7.

[34] Ibid. The most influential accounts in Anglo-American scholarship are the works by Milman Parry and Albert Bates Lord. Parry, an expert on the language of Homer's epics, aimed at putting together a collection of epic songs in a living tradition. Parry did his fieldwork in Yugoslavia (esp. Herzegovina) in the 1930s. He was assisted by A. B. Lord, one of his students at Harvard, who after Parry's death continued the work of collecting epics, adding his recordings from the 1950s and 1960s to the collection. Lord also initiated a monograph series – Milman Parry Studies in Oral Tradition. Probably the best known among Lord's works on the subject is *The Singer of Tales* (Cambridge, MA: Harvard University Press, 1960). See also Lord, ed., *The Multinational Literature of Yugoslavia* (Jamaica, NY: St. John's University, 1974), and others.

[35] Margaret Beissinger, "Epic, Gender, and Nationalism: The Development of Nineteenth-Century Balkan Literature," in *Epic Traditions in the Contemporary World: The Poetics of Community*, ed. Margaret Beissinger, Jane Tylus, and Susanne Wofford (Berkeley: University of California Press, 1999), 72; Wachtel, *Making a Nation, Breaking a Nation*, 101.

[36] Beissinger, "Epic, Gender, and Nationalism," 70.

romantic national revivalists. A number of collectors followed in Vuk's steps, and one can almost speak of a "collection frenzy" that marked the second half of the nineteenth century in the Balkans and continued well into the twentieth. With zeal, dedication, and competitiveness, various individuals and national institutions commissioned the recording of oral folk poems. Each time a distinct nationalist agenda was involved – some aimed to demonstrate the existence of cultural unity among the Yugoslavs; others to make claims about the creative and nation-building potential of a particular ethnoreligious group; still others to show that oral epic poetry was by no means an exclusive property of Serbs, as Vuk would have it. Numerous collectors thus set out to record what they considered to be either shared South Slavic or distinctly Serbian, Croatian, Muslim, Macedonian, or Slovenian oral folk expression.[37] It is worth stressing here that South Slav nationalist tendencies of the nineteenth and twentieth centuries can be grouped around two disjunctive ideological paths: the separatist ethnonationalist projects, on the one hand, and the integrative "Yugoslav" nationalist projects based on shared South Slavic linguistic and cultural heritage, on the other.[38] Both those propagating separate nationalisms and those who strove for South Slavic integration, however, drew upon the folklore foundation to validate their convictions.[39]

The South Slav epics, recorded by national revivalists and their followers in the nineteenth and twentieth centuries, are oral narratives, composed in strict metrically patterned lines, which were usually sung by peasant performers. Because they were sung, they have often been called "songs" in the literature in English.[40] The focus of the vast majority of

---

[37] For Croatian folk collections, see Stjepan Mažuranić, ed., *Hrvatske Narodne Pjesme, sakupljene stranom po Primorju a stranom po granici* (Senj: H. Luster, 18740; *Hrvatske Narodne Pjesme*, vols. 1–3 (Zagreb: Matica Hrvatska, 1896–8); for Muslim poems see *Hrvatske Narodne Pjesme*, vol. 3: *Junačke Pjesme, Muhamedovske*, see also Nasko Frndic, ed., *Muslimanske Junačke Pjesme*, ed. (Zagreb: Stvarnost, 1969); for Macedonian, see Miladinovci, *Zbornik 1861–1961* (Skopje: Kočo Racin, 1962); for Slovenian, Karel Štrekelj, ed., *Slovenske narodni pesmi*, vols. 1–3 (Ljubljana: Matica Slovenska, 1895–1907); vol. 1 features heroic poems; etc.

[38] For a discussion of various national ideologies in South Slavic lands that were to form Yugoslavia, see Banac, *The National Question*, pp. 70–115. On the issue of canonizing the folk tradition and the idea of Yugoslavism see Wachtel, *Making the Nation*, 31–8.

[39] For a discussion on how the folklore foundation provided key ingredients for nationalist narratives, see Beissinger, "Epic, Gender, and Nationalism," 70–1.

[40] For more on the performers of epic poems and on the Vuk's collection methods, see Milne Holton and Vasa D. Mihailovich, Introduction to *Songs of the Serbian People: From the Collection of Vuk Karadžić*, trans. and ed. Milne Holton and Vasa D. Mihailovich (Pittsburgh: University of Pittsburgh Press, 1997).

epic poems is expectedly "martial and male."[41] Vuk had a point when he introduced a gendered categorization of oral folk genres, naming the epics "men's poems" (as opposed to lyrical songs that he dubbed "women's"). Christian epic poems detail major battles, such as the 1389 Kosovo battle that, according to epic bards, signaled the denouement of the medieval Serbian state and the beginning of Ottoman rule in the Balkans; they sing about *hajduk*s and *uskok*s (outlaws and border raiders), portraying them not as pillagers but more amiably as righteous rebels against imperial misrule; they celebrate the participants of the First Serbian Uprising (1804), in which outlaw bands joined in the struggle for Serbia's independence. Slavic Muslim poems glorify Muslim heroes – feudal lords, local military notables, or border raiders – usually engaged in the fight against their Christian opponents.

The main characters of the majority of epic poems are bellicose males – *junak*s (heroes). In the tumultuous Balkans, divided among great empires for centuries and subject to frequent warfare, and within the context of relatively rigid social structures with a marked gender segregation, it is not surprising to find that both expressive forms and social practices glorify belligerent manhood in a manner consistent with hero worship. As incarnations of patriarchal masculinity par excellence – that of a heroic warrior – the *junak*s combine some features of medieval knighthood and chivalry with the tradition of peasant resistance and rebellion. Either as feudal lords, as bandits (*hajduks* and *uskoks*), or as rebel leaders of peasant uprisings, the epic heroes embody quintessential patriarchal values. Exceptional courage, honor, patriotism, endurance, strength, wisdom, and military prowess are among their typical traits. Yet they are by no means one-dimensional superhero characters. The epic heroes' vulnerability, insecurities, and often inferior position in the social hierarchy vis-à-vis their opponents made them characters to whom the peasants could easily relate.[42] Epic poetry's most important and most politically potent aspect was the hope that its heroes embodied – that resistance and dedication to a righteous cause would ultimately be victorious.

The link between the folk heritage and the communist narrative of the National Liberation Struggle is multifaceted. Most obviously, folk poetry provided an infinite repository of metaphors, which allowed the Partisans to represent themselves as the bearers of the great heroic tradition of the

---

[41] Wachtel, *Making a Nation*, 35.
[42] Wachtel makes this point in his excellent analysis of the role of Kraljević Marko; see ibid., 38.

Yugoslav peoples. It also helped them establish cultural authority among the peasants. Scholars have noted that "when great authority is invested in texts associated with elders or ancestors, traditionalizing discourse by creating links with traditional genres is often the most powerful strategy for creating authority."[43] In party rhetoric, the National Liberation War was the final and most-glorious episode of this centuries-long epic struggle for liberty. The oral heritage was especially suitable for the party's supranational platform because of its wider South Slavic character. The party made use of a spectrum of epic motifs: the heroism and self-sacrifice of a whole nation that is glorified in the Serbian epos of the Kosovo battle, the celebration of the *uskoks* and *hajduks* (border raiders and outlaws) as rebels against imperial rule (Ottoman, Venetian, and Habsburg), the legends of Croat and Slovene peasant revolts against feudal landowners, the freedom-loving spirit of the heroes of the First Serbian Uprising, and the Montenegrin paradigm of the necessity to fight against internal enemies and traitors featured in *The Mountain Wreath,* among others.

The epics were most readily invoked in party appeals to the Serbs, who constituted the majority of Partisan supporters in the first years of the war. The party elite recurrently invoked the Kosovo mythology in Serbia, Montenegro, and Serb-populated regions of Bosnia-Herzegovina and Croatia. An early party appeal to "the people of Kraljevo" (Serbia) insisted that the locals should continue in the steps of their glorious ancestors, reminding them of the "bravery of Serbian heroes, who have since Kosovo until today stood proudly on the bulwark of their fatherland." The appeal included the famous battle cry from one of the best-known epic poems of the First Serbian Uprising: "Serbia cannot be pacified!"[44] In their references to the Chetniks, the Partisans consistently evoked the image of Vuk Branković, whom the epics had remembered as a traitor and blamed for the Serbian defeat at Kosovo. "Patriotic Serb women!" reads a proclamation issued after the first Partisan conflicts with the Chetniks in Serbia, "scorn the new Brankovićs from the Ravna Gora and flock together as one into the strong and unified front for our people's freedom."[45] Similarly, a Partisan detachment in Bosnia invited Bosnian Serbs to "fight against the descendants of Vuk Branković," and "persist

---

[43] Charles L. Briggs and Richard Bauman, "Genre, Intertextuality, and Social Power," *Journal of Linguistic Anthropology* 2.2 (1992): 147–8.

[44] *Zbornik* 1.2, doc. 35, p. 131. "Serbia cannot be pacified!"[*Srbija se umirit ne može!*] is a famous line from one of the most beautiful poems on the first Serbian uprising (1804), "Boj na Mišaru."

[45] *Zbornik* 1. 2, doc. 65, p. 225.

in this Obilić-like [*obilićevska*] struggle."[46] The latter was a reference to the Serbian hero of the Kosovo battle, Miloš Obilić, who, according to the epic legend, killed the Ottoman sultan in a heroic act of self-sacrifice. Allusions to the Kosovo epics also figured in internal party documents.[47]

Among the Montenegrin Partisans, the preeminence of *The Mountain Wreath* was unquestionable. Milovan Djilas remembers how communists in Montenegro celebrated Orthodox Christmas Eve in January 1942 "with recitations against aggressors and traitors" from the *Wreath*. At the height of "left deviationism," Njegoš's verses about the necessity of confronting the internal enemy seemed particularly fitting. Himself a Montenegrin and a great admirer of Njegoš's work, Djilas admits that the *Wreath* was the only book that he always carried with him during the war.[48] In Montenegrin Partisan brigades, Njegoš's epic was the subject of educational lectures in history and literature.[49] In Montenegro's party declarations and appeals to the population, verses from the *Wreath* and references to Njegoš's male protagonists were commonplace.[50] Appeals to women invoked the image of the *Wreath*'s single heroine, the sister of the fallen hero Batrić, whose words mourning the death of her brother mark one of the most touching passages. An appeal to Montenegrin girls in a Partisan youth journal, for example, addressed them as "the sisters of Batrić."[51]

The epic imagery of the *uskok*s (border raiders) and *hajduk*s (outlaws) provided an equally potent symbolic pool, which could be used to appeal not only to the Serbs/Montenegrins but also to other groups. As Wendy Bracewell writes, common traditions of banditry were used to promote "brotherhood and unity" among the Yugoslav peoples – in the Partisan evocations, the images of epic heroes of Croat, Serb, and Muslim origin appear side by side. Perhaps more important, prewar nationalist

---

[46] *Zbornik* 4. 1, doc. 148, p. 333. See also the proclamation of the Bosnian Staff in *Zbornik* 4.1, doc. 12, p. 37.

[47] Tito himself could not resist the temptation – in an order sent to the Staff of the Durmitor (Montenegro) detachment, he made an allusion to Vuk Branković in reference to a Partisan commander who had switched sides and joined the Chetniks. See Zbornik 2. 3, doc. 44, p. 127, n. 7.

[48] Djilas, *Wartime*, 150, 276.

[49] See a report of the 3rd Proletarian Brigade in *Zbornik* 9. 1, doc. 104, 373.

[50] See, for example, the appeal of the Cetinje military committee to the people of the Cetinje district, in *Zbornik* 3. 1, doc. 9, p. 31. See also Proclamation of Provincial Committee of CPY for Montenegro, Boka and Sandžak, in *Zbornik* 3.1, doc. 69, pp. 182–3.

[51] Arhiv Jugoslavije (The Archive of Yugoslavia; AJ in the following text), SKJ 507, CKKPJ-1942/55, *Omladinski pokret: List Crnogorske narodne omladine*, god. II, br.1, 1 February 1942.

ideologues often elevated the outlaws to the status of freedom fighters against the imperial "yoke," thereby enabling the party to reinvent the epic bandits as "premature Partisans."[52] It was not unusual for a Partisan battalion to be named after an epic outlaw.[53]

Such imagery was admittedly less suitable for northwestern areas of the county. But even in these regions where the memory of the Ottoman conquest had faded away or where no *hajduk* tradition existed, such as Slovenia and northwestern Croatia, the party made use of the popular memory of peasant rebellions against feudal lords.[54] For instance, the Partisans adopted the cult of Matija Gubec, the leader of the peasant uprising of 1573. From the early stages of the war, the rhetoric of the party in Croatia was marked by references to Gubec, representing the Croat Partisans as his true successors. A 1941 issue of *Vjesnik*, the journal of the Croatian National Liberation Front, was dedicated to "the brave sons who honorably bear the flag of Matija Gubec and other Croat heroes."[55] The party named a Croat battalion after Gubec and invoked his image to attract the local peasantry and win over the left wing of the influential Croat Peasant Party.[56]

Even though the Partisans tried to accommodate the heroes and myths of all South Slavic constituencies, they were perhaps less sensitive to the rich epos of Bosnian Muslims. The Muslim epic poetry equally glorified military prowess and valor, and there were attempts to use it in the Partisan apotheosis of heroism.[57] Yet the Partisans seemed unwilling or unable to integrate Muslim heroes – *aga*s and *bey*s, who were portrayed in the Christian poetry as oppressors – into their wartime imagery. Moreover, while the epic imagery of the Kosovo battle, peasant

---

[52] Wendy Bracewell, "'The Proud Name of Hajduks': Bandits as Ambiguous Heroes in Balkan Politics and Culture," in *Yugoslavia and Its Historians: Understanding the Balkan Wars of the 1990s*, ed. Norman Naimark and Holly Case (Stanford, CA: Stanford University Press, 2003), 31.

[53] For example, a Bosnian Partisan battalion was named "Old Vujadin" [Starac Vujadin], after a Serb *hajduk* immortalized in the epics. See *Zbornik* 4.1, doc. 127, pp. 283–4; also ibid, doc. 134, 294–5; ibid., doc. 199, 483–4, and others.

[54] Also noted by Žanić, *Prevarena povijest*, 319–21.

[55] AJ, SKJ 507, CKKPJ-1941/133, *Vjesnik Hrvatske Jedinstvene NO Fronte*, December 1941.

[56] For instance, in an appeal to the CPP, the communists wrote, "The Communist Party offers you a brotherly hand and asks you to recall your glorious Croat traditions, the shadow [*sjeni*] of great Matija Gubec." *Zbornik* 5. 1, doc. 19, 62–5. For the battalion named after Gubec, see AVII, NOR, Muzej Like Gospic NOB 1/504, November 1943.

[57] Vladimir Nazor, for example, discusses the Muslim hero Alija Djerzelez alongside two *hajduks* – a Croat and a Serb. See Nazor, *Partizanska knjiga*, p. 107. Noted also in Bracewell, "The Proud Name of Hajduks," 31.

rebellions, or some *hajduk* heroism appealed to the Christian Slavic peasants, its overt anti-Islamic content could be alienating or even offensive to Yugoslav Muslims. Ivo Žanić writes that the Partisan leadership incorporated an implicit anti-Muslim bias both into its wartime rhetoric and into the postwar Yugoslav symbolic sphere.[58]

Besides providing a range of allegories about self-sacrifice, honor, and resistance that appeared ideal for any mobilizational rhetoric, the heroic traditions helped the party articulate its cause in a manner accessible to the peasantry. A former Partisan remembers how a female communist, Rada Vranješević, explained the Partisan struggle to a group of Bosnian Serb peasants in 1942: At first she talked about the Serbian heroes in the fight for national liberation against the Turks, and then she "beautifully and cleverly linked it to our struggle."[59] Djilas recounts how he consoled the Serb peasants of Banija (a region decimated by the Ustashas) "in the language and values of their heritage." He first stated that the Serbs could never free themselves except by death and sacrifice, and then recalled the heroes of Kosovo, the First Serbian Uprising, and World War I.[60] In order to attract the masses and present their cause in an accessible manner, the Partisans sometimes organized cultural events around themes from traditional folk poetry.[61] According to a Montenegrin veteran who often addressed youth conferences during the war, the strategy of evoking the heroic traditions indeed found a welcome response in the masses. "I mention by name the rebels from each clan of this region about whom I heard stories in my childhood," she remembers. "The youth warms up, they get carried away by the old and new heroic deeds of our *junaks*"[62] (Figure 2).

The Partisan cultural activity was itself based on the folk heritage of the peoples of the region. In the minds of Party leaders, the living traditions of epic singing agreed so well with guerrilla lifestyle that their "rules of Partisan warfare" recommended that each unit be equipped

---

[58] Žanić, *Prevarena povijest*, p. 339. On the problems of reconciling the *hajduk* and Turk/ Muslim imagery, see pp. 335–43.

[59] Stevo Ćulibrk's recollection, in Mila Beoković, *Žene heroji* (Sarajevo: Svjetlost, 1967), 411. There was some confusion, though, either in Ćulibrk's interpretation or in her speech about Saint Sava, whom she represented as a "fighter against the Turks," although he had lived well before the Ottoman arrival in the Balkans.

[60] Djilas, *Wartime*, 321; italics in the original.

[61] AVII, NOR, IRP BiH 12/119–20, Obl.kom. za Ist. Bosnu, pomoćniku komesara XVI Muslimanske brigade, 4 January 1945.

[62] Jelisavka Komnenić-Džaković, *Staza jedne partizanke* (Beograd: Narodna knjiga, 1980), 27.

FIGURE 2. Villagers of Glamoč (Bosnia and Herzegovina) attending a Partisan cultural event, 1942. Photographer Žorž Skrigin.
Courtesy of Jugoslovenska Kinoteka and Muzej Istorije Jugoslavije.

with "combat songs and a *gusle*" (traditional one-string musical instrument used by epic bards).[63] The oral heritage inspired many a Partisan writer; the majority of literary works that emerged from the Partisan war were poems in folkloric form. As Andrew Wachtel points out, "They had the undeniable advantages of brevity, spontaneity, and a connection to a living oral tradition familiar to a large number of the partisan fighters."[64] One can find published collections of epic poems about the Partisan struggle written in the traditional style.[65] The most prominent Partisan literary figures, including Skender Kulenović (about whose work more

---

[63] AJ, SKJ 507, CKKPJ-1941/37, A. Ranković, *Pravila partizanskog ratovanja koje je izradio naš štab u Srbiji*, 15 August 1941.

[64] Wachtel, *Making a Nation*, 149.

[65] See for example Momir Petronijević-Moša, *Borba Šumadijskog Partizanskog Odreda* (Aranđelovac: "Napredak," 1967).

will be said later), Ivan Goran Kovačić, Branko Ćopić, and many others, drew upon the folk tradition in their works.[66]

Partisan folklore bears an even greater imprint of the oral heritage. In her essay on Partisan folk poetry, the literary critic Maja Bošković-Stulli explores its parallels with the old oral poetic tradition.[67] Partisan songs mimicked traditional ones in style, narrative form, and, to a degree, content. They were equally imbued with the spirit of heroism and self-sacrifice. However, the new heroes were now Tito, Stalin, various communist leaders, and anonymous Partisan men and women.

Thanks to the party's efforts, a large corpus of wartime folk songs has been preserved. Like the national revivalists of the romantic era and their many nationalist followers, the party's leaders made sure that the heroic poetry of their times was recorded. The lore that they were interested in preserving celebrated the Partisan struggle. "Dear Comrades," read a 1943 party directive issued in the Karlovac district of Croatia, "Our people have always sung poems about various heroes, and thus also during this year's struggle against the occupiers, the Ustashas, and the Chetniks, our people have composed many songs about these struggles and today's heroes." The directive instructed local party committees to start collecting the new lore and asked them "to approach this task most seriously."[68] Similar orders were issued elsewhere, putting party committees and Partisan mass organizations in charge of collecting songs.[69] In addition, political commissars in the army were told to promote dances with villagers and record folk poetry.[70] Already during the war, the party managed to publish several smaller collections of Partisan songs in the

---

[66] Literary critics have pointed to the similarities between the traditional epics and the work of these writers. For instance, about the poetry of Ivan Goran Kovačić, whose poem *The Pit* (*Jama*) about the Ustasha massacres remains one of the best-known wartime works, A. B. Lord writes, "The same basic notes [as in the epic tradition] are to be found in I. G. Kovačić's poem *The Pit*, written during the Second World War, but the old myth is here reshaped in terms of the twentieth-century Yugoslav situation and sensibility." A. B. Lord, ed., *The Multinational Literature of Yugoslavia*, 12.

[67] Maja Bošković-Stulli, "Narodna poezija naše oslobodilačke borbe kao problem suvremenog folklornog stvaralaštva," in *Usmena Književnost: Izbor studija i ogleda*, ed. Bošković-Stulli (Zagreb: Školska knjiga, 1971), 334-48.

[68] AVII, NOR, CK HRV 18/261, Agitprop OK Karlovac Kotarskim komitetima, 13 July 1943.

[69] AVII, NOR, IRP BiH 5/557-8, Pokr. kom. SKOJ za BiH Oblasnim i okr. komitetima SKOJa, 17 March 1943. The directive puts the Communist League members in charge of the task.

[70] AVII, NOR, IRP BiH 12/148-150, Obl.kom. za Ist. Bosnu Pomoćniku kom. XXI NOU brigade, 4 January 1945.

liberated territories; the first comprehensive collection appeared in 1944 and was followed by innumerable anthologies afterward.[71]

In Yugoslav scholarship of Tito's era, the cultural production of the Partisan movement is seen as spontaneous. This notion that Partisan culture had had its sole origins in the masses was proposed during the war itself. Already in 1941, *Vjesnik* noted that in Lika, one of the early strongholds of the uprising, old folk songs and tales were being pushed aside by new ones about the Partisan struggle.[72] According to Dedijer, who recorded several wartime Partisan songs in his diary, "most of them are made up by the people themselves, and then there are the old folk songs adapted to the times. Finally, there is the poetry of Branko Ćopić and other poets, which the people have taken and turned into their own."[73] Many Yugoslav scholars simply adopted the official view of the authorship and spontaneity of Partisan folklore, representing it as an independent and authentic expression of the common folk.[74]

This idealized picture needs some revision. Actually, the Partisan cultural output was to a large extent directed and controlled from above. Throughout the war, agitprop (agitation and propaganda) party sections were in charge of cultural and educational activities in the movement.[75] Internal Party documents contain numerous instructions about the ways that the so-called cultural-educational activities should be organized. According to these instructions, every company was to form its own choir and its "dilettante" group (*diletantska grupa*, an amateur theater troupe). Choirs were considered particularly important, since

[71] Among the wartime collections are *Pjesme borbe* (CK KPH, 1942), *Pjesme koje pjevamo* (1943), *Pjesmarica* (Agitprop Požeškog područja), *Naše pjesme* (ZAVNOH, 1944), and others. The first comprehensive collection was *Druže Tito, ljubičice bijela* (ZAVNOH, 1944); its second, extended edition appeared in 1947 under the title *Narodne pjesme borbe i oslobodjenja* (Zagreb: Prosvjeta, 1947). See Maja Bošković-Stulli, "Narodna poezija," 318.

[72] AJ, SKJ 507, CKKPJ-1941/133, *Vjesnik Hrvatske Jedinstvene NO Fronte*, br. 9, December 1941, p. 44.

[73] Dedijer, *The War Diaries*, vol. 2, 430.

[74] These scholars do not necessarily approach the Partisan folk literature uncritically. They argue, for example, that the Partisan folk poetry lags behind the traditional one in terms of its literary value, complexity, and artistic imagination. But they do not question its origins or spontaneity. See, for example, Maja Bošković-Stulli, "Narodna poezija," 317–55. See also Nikola Cvetković "Likovi žena u narodnoj poeziji oslobodilačkih ratova," in *Srbija u modernizacijskim procesima*, vol. 2, pp. 367–71.

[75] Agitprop departments continued their activity after the war; for more on agitation and propaganda activities in Tito's Yugoslavia, see Carol Lilly, *Power and Persuasion: Ideology and Rhetoric in Communist Yugoslavia, 1944–1953* (Boulder, CO: Westview Press, 2001).

the agitprop recognized that through songs it could "make an impact morally, politically, and culturally."[76] Activists responsible for the cultural-educational work were in charge not only of recording the existing songs sung in the units, but also of asking the Partisans to write new lyrics and compose new melodies; for the creation of new songs, the agitprop itself often provided some "material."[77] Works of individual, mostly anonymous, Partisan poets were sent to the agitprop for evaluation and performed only if approved.[78] The lyrics of existing folk songs were similarly subject to control and alteration. The party committee for eastern Bosnia instructed political commissars to collect folk poems sung in the units and villages, *and* to inject some Partisan content into them.[79] The Partisan journals, which published these newly recorded lyrics and tales, were either run by agitprop activists or placed under their censorship.[80] There is, in short, little doubt that the party administered the movement's culture. Wartime songs, much like the Partisans' cultural production in general, may thus be considered party-coordinated folklore. The traditional lore shaped Partisan culture not only from below – from the mass of rank and file peasant Partisans and their covillagers in the rear – but was also inserted and manipulated from above.

Perhaps the most succinct appraisal of the ways that the party appropriated traditional culture is that of the wartime head of the agitprop department, Milovan Djilas. According to Djilas, in its propaganda the party consciously used the time-honored heritage and myths, "composed new poems about the Partisans in the traditional style," and emphasized their "ties with the centuries-old struggle of our freedom-loving peoples."[81] Comparing Greek and Yugoslav resistance songs, Janet

---

[76] *Zbornik*, 9.3, doc. 152, p. 639.

[77] *Zbornik*, 9.3, doc. 42, pp. 166–7.

[78] AVII, NOR, CK HRV 18/240, Agitprop CK KPH, Okr. kom-u KPH Karlovac, 6 July 1943, for example, presents the case of the Partisan Ivan Pekin's poem being evaluated and approved by the agitprop.

[79] AVII, NOR, IRP BiH 12/119–120, Obl. kom. za Ist. Bosnu Pomoćniku komesara XVI Muslimanske brigade, 4 January 1945.

[80] One could find some diversity and spontaneity in the Partisan press in the earlier stages of the war, especially in local units' journals, thanks in part to difficulties of imposing firm control over a large body of publications and in part to the fact that lower party officials, rank-and-file Partisans, and common people were encouraged to contribute. But early in 1944, Tito ordered the cessation of all local periodicals, after which most company and battalion journals were discontinued, and censorship in general became stricter. On the banning of local journals, see AVII, NOR, IRP BiH 6/269–274, 272, Pol. komesar XVII Divizije, Obl. Kom.-u za Ist. Bosnu, 10 February 1944.

[81] Djilas, *Wartime*, 227.

Hart finds that the Yugoslav ones "stressed an indigenous nationalism combined with orthodox Communist references." She writes that in the Greek case, dealing with a country much less ethnically heterogeneous than Yugoslavia, references to the Soviet Union were far less frequent. But in Yugoslavia, they were omnipresent, as "Tito was obliged to employ relatively 'neutral' rhetoric, choosing symbols that could be used to promote wholesale allegiances because they were not part of any particular group's repertoire."[82] Actually, the Yugoslav leadership chose symbols that were part of almost every group's repertoire, in each case with considerable nationalist baggage, which was neutralized by replacing traditional ethnic heroes with communist ones, be they Yugoslav or Soviet. In what follows, we shall see how heroines figured in this party-coordinated culture.

HEROINES IN THE CULTURE OF HERO WORSHIP

At the 1945 celebration of International Women's Day, March 8, in Jajce, Dr. Vojislav Kecmanović greeted the people of liberated Bosnia. Echoing Nazor's speech about the *partizankas*, yet referring not to female fighters but to women who had supported the Partisans in other capacities during the war, he presented the nonmartial complement of the Yugoslav New Woman. "We have admired the Jugović Mother who lost nine children without shedding a tear, but her heart burst out of sorrow," he said. "Our women experienced the same blows as she had, but their hearts did not burst, rather, they got stronger."[83]

These two statements by two prominent male political figures, Nazor and Kecmanović, denote the female idiom of wartime Partisan cultural production.[84] They reveal the two pillars of Partisan womanhood: the *martial* and *maternal* ones. The two roughly correspond to the roles that women played as combatants and as those who provided support in the rear, and both were based on their lived experiences. But rather than merely reflecting wartime women's activity, this imagery reveals the set of gender norms that the party promoted. It is significant that the referential

---

[82] Janet Hart, *New Voices in the Nation: Women and the Greek Resistance, 1941–1964* (Ithaca, NY: Cornell University Press, 1996), 213, 85.

[83] "Slobodoljubive žene svijeta," *Žena Danas*, June 1945, 28.

[84] Both Nazor and Kecmanović were, at the time of these statements, holding the leading posts in the Partisan administration. Nazor was president of ZAVNOH (The Land Antifascist Council of National Liberation of Croatia); Kecmanović was president of ZAVNOBIH (the equivalent for Bosnia-Herzegovina).

points for both Nazor and Kecmanović were epic heroines, as archetypes against which to define the "new woman."[85]

The Partisans invoked the images of epic heroines primarily to mobilize women in the rear, who contributed through an extension of their traditional tasks to the Partisan war effort. When the appeal of the Valjevo detachment to Serbian women quoted earlier recalled the Kosovo Maiden – who, according to the epic legend, roamed the battle-ground after the Kosovo battle, tending and comforting the dying Serbian heroes – it did so to invite women to nurse the wounded and sick Partisan men. When the party mentioned the Jugović Mother, whose heart collapsed upon learning of the death of her nine sons in the Kosovo battle, it did so to remind women of their patriotic duty to send their sons to the units.[86] The Jugović Mother was the traditional heroine most frequently mentioned in Partisan addresses to women. She served as a model for the Partisan notion of motherhood, which is exemplified by the main character of the best-known wartime poem about the National Liberation Struggle, Skender Kulenović's "Stojanka Majka Knežopoljka" (Stojanka, Mother from Knežopolje).

Patriotic Mothers: When, in 1942, Kulenović wrote his "Stojanka," he probably could not anticipate that this work was to make him one of the most famed poets in Yugoslavia in the following decades. Kulenović was a prewar communist, an agitprop activist, and a Partisan himself. His poem was written in a bout of inspiration after the German-Ustasha offensive against the Partisans on the mountain of Kozara. During the war, it was published in Partisan periodicals and recited at cultural events in liberated territories.[87] Kulenović himself frequently read or recited his work

---

[85] The authors who glorify "the new woman" often refer to the women of the South Slavic epic poetry. Svetozar Rittig, for instance, traces the history of women's heroism that culminated with the Partisan women back to the Biblical times; yet the only South Slavic women that he mentions are epic heroines – the Mother of the Jugovićs, Mother Margarita, the Kosovo Maiden, and the wife of Hasan-aga. See Rittig's text in *Žena u borbi*, Dec. 1944/Jan. 1945, 4–6. Jovan Popović's famous article "Legenda o Hanifi," in *Žena danas* similarly refers to the legendary women, including the Jugović Mother. See *Žena danas* (January 1943), 10.

[86] The literature on the Jugović Mother and the Kosovo Maiden in Serbo-Croatian is too vast to be cited here. For a brief discussion of the epic poem about the Jugović Mother in English see Wachtel, *Making the Nation*, 35–6; on the Kosovo Maiden in English see Ronelle Alexander, "The Poetics of Vuk Karadžić's songs: An Analysis of 'Kosovka Devojka,'" in *Kosovo: Legacy of a Medieval Battle*, ed. by Wayne S. Vucinich and Thomas A. Emmert (Minneapolis: University of Minnesota Press, 1991), 189–202.

[87] AVII, NOR, IRP BiH 5/604, Kult.prosvetna ekipa USAOJa okruga Podgrmeč, 1943.

to the units.[88] Throughout the communist era in Yugoslavia, "Stojanka" was required reading in the elementary and high school curricula. Critics praised the rugged yet rich folkloristic language of the poem as well as its fine rhythm mimicking the traditional Bosnian lament songs. The literary quality of the poem notwithstanding, its prestigious place in Yugoslavia's postwar culture is due primarily to Kulenović's ability to capture, as one commentator described it, "the spirit of Partisanhood" – the feeling of national tragedy under occupation and the resistance it produced.[89]

Kulenović's heroine is a mother, who, as the poem's subtitle states, "calls for vengeance, looking for [the bodies of her] sons Srđan, Mrđan, and Mlađen who perished in a fascist offensive." Mourning her sons and cursing the enemy, she foresees a clamor arriving from the east, from Moscow. This clamor is to answer her call for retaliation. At the end of the poem, she declares that if she could again give birth to sons, she would give them up for the struggle.[90] The poem's theme and style, critics have pointed out, suggest continuity with the best of South Slavic folk poetry – specifically, with "The Death of the Mother of the Jugovićs."[91] Kulenović himself makes an explicit link with the traditional epos, likening the mother's three Partisan sons to Miloš Obilić, the most celebrated Serbian hero of the Kosovo battle.[92] Unlike the Jugović mother and unlike the defeat at Kosovo, though, Stojanka survives and calls for revenge and rebellion, which is to be victorious this time. Modeled after the epic heroine but also departing from her, the Partisan mother became both a symbol of the wartime catastrophe *and* an agitator for the Partisan cause.

---

[88] AVII, NOR, IRP BiH 3/511–512, 511, Izvešaj sreski kom. B. Petrovac Okr. Kom-u B Petrovac, 25 January 1943.

[89] Stevan Raičković "Pesnička ponornica Skendera Kulenovića," in Skender Kulenović, *Stojanka Majka Knežopoljka i druge pesme*, ed. Stevan Raičković (Belgrade: Prosveta, 1968), 10–13.

[90]

If my womb were to be impregnated	Kad bi se utroba moja oplodila,
I would to three other Mlađens	Još bih tri Mlađena
and three other Mrđans	i tri bih Mrđana
and three other Srđans	i tri bih Srđana,
give birth,	porodila,
and nurse them on my bitter breast	i ljutom dojkom odojila,
and all three [again] onto you bestow.	i sva tri tebi poklonila.

[91] Raičković, "Pesnička ponornica," 11.

[92] The mother refers to her three sons as the three Obilićs: "tri goda srpska u mom vijeku / tri Obilića u mom mlijeku" (three Serbian tree-rings in my lifetime / the three Obilićs in my milk).

The extent to which maternal imagery, championing this particular kind of tragic yet vengeful and activist motherhood, figured in wartime publications is striking. Numerous reports, articles, letters, and first-person testimonies retell the variants of the same story: that of grieving and vindictive mothers, who proudly give up their children to die for the righteous cause and funnel all of their pain and anger into rallying for the Partisan struggle. Here are some characteristic quotes from AFW journals:

"I gave three sons to the National-Liberation Army eagerly," declares an elderly woman in her seventies …. "I gave three sons to the struggle, and I would give more if I had any," says another elderly woman. (at an AFW conference, and *Istranka*, the journal of AFW Istria reports)[93]

"I had seven sons. Four of them joined the Partisans, one was killed – three are still young children and I am sorry that they have not [yet] grown [enough] to carry rifles, so that I could send them too into Tito's army." (a Bosnian mother at a conference of the Tuzla district AFW)[94]

"My three sons were shot by the Chetniks…. Although I am old, I will contribute to the struggle as much as I can." (words of a Montenegrin mother)[95]

"I do not mourn [my son], he fell for the freedom of the people. Death to the hated fascists!" (mother of a Croatian Partisan commander, at his funeral)[96]

In party propaganda, patriotic mothers not only talked about their own contribution to the war, but also encouraged other women to send their children to fight. *Žena danas* features the words of Marija Vegrin, the "hero mother" of four Partisan fighters, who reportedly told women gathered at an AFW conference: "I ask all mothers to send their sons into this honorable and holy struggle. My children fight, and whole groups of children have left. Be brave, send your sons into the struggle."[97] The Partisans also tried to reach mothers of their local adversaries. AFW publications depicted women who had influenced their sons to switch sides and join the Partisans.[98]

---

[93] "Konferencija AFŽ za kotar Motovun," *Istranka*, July 1944.

[94] These were, reportedly, the words of Tima Kurelić from Tuzla at a conference of the Tuzla district AFW, 22 October 1944. From "Konferencija antifašističkog fronta žena tuzlanskog okruga," *Žena kroz borbu* 2, 1944, 10.

[95] The words of Zorka Vujisić from Kolašin, reported in "Iz borbe Crnogorki," *Žena Danas*, September 1944, 12.

[96] The words of Ana, Trivun Vraneš's mother, at his funeral; Vraneš was the commander of a Partisan battalion. Reported in "Herojsko držanje jedne majke," *Rodoljupka*, July 1943.

[97] "Istranke drugu Titu," *Žena Danas*, September 1944, 5.

[98] See, for example, *Žena Danas*, January 1943, pp. 53–4; *Istranka*, July 1944, and others.

Such emphasis on Spartan motherhood was neither original nor unique
to the Yugoslav Partisans. A motherly figure who symbolizes national
tragedy or patriotic resistance is a well-established tradition in modern
cultures worldwide. The prominence of such imagery in the Soviet case
during World War II has been well documented: from the famous portrayals of the "Motherland" in wartime posters such as *Rodina Mat'
Zovet* (The Motherland Is Calling), to fictional heroines in films and literature, to depictions of actual mothers' suffering and calls for vengeance.[99]
In the latter group, the mother of Zoia Kosmodem'ianskaia, "the Soviet
Joan of Arc," is probably the most famous example. The Partisan girl
Zoia Kosmodem'ianskaia (also known as Tanya) was the most celebrated
wartime Soviet heroine. The story of her short life and heroic death cap-
tivated Soviet public imagination for decades. It is the story of a teen
Komsomol girl who volunteered for the Partisan movement when the
war started. She was sent behind the front lines near Moscow, caught by
the Germans, bestially tortured, and finally hanged. Despite the despi-
cable cruelty to which they subjected her, the Nazis were not able to
extract any information from Zoia. The Soviet media systematically built
up her legend after her death in 1941.[100] A key element of the myth was
the girl's mother, Ljubov, who became both the myth's propagator and a
mythical character herself. When Zoia was killed, her mother appealed to
the Soviet nation in a radio address. She told of her grief on the death of
her only daughter but also of her pride, and simultaneously appealed to
the Soviet people to seek revenge. Her words were widely reported in the
media. Ljubov then began touring the country and visiting schools, where
she told the story of her daughter's heroism. Her tours continued well

---

[99] For an analysis of the Soviet posters, including the famous "Rodina Mat' Zovet," see
Victoria Bonnell, *Iconography of Power: Soviet Political Posters under Lenin and Stalin*
(Berkeley: University of California Press, 1997). For an analysis of Soviet war films,
including those featuring vengeful mothers, such as *She Defends the Motherland* (1943),
see Peter Kenez, "Black and White: The War on Film," in *Culture and Entertainment
in Wartime Russia*, ed. Richard Stites (Bloomington: Indiana University Press, 1995),
157–75, esp. 167; for martial and maternal images of women in wartime culture
see Richard Stites, *Russian Popular Culture: Entertainment and Society since 1900*
(New York: Cambridge University Press, 1992), 83.

[100] Her case became the subject of journalistic reports, essays, stories, brochures, poems,
songs, and films in the wartime and postwar eras. On the Kosmodem'ianskaia legend
as a case of wartime propaganda, see Rosalinde Sartorti, "On the Making of Heroes,
Heroines, and Saints," in *Culture and Entertainment in Wartime Russia*, ed. Richard
Stites (Bloomington: Indiana University Press, 1995), 182–90; Julianne Fürst, "Heroes,
Lovers, Victims – Partisan Girls during the Great Fatherland War," *Minerva* 18.3–4
(Fall–Winter 2000): 38–74.

after the war was over. She also authored two books about Zoia, which were published in several languages, including English.[101]

Zoia Kosmodem'ianskaia's fame reached the Yugoslav Partisans, who named a labor unit after her.[102] Yet perhaps even more than the Soviet *partizanka* herself, it was the character of her mother that gave the Yugoslavs a propagandistic motif to pursue. The Yugoslav mothers featured in the Partisan and AFW press tread in the steps of Ljubov Kosmodem'ianskaia. The CPY was careful, however, not simply to project the Soviet imagery onto the Yugoslav context, but rather to ground the images of Yugoslav mothers in local traditions. This was done, in part, by linking patriotic Partisan mothers with epic heroines.

Although this maternal imagery was designed and promoted by the party, not everything was tendentious about it – thousands of Yugoslav women did lose their sons and daughters in the war. Besides, these women whose family members had joined Tito's army were the most likely supporters of the Partisan cause. Such women were most often elected to AFW councils. The living embodiment of the character from Kulenović's poem and the archetype of an AFW activist was the very person presiding over the organization's Central Council, Kata Pejnović. Pejnović was a peasant Serb woman from Lika (Croatia) and a prewar communist. At the beginning of the war, her three sons were murdered by the Ustasha fascists. Thereafter she became one of the most prominent women of the resistance and one of the leaders of the AFW. At the founding conference of the Yugoslav AFW, in 1942, Pejnović described her tragedy in the spirit of epic poetry: "They have killed my three sons and my husband. My heart collapsed out of sadness and grief. But one needed to avenge my golden apples and thousands of those who had perished. I clenched my heart and my fist."[103] Widely reported in the Partisan press, her words became legendary, and so did their author, the revered "Mother Kata," as the fighters used to call her (see Figure 3).[104]

---

[101] Sartorti, "On the Making," 183–4.

[102] The third youth labor brigade of Bosanska Dubica, Bosnia, was named after Zoia Kosmodem'ianskaia. See Safija Redžepović, "Žene Bosanskodubičkog sreza u narodnooslobodilačkoj borbi," in Hurem, *Žene Bosne i Hercegovine*, 106.

[103] *Borba*, 13 Dec. 1942, 1.

[104] Pejnović also became the only woman elected to the first Antifascist Council of Yugoslavia and was later proclaimed a national hero. For Pejnović's biographies, see Milenko Predragović, *Kata Pejnović: Životni put i revolucionarno delo* (Gornji Milanovac: Dečje novine, 1978); and Marija Šoljan, *Žene Hrvatske*, 184–5. For brief accounts in English, see Barbara Jančar-Webster, *Women & Revolution*, 143; and Lilly, *Power and Persuasion*, 85.

FIGURE 3. Kata Pejnović, circa 1945.
Courtesy of Muzej Istorije Jugoslavije.

Maternal imagery had, at first sight, an enormous emancipatory potential during the war. Most obviously, it turned the mothers of heroes, the passive witnesses or victims of national tragedy, into active political subjects – into heroines in their own right. Through stories about patriotic mothers, the party gave political significance and recognition to women's traditional tasks. The AFW press acknowledged and praised the contribution of women in the rear, which employed mostly their traditional skills. But the primacy of traditionally male roles and the priority of the battlefront were never called into question in party rhetoric. Women's work was considered important, but only as an adjunct to the "real" contribution of armed combatants. The concept of patriotic motherhood thus challenged neither the notion of "natural" gender roles nor the traditional hierarchy associated with them.

Female Warriors: Alongside the maternal one, another pillar of ideal Partisan womanhood was the martial imagery representing women soldiers. The *partizankas* were the ultimate heroines of the communist master narrative of the National Liberation War. The link between them and female protagonists of the traditional folk epics is less apparent because the party elite seldom evoked the names and images of epic women warriors in an explicit manner. But the way Partisan propaganda represented women in the units replicated the major tenets of the epic motif.

Who, then, were the martial epic heroines? As noted previously, heroic poems celebrate a specific set of patriarchal values – honor, courage, chivalry, endurance, strength, wisdom, and military prowess – as embodied by the epic *junaks* (heroes). These values are gendered, as they are associated with the patriarchal ideal of manhood, but they are not sex exclusive. A person who possessed these characteristics and proved capable of living up to the "heroic" standards could be, regardless of sex, considered a *junak*. There exists a series of epic poems with a common motif of a young woman who in exceptional circumstances assumes the identity of a bellicose male hero.[105] Armed and dressed as a male warrior, she proves her valor by defeating her male opponents on the battlefield, thus earning the admiration reserved for a *junak*. This theme could be

---

[105] For a brief discussion of this motif in Serbo-Croatian, see Maja Bošković-Stulli, "Pjesma o prerušenoj djevojci," in Bošković-Stulli, ed., *Usmena književnost*, 107–12. For a more thorough analysis of this motif in Muslim poems recorded by Milman Perry, A. B. Lord, and David E. Bynum, see David E. Bynum, *Serbo-Croatian Heroic Poems: Epics from Bihać, Cazin and Kulen Vakuf*, trans. David E. Bynum, Milman Parry Studies in Oral Tradition (New York: Garland, 1993).

found in poems collected in different regions and among various South Slavic groups.[106]

The narrative of these poems begins with a young female in extraordinary conditions. She may be a daughter in a family without sons, whose elderly father is called into the army. Or she may be a woman whose lover or male family member was captured and held by the enemy for years. To liberate or replace her loved one, she assumes the role of a male *junak*. She covers or cuts her hair, dresses as a male warrior, and takes up weapons – a disguise that transforms her beyond recognition. Then she shows her exceptional wisdom or military prowess and, after defeating her male opponents, accomplishes her goal. All of those poems end with the triumphant revelation of her original identity, and most also with her resumption of traditional women's roles. A typical example is the Serbian poem "Ljuba Hajduk-Vukosava" (Hajduk Vukosav's Lover). The Serbian *hajduk* (outlaw) Vukosav is imprisoned by a Turkish aga, and his nameless lover decides to liberate him. She cuts off her hair, dresses as a man, and arms herself, assuming an impressive "heroic" appearance. After deceiving the Turkish aga, who runs away in fear, she frees her lover. Until the very end of the poem no one – not even her lover, who admires her courage and wisdom – recognizes her. An interesting detail shared by most of those poems is the unexpected passivity of the women-heroes' male companions. As the *junak* of the poem, the woman alone performs all the heroic deeds without any help from her male partner. In this way, the inversion of traditional roles and expectations is complete, while the performative character of gender is accented. Such imagery of female cross-dressers turned heroic warriors is not unique to the South Slavic oral heritage.[107] But although the motif of women's

---

[106] For instance, in Vuk Karadžić's collection of the so-called poems of the midperiod, *Srpske Narodne Pjesme* vol. 3, this theme appears in the following poems: "Kunina Zlatija," "Zlatija Starca Ćeivana," "Ljuba Hajduk Vukosava," "Sestra Đurkovic Serdara," and "Ženidba Jova Sarajlije." For examples from Croatia, see "Sekula u carevoj tamnici" in Matica Hrvatska's collection, *Hrvatske Narodne Pjesme* (1896) vol. 1, 432–5. In folk poems from Istria, there is one about Sultanija, who replaces her elderly father, Vidulin, in the emperor's army. See *Istarske narodne pjesme* (Abbazia-Opatija: Istarska književna zadruga, 1924), 8. Among Macedonian poems, an example is "Marko, Arapin, i Markoica" in Miladinovci, *Zbornik 1861–1961*, pp. 135–9. Among Muslim poems, this motif is found in the poem "Junaštvo i udaja Zlatije Dungalića," in Frndić, *Muslimanske Junačke Pjesme*, 485–516, and others.

[107] It existed in the medieval, Renaissance, and baroque European literature. Such motifs can also be found in Asian cultures; the Chinese ballad of Hua Mul'an is a famous example. It figured in Middle Eastern literature as well, most prominently in *The Thousand and One Nights*. The latter might have served as a source for the South Slavic epics. On

cross-dressing might have originated in the international repertoire, it was, as Maja Bošković-Stulli tells us, adapted to the social, cultural, and historical contexts in the Balkans.[108] The South Slavic epos clearly reflected local patriarchal values.

It is worth stressing that, as they arm themselves, fight, and perform heroic deeds, the South Slavic epic heroines assume a men's identity. In this respect, they differ from the mythical Amazons. The myth of the Amazons, female warriors, has successfully outlived many other ancient legends and persists in present-day Western cultures. Yet such imagery of Amazons, of women who as *women* become warriors, is atypical in the South Slavic oral tradition. As mentioned, the South Slavic women turn into warriors only after assuming the opposite gender. In other words, they become warriors and perform heroic deeds as *men*, not women. Their sex is female but their gender becomes male. In this sense, the epic *junak* exemplifies patriarchal masculinity par excellence, but this identity is not sex exclusive. Those, including some exceptional women, who could prove capable of living up to the heroic standards could become *junaks*.

There are two features of the concept important for my analysis. The first one defines the heroic warrior as a masculine figure and a woman's adoption of the heroic identity as *temporary* and *extraordinary*. In other words, in traditional culture, a woman's assumption of this ultimate male role is provisional and occurs only in particular conditions; when these conditions end so does the gender inversion, and the woman resumes her original identity and roles. The second characteristic deals with the logic of "proving worthy": A woman is granted respect reserved for men only if she proves worthy of it by passing the ultimate test of masculinity on the battlefield. Those features will be central to my discussion of the communist appropriation of the heroic tradition later.

A society's expressive forms are often consonant with its social practices, and rural patriarchal societies in the Balkans were no exception. In fact, Balkan mountain folks provide a prime example of this interplay between peasant custom and the preoccupations of an expressive medium, between social practice and cultural scripts, between poetic representation and lived experience in traditional peasant communities. The

---

the other hand, it is not impossible that this motif entered the epics through European Mediterranean literature. Among the historical models in the broader European context, there is, of course, Joan of Arc. For instances in which women dressed, lived, and fought as men, see Julie Wheelwright, *Amazons and Military Maids: Women Who Dressed as Men in the Pursuit of Life, Liberty and Happiness* (London: Pandora Press, 1989).

[108] See Bošković-Stulli, "Pjesma o prerušenoj djevojci," 107–11.

veneration of mothers and the respect for female cross-dressing warriors as described in the folk poetry, we shall see, have their counterparts in local customs.

The reader will recall that the characteristic traditional Balkan peasant household structure was the so-called *zadruga*.[109] With the exception of Slovenia, the *zadruga*s could be found in practically all lands that would form Yugoslavia and were particularly prevalent in the mountainous Balkan areas, including the former Habsburg Military Frontier. In some regions, such as Herzegovina, they survived well into the twentieth century. Elsewhere, they dissolved gradually over the past two centuries with rising urbanization, industrialization, and increase in wage labor opportunities, but the traditional patriarchal values proved persistent.[110] Although there were considerable regional variations, the South Slavic *zadruga*s had some widely shared characteristics. The typical *zadruga* was a patrilocal, patrilineal multigenerational family household in which power and authority were vested in the male head of the family – the peasant patriarch (*gospodar* or *starešina*) – to whom all men and all women were subordinated. The *zadruga* was organized along the lines of gender and age hierarchy, with women being subordinated to men and children to parents. The lowest status was typically reserved for the newest daughter-in-law. The division of labor within the extended family unit ensured a relative economic viability of the household and provided a welfare system that protected the elderly, children, the sick, and other inactive family members. Work within the household was exclusively women's domain, but women also assisted with agricultural work in the

[109] For more on traditional South Slavic peasant societies, see Philip E. Mosely, *Communal Families in the Balkans: The Zadruga*, ed. by Robert F. Byrnes, introduction by Margaret Mead (Notre Dame: University of Notre Dame Press, 1976); on the impact of modernization on Balkan family patterns, see Vera St. Erlich, *Family in Transition: A Study of 300 Yugoslav Villages* (Princeton, NJ: Princeton University Press, 1966); Joel M. Halpern, "Yugoslavia: Modernization in an Ethnically Diverse State," in Vucinich, *Contemporary Yugoslavia*, 316–50. Maria Todorova's study on Bulgaria challenges the view of the traditional Balkan family structure as markedly different from the European pattern. It also offers an excellent analysis of scholarly debates and mythologies about the *zadruga*. See Maria Todorova, *Balkan Family Structure and the European Pattern* (Washington, DC: American University Press, 1992). A brief introduction to women's position in the Yugoslav rural culture is also provided in Jancar-Webster, *Women & Revolution*, 27–31.

[110] For a discussion of the limited impact of modernization on peasant women in interwar Croatia, see Suzana Leček, "'Ženske su sve radile': Seljačka žena između tradicije i modernizacije u sjeverozapadnoj Hrvatskoj između dva svjetska rata," *Žene u Hrvatskoj: Ženska i kulturna povijest*, ed. Andrea Feldman (Zagreb: Ženska infoteka, 2004), 211–34.

fields, took care of animals, and carried water. Even though they were subordinate to men, women could find a sense of security in the family household. The *zadruga* provided compensatory power bases for them, allowing them to establish their own spheres of authority and influence. The highest place on the hierarchical ladder was reserved for the wife of the *zadruga*'s head, who assigned and coordinated all women's work in the household. Another sphere of authority for women was the role of the mother. In traditional peasant societies special reverence was reserved for mothers, so that some historians talk about the South Slavic "cult of motherhood." In some regions, an adult son would continue to obey his mother even after he had become head of the household himself.[111] This tradition is reflected in the epics, which, as noted, celebrate the wise and noble mothers of heroes.

Access to the role of warrior was reserved for men, yet even within the patriarchal constraints, women were in certain circumstances allowed to take part in combat. In a striking parallel with the epic model, there existed peasant customs that permitted women in specific conditions to enter into the most secluded male domain. Local histories document a number of real women who, like the epic heroines, became warriors in the centuries preceding World War II. Most recorded cases of women's participation in combat occurred in Montenegro, Bosnia-Herzegovina, Serbia, and Macedonia.

In Montenegro's tribal society, patriarchal hierarchy defined gender relations in a highly rigid manner. Although the traditional clan-based organization of communities started to give way to new influences in the mid-nineteenth century, old values, in which warlike masculinity was idealized, continued to shape gender relations well into the twentieth century. Women were confined to the domain of the home and were excluded from political affairs and decision making; they were not allowed to bear arms and were not subject to blood feuds. Yet it was not unusual for women to assume male roles in certain situations. If a man was killed in battle, for example, his wife was allowed to become a warrior and avenge his death. Ethnographers often stress another custom that permitted women's entry into the men's world: In a family without sons, a daughter would vow not to marry, dress as a man, and take over men's duties, including participation in warfare. Such females were granted the rights reserved for men. Among the first documented cases is that of

---

[111] This reverence of mothers was particularly pronounced in Montenegro. See Bojović, *Žene Crne Gore*, 12.

Milica Bulatović from the Montenegrin Rovci tribe, who, having lost her brothers in the mid-nineteenth century, pledged to remain unmarried and become the son of the family. She wore men's clothes, carried weapons, smoked, participated in fighting, and attended men's gatherings. The men respected her vow.[112]

Similar cases have been reported from the early nineteenth century into the present day, and not only in Montenegro. This custom of the female vow has actually been recorded throughout the Dinaric mountain range from Bosnia-Herzegovina to central Albania, among the rural population of both South Slavic and Albanian origin. Recorded cases include women of the three predominant denominations in the region – Orthodox, Catholic, and Muslim. Ethnographic literature notes many variations in the custom as well as several local names for it: "person bound by a vow" (*tobelija* or *tombelija*, used by both Slavs and Albanians), "female committed to virginity" (Slavic *virdžina* or Albanian *virgjinéshë*), unmarried woman (Slavic *ostajnica*), and "sworn virgin" (Slavic *zavjetovana djevojka* and Albanian *vajzë e betuar*). The reasons behind the women's vows vary. Some took the pledge because of the lack of male children or death of male heirs in the family; others to replace younger brothers until they become of age; still others to protect male family members from the threat of a blood feud, or to break off an existing engagement. Depending on the circumstances and the type of vow, the assumption of male roles could be temporary or permanent.[113] Living examples of such female men could be found during the war. The ethnographer René Grémaux, who did fieldwork in the Balkans in the 1980s and 1990s, mentions a particularly interesting case of a person who was recruited, as a man, by the Partisans during World War II. She was discharged from the military service two years later, after having been exposed as a female in a medical examination. After that, she was appointed a member of

---

[112] Milorad Medaković, *Život i običaji Crnogoraca*, Novi Sad 1860, cited in Bojović, *Žene Crne Gore*, 13.

[113] Based on René Grémaux, "Woman Becomes Man in the Balkans," in *Third Sex, Third Gender: Beyond Sexual Dimorphism in Culture and History*, ed. by Gilbert Herdt (New York: Zone Books, 1994); Predrag Šarčević, "'Tobelija': A Female-to-Male Cross-Gender Role in the 19th and 20th Century Balkans," *Studies on South Eastern Europe, vol. 1: Between the Archives and the Field: A Dialogue on Historical Anthropology in the Balkans*, ed. by Miroslav Jovanović, Karl Kaser, Slobodan Naumović (Münster: Lit, 2004), 35–46; and idem., "Sworn Virgins," in *Studies on South Eastern Europe, vol. 3: Gender Relations in South Eastern Europe: Historical Perspectives on Womanhood and Manhood in 19th and 20th Century*, ed. by Miroslav Jovanović and Slobodan Naumović (Munster: Lit, 2004). See also Antonia Young, *Women Who Become Men: Albanian Sworn Virgins* (Oxford, New York: Berg, 2000).

the revolutionary council, in which capacity she took part in the struggle for Muslim women's rights. She reassumed a woman's identity in the
1950s.[114]

Sworn virgins were not the only females who fought as *men* alongside
men in the Balkans. Some married women also assumed a male identity
in times of war in order to appease the traditional gender expectations
yet to be able to participate in fighting. A well-known example is Shota,
the wife of the Albanian guerrilla resistance leader against the Serbian
rule in Kosovo, Azem Behta, during and after World War I. Shota was
a "shepherdess" who fought alongside her husband and "hid her sex by
assuming a male name and attire as not to offend the patriarchal mores of
her people."[115]

Historically, women's participation in combat tends to be greatest in the
context of irregular warfare and nationalist insurgency. A number of Serbian
women participated in the First Serbian Uprising against the Ottomans in
1804. One of the most prominent among them was Čučuk Stana, the lover
and later wife of the famous *"junak"* Veljko Petrović (popularly known
as *hajduk* Veljko), with whom she rode and fought. Women's presence
was also notable in the Internal Macedonian Revolutionary Organization
(IMRO), which aimed at establishing an autonomous Macedonia independent of Ottoman rule at the turn of the twentieth century. IMRO instituted women's revolutionary committees, organized in groups of ten. Some
IMRO women fought alongside men, took part in terrorist and guerrilla
actions, and became the national legends of the Ilinden rising in 1903.[116]
During the Austrian occupation of 1916–18, sixteen Montenegrin women,
in soldierly outfits, actively participated in armed guerrilla struggle (the
so-called *komitski* movement).[117]

Although it was less likely to find women in regular armies, some did
join the Serbian Army as soldiers during the Balkan wars of 1912–13 and
the Great War. One of them, Milunka Savić, became a legendary figure in
Serbia. Much like a sworn virgin or an epic heroine, she was a peasant
woman who, disguised as a man, signed up to replace her sick brother. By
the time she was wounded and exposed as a female in 1913, she had already

[114] Grémaux, "Woman Becomes Man," 270.

[115] Alan Palmer, *The Lands Between*, 1970, as quoted in R. J. Crampton, *Eastern Europe in the Twentieth Century – and After*, 2nd ed. (New York: Routledge, 1997), 21–2; Banac, *The National Question*, 303.

[116] Veskovik-Vangeli, *Ženata vo osloboditelnite borbi na Makedoniia*, p. 42, 49. Also Jancar-Webster, *Women & Revolution*, 30.

[117] Bojović, *Žene Crne Gore*, 15; also Kovačević, *Borbeni put*, 76, Jancar-Webster, *Women & Revolution*, 29.

distinguished herself in battle. She was awarded the highest Serbian and
French war decorations for her service in World War I.[118] The Serbian military in World War I could boast of having another heroine – and a foreigner
at that – among its ranks. Flora Sandes was a British middle-class woman
who became a common soldier of the Serbian Army, eventually advancing
to the position of captain.[119] In her autobiography, she notes that to the
Serbian soldiers' minds there was nothing especially strange about peasant
women joining up, as they seemed to take it for granted that anyone who
could ride and shoot would be a soldier in a crisis of such a proportion. The
only characteristic that set her apart was her willingness as an outsider to
die for their country.[120]

The preceding instances of women's military activity are impressive.
But they are also isolated. These women were, for the most part, exceptional, and all of them together do not constitute a "female military tradition." Yet they did provide a set of precedents for the Partisans. More
important for this discussion, they offered a confirmation of the cultural
model that had been perpetuated in the epics. It is this model that the
party was to appropriate, replicating some of its basic characteristics in
the imagery of the *partizanka*.

As noted earlier, two common features characterize the representation
of warrior women in the oral epics: First, heroism is associated with masculinity; women assume the identity of a heroic warrior only temporarily and in extraordinary conditions. The second deals with the "proving
worthy" logic – only by equaling or outdoing men in heroism does a
woman earn respect and privileges traditionally reserved for men. The
wartime image of Partisan women, as propagated by the party, shares
both of these characteristics.

Much like the epic cross-dressers in the traditional lore, female
Partisan fighters in party propaganda were portrayed as desexualized
figures equaling or surpassing men on the battleground. Partisan publications accentuate and, not infrequently, magnify their "masculine

[118] Antonije Djurić, *Solunci Govore and Žene Solunci Govore* (Beograd: Književne
Novine, 1987).
[119] Sandes was among some six hundred Western, mostly British, women who traveled to
Serbia as nurses, doctors, or medical orderlies during the Great War. Most of the women
who spent the war years in Serbia were nursing volunteers, who had joined the British
medical teams to help the war effort. Among them, Sandes was the only one who signed
up in the army. See Monica Krippner, *The Quality of Mercy: Women at War, Serbia
1915–1918* (Newton Abbot: David & Charles, 1980).
[120] See Flora Sandes, *The Autobiography of a Woman Soldier: A Brief Record of Adventure
with the Serbian Army, 1916–1919* (New York: F. A. Stokes Company, 1927).

virtues" – their endurance, courage, and military prowess. A 1942 issue of *Slavonski Partizan* begins its article entitled "The Partisan Women" with the words "Heroism is for them a daily routine" and continues with examples from battles depicting how young females overpowered their male enemies.[121] The following is a typical passage depicting a *partizanka* in action (in this case against the Ustashas):

> Mileva Jorgić ... in a forcible charge, was the first to enter the bunker in which there were 12 bandits. With a pistol grip and knife this brave comrade attacked those villains and she alone killed five of them. One Ustasha, when he heard that our comrades refer to this heroic female comrade by the name Mileva [a Serbian name], started to call her desperately: "Mileva, I am also a Serb from Srijem, please don't kill me." Hatred and scorn filled the heart of the brave *partizanka* ... and with one well-aimed bullet she punished the culprit the way he deserved.[122]

It is helpful to note here that in Slavonia – where, because of the initial prevalence of Serbs in the units, Croats viewed the Partisans as a Serb movement and were reluctant to sign up – such depictions served to appeal to the Croat population by showing that the Partisans were far from privileging the Serbs. Yet it is the inversion of gender expectations that is the most striking feature of this account: The extraordinary bravery, strength, and martial skills of the young woman are juxtaposed to the weak "bandits" (she alone kills five of them with a knife!) and to the cowardly Serb man who begs for his life. Such representations ascribed a surplus of what had been traditionally considered a masculine quality to Partisan women, and a lack of masculinity to their male adversaries.

The imagery of the *partizankas'* heroism in combat had obvious similarities with the epic motif. For the peasantry, such imagery occasionally implied that female Partisans had assumed the male warrior identity, which necessitated a break with traditional women's roles. At a 1943 AFW conference, for instance, Partisan delegates talked about their absent comrades, female fighters, portraying them as "heroines" [*junakinje*], "who do not quail before obstacles, but are the very paradigm of bravery and heroism." After she had heard their stories, a peasant woman demanded to speak: "We [the peasant women in the rear] pledge that, as of today, our comrades female-fighters will not do the laundry, neither for themselves nor for other comrades. [We will do their laundry]."[123] Once

---

[121] *Slavonski Partizan*, 20 December 1942, 17. In *Izbor iz štampe*, p. 289.
[122] *Udarnica*, Jan/Feb 1944, p. 9. In *Izbor iz štampe*, p.324.
[123] *Udarnica* 7, 1943, p. 1. In *Izbor iz štampe*, p. 312.

they adopted the heroic identity and consequently the opposite gender, in this peasant woman's mind, it seemed unbecoming for the Partisan women to resume their traditional duties such as doing the laundry. That party portrayals of the *partizanka* resonated with the folk imagery in the mind of the local rural population – or rather, that this is what party officials tended to believe – confirms the recollection of one such official: "For the people of Krajina, [the Partisan woman] Đina represented a character from folk poetry. They attributed to her the features of a man.... I heard them saying: 'Everything fits her, just like [it would fit] a man.' "[124]

Partisan women's assumption of male roles sometimes caused some real gender confusion; in veteran reminiscences such stories are told with the same sense of frivolity that accompanies the folk motif of cross-dressing. A former *partizanka* remembers the consternation that was caused by the appearance of female fighters from the 5th Proletarian Brigade in a small Bosnian village, Zijamet, in 1942:

At first, the people of Zijamet found it to be very strange – how come women fight? They could not believe she [the *partizanka* Maša Lakić] was a woman ... in a man's outfit, with a cap on her short hair ... one of the peasants, believing she was a young man, addressed her with the words: 'Hey you, my fellow-man, come here.'[125]

Note the amazing repetition of the epic motif here: once they cut their hair short, dress as men, and arm themselves, thus transforming themselves into soldierly figures, the women are perceived as men.

Yet the *partizanka*s – both as propaganda icons and as a real constituency – differed from their mythical and historic predecessors in the Balkans. When a cultural model is invoked in a new setting the fit is never exact. Most obviously, unlike the cross-dressers from the epic myths, and unlike the "sworn virgins" and female avengers in peasant customs, Partisan women did not pass as men. Nor were the traditional markers of their womanhood eliminated in the CPY's representations. In fact, party propaganda often emphasized the persistence of their feminine attributes and skills alongside their excellent performance in battle. At a conference in Srem, among the speeches about female Partisans' courage and strength, the peasants could also hear how "it is touching to watch them

---

[124] According to Radoš Raičević, a wartime member of the district committee for Jajce (Bosnia), in Beoković, *Žene heroji*, 480.

[125] According to Jovanka Pavicević-Vuković, in *Peta Proleterska Crnogorska Brigada: Knjiga Sjećanja*, vol. 1 (Belgrade: Vojnoizdavački zavod, 1972), 430.

as they, in their free time, take the clothes of male comrades to mend and wash."[126] Judging by the AFW press, the lasting femininity of Partisan women seems to have impressed male observers. A Croatian male commissar reportedly had this to say about the *partizanka*s in his division:

Our female comrades are tough, and in many cases more persistent and resilient than male comrades themselves.... She [the *partizanka*] is not only a fighter in her unit but also mother and sister [to other soldiers]. Voluntarily, in addition to her soldierly duties, she mends male fighters' clothes, she washes, tends to hygiene, and in her gentle care, she has retained all the characteristics of a woman.[127]

If another analogy is to be made with the epics, the *partizanka* is best described as an ideal combination of the cross-dressing warrior and the Kosovo Maiden. Partisan propaganda sometimes made a direct link between the female icon of the traditional epos about the Kosovo battle and the *partizanka*. The Serbian AFW journal, *Zora*, for instance, named the *partizanka* "today's Kosovo Maiden," who surpassed her legendary predecessor in that she not only offered first aid but also fought.[128] And, as noted earlier, the image of the Kosovo Maiden tending the wounded seemed particularly well suited for Partisan nurses. In the words of a Partisan doctor, "The female Partisan nurse adjusted quietly to the struggle, each a Kosovo maiden in her own way, and as needed, she tended and encouraged the wounded, she cooked, washed the dishes, floors, and laundry, she served.... Who would have washed out all these layers of dirt and lice on us, who would have done all that women's work, had Partisan nurses not been with us?"[129] Remarkably, even when departing from the epic model – that of the female cross-dressers – to emphasize the presumably unchanging femininity of the female Partisan soldiers, party propaganda still drew on the folk heritage, making use of another traditional icon: the quintessential epic maiden.

The CPY's emphasis on women's excelling as warriors while retaining their femininity was in line with general trends in European-wide communist propaganda, which followed the Soviet example. Since the revolution, the Soviet press had celebrated the emancipation of Soviet

---

[126] AVII, NOR, IA PK SKS za Vojvodinu 4/262–3, Okružna konferencija AFŽ za Zapadni Srem, 1944.

[127] "Iz izveštaja vojnih rukovodilaca. Komesar XIX divizije VIII Korpusa o ženi-vojniku u njegovoj diviziji," *Žena vojnik* (Zagreb: AFŽ Hrvatske, 1945), 35.

[128] "Spremamo se!" *Zora* 1.1 (1945): 16, as quoted in Wiesinger, *Partisaninnen*, 61, n. 88. For a brief discussion on the image of the Kosovo Maiden in party propaganda concerning female nurses, see Wiesinger, 60–1.

[129] Dr. Oskar Ginsberger, "Uz tifusare," in Stana Džakula Nidžović, *Žene borci NOR-a Sedme banijske udarne divizije*(Čačak: Bajić, 1999), 69.

women through the imagery of women performing traditionally male jobs, as industrial and agricultural workers, miners, pilots, and, during the war, combatants. The New Woman, however, also managed to preserve her female traits – maternal and nurturing drives, physical attractiveness, concern for cleanliness.[130] Similar imagery was present in the initial stages of the Spanish Civil War, when the republican *miliciana* emerged as a symbol of bravery, decisiveness, and heroism, at the same time retaining her "essential" feminine features.[131] The accentuation of women combatants' femininity, scholars have noted, served to preserve the "natural" hierarchy of the sexes when this hierarchy was called into question by women's presence on the front lines.[132]

Although feminine qualities were not eliminated from the party's representation of women warriors, the symbolic triad linking heroism, combat, and masculinity remained prevalent. According to Victoria Bonnell, who analyzes Soviet visual propaganda, "women in the Bolshevik system of signification acquired heroic status" only in male roles.[133] In a similar manner, the imagery of combative Partisan women did not undermine the notion of combat as masculine nor the connection of heroism with the battlefield; what was heroic about the *partizanka*s was not their sisterly care for their male comrades – it was their "manly" performance in battle.

Nor did the propaganda that stressed women's capability to outdo men on the battlefield subvert all established ideas about gender difference. Traditional women's tasks were still portrayed as naturally suited to women, and characteristics such as kindness and cleanliness as unchangeable female qualities. What was changeable and temporary – much as in the epic myths – was women's participation in combat, which was reserved for such extraordinary conditions as those caused by the

---

[130] For the imagery that underlined the femininity of Soviet combat women, see Susanne Conze and Beate Fieseler, "Soviet Women as Comrades-in-Arms: A Blind Spot in the History of the War," in *The People's War: Responses to World War II in the Soviet Union*, ed. Robert W. Thurston and Bernd Bonwetsch (Urbana and Chicago: University of Illinois Press, 2000), 215, 223–5. On women in men's jobs in the Soviet Union see Lynne Attwood, *Creating the New Soviet Woman: Women's Magazines as Engineers of Female Identity, 1922–53* (New York: St. Martin's Press, 1999). On the imagery of women miners in Stalinist Poland, see Malgorzata Fidelis, *Women, Communism, and Industrialization in Postwar Poland* (New York: Cambridge University Press, 2010), 147–8.

[131] Mary Nash, *Defying Male Civilization: Women in the Spanish Civil War* (Denver: Arden Press, 1995), 109–10.

[132] Conze and Fieseler, "Soviet Women as Comrades in Arms," 224.

[133] Victoria Bonnell, *Iconography of Power*, 77.

calamity of World War II. Indeed, Partisan women were demobilized shortly after the war, and females were never included on conscription lists for the Yugoslav army.

The image of the combat heroine fit neatly into the Partisan imagery during the second year of the war, when the Partisans began accepting women as fighters. At the same time, the party shifted its emphasis from class war to patriotic struggle, and its rhetoric regarding women's participation was modified accordingly. As the war progressed, the party increasingly turned to the logic of "proving worthy": Instead of the original argument that women should support the Partisan movement because it would ensure their future emancipation, the CPY developed an inverted formula. It now claimed that women first needed to – and did – prove worthy of emancipation through their sacrifices in the struggle. In other words, women were not simply granted equality with men. Nor did they join the Partisans in order to fight for it. Rather, they *earned* it through their sacrifices, their devotion, and, most important, their valor on the battlefield.

It was, as usual, Tito who announced this shift in rhetoric. In his speech at the First National AFW Conference, in December 1942, Tito declared:

I am extraordinarily happy to be able to ... see the delegates of our heroic women of Yugoslavia, who, in this ... struggle sacrificed so much and gave so many examples of heroism.... In this uneven, superhuman struggle they have proven that they were right to demand equality, *they have proven it by their lives, by their blood on the battlefield* against German, Italian, and Hungarian fascists and other conquerors.... Perhaps someone abroad dreams that everything in Yugoslavia will return to the old ways after the war, that women will return to the kitchen and will not make decisions about anything. But women have, comrades, *passed the maturity test*; they have shown that they are capable not only of working in the home but also of *fighting with rifles in their hands*, that they can rule and hold power in their hands.[134]

Note that equality is deserved by one's blood on the battlefield, and that one's "maturity test" is passed by one's capability to fight with a rifle in hand.

Tito's words were echoed in the speeches of other party officials, and in flyers, pamphlets, the Partisan and AFW press, and other propaganda material. Anka Berus, one of the leading party activists, reported to the first conference of Croatia's AFW that women's newly acquired right

---

[134] Tito, "Govor na Prvoj Zemaljskoj Konferenciji Antifašističkog Fronta Žena," 6 December 1942, In *Tito-Ženama Jugoslavije* (Beograd: Centralni odbor Antifašističkog Fronta Žena Jugoslavije, 1945), 3–9.

to participate in public life had not resulted from demands for equality, but rather from women's dedication to the struggle.[135] AFW appeals to women frequently reminded them that their equality had been earned in battle.[136] "Fighting shoulder to shoulder with men and withstanding the same hardships," reads the resolution of a 1943 AFW conference in Srem, "women have in this struggle achieved equality."[137] A 1943 article in the Slavonian AFW journal *Udarnica* insists, "Women *did not* join the struggle with the intent of fighting for equality. No, they joined the struggle against fascism, for national liberation, and it is because of their heroic conduct that impresses the people that they have won the people's trust and earned equality."[138] Perhaps the best expression of the new paradigm is to be found in the words of Ivan Ribar, president of AVNOJ, at the first meeting of antifascist women of Serbia in 1945: "You did not ask for your rights in this struggle. You asked for neither political nor civil rights, nor for equality; you, female comrades, have rather through your struggle and your blood earned for women all the rights of men.... Nobody can change that."[139]

Thus, instead of simply promising equality to attract women as some historiographical interpretations stress, the party adopted a modified rhetoric according to which equality first needed to be earned by women's military prowess and their capability to outdo men in traditionally male roles. This almost apologetic approach made the enlistment of women as fighters acceptable within the predominant patriarchal mores. Since the notion of gender equality was alien to the rural population, it was justified by women's capability of passing the ultimate test of worthiness (and manliness) in the traditional value system – that which took place on the battlefield. Once women had passed this test, they deserved and won equality as honorary men. With this shift, the party's rhetoric reconciled the contradictions between the two mutually opposed cultural models – the communist egalitarian and the traditional, epic-based, patriotic ones. The battlefield still appeared as a prerogative of a preordained male world, into which women were temporarily allowed on the condition that they prove worthy of it. The gains that women thus made,

[135] AVII, NOR, CK SK Hrvatske 32/479–489, 1943. Also *Žena u borbi* 2, July 1943, 11–13.
[136] AVII, NOR, CK SK Hrvatske 52/501–2, AFŽ appeal to the women of the Varaždin district, 1943.
[137] AVII, NOR, k. 12, f. 12, doc. 21, Rezolucija okr. konferencije AFŽ za I. Srem, May 1943.
[138] *Udarnica*, year I, no. 8, November 1943, p. 10–12. In *Izbor iz štampe*, p. 318
[139] *Politika*, 29 January 1945, as quoted in Dr. Vera Gudac-Dodič, "Položaj žene u Srbiji (1945–2000)," *Srbija u Modernizacijskim procesima XIX i XX veka, vol. 4: Žene i deca*, ed. by Latinka Perović (Beograd: Helsinški odbor za ljudska prava, 2006), 35.

however, were to be permanent. The party's rhetorical shift ultimately changed the argument for gender equality from a modern one centered on the concept of rights to one accommodating traditional notions of duty and sacrifice.

This "proving worthy" argument was to survive the war and become one of the tenets of the master narrative of the National Liberation War. It became so pervasive that Partisan veterans found no alternative ways to depict women's position and gender relations in the movement; it is often difficult to sort out facts in their recollections from the attempts to tell their stories in a manner that fits the master narrative. Numerous anecdotes about female Partisans, published after the war, present variants of the same story about the women's initial experiences in the units – the story about a young heroine who, upon signing up, finds herself facing prejudice, mistrust, or even open hostility from her male comrades. Only when she proves her superior courage or military prowess do their attitudes begin to change. In such narratives gender equality is never an a priori state of affairs in the units – it is not even an a priori expectation on the part of the story's female characters – but rather the result of their heroic deeds.

Each among the legendary Partisan heroines had at least one "proving worthy" anecdote in her biography. Veteran reminiscences about Rava Janković, a *partizanka* posthumously decorated with the title of national hero, provide a representative illustration. A key character in one of the recollections is a peasant fighter, Luka, who believed that women should stay at home and not meddle in men's business. His initial reaction to Rava Janković, who was the first female fighter in his brigade, was rather negative. But Rava's performance in a battle made him reconsider his views. Shortly thereafter, at a meeting about women's social position, Luka argued in favor of gender equality: "Rava does not lag behind the best fighters.... So how could we refuse to treat her as our equal?" According to the Partisan veteran Dušan Blagojević, who recounts this story, "through Luka our whole army, our people spoke.... Our fighters, these common, half-literate people, who had never heard of women's rights before ... once having seen women fighters [in combat] ... accepted them as equals."[140]

Few military exploits could do a better job of proving a woman "worthy" than her heroic death. The imagery of heroic death had a long tradition in the interwar communist subcultures throughout Europe;

---

[140] Dušan Blagojević in Beoković, *Žene heroji*, 79.

wartime conditions only added to its prominence. In the case of Yugoslav *partizanka*s, this communist tradition was often combined with the "proving worthy" argument. Some reminiscences go as far as to suggest that most women were not seen or treated as equals while alive – only by their heroic deaths did they earn respect for themselves and women in general. A typical example is the tragic story of another national hero, the Bosnian peasant-*partizanka* Danica Materić (also posthumously awarded the title of "national hero"), who became the deputy polit-commissar of a company in Krajina. Her unit was known as the "mustached brigade" because it included many older, mustached men who had fought in World War I. As her comrade Rahela Albahari remembers, some of these men shared the superstition that a woman's presence in the company was bad luck; some felt offended by having to obey a young peasant woman's commands; others treated Danica scornfully and mockingly. After an unsuccessful attack on a strong Chetnik base, Danica's company was surrounded. Badly wounded but still alive, she was captured while covering her company's retreat. She died after having been unspeakably tortured. Her heroic death soon became legendary in the Partisan units. In Albahari's words, "This death had a miraculous impact on our male fighters. They began to behave differently to all women in [our] army ... [in their eyes] the value of other women comrades grew ... by her death, Danica contributed to the destruction of old customs and prejudices about women."[141]

According to such stories, women were not accepted and granted equality a priori among the Partisans. They had to earn both equal treatment and respect, and, like the epic heroines, they did so by proving capable of performing traditional men's roles – by passing the ultimate test of masculinity on the battlefield and in the face of death. There certainly is a great deal of truth in these reminiscences; internal party documents record numerous instances of lasting prejudice and "sectarianism" against female volunteers in the units.[142] None of this is surprising per se; any student of gender history could expect to find examples of the persistence of old discriminatory practices in nominally egalitarian movements. What is striking is that this rather unflattering version, emphasizing the lack of equality and respect before women's heroic performance in battle, remained an officially sanctioned segment of the communist master narrative after the war. Its prevalence in communist rhetoric and popular memory attests to the power of traditional gender values.

---

[141] Rahela Albahari, quoted in Beoković, *Žene heroji*, 258–9, 231–2.
[142] See Chapter 3 for a discussion about the problems of women's integration into the units.

CONCLUSIONS

Since the former Yugoslavia disintegrated through a series of wars in the 1990s, much has been written about its bitterly opposed ethnic nationalisms. What all of them have in common is the perception of the country's communist era in negative terms. Nationalist ideologues tend to find the "essence" of national identity in certain historical episodes and heroes; periods between these episodes – the "meantimes" – are often seen as interludes of alienation from the original national being.[143] In nationalist histories, communism is viewed as one of those alienating phases. In the 1990s, nationalists on different sides called for "a return" from communism to the folk base and the true "nature" of their nation. References to the epic amalgam of militarism, heroism, and honor abounded in their calls for national unity.[144] Yet the communist Partisan movement had drawn upon that very same tradition some fifty years earlier. The epic tradition was equally suitable for ethnonationalist and transnational communist rhetoric because it provided a folkloric foundation and ethnic heroes, on the one hand, and a shared South Slavic heritage that transcended divisions along ethnic lines, on the other. Equally important, it provided a repository of metaphors that proved ideal for the conditions of wartime mobilization.

That a communist movement narrates its cause in nationalist terms and by invoking traditional symbols is not specific to World War II Yugoslavia. The Yugoslavs had only to look to their patrons, the Soviets, for models in this respect. A "neotraditionalist" trend in the Stalinist culture of the mid-1930s and 1940s – characterized in part by crafted historical parallels with Russia's prerevolutionary past, a glorification of tsarist patriotic heroes, invocations of heroic battles against foreign conquerors, and an emphasis on folklore – has been well documented.[145] Janet Hart notes a similar tendency in the communist-led Greek resistance (EAM/ELAS). Analyzing resistance testimonies and popular culture, she finds that "nationalism was the overall theme of these stories and the rallying cry that gave the EAM ... control of almost the whole country."

---

[143] Renata Jambrešić-Kirin, "Verbalno nasilje i (raz)gradnja kolektivnih identiteta u iskazima ratnih zarobljenika i političkih zatvorenika," *Narodna Umjetnost* 37.2 (2000): 183–4.

[144] Ibid, 184.

[145] See, for example Terry Martin, "Modernization or Neo-Traditionalism: Ascribed Nationality and Soviet Primordialism," in David Hoffman and Yanni Kotsonis, ed., *Russian Modernity: Politics, Knowledge, Practices* (New York: St. Martin's Press, 2000), 162; David Hoffmann, *Stalinist Values: The Cultural Norms of Soviet Modernity, 1917–1941* (Ithaca, NY: Cornell University Press, 2003), 163–6, 171–3.

According to Hart, the hero(ine) in the EAM's story is Greece, the enemy the Axis menace, and the struggle takes "the form of an epic drama in which sacrifice is for a righteous cause, harking back in the popular imagination to the ancient wars against the Persians, [and] the 1821 War of Independence."[146]

Nor was this "neotraditionalism" a specifically communist phenomenon. Rather, as David Hoffmann writes, the communists took part in what was a larger international trend of using traditions for distinctly modern purposes of mass mobilization. At the moment when modernity was about to destroy the last vestiges of traditional cultures, Hoffmann reminds us, the exigencies of mass politics led to the rise of "invented traditions" to mobilize the population. In order to generate legitimacy for state policies and ensure popular support on the eve of the war, various European governments used the mobilizing might of traditional symbols, tried to revive traditional institutions, and shifted the emphasis toward the folkloric.[147] Well before Tito led his Partisans into the woods, "neotraditionalism" had proven itself as a potent recruitment mechanism for the times of mass politics and modern warfare.

Yugoslav communists selected traditions that were ideal for wartime conditions *and* could be reconciled with both their revolutionary agenda and supranational platform. Attempting to attract the peasant population, the Communist Party's leadership consciously invoked the epic imagery of freedom fighters against foreign invaders. According to the CPY, the National Liberation Struggle was the last and most glorious chapter in the unified epos about the Yugoslav peoples' centuries-long pursuit of freedom, with Partisan fighters being its greatest heroes.

The mass mobilization of women cannot be fully explained without taking into account the party's appropriation of traditional culture. The leadership invoked epic heroines as models for women's wartime roles. References to traditional heroines served to inspire and legitimize women's participation in the Partisan war effort. In addition, the party adopted the narrative structures from South Slavic folklore to represent women in the Partisan movement. The folk imagery of patriotic mothers and female

---

[146] Janet Hart, *New Voices in the Nation*, 79, 89. On the imagery of the heroines of the 1820s during the Civil War, see Margaret P. Anagnostopoulou, "From Heroines to Hyenas: Women Partisans during the Greek Civil War." *Contemporary European History* 10.3 (November 2001): 483, 501.

[147] Hoffmann, *Stalinist Values*, 9–10, 172, 186. The phrase "invented traditions" originated with Eric Hobsbawm and Terence Ranger, ed., *The Invention of Traditions* (New York: Cambridge University Press, 1992).

soldiers thus reemerged as the main symbols of Partisan womanhood in wartime iconography. Yet the originality and success of the party's rhetoric lay not in a mere invocation of traditions, but rather in a deft combination of the old and the new, of traditional symbols and revolutionary ideas. The *partizanka* blended the features of her mythical predecessors in the Balkans with those of a communist revolutionary. In the course of the war, the leadership also modified its argument for women's emancipation from one focused on rights to one that emphasized traditional notions of sacrifice and duty. This skillful weaving of the traditional and the ideological was unique to the Partisans in the Yugoslav civil wars and could perhaps be credited for a good portion of their mobilizing success.

The party's reliance on Balkan traditions went beyond the realm of rhetoric. As we shall see in the following chapters, these traditions came to be incorporated in the Partisan institutional framework and accommodated in daily practice in the Partisan movement.

2

The "Organized Women"

Developing the AFW

Let's gather at a prelo,[1] *female comrades,*	*Drugarice, hajdemo na prelo*
to make clothes for the Partisans.	*Partizanim' praviti odjelo.*

(Verses from a wartime Partisan folk song)[2]

In order to win the war, the communists needed to involve the masses of the population, male and female, in their movement. In its appeals to the female populace, the CPY leadership made revolutionary promises of equality and mentioned other advantages that the new socialist Yugoslavia would accord women. It also made use of traditional peasant cultures: To win women over and legitimize their participation in its struggle, it appropriated the heroic imagery of freedom fighters from South Slavic folklore and represented the *partizanka*s as epic heroines treading in the footsteps of their legendary predecessors.

Unlike its local adversaries, the party did more than just appeal to the female masses. It authorized the formation of a special organization – the Antifascist Front of Women (AFW) – in charge of mobilizing women into the movement and channeling their labor toward the Partisan war effort. Much as in the CPY's rhetoric, peasant traditions found their place in its institutional practice: Females recruited by the AFW were asked to contribute to the Partisan struggle through an extension of their time-honored tasks within the family household and village communities.

[1] *Prelos* (singular *prelo*, plural *prela*) were traditional village gatherings, at which peasant women usually did some handwork – weaving, knitting, sewing, and the like – together.
[2] As quoted in *Vjesnik Hrvatske Jedinstvene Narodnooslobodilačke Fronte*, 9 (December 1941), AJ, SKJ 507, CKKPJ 1941/133.

The "organized women" knitted socks and sweaters, nursed the wounded; collected food, medicine, and donations; laundered and mended soldiers' clothes; and offered shelter for Partisan families and orphans. They peopled labor groups that carried provisions to the troops stationed in the woods. Through the medium of the AFW, the party put women's traditional skills and responsibilities in the service of a guerrilla army in a markedly modern way, on a mass scale that had no precedents or rivals in the region.

In setting up the front of women, the communists drew upon the organizational activity of the prewar Yugoslav feminist movement. Since the Communist Party had been banned in the Yugoslav kingdom, in the mid-1930s it adopted the Moscow-dictated popular front line and tried to infiltrate legal organizations. Female members of the Communist Youth League and the CPY thus joined forces with the feminist "ladies" of the Alliance of Women's Movements and ended up running the alliance's youth section. These young communist women who had been active in the interwar feminist movement then formed the skilled and experienced core of organizers responsible for the development of the AFW during the war.

The AFW was an original and unique wartime creation, which thrived on a surprising blend of communist ideology, peasant mores, and feminist organizational experience. In the four years of conflict on the Yugoslav soil, it served as the backbone of the support system in the rear and proved indispensable to the Partisan military. Besides functioning as an auxiliary of the army, the Partisan women's organization had a revolutionary political mission: to help transform the "backward" masses of Yugoslav, mostly peasant women into equal and deserving citizens of the future socialist state. The AFW balanced the two tasks without much guidance or support from the CPY and in the process became increasingly independent. Yet that was precisely what the party had *not* intended. The women's front was created as a section of the Partisan movement; it was never supposed to be autonomous. Fearing its independence, communist leaders used the charge of "feminist deviations" to reorganize the AFW, suppress its autonomy, and place it fully under party control.

PRECURSORS

Scholarship on the women's movement in the Yugoslav lands generally distinguishes two currents in women's organizational activity before

World War II: feminist and socialist (proletarian).[3] The Yugoslav literature of Tito's era recognized only the latter as the rightful predecessor of the AFW. In line with the general communist take on feminism, it dismissed feminist organizations in Yugoslavia as "bourgeois." They fought for the liberation of women within the confines of capitalism, which, in the communists' view, was incomplete at best. According to this interpretation, gender inequalities stemmed from the class-based organization of society and women's emancipation could be achieved only with a revolutionary change of that system – a fact that only the proletarian women's movement recognized.[4]

Scholars have since revisited the prewar Yugoslav feminist movement and several valuable studies on its hitherto neglected history have emerged. These newer works have not only contributed a fresh, more positive evaluation of nonsocialist women's organizations, but have also revealed that the two traditions had much more contact and much more similarity than previous accounts allowed. In the words of Lydia Sklevicky, the AFW – as the sole women's organization to survive the war, led by female communists with a record of prewar activism in feminist organizations – was the "legitimate successor" of both currents.[5] The front of women was in fact more than a successor: It was the place where the two traditions continued to coexist until the front's independence was crushed by the CPY.

By the time the AFW entered the stage, women's organizational activity in the region had had almost a century-long history.[6] The earliest women's organizations among the South Slavs emerged in the second half of the nineteenth century. They were closely tied with their respective national movements – either with the Slavs' struggles against imperial rule in the areas belonging to the Habsburgs, or, in the Serbian case, with the national politics of the nascent nation-state. Since the national question was the main concern in the region, as Vlasta Jalušić explains, it was "virtually impossible" for women not to associate themselves with

[3] This distinction was introduced by Jovanka Kecman. See Kecman, *Žene Jugoslavije u radničkom pokretu i ženskim organizacijama* (Beograd: Narodna knjiga, 1978).

[4] Thomas Emmert, "Ženski Pokret: The Feminist Movement in Serbia in the 1920s," in *Gender Politics in the Western Balkans: Women and Society in Yugoslavia and the Yugoslav Successor States*, edited by Sabrina P. Ramet (University Park: Pennsylvania State University Press, 1999), 34; also Sklevicky, *Konji, Žene, Ratovi*, 79–81.

[5] Sklevicky, *Konji, Žene, Ratovi*, 79–81.

[6] The following discussion of the prewar women's movement draws on the writings of other scholars, primarily Thomas Emmert, Vlasta Jalušić, Neda Božinović, Lydia Sklevicky, Dušanka Kovačević, and others.

the national movements. In addition, the link between women's emancipation and national liberation provided a key source of legitimacy for
feminist organizations in the region.[7] These early women's societies were
made up of educated and affluent females belonging to the upper echelons of society, who tended to concentrate on cultural, humanitarian,
and educational work. The argument they most commonly made in favor
of women's education was that it would hone their domestic and maternal
skills, improving their ability to raise the future generations of patriots and
thus contribute to the national progress. Besides nationalism, some socialist
ideas and objectives gradually made inroads into the programs of women's
societies.[8] The result was that an ideological triad, combining, to varying
degrees, elements of nationalism, socialism, and feminism, marked the initial organizational efforts among the South Slavic women. Both the feminist
and proletarian women's movements in the region would stem from this
foundation.

The pioneers of the idea of women's emancipation in the lands that
were to become Yugoslavia could be found among the members of the
United Serb Youth (1866–1872), an organization of the Habsburg Serbs in
Vojvodina. Inspired by Mazzini's United Youth of Italy, its activists sought
to "enlighten the Serbs through education and culture." It was the first
South Slavic nationalist group to give space to the woman question and
establish a separate women's section.[9] Among its founders was Svetozar
Marković (1846–1875), a former Serb student in St. Petersburg, an admirer
of the Russian populists, and an avid reader of Chernyshevsky. In his later
studies in Zurich, he also discovered Marx, a process that led to his becoming the forefather and "apostle of Serbian socialism."[10] Much like his mentors, Marković believed that the position of women was the measure of a
nation's progress and that their emancipation was linked with the transformation of the social structure as a whole. In his views on the "woman question," Marković had a tiny but notable following among contemporaries.
Influenced by his ideas, the first females to advocate women's emancipation

[7] Vlasta Jalušič, "Women in Interwar Slovenia," in *Gender Politics in the Western
Balkans: Women and Society in Yugoslavia and the Yugoslav Successor States*, ed.
Sabrina P. Ramet (University Park: Pennsylvania State University Press, 1999), 53–4.

[8] Ibid, 54, 57.

[9] Ivana Pantelić, "Dejanović Draga," in *Biographical Dictionary of Women's Movements
and Feminisms in Central, Eastern, and South Eastern Europe: 19th and 20th Centuries*.
Ed. by Francisca de Haan, Krasimira Daskalova, Anna Loutfi (Budapest: Central
European University Press, 2006), 106–7.

[10] Ivo Banac, *The National Question in Yugoslavia: Origins, History, Politics* (Ithaca,
NY: Cornell University Press, 1984), 154.

were Milica Stojadinović-Srpkinja (1830–1878) and Draga Dejanović (1840–1871). The former's ideas were recorded in her poetry and diary. The latter, another poetess, was an active member of the United Serb Youth, an actress, and a public speaker. Her lectures on women's rights – imbued with both patriotic fervor and embryonic socialist ideas – earned her the title of the "first Serb feminist."[11]

The women's movement among the Habsburg Slavs in Slovenia and Croatia had its origins in the attempts of individual authors and teachers to raise the issue of women's position in society. The most radical and vocal advocate of women's emancipation was the Slovenian writer Zofka Kveder (1879–1926). The first women's organizations emerged within the framework of the national movement at the turn of the century. Among them, the major champion of women's emancipation was the General Woman's Society (Splošno žensko društvo), established in 1901 by "the nationally conscious" women of Slovenia with feminist and social goals in mind. The society's members argued that independent and educated women provided "the best support of the nation" in its struggles for autonomy in the Austro-Hungarian monarchy and hoped that, in turn, national liberation would yield the emancipation of women.[12]

In the kingdom of Serbia, the women's movement also had a national aspect, but in the context of an existing nation-state a different kind of nationalist politics was at play. Serbian women's organizations adopted their state's expansionist project to liberate and unite the Serbs still living under Habsburg or Ottoman rule. By far the largest and the most influential organization, the famous Circle of Serbian Sisters (Kolo Srpskih Sestara), for instance, was founded in 1903 with the aim of providing "material and moral aid to Serbs in unliberated … regions."[13] Although Serbian women seemed at first less concerned with women's political and legal emancipation, feminist ideas did gradually find proponents among them. In 1906, several humanitarian and educational societies joined forces to form a national association, the Serbian National Women's League (Srpski narodni ženski savez), which began advocating women's

---

[11] Pantelić, "Dejanović"; Latinka Perović, "Kako žena vidi sebe u vreme otvaranja 'ženskog pitanja' u srpskom društvu," *Tokovi istorije* 1–2 (2000): 9–18. For a fine discussion of the two women's writings, see also Celia Hawkesworth, *Voices in the Shadows: Women and Verbal Art in Serbia and Bosnia* (Budapest, New York: Central European University Press, 2000), on Stojadinović, 102–12; on Dejanović, 112–19.

[12] Jalušič, 52–54; see also Kovačević, *Borbeni put*, 189.

[13] Dragan Subotić, "Građanske i socijalističke ideje o ženskom pitanju u Srbiji (19. i 20. vek)," in Perović, ed., *Srbija u modernizacijskim procesima*, vol. 2, 446.

suffrage. By 1914, the league had coordinated the work of thirty-two organizations. It had also become a member of two international feminist associations, the International Women's League and the International Alliance for Women's Right to Vote.[14]

Yugoslav Feminists: When the Great War ended and the South Slav lands united in the new Kingdom of Serbs, Croats, and Slovenes, the movement for women's rights gained new momentum. In the interwar period, there were two major umbrella women's organizations on the national level with a feminist platform. The first, the Yugoslav Women's League (YWL), came into being as a successor to the prewar Serbian Women's League. The latter aspired to unite all women's societies in the new kingdom, and in September 1919, on this initiative, the National Women's League of Serbs, Croats, and Slovenes (later renamed the Yugoslav Women's League, YWL) was founded in Belgrade. From its Serbian predecessor, the now-enlarged organization inherited membership in international feminist associations. Shortly after its establishment, the YWL could boast of gathering together some four hundred groups and societies from all regions of the new state. It nevertheless fell short of reaching all women. As it adopted the official state's ideology of unitary Yugoslavism, which many non-Serbs saw as a screen for Serbian domination and centralization, it failed to attract the largest women's association in Croatia, the Croatian Woman Society (Društvo Hrvatska žena), a branch of the immensely popular Croatian Peasant Party of Stjepan Radić. In addition, the majority of clerical Croatian and Slovenian women's associations refused to join.[15]

Divisions among women's organizations existed with regard to not only ethnonational ideologies, but also the "woman question." Not all of the YWL's member societies were feminist oriented. In fact, the organizations that entered the league were extremely heterogeneous, ranging from conservative confessional groups to those with a radical feminist agenda. In 1922, influenced by the international organizations in which it claimed membership, the YWL's leadership opted – in the words of Neda Božinović – for a "sort of moderate feminism," including in its program a number of demands: legal equality between men and women, equal educational opportunities for female and male children, and the establishment of equal moral norms for the two sexes. Such a program

[14] Emmert, 35; Neda Božinović, "Žene u modernizacijiskim procesima u Jugoslaviji i Srbiji," in Perović, *Srbija u modernizacijskim procesima*, vol. 2, 513.

[15] Božinović, "Žene ... ," 515.

appeared too revolutionary for some of the members. In 1926, several conservative organizations broke away to form an organization of their own – an event that weakened the league significantly. Still, it remained the largest umbrella association of Yugoslav women, and, preserving a relatively heterogeneous character, continued its activities throughout the interwar period.[16]

The second, and for our discussion more important, interwar women's association was the Alliance of Women's Movements (Alijansa ženskih pokreta). It was in fact an umbrella organization within the largest umbrella organization, a member of the Yugoslav Women's League, gathering together the most radical, most active, and most vocal proponents of feminism in interwar Yugoslavia. The alliance was born when, at a meeting in Ljubljana in 1923, three feminist groups united: the Society for the Enlightenment of Woman and Protection of Her Rights – the Women's Movement (Društvo za prosvećivanje žene i zaštitu njenih prava – Ženski pokret) from Belgrade, the Association of Yugoslav Women (Udruženje Jugoslovenskih žena) from Zagreb, and the General Slovenian Women's Society from Ljubljana.[17] Other, smaller groups joined the founding members later. The major admission criterion was that the candidate organization supported women's suffrage.

The alliance saw itself as a "cultural movement." It had a left-leaning agenda: It defined feminism as "form of political, social and cultural work for socialist and humanist ideals."[18] Its chief goals included legislation that would give women political rights and the elimination of discriminatory laws, such as the Serbian civil code of 1844, in which inequality between the sexes in an extreme and outdated form was sanctioned. Its political activity primarily took the form of appeals and petitions to the government. The alliance also took an interest in social and humanitarian issues, especially in the protection of the poor and oppressed. Its journals featured numerous pieces on war orphans and widows, unwed mothers, female workers, and prostitutes, while its activists helped set up orphanages, maternity centers, and employment bureaus for women. This line of campaigning gave the feminists more influence with the state, and various ministries began assisting in their humanitarian projects. The feminists' educational efforts were notable as well. In the cities, they offered literacy courses for workers and training in tailoring for underprivileged girls. In

[16] Ibid., 515.
[17] Emmert, 48.
[18] Jalušič, 61.

the countryside, they organized domestic courses for female peasants. They also sponsored lectures on women's rights and the history of the women's movement. The alliance may not have been successful in achieving its primary objective of political and legal equality, but, as Thomas Emmert concludes, it did have a large impact on the lives of the women and children it touched.[19]

More relevant for this discussion is that the alliance accrued enormous experience in organizational matters, campaigning, and social and educational activities. In the mid-1930s, this valuable knowledge would be passed on to young communist women, the future organizers and leaders of the wartime AFW. The "training" they received during their alliance years could be credited for much of the organizational skill and resourcefulness that they exhibited during the war.

Socialist Women: The phrase "proletarian women's movement" in Yugoslav historiography generally refers to women's sections that used to operate under the auspices of the Communist Party or its predecessors, various local social democratic groups. In party politics, the Social Democrats were indeed the first – and for a long time the only – advocates of women's emancipation in the region. Among the many social democratic organizations that emerged in the Yugoslav lands in the two decades preceding World War I, the most important were those of Croatia-Slavonia, Slovenia, Serbia, and Bosnia-Herzegovina. As Ivo Banac writes, the former two were reformist parties in the Austro-Marxist tradition, rooted in trade unions, and without a strong intellectual leadership. The parties of Serbia and Bosnia, in contrast, were more dogmatic, with the Serbian one in particular being dominated by intellectuals and "preoccupied with the purity of doctrine and class independence of the socialist movement."[20] Regional differences notwithstanding, similar demands on women's behalf – such as suffrage and equal pay for equal work – were included in the party programs of all of them.

The South Slavic Social Democrats' take on the "woman question" and their view on the need for socialist women's organizations, however, were neither uniform nor consistent. In Slovenia, for example, where they were linked to the Austrian Social Democratic Movement, Vlasta Jalušič tells us, the socialists readily "sacrificed" the demand for women's vote as a compromise during the 1907 elections. When, in 1911, minor legal changes allowing women to become members of political associations

[19] Emmert, 40–1, 46, 48–9.
[20] Banac, *The National Question*, 196.

were made on the initiative of the Social Democrats, the party press announced that the socialists' duty to women had been done and that women themselves should take over the struggle for their rights from then on. And when Alojzija Štebi, an outspoken prosocialist feminist and one of the founding members of the General Slovenian Women's Society, began editing the first socialist women's journal, *Ženski list*, she received no support from the party, and the journal ceased after only six issues.[21]

The Serbian Marxists – perhaps because they were more left-leaning and orthodox than their counterparts in the Habsburg lands – were somewhat more consistent in their attempts to politicize the female proletariat. The founding of the Serbian Social Democratic Party in 1903 was immediately followed by the establishment of a women workers' society, "The Consciousness" (Svest). The society focused on education and agitation: It offered literacy courses for female laborers and organized strikes and protests.[22] Its organizational efforts, however, were rudimentary and its significance no more than symbolic as the society dissolved less than two years after its birth.

The initiative for a more systematic and comprehensive party approach to women originated with one of the leaders of the left faction, Dimitrije Tucović. The need for the Social Democratic fight for women's equality, Tucović explained, not only was obvious "from the standpoints of morality and justice," but also stemmed from "historical development itself. Economic progress has effected a great revolution in the position of women," forcing them to "enter the political struggle."[23] In 1910, Tucović attended the Second International's Congress in Copenhagen. The Congress followed the famous socialist women's conference, which adopted Clara Zetkin's proposal of establishing a yearly international women's day. Upon his return from Denmark, an analogous meeting of Social Democrat women was held in Belgrade. The women elected their Secretariat, which joined the international organization of women Social Democrats and started publishing its journal *Jednakost* (*Equality*, named after *Die Gleichheit*, the German socialist women's journal edited by Zetkin).[24]

Following Zetkin's ideas, the female socialists of Serbia distanced themselves from "those ladies from higher circles who would like greater rights for women," that is, from nonproletarian women's organizations.

[21] Jalušič, 57; also, Kovačević, *Borbeni put*, 190.
[22] Kovačević, *Borbeni put*, 224.
[23] As quoted in ibid., 15.
[24] Cvetić, *Žene Srbije*, 9.

As *Jednakost* announced, the Secretariat's mission was the struggle of the exploited classes against their exploiters and not a struggle of women against men.[25] This view on the proper place of women's activism together with a similar denunciation of feminism would later become the official stance of the Yugoslav Communist Party. Therein lies the Secretariat's primary importance: It adopted the ideological line on the women's movement that would be followed by the Yugoslav Left for years. As an organizational force, however, the Secretariat's relevance was not comparable. Since Serbian Social Democracy had developed in an agrarian state where trade unions were relatively weak, it was largely "remote from the economic struggle of factory workers."[26] Its attempts to reach the female proletariat, noteworthy though they were, represented organizational activity that was only in its infancy, and one can hardly talk about the existence of an organized proletarian women's movement in the region before World War I.

After the war and the unification of the South Slav peoples into a common state, representatives of local Social Democratic parties met at the Unification Congress held in Belgrade, 20–3 April 1919, to form the Socialist Worker's Party of Yugoslavia (Communist).[27] The Social Democrats of Croatia-Slavonia, Vojvodina, and Slovenia split over their view of the Bolshevik revolution, and only their left wings decided to join the new party. In contrast, the Social Democratic organizations of Serbia and Bosnia entered the party almost in their entirety. Serbian communists in particular were preeminent in the new party, giving it a direction corresponding to their Marxist orthodoxy. Their approach to the woman question was similarly transferred into the Yugoslav party's program. A women's conference, held during the unification congress, adopted the Statute of Yugoslav Socialist Women, which had been prepared by the Serbian Secretariat. After the Serbian organizational model, the women of the new party founded an all-Yugoslav Secretariat. The statute clearly spelled out the position of party women, being particularly vocal about the fact that their Secretariat was *not* meant to be an independent and separate organization:

Women socialists (communists) adopt the maximal and minimal program of the Party ... and see themselves as a part of the Party whole. At the same time,

---

[25] As quoted in Jancar-Webster, *Women & Revolution*, 20.

[26] Ivo Banac, *With Stalin against Tito: Cominformist Splits in Yugoslav Communism* (Ithaca, NY: Cornell University Press, 1988), 47.

[27] My discussion of the First and Second Congresses is based on ibid., 46–50; also idem, *The National Question*, 328–30.

they exclude any separate women's organization, and consider themselves a *technical-executive committee for agitation and organizational activity among women [u agitaciji i organizovanju žena].*[28]

The party further consolidated along the leftist platform at its second congress, held in Vukovar, in June 1920. The centrist faction, which was as distant from communist radicalism as it was from the reformism of social democracy, was defeated and expelled, leaving the ultraleft in charge. In Vukovar the party changed its name to the Communist Party of Yugoslavia (CPY) and assumed its definitive ideological orientation as the Comintern's South Slavic section.[29] The second congress confirmed the communists' nominal dedication to women's issues; suffrage, equality in the workplace, protection for pregnant workers and mothers, and maternity leave were all on the party's list of demands.[30] The CPY also proceeded to establish women's secretariats attached to its provincial, regional, and local organizations.

In its first two years of existence, riding the pan-European postwar red wave, the CPY proved relatively popular among the Yugoslav masses. According to Ivo Banac, the party's showing at the 1920 elections for the Constituent Assembly was surprisingly strong; it was the fourth strongest political party in the kingdom, winning fifty-nine seats with 198,736 votes or 12.34 percent of the ballots cast. Its electoral success and political prominence, however, were not to last. In August 1921, following a series of communist-led miner's strikes and several assassinations of government officials, the National Assembly passed an anti-Communist act, thus formally outlawing the CPY. In the following decades, known activists were arrested and the leadership forced into exile. The ban decimated the party, its membership decreasing from more than 50,000 in 1920 to a mere 688 in 1924. In addition, the CPY was internally weakened by incessant factional struggles. The royal dictatorship of 1929 almost dealt a deathblow to the remaining minuscule organization, since its most active members either were imprisoned or perished in armed conflicts with the police. Most of the party's interwar history consisted of repeated attempts at recovery, which would prove difficult.[31]

Given the harsh conditions under which the party operated in the Yugoslav kingdom, it is perhaps not surprising that it paid little attention

---

[28] As quoted in Cvetić, *Žene Srbije,* 9; my italics.
[29] Banac, *With Stalin,* 50, idem, *The National Question,* 329.
[30] Kovačević, *Borbeni put,* 15.
[31] Banac, *With Stalin,* 50–1, 61; idem, *The National Question,* 332–9.

to women. The women's secretariats had barely been established when the CPY was banned; after 1921, any kind of communist agitation became difficult and most activities directed at women ceased. Congress after congress, party leaders took note of this dismal situation and called for a renewal of efforts, yet in practice they could achieve little. Following the resolution of the Fourth Party Congress, held in Dresden in November 1928, a special commission of the Central Committee for work with women was formed. The commission started its work by issuing directives regarding the establishment of provincial women's commissions and the organization of underground *kruzhok*s that would introduce female workers to revolutionary ideas. But the imposition of the royal dictatorship two months later put the implementation of these directives on hold.[32]

It was not until the appearance of the Nazi threat on the international political scene and the party's adoption of the popular front line in 1935 that any significant revival of the "proletarian" women's activism occurred. The popular front strategy demanded that the communists form broad alliances with parties and groups opposing the fascists; communists were supposed to be the leaders of this antifascist movement. One of the CPY's tactics at the time was the infiltration of existing legal organizations with the goal of gradual takeover. Members of the party and the Communist Youth League were given the task of entering trade unions, teacher societies, professional groups, student clubs, and peasant, youth, and workers' organizations – practically any legally operating association that was not under the fascist sway. Female members were in charge of infiltrating women's societies. In the party's view, the most "progressive" and most suitable women's organization was the Alliance of Women's Movements.[33] In 1935, communist girls joined forces with feminists to form the alliance's youth section. The two currents of the Yugoslav women's movement – feminist and proletarian – thus united for the first time in decades.

The presence of the communist youth activists energized and radicalized the feminist association, which launched several notable campaigns for women's political and civil rights in the ensuing five years. Demonstrations for women's vote in Belgrade, Zagreb, and Split in 1935, the first large public gatherings since the imposition of the dictatorship, were the result of an initial joint action of feminist "ladies" and

---

[32] Bojović, *Žene Crne Gore*, 58–63; Cvetić, *Žene Srbije*, 10.
[33] Cvetić, *Žene Srbije*, 57.

communist youths. With élan and enthusiasm, the alliance's youth section organized regular meetings, lectures, and discussions with women of all social backgrounds. It also offered courses in literacy, hygiene, and nursing for female workers and peasants.[34] In 1936, the section in Belgrade began editing *Žena danas* (Woman today), a women's periodical that propagated antifascist and leftist ideas in a popular and accessible manner. Two years later, the Zagreb youth section started its equivalent, *Ženski svijet* (Women's world). Combining articles about women's daily concerns with subtle political messages, the journals soon found loyal audiences: The circulation of *Ženski svijet* rose from two thousand to seventeen thousand in the last three prewar years.[35] The culmination of feminist-communist cooperation was the 1939 women's suffrage campaign sponsored by *Žena danas*. The journal launched a petition and called for the establishment of women's committees in charge of collecting signatures as well as organizing women's rallies. No other campaign of the alliance had seen such positive public response; reportedly, the turnout at rallies was massive and the petition boasted more than thirty thousand signatures. For young communist activists, such campaigns served as a school where they received training in organizational matters, mass propaganda, and public speaking, which would prove invaluable in the coming war.

In evaluating the proletarian women's movement, one must emphasize that the organizational experience that female communists gained before the war was due to their activism in legal women's organizations, not in the party's secretariats and commissions. The CPY's interwar record shows little more than a succession of sporadic, short-lived, and mostly failed attempts to organize women. To be fair, this failure can be largely attributed to political repression and harsh conditions in the interwar kingdom. But the party's approach to women's emancipation should also be taken into account. The Yugoslav Left began paying attention to women primarily because they were increasingly entering the labor force, thus constituting a reservoir of future revolutionaries. The party viewed women mainly as a *reserve team* of the revolution, to be drawn into the political arena as needed to replace men.[36] It was largely thanks to the

---

[34] For more on the section's activities, see ibid., 57–60.

[35] Šoljan, *Žene Hrvatske*, xiv.

[36] This point was explicitly made in party documents. For example, the Montenegrin party conference of 1939 called for the urgent training of females because of the approaching war danger. In a similar vein, the resolution of the 1940 Vojvodina party conference asked for special attention to women so that they could take over the organization if

core of skilled female activists, whose experience combined the feminist and communist organizational traditions, that this substitute revolutionary army would mobilize behind the Partisans when the Axis conquered the country.

DEVELOPMENT OF THE AFW

The beginning of the war made the importance of having a reserve team made up of women evident. The party realized that women would have to take over the rear to replace men who were drafted to the front. Unlike its local rivals, the Ustashas and the Chetniks, the CPY took steps to make sure women's energies were directed toward its war effort early on in the conflict. Already in the summer of 1941, in the initially liberated territories, party leaders began gathering peasant women at mass meetings, at which they talked about the need for an efficient rear support system and appealed for help. The first such conference took place in Drvar (Bosnian Krajina), where one of the earliest Partisan guerrilla detachments operated. The conference was initiated by communist activists working in the Drvar region and in neighboring Lika (Croatia), among whom was Marko Orešković, a veteran of the Spanish Civil War.[37] "In mid-August 1941, I worked at the staff of the Drvar guerrilla detachment as a courier for Lika," remembers Mira Morača, one of the most prominent female communists and a future AFW leader:

At that time, comrade Marko Orešković came to the detachment's staff.... One day comrades Marko [Orešković] and Ljubo Babić called on Vera Babić, Jela Bićanić, and myself and talked to us about the need to organize the rear, and especially women, who would have to bear the brunt of the whole rear organization, because men would increasingly leave for the front. We were told to organize women's conferences and speak about the issue. The comrades also told us that the first such conference would be held in a couple of days in Drvar and gave us concrete assignments in relation to that.[38]

---

needed. And the Slovenian party resolution of the same year noted the need for women activists, especially in times when men were mobilized for the "imperialist war." As reported in *Proleter* 1-2, January–February 1940, pages not numbered; *Proleter* 9-10-11, October–November–December 1940, 17-19; *Proleter* 7-8, August–September 1940, 10-12, respectively.

[37] Marko Orešković was an "independently minded" member of the Central Committee of the Croatian party and a former volunteer in the Spanish Civil War. He took charge of organizing resistance in his native Lika. For more on Orešković, see Hoare, *Genocide and Resistance*, 127-41.

[38] Mira Morača, "Prva konferencija žena u Drvaru," in Hurem, *Žene Bosne*, 136.

The Drvar conference, which took place on 21 August 1941, turned out so well that even its organizers were surprised. "Women were arriving from all sides of the town: old women carrying their peasant bags, young wives and girls in their national costumes.... The streets of Drvar were overflowed," continues Morača. "The conference room of the workers' house was completely full and around the building, under the windows, there were groups of those who could not get in."[39] This success was, in part, due to the fact that the villages of the Drvar valley, being the very first to be liberated in the war, hosted a large number of people with an acute reason to rise up against the Ustasha regime or the occupiers. These villages were home to numerous Serb communities that, with the news about the Ustasha massacres of the Serbs, produced many a militant to join the insurgents and take part in the uprising.[40] It is small wonder that the mothers, sisters, daughters, and wives of these rebels should prove their eager supporters. In addition, the larger Drvar environs at the time hosted a number of refugees from the Plitvice area in Lika (Croatia), who had fled before the Ustasha onslaughts, and a group of Slovenes whom the Nazis had expelled from Slovenia. In such circumstances, the communist appeal to help the guerrillas found many female sympathizers.

Under communist direction, the women of the Drvar valley issued a proclamation asking their "liberators and protectors" – their men in the Partisan units – to persist in the struggle until all peoples of Yugoslavia were freed from fascists. As for themselves, the women pledged to support the army primarily through their traditional responsibilities:

Today, we decided unanimously to cooperate with you in our common struggle in the best way we can. We, in the rear, will in every village, every factory, every street and every house, through our committees and representatives, organize to help you, so that you are not undressed, hungry and thirsty, so that you can persevere until the final victory.[41]

After Drvar, communist activists began preparing women's conferences in neighboring villages.[42] The party also formed ad hoc women's councils

[39] Ibid.

[40] One of the first guerrilla detachments was formed in the Drvar valley in July 1941, after the initial Ustasha massacres. The detachment managed to liberate several villages. The short-lived "Drvar republic" lasted until September 1941, when the Italians occupied the territory.

[41] *Zbornik* 4.1, doc. 43, pp. 94–5. On the success of the Drvar conference see *Zbornik* 2. 2, doc. 11, p. 43.

[42] Such actions took place in Lika (where their organization was facilitated by the fact that many local women had been present at Drvar), in the Podgrmeč area (Bosnia), and others. For Podgrmeč, see Miljka Štrbac-Bursać, "Aktivnost žena u Podgrmeču do ljeta

in charge of providing basic supplies for men on the front. In these early wartime days, the activity of such bodies was welcomed in the embryonic rebel army, as they supplied it with food and other provisions on a regular basis. They represented a prelude to the establishment of an organized women's association.

Before long, such an association was founded on the initiative of the Croatian Communist Party. Early in December 1941, the Croatian Central Committee released a circular authorizing the formation of the Antifascist Front of Women (AFW). This is a seminal document that in rough terms provided the first definition of the organization's outlook, raison d'être, and basic functions, many of which would remain in effect for the duration of the war. According to this directive, the AFW was to be created with the purpose of "activating and connecting the broad strata of women and involving them in the national-liberation struggle"; the front was to include "all women … regardless of their political, national, or religious affiliation." The AFW's organizational structure, like the party's own, was to be territorial and hierarchical, springing from local and regional groups up to the Main Council for Croatia as a whole, with lower councils being subordinated to the higher ones. The front's primary task was to ensure women's support of the Partisan detachments. The AFW was also to popularize the accomplishments of the USSR, disseminate antifascist propaganda, and organize women's resistance against all enemy measures (such as the requisitioning of food and clothing for the fascist bands and the sending of female laborers to Germany). Significantly, on the list of the AFW's tasks one could also find the struggle for equality between the sexes. Although depicted in vague terms and listed almost as an afterthought in the document, this struggle would remain one of the central purposes of the AFW throughout its twelve-year existence.[43]

Immediately after the directive was announced, activists operating in the liberated territories in Croatia started forming AFW councils. Probably the most active in the first wartime years was the district AFW of Lika, which could boast of remarkable achievements in supporting the Partisan war effort. The Lika council also managed to assemble and publish the first wartime women's journal, *Žena u borbi* (*Woman in*

1943. godine," in Hurem, *Žene Bosne*, 281–4. On Podgrmeč, Lika, and other regions see also Kovačević, *Borbeni put*, 49–50, 124.

43 AVII, NOR, CK SK Hrvatske NOB 32/500, CKKPH Okružnica br. 4, 6 December 1941. Also in Šoljan, *Žene Hrvatske*, vol. 1, doc. 37, p. 57.

the Struggle), in the midst of an enemy offensive in 1942. The journal, intended to connect and help recruit local women, proved a highly successful mobilizing tool.[44] It would serve as a model for the later periodical of the same title, issued by the AFW Croatia, and for many other women's journals that would be released by various AFW forums during the war.

Besides Croatia, notable achievements were recorded in early 1942 in eastern Bosnia, where Tito and the Supreme Staff were located at the time. "We have developed intensive political work around here ... especially work with women [*rad po ženskoj liniji*] has met with great success," noted Tito in a February letter to his fellow party leaders, Lola Ribar and Edvard Kardelj:

We have managed to get Serb and Muslim women to work together. On Sunday we held a women's gathering [*zbor*] at which female delegates from all over the liberated territory were present, most of them peasants ... over 500 women came.... There the Antifascist Front of Women for Bosnia and Herzegovina was created. It is most interesting that, in these most backwards Bosnian villages, there is mass enthusiasm among female peasants for our national-liberation struggle.... In Foča alone we managed, immediately, during the very first days upon our arrival, to gather 906 women who [now] frequent meetings. All this was accomplished thanks to our female comrades from the detachments, who incidentally happened to be around. They not only work with women here, but also visit distant villages where they successfully gather women.[45]

Tito's entourage shared his enthusiasm. "We have created a miracle," wrote Vladimir Dedijer in his diary on the occasion. "In this forgotten burg by the Drina [river] we have created a people's house of culture – and in it over 500 women have gathered! Peasants, Serbs, Muslims, Partisans."[46] Even though this initial phase of women's organizational activity was brief, as the Partisans had to leave the area before enemy attacks several months thereafter, the episode gave the party leadership great encouragement to persist in setting up AFW councils wherever circumstances allowed. Using women's traditional responsibilities, it turned out, was the best way to mobilize the female masses. "Pay special attention to the work among women," insisted Tito in his letter to other party leaders. "This work is best done on the basis of their support to the

---

[44] AJ, AFŽ, 141-10-53, Učešće žena Like u NOBi, Razvitak organizacije AFŽ, n.d.
[45] AJ, SKJ 507, CKKPJ 1942/82, Titovo pismo Loli i Bevcu, 23 February 1942. Also *Zbornik* 2.2, doc. 201, pp. 435–6.
[46] Vladimir Dedijer, *The War Diaries of Vladimir Dedijer* (Ann Arbor: University of Michigan Press, 1990), vol. 1, 92.

national-liberation struggle. Here we succeeded in gathering hundreds upon hundreds of women on the basis of aiding the front: knitting socks and sweaters, collecting donations, enlisting nurses."[47]

The AFW of Yugoslavia Is Born: In the fall of 1942, in preparation for its boldest political statement to date – establishing AVNOJ (Anti-Fascist Council of National Liberation of Yugoslavia) and declaring it the legitimate civil administration in war-torn Yugoslavia – the CPY leadership decided to consolidate its mass organizations. The front of women, the party determined, needed to expand to encompass the whole country, and disparate women's councils were to unite into a large nationwide organization, the AFW of Yugoslavia.[48]

Held in Bosanski Petrovac, 6–8 December 1942, ten days after the AVNOJ meeting in Bihać, the founding conference of the AFW of Yugoslavia assembled 166 female delegates from various parts of the country.[49] Replicating the theatrics and pomp of similar Soviet events, the conference opened by naming the AFW's "honorary presidium," which included such figures as Stalin, Tito, and Sima Milošević (in the name of AVNOJ), as well as the following female comrades: Dolores Ibarruri (the communist heroine of the Spanish Civil War, at the time in the USSR); the Soviet sniper Ludmila Pavlichenko; the Soviet activist and onetime editor of the women's journal *Rabotnitsa*, Klavdiia Nikolaeva; the Polish communist Wanda Wasilewska; the widow of Sun Yat-sen; Eleanor Roosevelt; the Romanian communist Ana Pauker; and two female Partisans, Mara Kusturić of the 2nd Proletarian Brigade, and Ranka Stepanović in the name of the wounded Partisans.[50] Tito greeted the congregation with a magnificent speech, a gem in his oratory record. He began by pronouncing Yugoslav women on par in valor with their Soviet sisters. "I can say that in this struggle, by their heroism and their endurance, women have been at the forefront. The peoples of Yugoslavia should feel honored to have such daughters," he continued, adding a powerful avowal: *"I am*

[47] AJ, SKJ 507, CKKPJ 1942/82, Titovo pismo Loli i Bevcu, 23 Feb. 1942; *Zbornik* 2.2, doc. 201, pp. 435–6.

[48] AJ, SKJ 507, CKKPJ 1942/625, Direktivno pismo CKKPJ, 2 November 1942. Also *Izvori za istoriju SKJ, Series A: Dokumenti centralnih organa KPJ: NOR i revolucija (1941–1945)* (Beograd: Izdavacki centar Komunist, 1985–96) (hereafter *Izvori*), vol. 8, 324–6.

[49] Delegates were from Bosnia, Croatia, Serbia, and Montenegro. As a result of harsh wartime conditions in their respective regions, women from Slovenia arrived after the conference while the Macedonians were unable to attend. Kovačević, *Borbeni put*, 25.

[50] AJ, AFŽ, 141-14-75, Rad I zemaljske konferencije AFŽ; Materijali o proslavi godišnjice I konferencije, 1952.

proud to be the leader of an army that includes an enormous number of women!"[51]

After Tito's address and speeches by representatives of various Partisan institutions, the congregation elected its Central Council. The voting procedure at the first AFW conference – and all the following wartime conventions and congresses – unfolded in accordance with the standard election scenario of Soviet-style mass organizations. Typically, such elections would begin by a reading of names from a list of candidates, all of whom were handpicked by the party. The congregation would approve each name by loud applause and thus give legitimacy to the list, which would then be adopted practically without any changes.

Yet despite the fact that most such mass meetings were staged performances, where party-designated candidates were elected and predrafted resolutions were adopted, there was some, if limited, room for authentic expression and spontaneous input from below. Even if prepared for their conference addresses, delegates from the villages often said what they meant, be it to the party's liking or not. Quick-witted peasant women in the audience sometimes intervened with their questions and comments, adding a dose of authenticity to the event. Dedijer's diary records several such instances. At the first women's conference in eastern Bosnia, for example, a party representative's speech was interrupted. "When he said that we will have a better future, one old peasant woman in the first row cried out: 'If God wills!' "[52]

Medium- and lower-level AFW councils were often elected at similarly staged mass gatherings. Even though ordinary women could and did end up being elected, they were typically preselected by the CPY among those most devoted to the Partisan cause. This does not mean that these bodies were not popular institutions. In fact, females who found themselves in women's councils often enjoyed respect and authority among their fellow villagers in the liberated territories. While there is little doubt that the AFW's organizational structure was communist controlled, it was also genuinely participatory, especially on the local level and in the regions where the masses were pro-Partisan.

The Profile of "Organized Women": The front of women mostly gathered older, married females above the age of thirty. This was party policy; AFW activists were specifically instructed to focus on older women rather

---

[51] Tito, "Govor na Prvoj Zemaljskoj Konferenciji Antifašističkog Fronta Žena," 6 December 1942, in *Tito-Ženama Jugoslavije* (Beograd: Centralni odbor Antifašističkog Fronta Žena Jugoslavije, 1945), 6.

[52] Dedijer, *The War Diaries*, vol. 1, 93.

than the female youth. While the most numerous and most active female sympathizers of the Partisans in the rear were very young, in their teens and early twenties, they were real or potential members of Partisan youth organizations, and the party believed that the AFW should target women who were otherwise uninvolved in the movement.[53]

The vast majority of "organized" women were of peasant background, because the AFW worked best in the territories where the Partisan units operated, which were rural peripheries rather than urban centers. There were attempts to organize women in occupied towns and cities, and sometimes these met with relative success, as was the case in Italian-held Split (Dalmatia). Yet examples of well-working urban councils were comparatively rare.[54] The AFW thus ended up serving as a vehicle for the mobilization of the segment of the female populace that was considered particularly backward, inert, and difficult to reach: peasant housewives.

Why did female villagers join the AFW? Accounts and recollections directly from women on the rank-and-file level are scarce, and they tell us little about their motivation to take part in AFW activities. Judging by party records, it seems that for most women the decision to support the Partisans was not the result of a political inclination toward communism but rather a spontaneous reaction to the wartime calamity. The majority of "organized" women in the first years of the war were from endangered communities living in the so-called insurgent regions (*ustanički krajevi*) that provided the Partisans with the bulk of their initial manpower (Lika, Kordun, Bosnian Krajina, etc.). The most active AFW organizations proved to be those in which local women were connected to the Partisan army through their family members. The observation of the Makarska (Dalmatia) Party committee, complaining that even dedicated women lacked conscious *political* affiliation with the Partisan cause, speaks for most regions:

Although women are organized, they are neither politically solid nor sufficiently conscious, but all of their devotion to our movement came spontaneously, with the enlargement of our movement and with the direct link to our struggle, through their loved ones among the ranks of our fighters.[55]

[53] AVII, NOR, Muzej Like Gospić NOB 1/401–403, 402, Okr. KPH Lika kotarskom kom.-u Gospić, 16 July 1942; AVII, NOR, IRP BiH 5/740–741, Okr. kom. KPJ Sev. Herzegovina Ob. kom. u Herzegovina, 4 January 1944; AVII, NOR, IRP BiH 6/505–8, 508, Ob. kom. SKOJ za Hercegovinu svim org. SKOJa u Herceg., February 1944, and others.

[54] AFW documents abound in complaints about the problems the front encountered while attempting to organize women in cities. See, for example, AVII, NOR, k. 12, f. 1, doc. 21, Rezolucija okr. konferencije AFŽ za I. Srem, 31 May 1943, and others.

[55] AVII, NOR, Muzej NR Split NOB 7/182–9, 188, Kotarski kom. KPH za Makarsku Okr. kom. u KPH za Makarsku, 3 November 1943.

In short, the typical AFW council member on the local level was a female peasant in her thirties or forties, whose sympathies were on the Partisan side as her community was endangered by the occupiers or one of the local factions, and whose family members (usually children and/or husband) were in the Partisan units or in the CPY. This profile was also present in councils on the medium and higher levels. In Vojvodina, for example, the first provincial AFW conference chose Emilija Kolarov, the mother of the fallen Partisan hero Vladimir Kolarov, as president and, as vice president, Manda Agbaba, mother of seven – six daughters and a son – all of whom were at the time either among the Partisan ranks or captured by the enemy. In Srem, the first regional AFW council elected as president Krista Badanjac, mother of nine Partisan fighters.[56] As noted earlier, the archetypal AFW member was the very woman presiding over the organization's Central Council, Kata Pejnović, a Serb peasant from Lika, who had lost her three sons and husband to the Ustasha terror at the beginning of the war. Party propaganda, we have seen in the previous chapter, put to good use the motherly figure of a typical "organized woman." The image of patriotic motherhood was placed on a pedestal in Partisan culture, and maternal feelings were targeted in much of party addresses to women. "Female comrades," started a typical AFW appeal, "let's help our children who are fighting in the most difficult of conditions."[57]

Most peasant women organized by the AFW were poorly – if at all – educated. Even the organization's president, Kata Pejnović, had little formal schooling. Born to a poor family with six children, she had to abandon studying after four years of elementary school. Outstanding among her village peers, she was a keen reader who discovered the so-called progressive literature in the 1930s and became a party member in 1938.[58] The vast majority of those below her in the organization's hierarchy had even less formal education and lacked her ambition and self-teaching skills. Many were illiterate.

Yet the highest AFW echelons on the state and federal levels deviated from this typical profile: They were neither peasants nor uneducated.

---

[56] Srbislava Kovačević Marija, "Antifašistički front žena u Vojvodini, 1941–1945," in *Žene Vojvodine u ratu i revoluciji, 1941–1945*, ed. Danilo Kecić (Novi Sad: Institut za istoriju, 1984), 122–3.

[57] AVII, NOR, k.12, f.1, dok. 37, Letak, okr. odbor AFŽ za Ist. Srem, n.d.

[58] For Pejnović's biography, see Milenko Predragović, *Kata Pejnović: Životni put i revolucionarno delo* (Gornji Milanovac: Dečje novine, 1978); for a brief biographical sketch see Marija Šoljan, *Žene Hrvatske*, pp. 184–5.

In these elite circles, the self-taught Lika peasant Kata Pejnović was exceptional. The majority of leaders were prewar CPY activists, mostly from the ranks of university students, professionals, and the intelligentsia, schooled in larger cities (Belgrade, Zagreb, Ljubljana). Among women of the highest ranks were Mitra Mitrović (a CPY activist and graduate of the University of Belgrade, long active in the youth section of the Alliance of Women's Movements, editor of *Žena danas*), Spasenija Cana Babović (a member of the CPY's Central Committee and a professional revolutionary, schooled in Serbia and Moscow before the war), Olga Kovačić and Vanda Novosel (activists from Zagreb, editors of the prewar women's journal *Ženski svijet*), Mira Morača (a law student before the war),[59] Djina Vrbica (a student of economics in Zagreb and later Belgrade, originally from Podgorica, Montenegro), Vida Tomšič (a Slovene lawyer, trained at the University of Ljubljana, and another CPY Central Committee member, who became president of the AFW after the war, replacing Pejnović), and others. Most of these female leaders had a record of activism in interwar feminist organizations. One symbol of continuity between their work in the Alliance of Women's Movements and the AFW was their decision to revive *Žena danas,* the journal of the alliance's youth section, as the organ of the AFW's Central Council. Mitra Mitrović served as editor of *Žena danas* in both of its incarnations.

The Dual Function of the AFW: The CPY launched its Partisan movement with two goals in mind: first, to liberate the country from the invaders and their local collaborators, and second and equally important, to seize power and establish a communist state. This politicoideological dyad was reflected in the AFW, whose purpose was twofold as well. The organization's most important objective was to provide a rear support system for the National-Liberation Army by mobilizing women's labor and channeling it toward the Partisan war effort. The second goal was political in nature and revolutionary in ambition: to transform the backward masses of women into equal and deserving members of the new socialist society that the CPY was intent on creating. It was the task of the AFW, as one directive stated, to help eliminate illiteracy among women, "raise" their "political consciousness," and "train them professionally, so that they could be of better use" in the building of the socialist nation.[60]

---

[59] For Mira Morača's personal CPY file (*karakteristika*) see AJ, SKJ 507, CKKPJ 1944/687, Ob. kom KPJ za B. Krajinu CK-u KPJ, 4 December 1944.

[60] AVII, NOR, Muzej NR Split NOB 7/143, Kotarski kom. KPH za Makarsku Op. kom.-u KPH za Makarsku, 23 September 1943.

In order to fulfill the first objective of supplying succor for the guerrillas, the AFW soon took on many responsibilities that, in the conditions of regular warfare, would be associated with the home front and coordinated by state organs.[61] The "organized women" collected money, food, clothes, and medicine for the Partisans, providing the necessary supplies for the army (Figure 4). They also sewed uniforms, knitted sweaters and socks, and made shoes. Many services for the army were provided by the AFW: The women laundered and mended soldiers' clothes and offered accommodation and care for the wounded and the sick. In addition, the AFW made a contribution to the medical corps as it mobilized and trained females to serve as Partisan nurses.

The sphere of social and humanitarian work, conventionally considered a women's province, remained so during the revolutionary war. The AFW ran orphanages and children's homes in liberated zones, the earliest such institutions emerging in Lika and Kordun in the first year of the uprising.[62] About one hundred homes, assisting nearly seventeen thousand children, were set up during the war in Croatia alone.[63] Providing aid and care to the families and widows of Partisan soldiers was another AFW job.[64] The organization also helped accommodate the exiled Partisan families and numerous peasant refugees that followed the units on the move.

The females recruited by the AFW in certain cases crossed the old gender divide. Since much of the agricultural work in the villages was now left to women, the AFW helped set up the so-called labor units that plowed the land, harvested the crops, and performed other agricultural tasks in the rear, thus keeping the local economies going; women's labor units also transported food, goods, and ammunition from the villages to the front.[65] For actions of sabotage and diversion – destroying roads and railways, cutting telephone lines, burning enemy crops, and the like – the AFW organized women's combat groups (*borbene grupe*) in the rear.[66]

---

[61] Jancar-Webster, *Women & Revolution*, 139.
[62] AJ, AFŽ, 141-10-53, AFŽ i briga o djeci, n.d.
[63] Kovačević, *Borbeni put*, 234; Jancar Webster, *Women & Revolution*, 140.
[64] AJ, SKJ 507, CKKPJ 1943/362, Prilog 3: Inic. Odbor AFŽ za CG I Boku svim org. AFŽ-a na teritoriji Crne Gore i Boke, n.d. (1943).
[65] AVII, NOR, IA PK SKS Vojvodine NOB 4/203–4, Okr. odbor AFŽ za Ist. Srem svim sreskim i mesnim odborima, 19 April 1944; on labor units staffed by women in Montenegro, see Bojović, *Žene Crne Gore*, 287; for Bosnia, see Safija Redžepović, "Žene Bosanskodubičkog sreza u NOB," in Hurem, *Žene Bosne*, 106, and others.
[66] AVII, NOR, CK SK Hrvatske NOB 51/581–586, OK KPH Karlovac Svim part.org. Karl. okruga, 31 July 1942; AVII, NOR, CK SK Hrvatske NOB 32/504–10, "Kako ćemo učvrstiti našu organizaciju" (Lička) *Žena u borbi* 3, 1942; AVII, NOR, IA PK SKS Vojvodine NOB 2/252–9, Inicijativni odbor AFŽ za Vojvodinu Pokrajinskom kom. KPJ za Vojvodinu, 25 November 1943.

FIGURE 4. Women carrying food to Partisans, n.d.
Courtesy of Muzej Istorije Jugoslavije.

In Vojvodina, women also served as village guards, who controlled the movement of people and goods in and out of their villages in order to prevent smuggling, spying, and sudden enemy attacks.[67] Finally, the AFW helped the Youth League and other mass organizations in enlisting girls for the Partisan army.[68] Yet the results of such activities that involved women's entrance into the male sphere were mixed, in part because of men's resistance and in part because of women's reluctance to undertake new kinds of duties.[69] The AFW functioned best when it engaged females through an extension of their tasks within the home: feeding, cleaning, nursing, and caring for others. The lion's share of women's contribution in the rear would indeed remain within the boundaries of their time-honored responsibilities.

It is a testament to the communists' exceptional wartime astuteness that they found a way to put peasant women's traditional labor skills to use in a systematic and organized fashion. In the Partisans' institutions, much as in their rhetoric, the traditional and the revolutionary blended. Rather than confronting village ways, party women tried to adapt and direct them toward the Partisan cause. AFW activists frequented traditional village gatherings and joined women's conversations about their daily concerns. The so-called *prela* and *sijela* – at which peasant women customarily gathered to socialize and do handwork – were thus transformed into Partisan workshops of sorts. It is largely thanks to this willingness to appropriate peasant traditions and build them into the movement's structure that the AFW succeeded in fulfilling its first task of supporting the army.

To fulfill its second, revolutionary objective to politicize women and facilitate their inclusion, as equals, in the new socialist society, the AFW became a women's rights agitator and political educator. For this purpose, the front could rely on the skill and resourcefulness of the party women, who had amassed substantial experience in this kind

[67] AVII, NOR, IA PK SKS Vojvodine NOB 4/197–8, 198, Okr. odbor AFŽ Ist. Srem Okr. kom.-u KPJ Ist. Srem, 8 February 1944; AVII, NOR, IA PK SKS Vojvodine NOB 4/316, Glavni NOO Vojvodine Glavnom Štabu NOV I PO Vojvodine, 23 April 1944.

[68] AVII, NOR, IA PK SKS Vojvodine NOB 3/173, Sreski kom. Ruma Svim part. Organizacijama sreza, 3 November 1943; AVII, NOR, k. 12, f. 1, doc. 21, Rezolucija okr. konferencije AFŽ za Srem, 31 May 1943; AVII, NOR, CK SK Hrvatske NOB 19/277, Okr. odbor AFŽ Karlovac kotarskom odb. AFŽ Slunj, 12 October 1943.

[69] For women's reluctance to join labor groups and do the hard work in the fields, AVII NOR IRP BiH 5/540–3, Okr. kom. SKOJa za Vlasenicu Ob. kom. u SKOJa za Ist. Bosnu, 15 December 1943. For the questionable success of female village guards in Vojvodina, see note 67.

of activism in the course of their interwar engagement in the feminist alliance.

Special education for women was, in the party's view, necessary, since they were perceived as a more backward, passive, narrow-minded, and oppressed sex. The position of the illiterate, subordinate village woman was the prime symbol of the primitivism and injustice of the old system. The female peasant was considered the embodiment of much of what needed to be altered in the socialist Yugoslavia, and the AFW was to serve as an instrument of her transformation. In order to enlighten women, the AFW organized a number of cultural-educational programs. Among the most popular were courses for illiterate female villagers, at which thousands of peasants learned their first letters – many, reportedly, with great enthusiasm. "It was rather demanding and arduous work," remembers a Bosnian AFW activist. "During the day, women did the heaviest physical labor, while at night, in poor lighting, they learned how to draw their first letters."[70] The women's press praised those who managed to conquer the alphabet for fulfilling yet another major patriotic duty. Special "political" AFW courses were reserved for female villagers who were particularly devoted to the Partisan cause and who were deemed sufficiently bright and capable. These courses aimed to create a new, trained cadre of local activists capable of replacing the overburdened party women. At "political" courses, students learned about the Partisan movement and women's role in it, together with some basics about the current situation in the country and the world.[71]

"Cultural-political education" for women was provided also by AFW publications, which, besides being tools for the dissemination of propaganda, featured educational pieces and political texts in a simple, accessible language. They offered rudimentary lessons on Yugoslav history and culture together with explanations of recent developments and new decisions made by the party leadership. At meetings and mass conferences, besides the topics immediately related to the war and revolution, female peasants could hear about the advantages for their sex in the future regime. The AFW also tried to inculcate modern values of hygiene, literacy, and efficiency into the "backward" female masses, who heard lectures about the necessity to study and about the importance of personal and communal cleanliness and health. Before the first elements

---

[70] Safija Redžepović, "Žene Bosanskodubičkog ... ," in Hurem, *Žene Bosne*, 108.
[71] A typical outline of a lower AFW course published in *Žena danas* 32, September 1943, 53.

of communist statehood emerged in Yugoslavia, the Partisan movement acted as a modernizing force determined to transform not only the political system but also all social relations and the citizenry itself. At the same time, though, it incorporated peasant traditions in its organizational structure and daily practice.

Organizational Problems: As a result of the changing fortunes of the Partisan struggle, the wartime evolution of the front of women was neither smooth nor even. Regional differences in the organization's development were dramatic. For much of the war, Croatia had the best-developed and best-organized AFW network, which, by mid-1943, had been fully integrated and centralized into the newly elected Main Council. Other areas gained their permanent provincial and state leaderships later, although many had long-established local councils. The Main Council for Bosnia-Herzegovina, for instance, was set up only in 1945. The same could be said for Serbia, where the organization could not be founded before the liberation in the winter of 1944–5.

In addition to the regional unevenness, AFW activists faced a number of smaller organizational problems on the ground. One of them was a cultural gap between female party members who were the leaders of the women's front, and the masses of peasant women below them. As noted, the initial establishment of the AFW network for a particular region rested on the shoulders of party women. Because of the CPY's urban base prior to the war, most of these female activists were educated youths from Yugoslavia's metropolitan areas. The fact that they were put in charge of working with older, illiterate peasant women – with whom they had little in common and who often viewed city dwellers with suspicion and mistrust – proved a significant obstacle. City girls often knew little about village conditions and still less about how to communicate with the peasantry. "Some female comrades, unfamiliar with the circumstances and lives of women in the village, alienate women with their speeches," reported the Kordun AFW in early 1942, adding that "some explain the question of hygiene in such an awkward way that women feel insulted. One must not approach a woman with the words: 'do you wash yourself? I can see that you do not,' etc. This manner offends her and she begins to see in us not a friend but an adversary."[72] Dedicated to communism, many party women had little understanding and tolerance of

---

[72] AJ, AFŽ, 141-10-53, Odbor AFŽ za Kordun Odboru AFŽ za kotar Slunj, 22 February 1942.

those who still adhered to traditional religion. At times they entered into long debates with female peasants about the existence of God; some even failed to control their tempers – they scolded the persistent and pious villagers, thus losing their sympathy forever. In addition, they sometimes approached their organizational work with rigor that did more harm than good, introducing threats and penalties for peasant women who missed AFW meetings.[73]

Besides criticizing those responsible for such excesses, the leadership introduced preventive measures. Whenever possible, it tried to select activists who were still connected to the village and familiar with local peasant ways, such as peasant-born university students. They often proved the best organizers. A good example is Mira Morača, originally from Bosnian Krajina, whose first appointment was in the environs of her native Drvar. Only upon gaining significant experience with Krajina's peasant women was she sent to Vojvodina to help set up the organization there. Other city activists were asked to accept – even adopt – peasant customs, lifestyle, and language in order to be able to communicate better with female villagers.

Another widespread obstacle on the ground was prejudice among male CPY officials, which went hand in hand with their unwillingness to help the women's organization. Equally important was that many party women themselves saw "work with women" as a lesser assignment – an attitude that predated the war.[74] For a female party member, who could hope to become a political commissar in a brigade or otherwise rise in the hierarchy, "work with women" might indeed seem an inferior assignment akin to demotion. Comments about female communists who accepted this duty without much enthusiasm were not uncommon in internal party reports. "Comrade Vera," noted the Jajce committee in such a report, "likes to work on all lines of Party activity except the AFW line, to which she has been assigned."[75] The party recognized the problem and occasionally took steps to alter negative attitudes. A Montenegrin directive, for example, insisted that activists must "liquidate the weakness of

[73] Okružnica odbora AFŽ za Kordun, 15 June 1942, doc. 76 in Šoljan, *Žene Hrvatske*, 107. Similar complaints about the city women's difficulties in approaching the villagers were voiced elsewhere. For example, AVII, NOR, IRP BiH 5/259–65, 263, Okr. kom. KPJ za Majevicu Ob. Kom.-u za B. Krajinu, 26 November 1943, and others.

[74] On this attitude before the war, see Uglješa Danilović, "Pitanje ravnopravnosti žena u politici KPJ," in Hurem, *Žene Bosne*, 15.

[75] AVII, NOR, IRP BiH 6/325–330, 329, Okr. kom. Jajce Travnik Ob. kom. u za B. Krajinu, 16 February 1944.

underestimating this work."[76] Such steps were sporadic, however, and the AFW remained the least important and least respected Partisan institution in the eyes of many communists.

Still another challenge for AFW activists was interethnic animosity. Much as the Partisan movement as a whole did, the AFW recruited most efficiently among the Serbs under the Ustasha regime in Bosnia-Herzegovina, Croatia, and Srem, and among the Croats of the Italian-occupied regions of Dalmatia and Gorski Kotar. It took time and effort on the part of the party to win over the Croat and Muslim masses in the regions nominally under Ustasha control in the Independent State of Croatia. In the first years of the war, the Serb/Montenegrin element was represented disproportionately in the Partisan units and institutions. In eastern Srem, for instance, of 13,500 women who had been "organized" into the AFW by late 1943, only 500 were non-Serbs.[77] The initial preponderance of Serbs proved an obstacle in attracting other groups, who perceived the Partisans primarily as a Serb movement. On the other hand, Serbs were often hostile to the peoples of other ethnoreligious backgrounds, particularly toward Croats and Muslims, whom they indiscriminately considered pro-Ustasha. Thus when a Croat girl was about to join the youth league in a Lika village, Serb girls protested and threatened to resign: "If she gets in, you may as well admit [the Ustasha leader] Ante Pavelić!"[78] Nor was winning over the Serb masses always easy. Not only were their loyalties divided between the Chetniks and the Partisans, but also they often viewed the Croat party leaders with suspicion. That a large number of female party activists in Croatia were Croats meant that they had to find ways to overcome mistrust in Serb villages.

Notwithstanding the problems described, the organization managed to involve tens of thousands of women, whose contribution to the

---

[76] AJ, SKJ 507, CKKPJ 1943/362, Prilog 3: Inic. Odbor AFŽ za CG i Boku svim org. AFŽ-a na teritoriji Crne Gore i Boke, n.d. (1943). Also *Izvori* 14, 218–36.

[77] AVII, NOR, IA PK SKS Vojvodine NOB 2/252–9, Inicijativni odbor AFŽ za Vojvodinu Pokrajinskom kom. KPJ za Vojvodinu, 25 November 1943. Examples abound and are not limited only to the first years of the war. In western Srem a year later, of 8,000 organized women, more than 7,000 were Serbs (women of other backgrounds included 200 Croats, 300 Ukranians, 250 Slovaks, 10 Slovenes, 12 Hungarians, and 3 Germans). AVII, NOR, IA PK SKS Vojvodine NOB 4/240–3, Izvadak iz izveštaja Okr. odb. AFŽ Zapadni Srem Odboru AFŽ-u za Vojvodinu, 9 October 1944. For examples from other regions, see AVII, NOR, CK SK HRV 19/295–7, Općinski biro Cetingrad Kotarskom kom. KPH Slunj, 4 November 1943; AVII, NOR, IRP BiH 6/312–402, Obl. Kom. za Hercegovinu Pokr. Kom.u za BiH, 22 February 1944, and others.

[78] AVII, NOR, Muzej Like Gospić NOB 1/571–2, 571, Kotarski kom. SKOJ Gospić Okr. kom. u SKOJ Lika, 6 July 1944.

Partisan victory was invaluable – a fact recognized by the party bosses. "Without the women the Partisans could never have won," they readily admitted to scholars after the war.[79] That the AFW did reach the female masses is largely due to its strategy of approaching women through their traditional areas of interest and employing their customary labor skills. By linking women's daily concerns and hopes regarding their families and communities with those of the movement, the party managed to win them over. By creating an opportunity for them to contribute through an extension of their duties within the home, the AFW involved the female peasantry in the war on a scale unseen before. Women could easily undertake looking after the wounded and supplying the Partisans in part because these activities corresponded with their traditional responsibilities. As an extension of serving the family, managing the household, and defending the home, women's resistance activity provided the core of the Partisan support structure.[80]

SUCCESSES AND FAILURES

During the first three years of its existence, the AFW proved indispensable to the party's war effort. With respect to its primary task of providing supplies and services for the Partisans, the women's front could claim major accomplishments. By 1944, the organization had spread throughout the regions where the units operated, gathering masses of females and funneling their labor toward keeping the army fed, clothed, washed, and cared for. Though it is difficult to quantify the aid – in supply and work hours – that the AFW provided to the units, some numbers are telling. During a month in Srem (Vojvodina), for instance, peasant women of three villages laundered twenty thousand to thirty thousand pairs of underwear for the troops temporarily stationed there.[81]

The AFW's contribution to Partisan success was no secret. Even the Partisans' rivals took notice. In 1944, the conservative Chetniks, who

---

[79] Tomasevich, *The Chetniks*, 188; similar quote in Jancar-Webster, *Women & Revolution*, 183.

[80] That women contributed to the resistance through an extension of their traditional roles is not unique to Yugoslavia. For similar observations about the nature of women's roles in the French Resistance, see Paula Schwartz, "Redefining Resistance: Women's Activism in Wartime France," in *Behind the Lines: Gender and the Two World Wars*, ed. Margaret Higonnet et al. (New Haven, CT: Yale University Press, 1987), 141–53. Julian Jackson, *France: The Dark Years, 1940–1944* (Oxford: Oxford University Press, 2001), 493.

[81] AVII, NOR, IA PK SKS Vojvodine NOB 4/240–3, Izvadak iz izveštaja Okr. odb. AFŽ Zapadni Srem Odboru AFŽ-u za Vojvodinu, 9 October 1944.

had initially been uninterested and reluctant to recruit women, decided to found a women's organization of their own. In February that year, Draža Mihailović ordered the creation of the Yugoslav Organization of Ravna Gora Women (Jugoslovenska Organizacija Ravnogorki, JUORA). The organization was to have a range of political and social tasks, such as "raising national consciousness" and educating children, alongside providing "sisterly support" for the Chetniks. In spring, in preparation for general mobilization, the Chetnik Supreme Command also formed the Women's Ravna Gora Organization of the Sanitet (Ženska ravnogorska organizacija saniteta, ŽROS), which was intended as a military organization providing medical service, staffed exclusively by women. Though little documentary material about them survived the war, it seems that the Chetnik organizations took some root in Serbia. Much like the AFW's, their primary purpose was aiding the units. JUORA women were mostly engaged in making clothes, knitting, sewing, mending, and doing "everything that falls under women's work," and some attempts were also made at courses in nursing and hygiene. But when it comes to mass mobilization of females, the Chetniks undertook too little, too late. Just months later, in the fall of 1944, they were defeated in Serbia and their women's organizations disbanded.[82]

Besides providing for the army, the Partisan women's front should be credited with some successes in the educational and political domains. Literacy programs reached many hitherto illiterate female peasants, equipping them with basic reading skills. The "political education" of women helped disseminate party propaganda to the female masses. So did the local AFW journals, the sole Partisan medium specifically addressing women and their current concerns. Focused, systematic, and organized work on women's political education – where it existed – did produce results, at times even impressive ones. In some regions, because of the AFW's effort, women reportedly proved more active, politically sophisticated, and attuned to the

[82] For women and the Chetnik movement, see Žarko Jovanović, "Žene Srbije u ratu 1941–1945," 331–41; Mihajlo Stanišić, "Stavovi (Ravnogorskog) Četničkog pokreta prema ženi," 342–52; and Bojan Dimitrijević, "Žene ravnogorskog sela 1943–1944," 353–66, in *Srbija u modernizacijskim procesima 19. i 20. veka, vol.2: Položaj žene kao merilo modernizacije*, ed. Latinka Perović (Beograd: Institut za noviju istoriju Srbije, 1998); on the Chetnik women's organizations (JUORA and ŽROS) see esp. pp. 335–6; 348–9; 359–66, which inform my discussion. Quotes from Dimitrijević, 359–60. On women and the Ustasha movement, see Yeshayahu Jelinek, "On the Condition of Women in Wartime Slovakia and Croatia," in *Labyrinth of Nationalism, Complexities of Diplomacy*, ed. Richard Frucht (Columbus, OH: Slavica, 1992), 190–213. On women and right-wing movements, see Carol Lilly and Melissa Bokovoy's articles on Yugoslavia, Serbia, and Croatia in *Women, Gender, and Fascism in Europe, 1919–45*, edited by Kevin Passmore (New Brunswick, NJ: Manchester University Press, 2003), 91–123.

party's message than their menfolk, prompting some CPY officials to lament
the absence of a similar organization for men. "The response of women and
youth," reported the committee from Crikvenica (Croatia), "is much more
correct than that of adult men. Women interpret well the political questions
of the national liberation struggle, they lead the actions in the rear." Lacking
an equivalent organization of their own, complained the committee, adult
male villagers were more difficult to reach and remained largely uninvolved
in the movement.[83]

As far as peasant women were concerned, perhaps the most remarkable achievement of the AFW lay in the public recognition it accorded
to their work *and* their words – a recognition without precedent in the
Yugoslav lands. The organization gave political significance to traditional
women's tasks; weaving, knitting, sewing, laundering, and mending now
became legitimate ways to contribute to the people's liberation. Those
who had performed such tasks most of their lives without any acknowledgment were now praised as heroines of the war. Just as important,
many female peasants were for the first time given both authorship and
an audience in public. They were encouraged to speak at conferences,
their words being heard by the masses and quoted in Partisan periodicals
(Figure 5). "It is hard to recognize the women of [the village of] Šekovići
as they hold AFW conferences independently, speaking convincingly and
with confidence," noted party officials in eastern Bosnia with enthusiasm
and a degree of surprise.[84] In addition to public speaking, village women
were invited to contribute to AFW journals, local periodicals, and wall
newspapers. For most female peasants, those were the very first attempts
at writing. Seeing their words published was a rewarding experience. Even
a minor contribution was a source of elation for some. During a political
course that the AFW organized in Srem, for example, the women were
reportedly delighted upon seeing the wall newspaper they had helped create, "The *Partizanka* of Srem," which gave them new élan for activism.[85]

Despite the existence of some shining examples of progress, the AFW's
accomplishments in realizing its political mission remained limited
at best. Of the two major assignments that the party presented to the
organization – providing support for the Partisan units and serving as
a vehicle for women's political education and integration into the new

[83] AVII, NOR, CK SK HRV NOB 52/197–199, 198, Izveštaj KKKPH Crikvenica, n.d.
[84] AVII, NOR, IRP BiH 13/184–98, 196, Okr. kom. KPJ za Birač Ob. kom. u za Ist. Bosnu,
4 March 1945.
[85] AVII, NOR, IA PK SKS Vojvodine NOB 4/190–1, Okr. Odbor AFŽ Ist. Srem OK-u KPJ
Ist. Srem, 19 September 1943.

FIGURE 5. A peasant woman speaking at an AFW conference, Croatia, May 1944.
Courtesy of Muzej Istorije Jugoslavije.

governmental structure – the latter proved far more difficult to achieve. During the war, the AFW never moved entirely beyond functioning as an auxiliary of the army to become a political organization in its own right. It remained the most underestimated mass organization within the national-liberation front. In addition, it witnessed the party leadership's failure to ensure equal participation of women in the national liberation councils and the CPY – the failure of which the women activists were painfully aware.

The limited success of the AFW in the political domain was in part due to the fact that Party officials tended to give an absolute priority to the organization's first objective – supplying the army – and relegated the enterprise of women's emancipation to a secondary position or ignored it altogether. Even a superficial glance at internal documents reveals the extent to which the CPY neglected the political aspect of women's participation in the movement. Time and again officials on the ground reported that party work "along the AFW line" headed primarily in the direction of mobilizing women's labor. The problem was recognized as such already in the organization's infancy, in 1942. In Kordun and Banija (Croatia), the party reported great successes in attracting female peasants, but work with them was reduced to the most basic tasks surrounding the support for the Partisan men.[86] In Lika, too, CPY officials confessed half a year later, the AFW served "only for the gathering of material aid and not as the leader of political and cultural-educational work among women."[87] Similar concerns were raised in practically every region where the organization took root – in Bosnian Krajina, Herzegovina, on the Adriatic islands, in Srem (Vojvodina), and elsewhere.[88] The problem was as persistent as it was widespread, bothering the AFW's leadership until the very end of the war.[89]

Despite the best efforts of some female activists to demonstrate the importance of their organization for the Partisan movement, most men saw the front of women in derisive terms. The very idea of a political organization for women was alien to villagers and many CPY members themselves; attempts to gather peasant women at conferences and political courses brought condescending smiles to the faces of male officials. AFW activists complained over and over again about the resistance and ridicule they faced on the ground. "Many Party men have no understanding for the AFW," one activist noted. "They laugh at us [*oni se ismijavaju*]."[90] In some cases these attitudes undermined the authority of the women's front to such an extent that the party had to react. "In almost all villages our AFW organizations are viewed somehow in a humorous manner [*sa šaljivog stanovišta*]. What's much worse, not only individuals but also entire organizations relate incorrectly, even with enmity, toward the AFW," noted a Vojvodina committee ordering an immediate change in the attitude of CPY members.[91]

[86] AVII, NOR, CK SK HRV NOB 12/619–20, Odbor AFŽ za Kordun Okr. Kom.-u KPH Karlovac, July 1942; also AVII, NOR, CK SK Hrvatske NOB 16/2–5, 5; KK KPH Dvor svim partijskim organizacijama i članovima KP kotara Dvor, 20 December 1942.

[87] AVII, NOR, CK SK Hrvatske NOB 20/111–116, Referat o AFŽ, III Okr. Konf. KPH Lika, 1 and 2 July 1943.

[88] For Bosnian Krajina, AVII, NOR, IRP BiH 5/418–22, Okr. kom. KPJ Ključ-Mrkonjić Ob. Kom. u za B. Krajinu, 7 December 1943; also AVII, NOR, IRP BiH 5/572–4, 573, Okr. kom. za Banja Luku Ob. Kom.-u za B. Krajinu, 19 December 1943. For Herzegovina, AVII, NOR, IRP BIH 9/204–10, 208. Okr. kom. za S. Hercegovinu Ob. kom-u KPJ za Hercegovinu, 20 August 1944. For the islands, AVII, NOR, Muzej NR Split NOB 7/763–7, Kot. Komitet KPH Vis-Lastovo Okr. kom. u Srednje Dalm. Otočja, 4 November 1944. For Srem, AVII, NOR, IA PK SKS Vojvodine NOB 4/240–3, Izvadak iz izveštaja Okr. odb. AFŽ Zapadni Srem Odboru AFŽ-u za Vojvodinu, 9 October 1944.

[89] For reports on the problem dating as late as spring 1945, see AVII, NOR, IRP BiH 13/201–4, 203, Sreski kom. za Ključ Okr. kom. u za Podgrmeč, 5 March 1945; AVII, NOR, IRP BiH 13/449–51, 450, Sreski kom. KPJ za Prijedor Okr. kom. u za Banja Luku, 31 March 1945.

[90] AVII, NOR, IRP BiH 12/402–11, 407, Zapisnik sa I konf. komunista sreza Tuzlanskog, 30 December 1944.

[91] AVII, NOR, IA PK SKS Vojvodine NOB 2/123, Sreski kom. KPJ Sremska Mitrovica Svim partijskim organizacijama u srezu, 31 January 1944.

In extreme cases, the mockery and neglect of the organization's political objectives were accompanied by a blatant exploitation of women's work. In the minds of some men of authority, AFW councils served as a pool of free labor for the most tedious manual jobs. "Women ... have been taken into account only when something needed to be done, when the command [office] floors needed to be scrubbed," noted a village party committee in Bosnia.[92] Another added, "[Our] AFW council has been transformed into a labor market and quartermaster quarters of sorts [*burzu za traženje radne snage i kao u neku vrstu intendanture*]."[93] Those responsible for such practices were most often local party bosses, who, as the Krajina district committee explained, "abused women's enthusiasm" for the Partisan cause to get the common chores around the army done.[94]

Such treatment of the AFW was a constant source of frustration to its leaders. In vain did they insist that the women's front should be seen first and foremost as an organization political in nature: a vehicle for women's activation, politicization, and inclusion in public affairs on an equal level. As early as December 1942, Mitra Mitrović wrote in *Proleter* that the tendency of reducing the women's front to "an organization that performs only the crudest work for the army" should be suppressed "in the most decisive manner."[95] Rather, as the AFW's Central Council underlined in a letter the next year, the front should become "a powerful political factor in the national-liberation movement" and "a political organization ... capable of being a pillar [*oslonac*] to women today and in the future."[96] Despite various statements to that effect, the treatment of the AFW did not improve significantly in the course of the war.[97] Nor did the organization's political accomplishments ever approach those in the practical, material domain.

[92] AVII, NOR, IRP BiH 5/510–11, Op. kom. KPJ Prekaja-Podić Svim partijskim jedinicama, 14 February 1943.

[93] AVII, NOR, IRP BiH 3/428–31, 430, Okr. kom za Bihać-Cazin Obl. Kom-u KPJ za B. Krajinu, 4 January 1945.

[94] AVII, NOR, IRP BiH 3/715–25, 722–3, Obl. Kom za B. Krajinu Pokr. kom-u. KPJ za BiH, 14 May 1943.

[95] Mitra Mitrović, "Uloga Anitfašistčkog Fronta Žena u Oslobodilačkom ratu," *Proleter* 16, December 1942, 29.

[96] AVII, NOR, k. 12, f. 1, doc. 25, Centralni odbor AFŽ Jugoslavije, Pismo svim odborima, 15 September 1943; also in AVII, NOR, k. 1143, f. 5, doc. 2; also AJ, AFŽ, 141-10-50; AVII, NOR, CK SK Hrvatske NOB 32/488–9, and others.

[97] Croatia's women leaders were particularly vocal about the issue. For their statements, see AVII, NOR, k. 12, f. 1, doc. 25, Centralni odbor AFŽ Jugoslavije, Pismo svim odborima, 15 September 1943; also in AVII, NOR, k. 1143, f. 5, doc. 2; also AJ, AFŽ, 141-10-50; AVII, NOR, CK SK Hrvatske NOB 32/488–9, and others.

When attributing the factors that hampered the AFW's development in the political realm to the confusion, traditionalism, and discrimination on the ground, one needs to add the lack of guidance and help from above, from the CPY's higher rungs. Party organizations on all levels, starting from the provincial leaderships down, gave only minimal, if any, assistance and direction to women activists – a tendency for which they openly criticized themselves and their lower forums.[98] But besides these self-critical statements little was done to correct the situation. Women activists were for the most part left to their own devices, and the organization they developed was the result solely of their resourcefulness and dexterity.

Another source of frustration for female activists and of self-criticism for the CPY leaders was their failure to ensure equal representation of women in the organs of the new government and the party itself. As we have seen earlier, the party was true to its promise of political rights for women, giving them early on in the war the right to vote and be elected in the national liberation councils. Many peasant women thus became politically active in a manner unthinkable prior to the war. Some managed to earn respect and command authority among their fellow villagers. In a village in eastern Bosnia, for example, a female candidate received more than three hundred votes in local elections – a remarkable success given the persistence of the traditional culture that barred women from participation in village affairs.[99] The prospect of a peasant woman holding office – for the first time in the history of the Yugoslav peoples – incited popular imagination and gave rise to a number of wartime anecdotes. One of them recounted the story of a man whom a female-dominated national liberation council sentenced severely for wife beating. Some time in 1942, his battered wife reportedly complained to the Bukovača council, which was composed of four women and three men. By four votes (women's) against three (men's), the council decided that the husband be punished by twenty-five lashes, or – in one of the

---

[98] On the lack of guidance and help from the party, see AVII, NOR, IPR SFRJ 1/5–16, PK KPJ za Crnu Goru i Boku CKKPJ-u, 1 January 1944; AVII, NOR, Muzej Like Gospić NOB 1/381–2, OKKPH za Liku Kotarskom KPH Mogorić, 9 May 1942; AVII, NOR, IRP BiH 13/594–6, Sreski kom. za B. Dubicu Okr. kom. u za Banja Luku, 25 April 1945; AVII, NOR, CK SK Hrvatske NOB 20/111–16, Referat o AFŽ, III Okr. konferencija KPH Lika, 1 and 2 July 1943; AVII, NOR, IRP BiH 10/480–3, Referat o AFŽ na III Oblasnom Partijskom savetovanju za Ist. Bosnu, 26–28 September 1944; AVII, NOR, IA PK SKS Vojvodine NOB 2/636–47, 638, Izveštaj, pol. I org. stanje u okrugu Zapadni Srem, n.d. (1944); AVII, NOR, IRP BiH 9/574–80, 577–8, Okr. kom. za J. Hercegovinu Obl. Kom. u za Hercegovinu, 18 September 1944, and others.

[99] AVII, NOR, IRP BiH 6/89–96, 94, Okr. kom. za Vlasenicu Obl.kom za Ist. Bosnu, 29 January 1944.

versions – executed. Only upon the intervention of the district party leadership was the sentence altered to ten days in prison. Much to the amusement of the CPY elite, this anecdote was recurrently discussed at meetings and ultimately assumed the status of a wartime legend. According to Kata Pejnović, the party and AFW leader who had intervened in reducing the sentence, the story greatly entertained Tito. "What did you teach these women," he reproached her jokingly, "if they nearly killed the man for such a trifle – for beating 'his own' wife?"[100]

Anecdotes like this one, however, recorded exceptional cases and misrepresented reality. Councils where women outnumbered men and where their voices mattered did exist but were far from being the norm. In fact, a chronic lack of female representation and discrimination against female council members were commonplace characteristics of the "national liberation government."[101] The problem was recorded on all levels with the general trend being the following: the higher the level of the council the smaller the percentage of women.[102] On the national level, at the first meeting of AVNOJ in 1942, only one female delegate was present; at its second meeting in 1943, of 269 delegates, 11 were women, constituting about 4 percent of the legislators.[103]

Just as important, even where women entered national liberation councils, they were often not considered full and active members, their participation reduced to mere posturing for convention's sake. "Women often sit in the national liberation councils," protested the Dalmatian party committee, "only for the sake of form ... , yet the entire work of the councils unfolds without them."[104] The Dalmatian assessment was echoed elsewhere: The few women present in organs of the people's government did not feel that they were equal members;[105] their participation

[100] In various versions, the story appears in Dedijer, *The War Diaries*, vol. 2, p. 38; Kata Pejnović, "Istorijskih dana u Bihaću i Bosanskom Petrovcu," in Hurem, *Žene Bosne*, 514. Mitra Mitrović, *Ratno putovanje* (Beograd: Prosveta, 1962), 150; Vladimir Dedijer, *The Beloved Land* (London: MacGibbon & Kee, 1961), 318, and others.

[101] Reports that complain about the insufficient representation of women are too many to list here. Among them are AVII, NOR, Muzej NR Split NOB 7/226, Kotarski o. AFŽ za Muć-Lećevicu Okr. odboru AFŽ za Srednju Dalmaciju, 16 April 1943; AVII, NOR, CK SK Hrvatske NOB 32/477–8, Rezolucija I konferencije AFŽ Hrvatske, 12 June 1943; AVII, NOR, IA PK SKS Vojvodine NOB 4/240–3, Izvadak iz izveštaja Okr. odb. AFŽ Zapadni Srem Odboru AFŽ-u za Vojvodinu, 9 October 1944, and others.

[102] Also noted by Jancar-Webster, *Women & Revolution*, 120.

[103] Pantelić, *Partizanke kao građanke*, 37–8.

[104] AVII, NOR, Muzej NR Split NOB 7/4–5, Oblasni NOO Dalmacije svim NOO Dalmacije, 6 March 1944.

[105] AVII, NOR, CK SK Hrvatske NOB 20/111–16, Referat o AFŽ, III Okr. Konf. KPH Lika, 1 and 2 July 1943.

was passive and formal at best;[106] they merely posed [*statiraju*] instead of being treated as rightful members.[107]

Part of the problem lay in the novelty of the practice. As there was no tradition of female participation in village politics, Mary Reed suggests, peasants of both sexes preferred to vote for men and the females who had managed to get into the councils tended to accept passively instructions from their male peers. Yet the major reason for women's poor representation was the persistence, on all levels, of prejudice and discrimination.[108] Village men often interfered to prevent their wives', daughters', and sisters' political activism, forbidding them to attend AFW meetings and take part in the national liberation councils.[109] Even higher-ranking female officials were vulnerable. For example, the president of a county AFW council in Srem had to step down because her husband hindered her work, and the female president of a national liberation council in Slavonia was not permitted to attend the meetings.[110] To make matters worse, there were many such cases in which party men were involved.[111] As for the fact that females took only a passive role in the work of the people's government, the negative attitude of male council members was most often the reason:

Some council members think ... that women entered the councils only pro forma. They don't introduce female members to the life and work of the councils.... Women often do not attend all meetings and do not participate in the making of all decisions. In this manner, the strengths, efforts, and experiences of a good portion of female cadres remain unused.[112]

[106] AVII, NOR, IRP BiH 13/726–8, 728, Sreski kom. KPJ Ljubinje Obl. Kom.u za Hercegovinu, 15 May 1945.

[107] AVII, NOR, IA PK SKS Vojvodine NOB 4/578–83, Okr. NOO za Ist. Srem svim sreskim NOO, po sastanku odr. 31 August–1 September 1943.

[108] Mary E. Reed, "The Anti-Fascist Front of Women and the Communist Party in Croatia: Conflicts within the Resistance," in *Women in Eastern Europe and the Soviet Union,* ed. Tova Yedlin (New York: Praeger, 1980), 130.

[109] For AFŽ meetings, AVII, NOR, CK SK HRV NOB 12/596–8, Odbor AFŽ za Kordun Okr. Kom KPH Karlovac, 9 July 1942; AVII, NOR, IA PK SKS Vojvodine NOB 2/252–9, Inicijativni odbor AFŽ za Vojvodinu Pokrajinskom kom. KPJ za Vojvodinu, 25 November 1943; for national liberation councils, AVII, NOR, IRP BIH 6/89–96, 94, Okr. kom. za Vlasenicu Obl. kom za Ist. Bosnu, 29 January 1944.

[110] AVII, NOR, IA PK SKS Vojvodine NOB 4/214–16, 215, Sreski odb. AFŽ Sr. Mitrovica okr. odboru AFŽ Ist. Srem, 5 May 1944. For Slavonia, Reed, "The Antifascist Front ... ," 130.

[111] AVII, NOR, IRP BIH 9/392–6, 395. Okr. kom. Prozor Obl. Kom. u za Bosansku Krajinu, 2 September 1944; AVII, NOR, IRP BiH 12/402–11, 407, Zapisnik sa I konf. Komunista sreza Tuzlanskog, 30 December 1944; AVII, NOR, IRP BiH 9/204–10, 208. Okr. kom. za S. Hercegovinu Obl.kom-u KPJ za Hercegovinu, 20 August 1944, and others.

[112] AVII, NOR, Muzej NR Split NOB 7/4–5, Oblasni NOO Dalmacije svim okr., kotarskim, seoskim NOO Dalmacije, 6 March 1944. For complaints about the attitude of male

The situation was not much better in the party itself. Although the leadership insisted that the female masses were the key reservoir for new CPY cadres, "sectarianism" toward women remained the dominant feature of party admission politics. "Out of 7000 women who are involved in the AFW only 36 are in the Party," reported the Karlovac (Croatia) committee.[113] Similar self-criticisms were voiced in numerous internal communiqués throughout the country. "We have neglected our female comrades within the Party itself," admitted the provincial committee for Montenegro, so that "we don't have a single woman in leadership starting from municipal committees up" despite the existence of many "good and devoted female comrades."[114] The backwardness, illiteracy, and traditionalism of peasant women were often cited as the grounds for their exclusion. But the CPY also admitted that the major reason was the resistance of party men. "Patriarchal views of our [male] Party members prevent them from dedicating more attention" to women's candidacy in the CPY, contended officials in eastern Bosnia.[115] The reluctance of the Party to accept and train female cadres led to a chronic shortage of AFW activists, which in turn hurt the organization's political development.

On the local level, old ideas about gender roles often coupled with a genuine lack of understanding of party expectations, leading to situations both comical and sad. Thus in a Montenegrin village, Dedijer's diary records, "The *president* of the NOO [national liberation council] simply orders the *president* of the AFW to sew his underwear. For a month now, she has mended 200 pairs of undershirts and shorts."[116] In some areas, women who entered the national liberation councils were expected not to serve as delegates but to do the "women's work" – to cook, launder, or clean for male council members. "Female comrades in [your] national liberation council have been getting practice in cooking rather than political work," a Dalmatian party committee reprimanded one of its lower

council members see also AVII, NOR, Muzej NR Split NOB 7/226, Kotarski o. AFŽ za Muć-Lećevicu Okr. o. AFŽa za Srednju Dalmaciju, 16 April 1943, and others.

[113] AVII, NOR, CK SK Hrvatske NOB 51/588–90, OK KPH Karlovac svim part org. Karl. okruga, 15 October 1942.

[114] AVII, NOR, IPR SFRJ 1/5–16, PK KPJ za Crnu Goru i Boku CKKPJ-u, 1 January 1944. See also AJ, SKJ 507, CKKPJ 1943/362, PK KPJ za Crnu Goru i Boku CKKPJ-u, 17 November 1943. Prilog 1: Zaključci proširenog sastanka PK KPJ za Crnu Goru i Boku odr. 17 Avgusta 1943, p. 10, point (z). Also *Izvori* 14, 218–36.

[115] AVII, NOR, IRP BiH 10/282–91, Okr. kom za Vlasenicu Ob. kom. u za Ist. Bosnu, 16 October 1944. See also AVII, NOR, IRP BiH 9/264–75, 274, Obl. Kom. za Hercegovinu Pokr. Kom. u za BiH, 26 August 1944.

[116] Dedijer, *The War Diaries*, vol. 1, 176. My italics.

forums in an angry letter. "You are presumably in a greater need of a cook than of a comrade capable of working in the people's government."[117]

Even where local institutions were set up in accordance with CPY instructions, female officials were more likely than men to find themselves doing traditional women's chores. As committee members were each given their areas of responsibility, the sector of "hygiene" – often a code name for laundering and cleaning – was likely to be the preserve of a female delegate. Reports from the weekly meetings of a party cell in a North Herzegovina village provide a vivid illustration of this division of labor within party organizations. During such meetings, each member had to account for his or her work in the past seven days. At a typical session, a male member reported that he had issued radio news; another member mentioned that he had organized a conference for Partisan couriers. Female comrade Njega, however, reported that she had worked on having the laundry done and food distributed. Next week, the same scenario was repeated: The male members talked about their publishing activities and collaboration with the Communist Youth League, while comrade Njega reported "that she had helped in the kitchen, laundered, and swept the office floors." And thus week after week, laundering and cleaning remained the essence of comrade Njega's political activity.[118]

In sum, the AFW's accomplishments in the political realm lagged behind its successes in supporting the army. The reasons behind the setbacks in reaching its political goals were manifold: the persistence of traditional values, resistance to change, discrimination, confusion and misunderstanding on the local level accompanied the lack of interest and determination on the part of the party leadership. This neglect of the front's political development, however, did not prevent CPY leaders from launching a highly political charge of "feminist deviations" against the organization when it appeared to have gained a momentum of its own.

THE CHARGE OF FEMINISM

The difficulties that the AFW encountered in its political mission did not necessarily translate into organizational weakness. From the time the Croatian party authorized its formation in 1941, the front of women

---

[117] AVII, NOR, Muzej NR Split NOB 7/113, Kotarski kom. KPH za Makarsku Op. kom.-u KPH za Makarsku, 18 April 1944.
[118] AVII, NOR, IRP BiH 9/25–6, Izveštaj sa sastanka part. ćelije pri Okr. komitetu za S. Hercegovinu, 4 August 1944; AVII, NOR, IRP BiH 9/95–6, Izveštaj sa sastanka part. ćelije pri Okr. komitetu za S. Hercegovinu, 11 August 1944, and others.

grew slowly but steadily in membership and strength. In the second half of 1943, after the failure of two major German offensives against the Partisans and the capitulation of Italy, the AFW, much as the Partisan movement as a whole did, experienced a significant increase in size and organizational sophistication. Despite the neglect that they often suffered from CPY officials, its activists managed to form a relatively stable and self-sustaining organization with a working network of councils and a centralized administrative apparatus. Not only did the organization develop an autonomous structure – with its own hierarchy, dedicated leadership, permanent staff, active membership, and bureaucracy – but it also reached relative financial independence through fund-raising.[119] This was particularly the case in Croatia, where, unlike in other regions, wartime conditions allowed for the early establishment of a complete organizational pyramid, springing from local organizations up to the Main Council.

Fearing the emergence of feminist tendencies and divisions within the movement, the party, as we have seen, never intended to allow the creation of an autonomous women's organization. The AFW was conceived not as an independent agent, but as an arm of the National Liberation Front designed to mobilize masses of females into the movement. Any separation of women's issues from the common goal was seen with suspicion in party circles, and any conflicts that the AFW might have with other mass organizations were taken as potential signs of feminism. Already in the organization's infancy, in 1942, communist officials in Croatia expressed concerns over developments of this kind. In some regions, complained the Karlovac committee, because of the lack of party control, the organization began assuming "the character of a [separate] women's front" and friction between the AFW and national liberation councils emerged.[120] "There is danger that the movement may assume a feminist character because Party control has not been sufficiently strong," the Croatian party dutifully reported to the CPY's Central Committee in December.[121]

Such fears only intensified with the growth and strengthening of the AFW in the following year, exploding in the winter of 1943–4. In January, the Central Committee of the CPY issued its famous circular #5, which

---

[119] For more on the organization's financial autonomy, see Sklevicky *Organizirana djelatnost*; also Jancar-Webster, *Women & Revolution*, 151.

[120] AVII, NOR, CK SK Hrvatske NOB 51/588–90, 590, OK KPH Karlovac Svim part. org. Karl. okruga, 15 October 1942.

[121] Šoljan, *Žene Hrvatske*, doc. 116, Pismo CK KP Hrvatske CK-u KPJ, 12 December 1942, pp. 162–3.

featured a list of "errors" that had evolved in the AFW. This directive has been widely cited in the existing revisionist literature, and rightly so. There is no doubt that the party leadership considered the issue of feminism to be of major significance for the movement. During the war, the directive was widely circulated and intensely studied at communist meetings. As is rarely the case with other documents, one could find numerous extant versions of the circular in the archives – obviously intended for wide distribution, it was printed in various forms, ranging from a letter to a booklet, in both scripts (Cyrillic and Latin) and almost all local dialects.[122] Once they received it from the Central Committee, Provincial Committees passed it down the hierarchical ladder, often with a note "important" and sometimes with special instructions as to how the directive applied to their own region.[123]

As outlined in circular #5, the errors that so troubled the Central Committee consisted of the following: First, an extremely "damaging tendency" had developed in the AFW – the tendency toward its centralization and transformation into a "distinct and rigid organization" that was increasingly losing its connection with the national-liberation movement. Second, the organization's leaders had begun constructing an apparatus of offices, instructors, and functionaries, which was isolated from the political life of the movement. The very existence of such an apparatus, warned the Central Committee, led to the separation of the AFW from the common resistance against fascism. Third, on the basis of this apparatus a certain "women's group" [ženski aktiv] had developed within the party. Members of this group were now working exclusively with women, and they had even begun creating their own party cells within the AFW, thereby isolating themselves from the internal life of the party. Under the circumstances, the development of these female comrades was "incorrect and one-sided," promoting the already harmful transformation of the AFW into a centralized "militant political organization."

---

[122] See AJ, SKJ 507, CKKPJ 1944/23, Direktiva CKKPJ centralnim, pokrajinskim, i oblasnim komitetima KPJ, January 1944. The version sent to Croatia's Central Committee has been published in Šoljan, *Žene Hrvatske*, vol. 1, doc. 264, pp. 439–40.

[123] Dalmatia: AJ, SKJ 507, Hrvatska II/118, Cirkular OK KPH Dalmacije svim okr. komitetima KPH, 27 February 1944. Also AVII, NOR, Muzej NR Split NOB 7/265–8, and others; Bosnian Krajina: AJ, SKJ 507, CKKPJ 1944/729, Obl. Kom za B. Krajinu svim okr. komitetima KPJ, 16 January 1944; also AVII, NOR, IRP BiH 5/827–9; AJ, SKJ 507, BiH II/34, and others. Herzegovina: AVII, NOR, IRP BIH 6/710–13, Ob. kom. za Hercegovinu svim okr., sreskim, mjesnim, opštinskim komitetima, 12 April 1944; Vojvodina: AVII, NOR, IA PK SKS Vojvodine NOB 2/282–4, Cirkular br. 5, PK KPJ Vojvodine svim partijskim organizacijama u Vojvodini, 18 March 1944, and others.

Finally, lower AFW councils turned into narrow women's organizations that considered themselves more responsible to the higher AFW forums than to other Partisan institutions. These mistakes manifested themselves most intensely in Croatia, but they appeared in almost all Yugoslav lands. Clearly, these mistakes could lead to the separation of women from the national front. Should they be allowed to carry on, concluded the Central Committee, "certain feminist tendencies" were sure to emerge.

Some of these charges, wrapped as they were in communist jargon, deserve additional explanation. That the organization became rigid [*kruta*] meant that it was selective in accepting members. Its leaders allegedly considered for membership only those women who took an active part in the organization, while ignoring a large number of more passive sympathizers and excluding other female villagers. This prevented the AFW from turning into a truly mass-based organization that would involve *all* Yugoslav women in the movement, as the CPY leaders had intended. Instead, the AFW had developed a clear organizational identity and a pool of active members who identified themselves primarily with the women's organization.

Even more troubling in the Central Committee's eyes was the segregation of the organization's leaders within the CPY. Although they were party members, most of them now worked solely in the AFW, all their activities being focused on women. Creating their own party cells within the AFW was another step in the direction of their isolation. Party cells and committees were the CPY's primary means of keeping its membership in check, and if a cell was filled entirely by female AFW activists, the party would have no control over what they did in the women's organization. Most important, the fact that "organized women" felt a primary allegiance to the AFW rather than the Partisan movement made the organization dangerously secluded and independent. In short, what all these "errors" pointed to was the loss of direct party control over the front of women.

This, however, does not mean that the AFW ever openly confronted the CPY, challenged, or even simply disagreed with any party policy. A comparison with the Soviet *Zhenotdel* (women's section) may be instructive at this point, since some striking similarities could be noted in the fate of the two communist women's organizations. Both of them were formed in the revolutionary years, led by experienced and enthusiastic party women, and charged with feminism. Yet there were differences as well, one being of particular importance for our discussion here. As Elizabeth Wood has shown, the Soviet women's section, which was created in 1918 as an organ within the party, soon started taking on a life of its own. In the early 1920s, as more of its staff began lobbying on behalf of women and criticizing the Soviet regime for its failures, the party used the charge of feminist deviation and made the section take a more obedient position.[124] In Yugoslavia, in contrast, no such political challenge to the party was posed by the women's organization. The AFW never became a vocal critic of the CPY; its activists did not confront the party's leadership on women's behalf or call it to answer for its failings, as the *Zhenotdel* did. All that Yugoslav activists did was call for a greater political role of their organization. Neither the Central Committee's circular nor other documents suggest any political deviations from the official line or criticisms that the AFW might have launched from a "feminist" position against the CPY. What frightened the Yugoslav party leadership, it seems, was the *very possibility* of the AFW's organizational independence, and the reorganization order is best seen as a preemptive strike to ensure that the party's control over it was absolute.

At the core of the party's AFW problem lay an inherent contradiction in the communist project of "emancipating women from above" without drifting into feminism. Like its Soviet mentors, the CPY had long been ambivalent, even apprehensive, about gender difference for its potential to divide the revolutionary proletariat. Yet women were thought to be different enough to form a distinct, generic social group – a group presumably more backward, more passive and inert, more oppressed, and thus in need of special tutelage in order to be raised to the level of men.[125] Therein lies the conundrum. On the one hand, to be able to draw this social group into the common movement and prevent its separation through feminism, the communist parties – in Yugoslavia as in the Soviet Union – found it necessary to form special organizations for women. On the other hand, the very existence of a women's organization divided women's from common issues and could lead to feminist tendencies. In other words, the contradiction lay in the necessity to separate women with the goal of integrating them.

How did the CPY approach this contradiction? A hint is given in the circular's first version, written in December 1943. Curiously, this document, although of great importance, has been overlooked in the existing literature. Much more strongly worded than its final and revised version (circular #5), the original draft reveals the extent to which the AFW's

[124] Elizabeth Wood, *The Baba and the Comrade: Gender and Politics in Revolutionary Russia* (Bloomington: Indiana University Press, 2000), 4–5.
[125] On these concerns and contradictions in the Soviet context, see ibid., 2–3, 5, 79.

autonomy alarmed the party. It also explains under which circumstances a women's organization is permissible and when its usefulness to the party ends. "Our major goal," it states, "is not to create some women's organization but to ... activate women to take part, en masse, in the struggle:"

> We allow, as we have done before ... that women ... gather and work separately, with the aim of increasing their participation where the national liberation movement – and especially women's participation in it – is less developed.... But these can only be *transitional forms of work* that – in view of general circumstances and women's backwardness – would facilitate women's mass orientation towards the national liberation movement.... There is no doubt that this process of women's elevation and their activation ... leads – in the final instance – to the disbanding of separate women's organizations.[126]

Apparently, the CPY's solution to the contradiction was a *provisional* women's organization that would be under the strict control of the party. As to how long this provisional phase should last, the draft suggested that it was already coming to a close in the current stages of the war. In the liberated territories, it stated, where women had already been granted all rights, there was no need for separate work with them – and thus no need for AFW councils. Upper-level AFW forums were to remain in operation only as organs for issuing women's periodicals and holding mass conferences. The suggestion, in short, was that the process of the organization's dismantling should begin immediately.

It is unclear why the Central Committee changed its mind by January, when circular #5 was issued to replace the original directive. It might have concluded that the support the AFW had been providing was still essential to the Partisans. In any case, the language and directives that were issued in the final version were somewhat toned down: Circular #5 did not call for the dissolution of the AFW. It did, however, order its complete reorganization.

The AFW had to be restructured along the following lines: first, AFW councils had to have the widest possible form. The local councils were to be restructured to include *all* village women, while AFW functionaries – their numbers reduced to a few indispensable ones – were instructed *not* to think of themselves as representatives of women, but rather as activists of the national-liberation front in charge of women's mobilization.

---

[126] AJ, SKJ 507, CKKPJ 1943/405, Direktivno pismo CKKPJ svim centralnim i pokr. komitetima KPJ, December 1943, my italics. Also *Izvori* 14, 553–6. (For a short period, this directive letter was used as a required reading in lower party courses. See AVII, NOR, IRP BiH 5/685–7, Program za niže partijske kurseve, od CKKPJ [Ranković] PK KPJ za BiH, December 1943.)

Second, the role of higher AFW forums was to serve only as advisers for lower councils and to prepare women's journals. They were to be closely linked with the accordant party forums, from which they would receive instructions. They should in particular make sure that lower AFW forums be responsible to the corresponding national liberation councils, and *not* to them. Third, female CPY members in the higher executive AFW bodies were *not* to work exclusively in the women's organization; instead they were to be given various party assignments alongside those concerning women. Their cells within the AFW were to be disbanded and the women were to be dispersed to different party cells or committees.

The reorganization altered the very nature of the front of women. Although the AFW was not dissolved, its work was completely transferred into the hands of the party, national-liberation councils, and other mass organizations. The original local councils that had worked successfully in the countryside were now transformed into loose associations of all village women, thus losing their activist core and identity. The request that female party activists stop working solely for the AFW and be given other tasks diluted their focus. By dispersing them to other party cells, the CPY assumed direct control over their work. Perhaps the most dramatic change concerned the command structure: Lower AFW councils were no longer responsible to the upper ones but to the national liberation councils on the same level. The very organizational formula upon which the AFW had functioned was thus abandoned, and the organization itself was absorbed into the hierarchy of the people's government. The AFW's structure was, as Mary Reed characterizes it, "transformed into an amorphous channel through which women would contribute to the movement" but have no organizational independence.[127]

The reorganization succeeded in crushing the AFW's autonomous existence and was thus fully justified in the eyes of the party. Yet, it did little to correct other problems that the Central Committee had outlined in the circular. There is no evidence to suggest that the reorganization helped the movement in reaching the still uninvolved masses of women; in some areas in Croatia, in fact, it had the opposite effect of making all females, including former AFW activists, passive.[128] In these and many other regions the circular was incorrectly interpreted: Some CPY members thought that the organization was to be dissolved altogether and took steps in that direction;[129]

---

[127] Reed, 136.

[128] Ibid.

[129] AVII, NOR, IRP BIH 6/486–7, 486, Okr. kom. za Drvar Ob. kom. u za B. Krajinu, 29 February 1944; AVII, NOR, IRP BIH 6/601–10, 608, Zaključci sa II part. oblasnog savetovanja B. Krajina, 5 and 6 April 1944; also Reed, 136.

others prevented the formation of councils in the newly liberated regions where they had not existed before.[130] All this put an end to the momentum that the AFW had gained in the previous years, turning it into a mass of councils with minimal responsibility and that only on the local level. Perhaps most important, the limited institutional space that the AFW had to achieve its political mission – women's activation and emancipation – was now all but gone.

There was no resistance to the reorganization among the AFW ranks. Since the upper echelons of the AFW were – to borrow Elizabeth Wood's phase used in reference to the Soviet Zhenotdel – "the dutiful daughters of the revolution," their primary loyalty was to the CPY.[131] As expected, they proved obedient to party discipline and readily accepted other assignments. If the experienced activists, who had founded the organization, did not resist its devaluation, still less opposition could be expected from the rank-and-file members in the villages, and indeed there was none. Thus quietly ended the first phase of women's organizational activity under the party's rule. It was also the sole phase that could boast of any significant organizational autonomy.

CONCLUSIONS

The party's view of women as a reserve revolutionary team – to be used as needed if men were unavailable – found its unique application in the AFW experiment. The party began paying serious attention to women because they were needed in the rear to replace men drawn to the front. The result of this attention was the formation of a rear support system largely dependent on women's labor, skill, and resourcefulness, without which the Partisans could not have survived, let alone won the war.

The AFW's wartime success is due in part to its mobilizing strategy, the originality of which lay in the skillful use of peasant traditions and the old gender division of labor in a distinctly modern key. Contrary to the conventional view of the communist revolution as an attempt to eradicate traditional values and culture, in the Partisans' institutional setting and their rhetoric alike, the differences between the revolutionary and the traditional were often handled by adaptation and translation. What the communists did was use women's traditional concerns

---

[130] AVII, NOR, IRP BiH 12/204–7, 206, Part. Jedinica Vareš, Okr. kom.-u KPJ za Sarajevo, 11 January 1945.
[131] Wood, *The Baba and the Comrade*, 5.

and employ their time-honored duties and skills toward the Partisan war effort in a structured fashion. To be sure, traditional practices of female peasants aiding their warrior men were not simply revived in their original form, but were converted by modern organizational tools into catalysts of women's mass participation in warfare.

The AFW episode exposes with particular force the contradictions in the communist project of "emancipation from above." The involvement of women in the revolutionary struggle not only was a communist tenet but also proved a wartime necessity. Since the party perceived women as more backward and passive, it considered a special organization for women necessary. Yet any such efforts could divide the revolutionary masses along gender lines, undermine revolutionary unity, and exhibit feminist tendencies. The CPY's solution to this dilemma was to form a party-controlled women's organization as an arm of the Partisan movement. But then, except using it to provide basic support and services for the army, the party leadership neglected the organization and left its activists to their own devices to fulfill their many wartime tasks. And when the female activists became increasingly independent – in part thanks to the neglect, discrimination, and lack of guidance – the party leveled the charge of feminism against them. It is ironic that, for all the intensity with which the party denounced feminism, it drew upon the interwar organizational legacy of precisely *feminist* activism.

As far as women are concerned, the Partisan recruitment strategy was a double-edged sword. Once mobilized by the AFW, they took part in political affairs to a degree unheard of before the war, while their labor and voices received unprecedented public acknowledgment. On the other hand, gender remained not only one of the main organizational principles of the Partisan movement but also a marker of hierarchy in it. By putting the women's organization in charge of channeling old female duties to meet the wartime needs of a revolutionary army, the party simply bolstered the perception of these duties as uniquely women's. The AFW helped create a public version of feminized domesticity while reinforcing the traditional notion that men belong to the front and women to the rear. The inferior status of the women's organization within the movement confirmed the conventional hierarchy of gender roles. Worse still, through the AFW, the customary sexual division of labor and old gender stereotypes were institutionalized. As we shall see in the following chapter, they would not be abolished even when women crossed the gender barrier in the most extreme manner and entered the Partisan army as fighters.

3

The Heroic and the Mundane

Women in the Units

Your only daughter, dear mother of mine	*Majko moja, imaš me jedinu*
I leave you to carry a carbine.	*Ja ti odoh nosit karabinu.*

(verses from a wartime Partisan folk song)[1]

When the insurrection started in her Bosnian Krajina in 1941, a twenty-year-old peasant, Marija Bursać, decided to join the Partisan movement. After having worked in the rear for a while, she enlisted in the Partisan army as a fighter. Forged in battle, she soon turned into a skilled grenade thrower (*bombaš*). In the late summer of 1943, her brigade was given the task of taking over a German stronghold at Prkosi. In the course of action, her comrades remember, Bursać's platoon managed to seize two howitzers, disarm four enemy soldiers, and destroy three bunkers. Then, as she was approaching another bunker, Bursać fell, a grenade explosion shattering her right foot. Gravely wounded, she had to be transported to the nearest Partisan hospital, which was some forty kilometers away from the battle zone. It took several days for the column carrying the bleeding *partizanka* to reach its destination. Along the way, Bursać reportedly cheered her worried friends on, singing Partisan fighting songs:

Our struggle thus demands	*Naša borba zahtijeva*
That while dying, one sings	*Kad se gine da se peva*[2]

---

[1] As recorded in *Udarnik*, August 1945, 15.
[2] Verses from one of the most popular Partisan songs.

She passed away, her wound infected by tetanus, on 23 September 1943. The name of Marija Bursać, the singing Partisan heroine, thereupon became legendary in the Yugoslav lands.[3]

The martial heroine, so well represented by Bursać, came to be one of the fixations of the Partisan wartime rhetoric and postwar mythology alike. But what was behind the myth? Bursać was not an isolated example of female combativeness in the Partisan movement; she was among many thousands of Yugoslav girls who broke out of the patriarchal frame and fought alongside men in the Partisan units. Who were these Balkan female warriors? Why and how did the party decide to recruit them in the first place? How were they integrated into the army? What problems did their presence among the ranks cause and how were those solved?

Seeking to answer these questions, this chapter outlines the history of women's wartime mobilization. It focuses on women in Partisan military units, paying particular attention to two groups: female fighters and nurses. These two, although predominant among the ranks, were not the only roles in which females could be found in the Partisan army. Women were in fact employed in many other capacities. While some served as political commissars, many more worked in the agitation and propaganda departments attached to units' staffs; others could be found in administrative and communications positions as typists, secretaries, and telephone, radio, or telegraph operators; still others were used for intelligence gathering, as liaison personnel, and in various auxiliary services.

Of all these women, however, the two aforementioned groups were the most conspicuous: Female fighters stood out as a novelty, while female nurses owed their visibility in the units to their numerical preponderance. The term *partizanka* itself, although signifying all women in the Partisan movement, has been most often used in reference to female fighters and nurses. A typical representation of the female Partisan in postwar Yugoslav culture is an armed girl who fights *and* tends to the wounded. That the two functions merged in the revolutionary image of the *partizanka* was not entirely accidental. As is often the case with irregular warfare, the line between fighting and nonfighting tasks was blurred in the Partisan struggle. Many women served as both nurses and fighters.

---

[3] Based on Beoković, *Žene heroji*, 11–53. Bursać was the first of the ninety-two women decorated with the title of National Hero of Yugoslavia for distinguishing themselves by heroic deeds during the war. She was immortalized in the poem "Maria at Prkosi," written by the famous Yugoslav poet Branko Ćopić, a Partisan himself. The title in Bosnian/Croatian/Serbian is *"Marija na Prkosima"* – a wordplay, which also means "Maria, in spite" or "Maria defiant."

In addition, those women who were assigned exclusively to the medical sector were often armed and sometimes took an active part in combat.

Although they constituted only a fraction of the women involved in the resistance, female soldiers played an extraordinary role in the war. By entering the most secluded and cherished male realm, the military, the *partizanka* posed a radical challenge to the established norms and provoked reaction from all sides. She became one of the central icons of the Partisan struggle and the favorite target of enemy propaganda. The phenomenon of the *partizanka* provides exceptional insights into the Partisans' gender politics. As we shall see, it sheds light on the leadership's dilemmas concerning gender roles, exposes a sex-based hierarchy in the movement, and shows how gender remained a major organizational criterion even in a revolutionary guerrilla army.

In what follows, I trace the evolution of Partisan policy on women's recruitment into military units and probe problems of its implementation on the local level. My major concerns are, first, the persistence of traditional norms on the ground in the face of an egalitarian campaign from above, and, second, the limits of egalitarianism at the top. In addition, this chapter looks at the motivations and experiences of the *partizanka*s themselves. Whenever possible, participant voices are incorporated to illustrate how party decisions affected women and highlight the gender specificities of their experiences.

THE PARTY APPROVES FEMALE COMBATANTS

Among the many tasks that men and women could perform in the Partisan movement, the most highly regarded one was combat. This ultimate duty, "which all others were designed to prepare and support," as Paula Schwartz writes, "bore an unmistakable gender stamp, in peacetime as in war."[4] Perhaps more than any other activity, combat was universally seen as a male preserve. By granting women access to the front, the Communist Party consciously breached the traditional social order. The decision to do so, however, was made neither automatically nor easily, despite the party's egalitarian agenda.

The CPY's position regarding women's recruitment as combatants was in fact ambiguous at first. Some early appeals to civilians invited women to join Partisan detachments and take part in armed struggle. An announcement of the Montenegrin Staff, issued after a battle at which

---

[4] Paula Schwartz, "Partisanes and Gender Politics in Vichy France," *French Historical Studies* 16. 1 (Spring 1989): 128.

the Partisans suffered great casualties, asked each "sister to pick up her [fallen] brother's rifle and take his place."[5] Individual CPY committees and Partisan staffs also called for women's recruitment into the ranks.[6] It appears, however, that such calls originated in local initiatives rather than official policy. The vast majority of early party directives and appeals appointed women to support roles in the rear and men to the battlefield. A typical 1941 address to the masses reads:

> Our brothers, flock into the heroic partisan units! Join the people's army! Clean and prepare your weapons! ... Our sisters, your duty is as great as that of a soldier! You have to organize the *sanitet* [medical service], the cooking and carrying of food, the destruction of enemy connection lines, the securing of the people's government in the rear.[7]

The relatively few women Partisans at the onset of the uprising were mostly prewar party members and girls associated with the Communist Youth League. They served in noncombatant capacities, as political workers and nurses, or, in smaller numbers, as typists and telegraph operators. Surely, some of these early *partizanka*s took part in the actual fighting, but if any consistency were to be found in the party's recruitment practices in 1941, it would be that of *not* enlisting females as combatants.[8] There were even cases in which the recruitment of women volunteering for combat was obstructed from above. Since the fall of 1941, young women in Lika (Croatia) had insisted on being allowed to fight, but the party rejected their demands, even though the women had the support of the Communist Youth League. As a result of the resistance of Lika's party leadership, the league's initiative to form a female company was not put into practice before August 1942.[9]

---

[5] *Zbornik* 3.1, doc. 156, p. 347. Similarly, a Serbian detachment asked women to sign up. See *Zbornik* 1. 2, doc. 37, pp. 137–9.

[6] The committee for Vojvodina, for instance, ordered its lower forums to prepare women to serve as nurses and fighters. AVII, NOR, IA PK SKS Vojvodine 2/174–83, Cirkular PK KPJ za Vojvodinu, 1 February 1942. Similarly, according to recruitment instructions issued by the Partisan staff of the Sarajevo district, women were considered primarily as nurses and for intelligence, but they were to be admitted in the detachments as well. See *Zbornik* 4.1. doc. 86, p. 195. The Serbian party leadership suggested that women could be used for fighting in addition to other tasks. *Zbornik* 1.1, doc. 11, p. 66, and others.

[7] *Zbornik* 3.1. doc 28, pp. 76–7. See also *Gerilac* no. 5, 19 August 1941, in *Zbornik* 4.1, doc. 18, pp. 50–3; *Zbornik* 4.1, doc. 43, pp. 94–5, and others.

[8] According to the CPY committee for Montenegro, the "correct distribution" of female youth by the Partisan staffs was for medical training and sanitary or nursing assignments AJ, SKJ 507, CKKPJ-1941/85, Cirkularno pismo PK KPJ za Crnu Goru, Boku i Sandžak, 19 November 1941.

[9] Desanka Stojić, *Prva Ženska Partizanska Četa* (Karlovac: Historijski Arhiv u Karlovcu, 1987), 14–16. For cases in which individual women were not allowed to sign up as

Several factors accounted for this hesitation to accept female combatants: First, in the early months of the war the Partisans were in desperate need of nurses, as opposed to fighters, since male insurgents poured into their ranks once the uprising was launched, particularly in Montenegro, parts of Serbia, and the regions affected by the Ustasha terror. Second, the leadership feared that the appearance of female fighters – or even women in prominent political roles – might alienate the conservative public. One of the leading female communists, Mitra Mitrović, remembers the long debates in the Belgrade party committee in the spring of 1941 about whether it would be "politically opportune" to assign female commissars to the army.[10]

Third, the CPY received mixed messages from other European communist parties and the Comintern regarding female fighters. The latest precedent and most logical model was the Spanish Civil War, where many of the Yugoslav Partisan leaders had received their training in guerrilla warfare. The Spanish policy, however, was far from straightforward. Female fighters were welcomed in the militias when the civil war broke out in 1936, and the image of the *miliciana* in blue overalls became an international symbol of republican Spain's antifascist resistance. But less than a year later women were coerced to leave the front lines. The republican government ordered their withdrawal from the militias and warned foreign volunteers that women could not join combat units. The exclusion of females coincided with the reorganization of the militias into a regular, communist-dominated army. By 1937, the *miliciana*, once an antifascist heroine, had also disappeared from republican posters and propaganda.[11]

Besides the Spanish case, which weighed against women's recruitment, the most important reason for the party's reluctance lay in the fact that there had been no consistent policy on the issue and no uniform definition of wartime gender roles in Moscow until March 1942, when the Soviets began their campaign for women's mobilization into the Red Army. Before the war, the Soviet state provided paramilitary training for women on a large scale; women's journals featured articles on women's participation in combat in the Spanish and Chinese wars and reminded the female reader that "because of her greater degree of emancipation,

fighters, see for example, Slavko Borojević, "Sećanje na Zoru Zebić," in Stana Džakula Nidžović, *Žene borci NOR-a Sedme banijske udarne divizije* (Čačak: Bajić, 1999), 103.

[10] Mitra Mitrović, *Ratno putovanje* (Beograd: Prosveta, 1962), 40.

[11] Mary Nash, *Defying Male Civilization: Women in the Spanish Civil War* (Denver: Arden Press, 1995), 48–54, 110–16.

she was expected if need be to fight better and harder against fascism than her sisters in Spain and China." In the opening nine months of the war, however, the Soviet leadership's position on women's recruitment was as ambivalent as that of the CPY. State propaganda sent conflicting messages to women, inviting them to stay at the home front and at the same time celebrating female partisans and heroic Soviet nurses rescuing wounded soldiers at the front. Meanwhile, Soviet representatives abroad insisted that their state had no intention of using women for regular frontline duty. Women's potential service in the ranks of the Red Army was rejected on account of "natural" differences between men and women, which relegated the latter to the home front.[12]

The Yugoslavs made up their minds about women's participation in combat in February 1942. It was, as usual, Tito's decision that defined the CPY's policy. In a letter to the party leaders Edvard Kardelj and Ivo Lola Ribar, Tito announced his new position: "Since there are more and more demands by women to join the detachments, we have decided that they be admitted not only as nurses but also as fighters. It would really be a shame for us to forbid women to fight with rifles in hands for national liberation."[13] Women were indeed eager to fight. Several insisted on being assigned to combat duty; some even petitioned to Tito. But there could have been other reasons behind his decision. This was the period when the core Partisan units, the Supreme Staff among them, found themselves battered and driven out of their base in Serbia. After the rough winter of 1941–2 – during which they had barely survived two German offensives and several clashes with the Chetniks – the Partisans faced severe manpower shortages. In addition, the party was at the time in its most radical, hard-line revolutionary phase. Its adoption of communist orthodoxy, coupled with wartime necessity, might have made the leadership more attuned to women's demands. It is also possible that Tito received the green light from Moscow, where the Soviet government's campaign for the mobilization of female volunteers into the army was to be launched about a month later, in March.[14] Whether this is the case or not, the new

---

[12] Susanne Conze and Beate Fieseler, "Soviet Women as Comrades-in-Arms: A Blind Spot in the History of the War," in *The People's War: Responses to World War II in the Soviet Union*, ed. Robert W. Thurston and Bernd Bonwetsch (Urbana and Chicago: University of Illinois Press, 2000), 214–24; esp. 217, 219.

[13] AJ, SKJ 507, CKKPJ 1942/82, Titovo pismo Loli i Bevcu, 23 February 1942. Also *Zbornik* 2 2, doc. 201, pp. 435–6.

[14] I was not able to locate any document that would link Tito's decision with that in Moscow. However, the timing here suggests that more than just coincidence might be the case; preparations for the Soviet mass mobilization campaign had been well under way

policy on women combatants in Yugoslavia was likely informed by a combination of factors: women's eagerness, communist radicalism, and – similar to the USSR – manpower shortages after the first wartime winter.

Tito's decision opened the doors of the Partisan forces to masses of Yugoslavia's women. By mid-1942, shortly after the official approval from above, the units experienced a notable increase in the numbers of female Partisans – fighters and nurses alike – most of whom were peasant youths. A series of campaigns for women's mobilization, which began in earnest in the spring of 1942, proved a success, resulting in a relatively steady influx of female recruits for the rest of the war. Given the large numbers of females who signed up, it is surprising that there was no military ordinance that specified the conscription policy with respect to women or defined their status in combat units. The only official guidance was provided in the order of the Supreme Staff, issued on 9 January 1943, regarding the preparation of conscription lists for the National Liberation Army in liberated zones.[15] According to the order, all men eighteen to forty-five years old were to be enlisted; they were considered conscripts of the first order and their service was obligatory. Women of the same age were to be included only if they volunteered as fighters. Similarly, separate lists were to be kept for all male youths of seventeen to eighteen, to which only the names of female volunteers of the same age would be added.[16]

Once accepted, female recruits served together with men in mixed-gender units. The Montenegrin shock battalions, organized in early 1942, were the first to incorporate significant numbers of female fighters. Some of them would later enter elite Partisan units – the proletarian brigades. The 4th and 5th (Montenegrin) Proletarian Brigades, newly formed in June 1942, boasted a considerable percentage of women: It has been estimated that there were 220 females out of 1,082 soldiers in the

---

at the time Tito announced the new policy. On Soviet preparations, see Anna Krylova, *Soviet Women in Combat* (New York: Cambridge University Press, 2010), 144–57.

[15] AJ, AFŽ, 141-10-50, Žene u NOB, 433–5, n.d.

[16] Ibid.; also AVII, NOR, IRP BiH 3/456, Otsjek Vrhovnog Štaba za vojne vlasti u poza- dini, Uputstvo za pravilno popunjavanje mobilizacijskog materijala, 12 January 1943. Until the second AVNOJ session (November 1943), the Partisans recruited primarily on a voluntary basis. Several general mobilization orders for men older than 18 had been issued before late 1943, but these had mostly been limited to small operative zones and special conditions such as enemy offensives. On the basis of a decision made at the sec- ond AVNOJ session in November 1943, the National Committee (the new provisional government) announced the beginning of obligatory conscription for all adult males. This order notwithstanding, the Partisans could start carrying out mass conscription on a national level only in late 1944. *Zbornik* 2.2, doc. 153, note 7, p. 311; for earlier orders, see, for example, ibid.; *Zbornik* 4. 3, doc. 49, p. 147.

FIGURE 6. Fighters of the 2nd Batallion, the 4th Montenegrin Proletarian Brigade, with the party leader Ivan Milutinović, in Janj (Bosnia), 1942. Courtesy of Muzej Istorije Jugoslavije.

4th, and 160 out of 800 soldiers in the 5th at the time of these brigades' formation.[17] Although the number of females underwent many fluctuations in these units during the course of the war, Montenegro's women remained highly visible and earned a well-deserved reputation as heroines in the Partisan movement (Figure 6). Being the first and relatively numerous, the Montenegrin *partizanka*s were often mentioned as models in party propaganda and directives calling for women's recruitment into combat units elsewhere.[18]

On the whole, the proportion of women could range from zero to 25 percent, averaging about 12 percent in the Partisan units based on voluntary recruitment.[19] Fairly representative in terms of gender distribution are the

[17] Figures on the 4th Proletarian Brigade from Blažo Janković, *4. Proleterska Crnogorska Brigada* (Beograd: Vojnoizdavački zavod, 1976), 67, 634; on the 5th, Jovan Bojović et al., *Žene Crne Gore u revolucionarnom pokretu, 1918–1945* (Titograd: Istorijski institut, 1969), 174–5.

[18] AVII, NOR, CK SK Hrvatske NOB 16/2–5, 5; KK KPH Dvor svim partijskim organizacijama i članovima KP kotara Dvor, 20 December 1942.

[19] This proportion changed in the last months of the war, when the Partisans increasingly turned into a regular conscript army. The rapid growth of Partisan forces in late 1944 and early 1945 was due, first, to Tito's granting amnesty to his former enemies should they

TABLE 3.1 GENDER COMPOSITION OF THE 12TH
HERZEGOVINIAN BRIGADE, JANUARY 1944

	Men	Women	Totals
1st Battalion	53	6	59
2nd Battalion	72	11	83
3rd Battalion	60	7	67
4th Battalion	52	5	57
Technical unit	9	/	9
Correspondence	10	1	11
Ambulance	1	1	2
Total	257	31	288

Source: AVII, NOR, IRP BiH 6/125, Statistika iz jedinica XII Hercegovačke NOU brigade, 31 January 1944.

statistics from the 12th Herzegovinian Brigade, dated January 1944 (see Table 3.1).

Besides soldiering, female recruits were most often appointed to the medical sector as nurses. The Partisan medical corps was divided into two major branches: the *sanitet* among the troops and Partisan hospitals in the rear. Women's presence was most visible in the latter: The hospitals in the rear were in many cases staffed primarily – sometimes exclusively – by women. Data of the 6th Corps hospitals (Croatia) illustrate this well (see Table 3.2).

The *sanitet* among the troops was also often feminized. Ideally, a platoon had its own nurse, who remained with the platoon at all times and who was in charge of giving first aid to the wounded. And each brigade had its own medical unit (*bolničarska četa*), which was used for evacuating the wounded Partisans and taking measures related to hygiene and prophylaxis (preventive treatment such as vaccination) among the troops.[20] In selecting recruits for medical units, priority was given to men who had formerly served as medics in the Yugoslav royal army *and* to

switch sides, which drew entire Domobran (Home Guard) and Chetnik units into the Partisan ranks, and second and more important, to mass conscription that the Partisans carried out in liberated areas, which by then covered most of the country. Women were not subject to conscription, and their recruitment, unlike men's, remained voluntary. In the final stage of the war the proportion of females in the army thus dropped, probably to well below 10 percent, although women continued to sign up and their absolute numbers in the army grew.

[20] For more on the *sanitet* organization in Partisan divisions and corps in Slavonia, see *Zbornik sanitetske* 3, doc. 43, pp. 82–109.

TABLE 3.2 DISTRIBUTION OF MEDICS BY GENDER, HOSPITALS OF THE
6TH CORPS, CROATIA (15 OCTOBER–30 NOVEMBER 1943)

Hospitals of the 6th Corps	Male Medics	Female Medics
Hospital 1	5	21
Hospital 2	2	14
Hospital 3	7	26
Hospital 4	5	19
Hospital 5	5	7
Hospital 6	3	5
Total	27	92

Source: Zbornik dokumenata i podataka sanitetske službe u narodnooslobodilačkom ratu jugoslovenskih naroda (Beograd: Vojnoistorijski institut, 1952–78) (hereafter *Zbornik sanitetske*), vol. 3, doc. 145, pp. 264–5.

"healthy, strong girls," capable of carrying the wounded Partisans from the front lines to safety.[21] Medical units thus typically incorporated a larger percentage of women than other Partisan units. As a simple rule, if there were women in any given Partisan unit, they were most likely found in the *sanitet*.

THE PROFILE OF THE *PARTIZANKA*

Who were the typical female Partisans? Exact figures do not exist for any region, but personal narratives, archival sources, and secondary analyses suggest that the typical rank-and-file *partizanka* was a young woman of peasant origin. In the first units formed in 1941 and early 1942, most *partizanka*s were prewar communist activists from Yugoslavia's towns and cities – secondary school and university students, workers, intellectuals, or professionals – but in 1942 peasant women began increasingly swelling the Partisan ranks. Young peasant women constituted a large majority even in elite Partisan units – the so-called proletarian and shock brigades – although educated urban women continued to be overrepresented relative to their share of the population. Perhaps the best indicator for the elite units of the National Liberation Army is the statistical survey of the troops engaged in the Battle of Sutjeska (also known under

---

[21] On preference for former royal army medics, *Zbornik sanitetske* 3, doc. 1, p. 11. On "healthy, strong girls," *Zbornik sanitetske* 3, doc. 16, p. 41. On the reasons why physical strength was emphasized, *Zbornik sanitetske* 3, doc. 43, pp. 82–109.

its German code name, Operation Schwartz) in May–June 1943. In the sixteen brigades that formed the Supreme Staff's main operative group during the battle, there were 2,846 women, constituting about 15 percent of Partisan manpower. Among them, more than 61 percent were peasants (or "agricultural workers"). If we add to that the women dubiously classified as "housewives," the proportion rises to 74 percent.[22]

Particularly striking is the youth of female volunteers. "What we [female Partisans] had in common," remembers a former *partizanka* from the 4th Krajina Brigade (Bosnia), "was that all of us were young. I could claim with certainty that someone over 20 would have been an exception. Most were 17 or 18."[23] Existing statistical data agree with her observation. The average age of the seventy-five peasant women who formed the first female company in Lika in August 1942 was eighteen.[24] In the 7th Banija (Croatia) Division, of the 566 women whose age at the time of enlistment is known, 384 (68 percent) were younger than twenty, 152 (26 percent) were between twenty and thirty, 28 (5 percent) between thirty and forty, and only 2 (0.3 percent) were older than forty.[25] Of the 85 women who entered the 1st Proletarian Brigade at the time of its formation in the fall of 1941, 81 percent were less than twenty-five.[26]

As for national composition, there is little doubt that the Partisans were truly Yugoslav in orientation, attracting recruits of all ethnic and religious backgrounds. Yet sources also suggest a preponderance of women (and men) of Serb/Montenegrin origin, especially in earlier stages of the war. In central Serbia and parts of Montenegro, this was the case for the obvious reason of these regions' relative ethnic homogeneity. A disproportionate representation of Serbs, however, existed initially in most areas characterized by ethnoreligious diversity *and* a significant presence of Serb population, as were the cases of the Independent State of Croatia and Vojvodina. The Serb element was particularly strong in the

---

[22] The full breakdown includes 1,743 peasants, 426 pupils, 371 housewives, 178 workers, 46 university students, 34 white-collar workers, 21 teachers, 10 medical doctors, 6 professors, 2 engineers, 2 actresses, 1 pharmacist, 1 artist, and 5 children. Viktor Kučan, "Sutjeska – Dolina heroja – Žene borci (prvi deo)," *Vojnoistorijski glasnik* 39. 3 (1988): 214.

[23] Draginja Višekruna-Lukač, "Ženska omladina u IV krajiškoj udarnoj brigadi," in Hurem, *Žene Bosne,* 470.

[24] Stojić, *Prva Ženska,* 20.

[25] Stana Džakula Nidžović, *Žene borci NOR-a Sedme banijske udarne brigade,* 141–2.

[26] The exact distribution by age is as follows: 19 women were below 18 years of age, 24 were 18–20 years old, 26 were 20–25, 13 were 25–30, and only 3 were older than 30. On average, women Partisans in the 1st Proletarian Brigade were younger than their male comrades. Lagator and Čukić, *Partizanke Prve Proleterske,* 10.

units that recruited from the regions exposed to the Ustasha terror (such as Lika, Kordun, Banija, and Bosnian Krajina). Of the 811 women who served in the 7th Banija Division, for instance, 607 were Serbs, 32 Croats, 89 Jews, 4 Montenegrins, 2 Muslims, and 77 of unknown ethnicity.[27] The representation of Jewish women among the Partisans was also relatively high, and this was true for all Yugoslav lands.[28] Among other groups, the Partisans were particularly successful in attracting Croats from the regions annexed by Italy (Dalmatia, parts of Gorski Kotar) and in Istria, as well as among Slovenes in Slovenia and Macedonians in Macedonia. As the sympathies of many Bosnian Muslims turned to the Partisans, Muslim women also signed up, though in somewhat smaller numbers. The Partisans had the least success in attracting the non-Slavic minorities, many of whom had suffered injustice in the interwar period and for whom a favorable solution to the national question was offered by the occupying powers, such as the Kosovo Albanians, the Hungarians of Bačka (Vojvodina), and the Germans of the Banat (Vojvodina). The Sutjeska statistics, covering the sixteen core operative brigades surrounding the Supreme Staff in 1943, provides illustrative data on the early Partisan ethnic breakdown. Of the 2,846 *partizanka*s present at Sutjeska, 1,268 were Serbs, 635 Montenegrins, 608 Croats, 110 Muslims, 17 Jews, 8 Slovenians, 4 Czechs, 1 Slovak, 1 Russian, and 1 German; 193 declared themselves as Yugoslavs.[29]

What were the young women's motivations for joining the Partisan forces? For a minority of *partizanka*s – mostly those belonging to the urban nucleus of the CPY or the Communist Youth League before the war – the decision to sign up was based on their ideological commitment to the communist cause and affiliation with the party. Some joined the

---

[27] Stana Džakula Nidžović, *Žene borci NOR-a Sedme banijske udarne brigade*, 141–2.

[28] In the Yugoslav Kingdom there were about 76,000 Jews, with the largest communities living in interior Croatia and Slavonia, Vojvodina, Bosnia, Serbia, and Macedonia; on the eve of the war, their numbers increased to about 82,000 as a result of the influx of refugees from Germany and elsewhere. See Paul Benjamin Gordiejew, *Voices of Yugoslav Jewry* (Albany: State University of New York Press, 1999), 41. This estimate corresponds to the one provided by a Yugoslav Jewish historian, Jaša Romano. The total number of Jews in Yugoslavia on the eve of the war – according to Romano – was 82, 242 (12,500 in Serbia; 4,200 in Banat; 25,000 in Croatia; 16,000 in Bačka and Baranja; 14,000 in Bosnia-Herzegovina; 7,762 in Macedonia; 1,500 in Slovenia; and 1,280 from elsewhere). See Jaša Romano, *Jevreji Jugoslavije, 1941–1945: Žrtve genocida i učesnici narodnooslobodilačkog rata* (Beograd: Savez Jevrejskih opština Jugoslavije, 1980), 13–14.

[29] Kučan, "Sutjeska," 213–14. The data are not representative of the participation of Slovene and Macedonian women, since units from Slovenia and Macedonia did not take part in the battle.

units immediately, though a number of female CPY activists remained in occupied towns and villages. These so-called illegal activists (*ilegalke*) worked underground in enemy territory until they received a new assignment or until their cover was blown. In the latter case, if lucky, they would be able to escape and find refuge in the units. Others, captured by the enemy, found themselves in the army after prisoner exchanges or successful rescue missions. Among the *ilegalke*, who worked underground in constant danger and fear, the desire to move to the relative freedom and safety of the Partisan units was almost universal.

Female peasant recruits were often from war-ravaged villages, in which entire communities – men, women, and children alike – had been targeted on account of their ethnicity. To these displaced and bewildered peasants, the Partisans provided a refuge from persecution and terror back home. This was often the case with Serbs in the Independent State of Croatia: Whole families, sometimes whole villages, took to the hills in retreat before Ustasha onslaughts, where, after meeting the Partisans, many ultimately joined the troops.[30] Other victims of interethnic violence, including Muslims and Croats attacked by the Chetniks, also found protection in the Partisan forces. The same can be said for the group targeted everywhere in the former Yugoslav lands, the Yugoslav Jews, for whom reaching the Partisans was practically the only chance for survival.

In addition, a large number of women joined the Partisans for personal reasons. The desire for revenge, after having been exposed to violence, comes up frequently in reminiscences as motivation for joining. In their postwar recollections, the *partizanka*s sometimes note the "bestiality" of their adversaries, which was made manifest in part through sexual offenses and rape. However, the women never identify themselves as rape victims. The majority of such accounts vaguely refer to the general danger that women faced in captivity or in villages controlled by the enemy; occasionally, a female friend or a relative would be named the victim. In his diary, Dedijer mentions a headstrong, bitter young girl, who was motivated by vengeance to enlist. According to what she confided to him, all of her female cousins – though reportedly not she – were raped, and most of them were then murdered by the Ustashas.[31] As the literature on

---

[30] For a typical testimony, see Zora Popović-Smoljanović, "Rad za narodnooslobodilački pokret od 1941–1945. godine," in Hurem, *Žene Bosne i Hercegovine*, 249–59, 249. See also Dara Radujković-Vujnović, "Žene Kozare u slavonskim partizanima 1942. godine," in ibid., 536–8.

[31] Vladimir Dedijer, *The War Diaries of Vladimir Dedijer* (Ann Arbor: University of Michigen Press, 1990), vol. 1, p. 80.

rape elsewhere shows, this phenomenon of speaking about sexual assault in the third person is common among victims.[32] Women who do recount instances involving attempts at sexual coercion and rape as part of their own experience represent such events in terms of their successful escape.[33] The most explicit account is that of a Bosnian *partizanka* who explains the assault as the decisive factor behind her decision to join the Partisans. At the time of the incident, she was an eighteen-year-old employee of a merchant who was a Chetnik sympathizer:

> My most difficult moment was ... in the fall of 1942, when the Chetniks attempted to dishonor me. It is hard to even imagine what it was like for me, an already grown up girl, when a group of bearded men encircled me and started to roll up the sleeves of their shirts, I screamed, there was no one to protect me. Not even now can I explain to myself how I managed to run away from these beasts in human skin; I escaped and woke up in the woods. That night I made the decision: I'd take up a rifle and fight those bastards.[34]

Such stories of unlikely escapes suggest that the women may have left something out of their accounts. In the past three decades, much has been written on the issue of rape and the reluctance of victims to discuss or even report assaults. Feminist scholarship has tried to explain women's silence by pointing to the stigma associated with the label of rape victim, the significance of sexual honor to both a woman's identity and her social status, and the lack of collectively sanctioned narrative structures for victims to speak about their experiences, among other issues. All these factors apply to Yugoslav women, making it hard to believe that none of those speaking about the rapes of other women or their own escapes were victimized themselves. In any case – whether they were actual victims or witnesses, successful or unsuccessful escapees – some women were apparently prompted to seek revenge for sexual assaults by joining the guerrilla army that fought against the perpetrators.

Another major reason for signing up was a genuine attraction to soldiering. Some women desired the freedom, higher status, and respect reserved for military men; others wanted to taste the excitement and adventure they associated with military activity. "My parents ... wanted a son. I wanted to be that son, I wanted to be a soldier," remembers

---

[32] On this phenomenon among the exiled Polish women in the USSR during World War II and on other cases, see Katherine Jolluck, *Exile & Identity: Polish Women in the Soviet Union during World War II* (Pittsburgh: University of Pittsburgh Press, 2002), 168–9.

[33] This is another common occurrence. See ibid., 169–71.

[34] Duja Marić-Vujanović, "Koliko li je tvoje srce ... ," in Hurem, ed., *Žene Bosne i Hercegovine*, 601.

the Serbian *partizanka* Dana Milosavljević. "I ran a hundred times under the rainbow to turn male."[35] Occasionally the women couch this motive in the language of the epic heritage, placing it in the traditional hero-worship context. In her memoir, the Montenegrin *partizanka* Jelisavka Komnenić-Džaković describes growing up with epic poems about Montenegrin and Herzegovinian heroes. Her grandfather and father were, as she put it, *junak*s (heroic warriors) themselves. As a young girl she used to lament that she was not male, and that there was no war, for she too wanted to become a *junak*.[36] World War II and the Partisans gave her a unique opportunity to do so.

Finally, the enthusiasm and idealism of the latter phases of the war, when the fortunes of battle clearly turned toward the Allies, drew many women and men into the Partisans. The exhilaration of the approaching victory increased the desire to take part in the ousting of the occupiers. The youth, in particular, was eager to join in. With the fall of Italy, young men and women from Dalmatia and the Croatian littoral began signing up in droves. In 1944, the youth of Serbia and Vojvodina too volunteered in large numbers to contribute to the country's liberation.[37]

PROBLEMS OF INTEGRATION

Women's integration into the army presented a host of problems before the Partisan leadership. Judging by internal party documents, most problems of integration fall into four general categories: 1) women's military inexperience, 2) the persistence of old beliefs and hierarchies, 3) the perseverance of the customary sexual division of labor, and 4) the emergence of sexual tensions in the units. Each of these categories, except the last one, will be discussed in the following. The last issue, sexuality, is the subject of the next chapter. Suffice it to say here that enemy propaganda and actual tensions in the units forced the party leadership to spend time and effort to define the norms of sexual behavior. Although the Partisan code nominally did not differentiate between the sexes, on the level of implementation women were often held to a different standard than men.

Women's Military Skill and Training: One of the major problems the party encountered when it started accepting females in combat units

---

[35] Quoted in Pantelić, *Partizanke kao građanke*, 31, 45.

[36] Jelisavka Komnenić-Džaković, *Staza jedne partizanke* (Beograd: Narodna knjiga, 1980), 13.

[37] On mass volunteering in Serbia and Vojvodina, see AVII, NOR, IRPJ 1/539–40, PK KPJ Vojvodine CKKPJ-u, 20 September 1944.

was women's military inexperience. The Montenegrin brigades, which initially boasted the largest number of female fighters, were the first to raise the issue. "The most painful question regarding women ... is their poor or almost non-existent military training," wrote the CPY members of the 4th Montenegrin Brigade to the Central Committee, "which is why female comrades were often wounded or killed in battle when this was neither necessary nor unavoidable."[38] The high casualty rate among women alarmed the leadership. As a remedy, newly recruited females were kept out of combat in Montenegro.[39] Party leaders elsewhere advised commanders to start learning from previous battle experiences and stop "pushing those female comrades, who are completely unskilled and without any knowledge on how to use arms, into serious combat situations where they perish needlessly."[40] This ban on fighting was a temporary solution until women gained more experience in actions deemed less dangerous or until they received some military instruction. The latter was in most cases short and elementary. A rare exception to this rule took place in Lika in the second half of 1942. Five all-female companies were successively formed to prepare women for combat. After a month-long "political-military" course, the units were disbanded and the girls dispersed to various mixed Partisan detachments, where they experienced their first baptism by fire.[41] Even such exceptional courses for women as those in Lika were basic at best. It is doubtful that they could prepare inexperienced female youths for the conditions on the battlefield, especially in view of the fact that casualty rates continued to be high throughout the war. Medical training for women in the *sanitet*, on the other hand, was organized in a more systematic fashion. As early as the summer of 1941, the Communist Youth League began providing medical courses for girls, after which the young nurses were dispatched to Partisan ambulances and units.[42] As the war progressed, training for nurses further improved as the *sanitet* officials developed a network of

---

[38] *Zbornik* 9.1, doc. 129, p. 493.

[39] *Zbornik* 9. 1, doc. 131, pp. 503–4.

[40] AVII, NOR, IRP BiH 3/531-7, 536, Zapisnik sa sastanka i formiranja part. komiteta IV KNOU divizije, 1 February 1943.

[41] See Stojić, *Prva Ženska Partizanska Četa*, 19–54.

[42] Jelena Drecun-Kostić, "Kako smo se pripremale za ustanak 13. Jula 1941," in *Ustanak naroda Jugoslavije, 1941: Zbornik. Pišu učesnici*, ed. by Milinko Purović (Beograd: Vojno delo, 1962), vol. 2, 768–9. For training for nurses see also Julka Mešterović, *Lekarev dnevnik* (Beograd: Vojnoizdavački zavod, 1968), 58; also Zaga Umićević, "Godine 1941. s banjalučkim ženama," in Hurem, *Žene Bosne i Hercegovine*, 54; Mara Vinterhalter-Miletić, "Kurs za partizanske bolničarke u okupiranom Mostaru," in ibid., 142–3, and others.

courses at lower and intermediate levels, which were usually taught by
doctors or other trained medics. However, *military* instruction for nurses
was often not on the same level. A political commissar complained that
his brigade had lost most of its *sanitet* cadres in battle, because "little
attention had been given to the military development of this personnel."[43]
As we shall see, the high fatality rate among females – fighters and nurses
alike – would serve as a pretext for their withdrawal from combat units
in the final stages of the war.

This, however, does not mean that the *partizanka*s were not brave and
dedicated as combatants. On the contrary, positive appraisals of their military conduct dominate the documents. "There are 95 female comrades in
our brigade, 80 of them are fighters," reported the deputy commissar of
a Slavonian brigade. "With some exceptions, they have performed excel-
lently in battles. They have charged at bunkers bravely and in the front
lines."[44] A report from a Serbian brigade underlined the admirable conduct of women during the marches and struggles.[45] "It is characteristic
that female comrades in our brigade held extraordinarily well during the
offensive," stated the deputy commissar of the 6th Bosnian Brigade, adding that "not a single woman fell behind" in the course of the movement.[46]
And some Montenegrin *partizanka*s, according to a party official, "surpassed their male comrades" in courage and endurance[47] (Figure 7).

Party propaganda put to good use such examples of women's bravery
and military prowess. The Partisan press portrayed the *partizanka* as a
heroine who excelled in the art of war, thus proving herself worthy of
equality with men. This "proving worthy" argument served to legitimize
both women's presence in the units and the party's egalitarian policies in
the eyes of the traditionally minded populace. The official line, emphasized whenever male fighters refused to accept females as their equals, was
that women had earned equality by proving their valor on the battlefield.

Traditional Beliefs and Hierarchies: Yet rooting out conservative
ideas was difficult. The party had to battle the prejudice and opposition of male Partisans to the prospect of women's transformation into

---

[43] AVII, NOR, IRP BIH 9/121–6, 125, Pom. polkom. XXI NOU Brigade CKKPJ-u, 12
August 1944.

[44] *Grada za historiju Narodnooslobodilačkog Pokreta u Slavoniji* (Slavonski Brod:
Historijski Institut Slavonije, 1966), vol. 5, doc. 141, p. 314.

[45] AVII, NOR, IRP SFRJ 1/744–747, 747, Pom. polkom XIX Sr. brigade CKKPJ-u, 17
December 1943.

[46] AVII, NOR, IRP SFRJ 1/466–71, 471, Zam. polkom. VI bosanske NOU brigade CK
KPJ-u, 19 January 1944.

[47] *Zbornik* 4. 9. doc. 19, p. 60.

FIGURE 7. A column of fighters, the 3rd Sandžak Proletarian Brigade, in the area of Prijepolje-Pljevlja-Bijelo Polje (Montenegro), 1943.
Courtesy of Muzej Istorije Jugoslavije.

warriors. Individual Partisan commands refused to admit a large number of women into their units.[48] Many saw female soldiers as a burden.[49] "Sectarianism" toward women – as rejection of female volunteers and discrimination against them were labeled in party jargon – persisted well after Tito's directive, even in CPY circles.[50] In a self-critical manner, committee members in Lika noted that communists had failed to capitalize on women's eagerness to fight. "Women's combat morale is higher than that of men," they wrote. "This we have poorly used."[51] Some men in the units questioned the wisdom of the policy of women's recruitment into combat units; others openly disapproved. A male party secretary of a company in Croatia, for instance, publicly declared in reference to the *partizanka*s,

[48] Bojović, *Žene Crne Gore,* p. 163, 178.

[49] *Zbornik* 1.6. doc. 54, p. 208.

[50] See, for example, AVII, NOR, IRP BiH 3/531–7, 536, Zapisnik, part. komitet IV KNOU divizije, 1 February 1943; AVII, NOR, IRP SFRJ NOB 1/598–601, 601, Politodjel 25. divizije CKKPJ-u, 15 October 1944.

[51] AVII, NOR, Muzej Like Gospić NOB 1/381–2, OKKPH za Liku Kotarskom KPH Mogorić, 9 May 1942.

"it would be best if all of 'that' was expelled from the company."[52] Of particular annoyance to the party were incidents in which male communists forbade their wives, sisters, mothers, daughters, or other female relations to enlist. Some men of influence intervened to have "their" women released from the units, even when doing so was against a woman's will. A company commander in Herzegovina, for example, used his authority and connections to have his sister withdrawn from a youth brigade.[53] In Croatia, men tried dissuading their female family members from enlisting with the pretext that "all kinds of things happened in the army."[54]

The CPY's declaration regarding incidents of this kind was worded in a manner that left little room for speculation about the seriousness of the issue. The main organ of the Central Committee, *Proleter,* featured an article warning those who opposed women's recruitment that such views were "reactionary and aberrant," and that they represented "the attitude of the fifth column." The mobilization of women, the article stressed, was "the assignment of the first order for all party organizations."[55] Similar language characterizes party directives. In units that were yet to begin accepting females, political commissars were instructed to work on ending the prejudice in an organized fashion prior to women's arrival. Holding "discussions about whether women are fit or not for combat units, whether it is necessary or not" is "unacceptable" – states one such directive – adding that it is military commanders' duty to abandon their "ugly opinions about the female fighter."[56]

The implementation of the party's diktat regarding women combatants on the local level was, however, not consonant with the diktat's serious tone. To my knowledge, this was a unique case that such grave terms as *reactionary, fifth column,* and *duty of the first order* were consistently used at the top with so few consequences on the ground. Male communists with "unsound attitudes" were reprimanded or punished only on occasion.[57] Ordinarily, men from the units were sent to conferences

---

[52] *Zbornik*, 9. 3, doc. 216, p. 903.
[53] AVII, NOR, IRP BIH 9/204–10, 209. Okr. kom. za S. Hercegovinu Obl.kom-u KPJ za Hercegovinu, 20 August 1944.
[54] AVII, NOR, Muzej Like Gospić NOB 1/564, Okr. Kom. KPH za Liku Kotarskom kom. za D. Lapac, 6 February 1945.
[55] "Važnost učešća žena u narodno-oslobodilačkoj borbi," *Proleter* 14–15, March–April 1942, 16.
[56] *Zbornik* 9.3, doc. 13, p. 53.
[57] For an example of a male communist who was punished for his "unsound attitude toward female comrades," see AVII, NOR, IRP BiH 3/827, Politodjel X KNOU brigade Oblasnom kom. KPJ za Bos. Krajinu, 20 June 1943.

and lectures on the importance of women's participation in the national liberation war.[58]

In addition to the resistance to female enlistment, the party had to deal with discrimination against women once they entered the army. The countless cases of discrimination recorded in internal party correspondence reveal how widespread and persistent traditional gender norms were in Yugoslav society. Typically, documents note that female Partisans were considered inferior, treated improperly, and "politically and militarily neglected (*zapostavljene*)."[59] "Male comrades do not approach female comrades correctly; they underestimate them or are cruel towards them," reads a report from a Croatian brigade.[60] Women "are neglected and not seen as equal fighters," states another.[61] The highest-ranking men were often responsible for such a state of affairs in the units. Military commanders reportedly made "the crudest mistakes concerning the female comrades' rights and authority."[62] Battalion commanders in the 12th Brigade in Bosnian Krajina, for example, were noted for their disrespect for the *partizanka*s, whom they used as their personal servants or assigned as cooks and horse keepers (*konjovoci*).[63]

CPY representatives in the troops sometimes made an effort to correct such attitudes and give women the attention they needed. In such cases when extra energies were dedicated to eradicating discriminatory practices and attitudes, significant improvement reportedly ensued.[64] Officials

---

[58] AVII, NOR, IRP BiH 10/105–7, Kom. SKOJ-a IX KNOU brig. Ob. Kom.-u SKOJ-a za B. Krajinu, 4 October 1943; AVII, NOR, IRP SFRJ NOR 1/197–201, 200, Zam. Politkoma V Vojvodjanske brigade CKKPJ-u, 15 February 1944, and others.

[59] See, for example, AJ, SKJ, 507 CKKPJ 1943/283, Politodjel XII KNOU brigade, Izveštaj za CKKPJ, 8 September 1943, also *Izvori* 13, 61–4; AVII, NOR, IRP BiH 9/188–91, 191, Brigadni komitet SKOJa IX Kraj. Brigade, Oblasnom kom.-u SKOJa za B. Krajinu, 18 August 1944; AVII, NOR, IRP BIH 10/592–3, 593, Pom. Politkom. VI Brigade Oblasnom kom.-u za B. Krajinu, 5 November 1944; AVII, NOR, IRPBIH 12/148–50, 149, Ob. Kom. za Ist. Bosnu pomocniku kom. XXI NOU Brigade, 4 January 1945, and others.

[60] *Zbornik*, 9. 3, doc. 216, p. 903.

[61] AVII, NOR, IRP BiH 10/105–7, 107. Kom. SKOJ-a IX KNOU brigade Oblasnom kom. SKOJ za B. Krajinu, 4 October 1944.

[62] AVII, NOR, IRP BiH 12/438–43, 439, Izveštaj Part. Rukovodilac V Korpusa NOVJ Ob. kom.-u za B. Krajinu, December 1944–January 45.

[63] AJ, SKJ, 507 CKKPJ 1943/283, Politodjel XII KNOU brigade, Izveštaj za CKKPJ, 8 September 1943; also *Izvori* 13, 61–4.

[64] A division Politodjel, for example, reports that the relationship to women, formerly sectarian, has improved since the party started paying attention to women. See AJ, SKJ 507, CKKPJ 1944/179, Politodjel XXVIII NOU Divizije CKKPJ-u, 12 May 1944; also *Izvori* 17, 286–97. Some conferences and lectures on women's role in the national liberation war also met with good results. AVII, NOR, IRP BiH 9/188–91, 191, Brigadni komitet SKOJa IX Kraj. Brigade, Oblasnom kom.-u SKOJa za B. Krajinu, 18 August 1944.

in several units felt confident enough to pronounce the problem solved.[65] The CPY's efforts, however, were neither uniform nor consistent, and the problem was never eliminated from the ranks. Indeed, internal reports kept noting instances of unsatisfactory treatment of women until the very end of the war.

Although all females in the units could experience negative attitudes or "neglect," it appears that women of the *sanitet* were exposed to dual discrimination. "Everyone used to lash out at the female nurses: the healthy and the sick, the wounded and the typhus-stricken and the recovered, and often the doctors and the leaders themselves," remembers the Partisan doctor Oskar Ginsberger.[66] The contribution of nurses, although crucial to the army, was not valued as much as that of combatants. For the most part, their place was in field hospitals, ambulances, or medical companies, and they would find themselves in combat to the extent that a wounded soldier needed treatment on the spot or had to be removed from the battle zone. Although the nurses in such circumstances frequently took part in the fighting, their primary duty was considered to be off the battlefield. Female nurses were also referred to as *partizanka*s, they wore the Partisan insignia and swore the same oath as soldiers, yet their status was inferior and their duty viewed as lesser[67] (Figure 8).

Part of the problem lay in the fact that, traditionally, the medical corps was considered a lesser, ancillary sector of an army. Whether staffed by men or women, the Partisan *sanitet* was often subject to "neglect" or disrespect, and its officials had to struggle for authority among the ranks. A report from Croatia voiced concerns over "the mocking attitude among Staff members" toward the higher-ranking *sanitet* officials (who were male).[68] The attitude among the rank and file was often not much better.[69] The medics, especially men, were labeled "slackers" and viewed as "inferior individuals" who avoided combat, even though they were

---

[65] On the successful "removal" of "incorrect opinions" about females as lesser soldiers, AJ, SKJ 507, CKKPJ 1943/379, Izveštaj Part. Komitet IV Divizije I Korpusa NOVJ CKKPJ-u, 3 December 1943; also *Izvori* 14, 394–406. See also AVII, NOR, IRP BiH 3/651–2, Politkom VI KNOU brigade Ob. Kom.-u za B. Krajinu, April 1943.

[66] Oskar Ginsberger in Stana Džakula Nidžović, *Žene borci NOR-a Sedme banijske udarne brigade*, 81.

[67] Bojović, *Žene Crne Gore*, 160.

[68] *Zbornik sanitetske* 3, doc. 40, pp. 76–9.

[69] Among the Partisans of the 12th Croatian Brigade, for instance, the medics were not seen or treated as "comrades cofighters" but rather as "gravediggers." *Zbornik sanitetske* 3, doc. 46, p. 115.

FIGURE 8. Savka Bursać, nurse of the 6th Krajina Division, bandaging a wounded soldier, Vučja Gora near Travnik, Herzegovina, January 1945.
Courtesy of Muzej Istorije Jugoslavije.

present in battle zones, where they fought and charged at enemy bunkers in addition to performing their medical duties.[70]

That women were assigned primarily to the medical corps did not help. In fact, the feminization of the *sanitet* seems to have led to its further devaluing. Newly recruited peasant *partizanka*s appointed to the *sanitet* – young, female, and often inexperienced – were not likely candidates for respect and authority in a Balkan army, even if it was a revolutionary one. Reports from the units ordinarily noted that medical personnel, consisting of young women, lacked the necessary authority among the men.[71] This want of deference toward female medics existed regardless of their actual performance on duty. "In spite of the excellent

[70] *Zbornik sanitetske* 3, doc. 104, pp. 203–4. As a remedy, the staff ordered that the medics who distinguished themselves in battles be publicly commended in front of all fighters.
[71] See, for example, AVII, NOR, IRP SFRJ 1/246–50, 250, Politodjel IV div. V korp. Izvestaj Obl. Kom.-u za B. Krajinu, prepis poslat CKKPJ-u, 29 February 1944.

conduct of [our] female comrades in battle and at work," wrote the *Politodjel* of the 11th Division, "the *sanitet* is not appreciated sufficiently."[72] And the medics in a Bosnian brigade were reportedly "young female comrades who perform[ed] their tasks with great élan," yet without being accorded much authority.[73] Besides, women of the *sanitet* often suffered neglect in political and military instruction, which hindered their chances for promotion in the ranks.[74] In sum, it appears that the already inferior standing of the *sanitet* in the army led to its feminization, which in turn undermined its status twice over.

Once the Partisans began admitting women as fighters, being assigned to any other job proved a major disappointment for young female recruits. A Slovenian *partizanka*, Albina Hočevar Mali, remembers her reaction when she discovered her first assignment was as a nurse: She was so frustrated she started to cry. A Serbian veteran, Danica Milosavljević, having spent six months as a nurse in the 1st Proletarian Brigade, decided to petition Tito personally for permission to become a fighter. His approval marked, as she recalls, "one of the greatest days of her life."[75]

Women's preference for combat over nursing led to occasional breaches of discipline, forcing the party to react. In Srem (Vojvodina), for instance, many female recruits reportedly "declined to perform the duties of nurses and demanded to be sent to the unit as fighters."[76] The problem was noticed even among the highly disciplined *partizanka*s in elite Partisan units: the proletarian brigades. "We have in the brigade close to 100 female comrades," complained the deputy commissar of the 2nd Proletarian Brigade in 1942, "all of whom want to be fighters and

---

[72] AJ, SKJ 507, CKKPJ 1944/731, Politodjel XI Divizije CKKPJ-u o stanju u V KNOU brigadi, 2 March 1944; also *Izvori* 16, 179.

[73] AVII, NOR, IRP BIH 10/93-7, 96, Pom. komesara XVII Majevičke NOU brigade Ob. Kom.-u za Ist. Bosnu, 3 October 1944.

[74] For reports on the lack of political work with women in the *sanitet* see: AJ, SKJ 507, CKKPJ 1944/116, Zamenik politkomesara VI Bosanke NOU Brigade CKKPJ-u, 28 March 1944; also *Izvori* 16, 418–28. AVII, NOR, IRP SFRJ 1/628-31, 630, Pol. kom. XXI NOU Brigade Ob. kom.-u za Ist. Bosnu i CKKPJ-u, 1 November 1944. For reports on poor military training of the *sanitet* personnel, see: AVII, NOR, IRP BIH 9/121-6, 125, Pom. polkom. XXI NOU Brigade CKKPJ-u, 12 August 1944. For documents reporting some improvement regarding the authority of the female nurses and the attention to their political education, see AJ, SKJ 507, CKKPJ 1944/179, p. 2, Politodjel XXVIII NOU Divizije CKKPJ-u, 12 May 1944, also *Izvori* 17, 286–97. AVII, NOR, IRP SFRJ 1/466-71, 470, Zam. polkom. VI bosanske NOU brigade CK KPJ-u, 19 January 1944.

[75] Jancar-Webster, *Women & Revolution*, 81, 87. On Milosavljević, see also Pantelić, *Partizanke kao gradanke*, 45.

[76] AVII, NOR, IA PK SKS Vojvodine NOB 2/561-2, OKKPJ Ist. Srem Okr. odboru AFŽ-a, 9 November 1943.

under no circumstances [*nikako*] agree to be nurses, and for that reason our *sanitet* suffers."[77] To prevent similar incidents, the party in Srem tried to confront the notion of medics' inferiority by educating new recruits about the female nurses' great responsibilities and importance for the war effort.[78] In order to popularize the Partisan nurse, the women's front initiated a campaign for collecting stories about the heroic deeds of female medics, which were then published in women's journals.[79] Such attempts, sporadic and unsystematic as they were, had little long-term effect, and nurses never acquired the recognition matching that of Partisan fighters.

"Sectarianism" toward females in general remained an unresolved issue within the CPY itself. One's combativeness, military discipline, and devotion to the struggle were the principal criteria for one's admission to the party from the troops, yet it appears that women were often held to different standards.[80] "Since our brigade was founded, we've admitted to the Party only one female comrade although many stand out in combat as real heroes," confessed CPY representatives in the 1st Dalmatian Brigade, echoing many similar complaints and self-criticisms in party documents.[81]

The oft-cited "neglect" of women in the units meant that they received less instruction in military and political matters and were thus less likely to advance.[82] It also meant that they were assigned to do the most tedious, often physically strenuous, and least rewarded tasks such as fetching water, doing the laundry, cooking, cleaning, and the like. Finally, it meant that females were often the last in line to receive arms, clothing, shoes, and other provisions. Shortages of clothes and shoes proved perennial problems in the units, with dire consequences in cold weather, as captured uniforms, boots, rifles, and other material provided the main source of Partisan armament and supply.[83] "For a long time, men saw

---

[77] *Zbornik* 9.2. doc. 33, p. 218.
[78] AVII, NOR, IA PK SKS Vojvodine NOB 2/561–2, OKKPJ Ist. Srem Okr. odboru AFŽ-a, 9 November 1943.
[79] *Zbornik sanitetske* 3, doc. 78, pp. 161–2.
[80] For the party's admission criteria in the army, see, for example, *Zbornik* 9.2, doc. 77, p. 389.
[81] *Zbornik* 9. 2, doc. 83, p. 416. Similarly, of more than 120 women in another Dalmatian brigade only 7 were accepted into the party, reported the brigade's deputy commissar, attributing this poor representation to "neglect" and promising to break the pattern. AVII, NOR, IPR SFRJ 1/157–61, Zam. pol.kom-a II Dalmatinske NOU Brigade CKKPJ-u, 6 February 1944.
[82] Indeed, women did not rise through the ranks in large numbers to hold commanding positions. For a discussion of military rank attained by women, see Lydia Sklevicky, *Konji, Žene, Ratovi*; see also Jancar-Webster, *Women & Revolution*, 90–4.
[83] See AVII, NOR, IRP BIH 10/457–8, Pom. pol. kom. XX Brigade Ob. kom. u za Ist. Bosnu, 25 October 1944; AJ, SKJ 507, CKKPJ 1943/379, Div. Kom. IV divizije I Proleterskog

to it that their needs for arms and clothes were met first," remembers the *partizanka* Kosa Šoć, "and we went in whatever rags we had" [*a mi smo dronjale kako bilo*]. Only upon direct intervention from above were such practices discontinued. In Šoć's case, it was reportedly Tito himself who noticed that women in her unit lacked adequate clothing and ordered that, after the next battle, captured enemy uniforms be allocated to them.[84]

Not all *partizanka*s, however, could boast of Tito's intervention. The practice of overlooking women when it came to the distribution of provisions would continue in some units until the final months of the war. In a particularly dramatic case that took place in the 21st Brigade during the winter of 1944/45, the command's failure to provide female volunteers with the basic garments that would protect them from exposure resulted in several instances of women's desertion (otherwise extremely rare).[85] The bleakness of women's position in the units where they suffered "neglect" is best summed up in the following report:

> Female comrades in the brigade are in a subordinate position ... they are viewed as an unnecessary burden. Thus it happens that they are used for "auxiliary women's tasks" such as laundering, cooking, etc, that they are as a rule the worst dressed, that little is done to prevent their being physically overtaxed, etc. Such attitude originates with the leaders and has spread among the fighters.... Due to such attitude, male fighters and even the female comrades themselves have adopted a flawed opinion about women in general. This has turned our female comrades passive, so that they do not participate in political life, and this is, ultimately, the reason why we have a relatively small percentage of women in the Party.[86]

"Women's" Work: The persistence of traditional notions about gender roles was perhaps nowhere more obvious than in the mundane matters involving daily chores in the units. The official party position was that of equal participation in all tasks by both sexes, but in almost all units it was expected that women, albeit fighters, also perform their traditional chores: cooking, laundering, washing dishes, fetching water, sewing,

Korpusa NOVJ CKKPJ-u, 3 December 1943, also *Izvori* 14, 394–406, and others. The former document, reporting from the XX Brigade, notes that nearly 50 percent of fighters were practically barefoot, and about 65 percent poorly clothed.

[84] Kosa Šoć in Ljiljana Bulatović, *Bila jednom četa devojačka* (Beograd: Nova knjiga, 1985), 36.

[85] AVII, NOR, IRP BiH 12/148–50, 149, Obl. Kom. za Ist. Bosnu pomocniku komesara XXI NOU Brigade, 4 January 1945.

[86] AVII, NOR, IRP BiH 6/469–73, 471–2, Politodjel IV div. V korp. Izvestaj Obl. Kom.-u za B. Krajinu, prepis poslat CKKPJ-u, 29 February 1944. Also AVII, NOR, IRP SFRJ 1/246–50, 248.

mending, and cleaning. In the initial Partisan bands with little regulation from above, this division of labor seems to have been the result of
inertia: The few women present in the units simply resumed their prewar tasks. Rava Janković, at first the only woman in her company (in
the Vareš Battalion, Bosnia) early in 1942, served as both a nurse and a
fighter, and she alone did the laundry, hand washing it in a creek, for all
the men of her unit.[87] Duja Marić-Vujanović, although a platoon commander, sewed and washed the clothes of her fighters while they rested.[88]

Most *partizanka*s assumed those duties with few complaints, often
voluntarily. Mitra Mitrović writes that even the female party leaders, herself included, took it upon themselves to do domestic chores early on
in the war. She provides an interesting "theoretical" reason behind their
decision:

Female comrades alternate on duty, cleaning, setting the fire, and washing the
dishes. We exempt male comrades who live with us from such tasks, without res-
ervations and discussions about "equality." ... We explain our tenacity in a "theoretical" way: these domestic chores are a burden for us and for women in general,
and there is no reason to introduce male comrades to such ungrateful duties, since
some day – and we are fighting for that, too – these duties will disappear for us
women as well. Male comrades are apparently happy with our theory.[89]

But for the majority of Partisans, male or female, this division of labor
appeared only natural and no grand theory was necessary to justify it.
Dissenting voices were few. Peasant girls – who constituted the majority
of females in the units – were accustomed both to serving men and to
performing hard physical labor. For them, there was nothing extraordinary in the expectation that women's work should remain their domain.

It is perhaps more surprising to see the same willingness among the
urban, upper-class female recruits, unaccustomed to household tasks,
let alone manual labor. Major William Jones, a British officer who spent
a year with the Partisans, remembers that women arriving at a Partisan
camp in Slovenia from homes in the occupied towns started their new
life as *partizanka*s in the kitchen. His observations are reserved for those
exceptional, privileged women belonging to professional and intellectual
elites, who had before the war lived in relative luxury, usually surrounded
by maids or servants. "For the first few days, still wearing her skirt, she

---

[87] Recollections of Ljilja Prlja, in Beoković, *Žene heroji*, p. 76.
[88] Duja Marić-Vujanović, "Koliko li je tvoje srce ... ," in Hurem, *Žene Bosne i Hercegovine*, 602.
[89] Mitrović, *Ratno putovanje*, 90–1.

would be excited and happy at meeting old friends and hearing of others who were believed to be still alive," Jones describes the guerrilla debut of a typical urban elite woman:

It was not long before she felt the urge to do something, and, remarkable as it may seem, she usually began in the kitchen! One woman, the wife of a prominent lawyer, had been in the camp for a few days when we saw her collecting loads of firewood.... And the wife of a very well-known artist made herself responsible for cleaning the kitchen, and eventually took over the full duties of that department.... They would all wash-up, sweep the messroom and set the table, obviously strange to it all, yet with a willing spirit and a sense of humour ... so, in a very short time, the new arrival would be seen wearing a woolen shirt and heavy alpine boots in place of her fine shoes.... And within a few weeks she had become thoroughly acclimatized and acquired a completely new appreciation of life. The possession of a belt and pistol set the seal of her pride and satisfaction in being a Partisana.[90]

Jones's sympathetic account, however accurate and insightful, concerns but a tiny minority of *partizanka*s and overlooks a less amiable side of the story. For most female fighters, the persistence of "women's tasks" in the units meant taking on a double burden in the already strenuous conditions of guerrilla warfare. "To be a woman in the Partisans was very difficult in the beginning," recalls one of the few *partizanka*s who dissented:

I'd like that to be known. It was most difficult, I believe, in the Montenegrin units.... [Men] treated us as their laundry-women, knitters, cooks. Many female comrades then bore too heavy a burden. I could not: you go side by side with them in battle, and when the shooting stops you have to do the so-called women's work! I couldn't.[91]

The CPY condemned the practice of ordering women to do the chores as petit bourgeois, but this had little effect on the local level. Complaints about its perseverance were voiced in internal communiqués throughout the war. As late as August 1944, for instance, the communist youth of a Krajina brigade noted that male fighters expected their "female comrades to be as in old Yugoslavia, only for laundering and mending."[92] In some cases officials intervened to correct this attitude.[93] But just as often they

---

[90] William Jones, *Twelve Months with Tito's Partisans* (Bedford: Bedford Books, 1946), 83.

[91] Kosa Šoć in Bulatović, *Bila jednom*, 36. For similar veteran testimonies on women's double burden, see Draginja Višekruna-Lukač, "Ženska omladina u IV krajiškoj udarnoj brigadi," in Hurem, *Žene Bosne i Hercegovine*, 473–4.

[92] AVII, NOR, IRP BiH 9/188–91, 191, Brigadni kom. SKOJa IX Kraj. Brigade Ob. kom.-u SKOJa za B. Krajinu, 18 August 1944.

[93] A directive of a Partisan staff in Serbia, for example, insists on equality between female and male fighters: "Female comrades on military duty must not be given some additional

reinforced it. A directive of the Partisan staff of the 3rd operative zone (in Slavonija) insisted that the *partizanka*s of the medical units "could and should" do the laundry and iron the clothes for all fighters in the units.[94] In a similar vein, the staff of a Croatian division ordered the mending of fighters' clothes, underwear, and shoes and put "female comrades from combat and medical units" in charge of the task.[95]

It is worth noting that the Partisans viewed "women's" tasks with contempt. These chores were dull, repetitive, at times physically taxing; they provided little fulfillment and guaranteed neither high rank nor honors to those in charge of them. Male Partisan fighters, especially the experienced ones, were generally spared such duties. Yet most women, even the Partisan heroines who had long proven themselves "worthy" in battle, such as the legendary Marija Bursać, could expect to find themselves assigned to such jobs. According to her friend, Bursać felt offended and neglected when she was temporarily withdrawn from combat and appointed as a cook at a brigade's staff.[96] Seen as auxiliary and inferior, "women's work" had clear status implications.

But more than status was at stake regarding the division of tasks into men's and women's. Party documents and personal narratives reveal the prevalence of a normative view of the two genders, whose characteristics and roles presumably originated in nature. For many Partisans, proper adherence to traditionally prescribed gender roles had as much to do with identity as it did with social hierarchy. A female fighter put in charge of a women's task might have felt demoted (as Bursać did), but the stigma associated with "women's work" was much greater if it involved crossing gender boundaries. Being assigned to a women's task was accompanied with a sense of humiliation and debasement for men, who saw it not only as an inferior duty but also as an outright attack on their masculinity. The humiliation was particularly great if a man was given such an assignment in the presence of women who could have been employed instead. A communiqué that the CPY committee for Banat (Vojvodina) sent to all party forums in the region upon its liberation illustrates this well. The Banat committee reproached lower party officials for their poor treatment of ethnic Romanians and Hungarians in the liberated

auxiliary tasks such as laundering, cooking, mending, etc." *Zbornik* 1.7. doc. 154, p. 361. See also *Zbornik* 9. 1, doc. 129, p. 492.

[94] *Grada za historiju*, vol. 4., doc. 58, pp. 132–3. Also in *Zbornik sanitetske 3*, doc. 21, p. 49.

[95] *Zbornik sanitetske 3*, doc. 159, pp. 287–8.

[96] Pero M. Pilipović, in Beoković, *Žene heroji*, p. 32.

territories. "In some places," the directive states, "these peoples were not even treated as citizens with equal rights." Most worrisome, in the minds of committee members, was that the Partisan authorities assigned Romanian and Hungarian males to peel potatoes, "even though there were enough available female comrades around."[97] The committee saw this assignment as an abominable act of humiliation for men of ethnic minorities. For "female comrades," in contrast, it was a normal task.

In the later stages of the war, as the organization of the rear improved and Partisan guerrillas began resembling a regular army, local AFW councils and certain specialized sections in the units (such as the *sanitet*) were put in charge of some of the chores. The way that the division of labor in the movement was thus institutionalized – by using the women's organization in the rear or feminized sectors of the army for laundry, cleaning, ironing, and the like – only reinforced the traditional view of these jobs as specifically *women's*.

In sum, judging by the way that women's integration into the army proceeded, the CPY's egalitarian drive was remarkable in its aspiration, but not in its realization. Official proclamations pertaining to the equality of the sexes translated into policies only partially; moreover, these policies' implementation was beset with difficulties on the ground. Throughout the war, gender issues ranked low on the party leadership's agenda. Problems and obstacles to women's integration were recognized as such, yet attempts to solve them lacked the necessary vigor and consistency. It is obvious that, when it comes to daily life in the units, the party found it easier to accommodate than to challenge traditional beliefs and practices. The persistence of the customary sexual division of labor confirms that some old ideas about gender characteristics and duties survived, almost intact, in the revolutionary army. Most important, the belief that women's "natural" place was not in combat remained prevalent on all levels, including CPY circles. The leadership itself regarded women's presence in the units as temporary and reserved for the extraordinary conditions of the current crisis. As we shall see later, the process of women's elimination from combat was initiated even before the war was over. But before turning to the policy of the *partizanka*s' withdrawal from the ranks, we will take a look at cases when women's new role as combatants clashed most drastically with their traditional role par excellence: the cases of young mothers in the army.

---

[97] AVII, NOR, IA PK SKS Vojvodine NOB 2/709–11, OK KPJ Južni Banat svim sreskim komitetima za J. Banat, 27 November 1944.

"THE REVOLUTION HAS NO TIME FOR MOTHERHOOD"

Despite short interludes of relaxation and entertainment, life in the Partisan units was extremely arduous. It was characterized by constant danger, lethal battles, exhausting marches, scarcity of food and medicines, sleepless nights, exposure to brutal winter and hot summer weather, and periodic epidemics of typhus and other contagious diseases. Although such conditions affected the Partisans of both sexes, some experiences were gender specific. Thanks to the harshness of guerrilla lifestyle, many women ceased to menstruate – temporarily or permanently – or suffered from other difficulties related to the monthly cycle. Reporting that his brigade's medical company was cut in half by exhaustion and illness, a *sanitet* official from Croatia thus explained the situation: "There is a large number of women in the medical company, and it appears that most of them do not menstruate, i.e., they lose their period, and after that follows fever and inability to march any further."[98] It is reasonable to assume that, much like women elsewhere who found themselves in extreme conditions during the war, many female Partisans feared that the war might have affected their ability to bear children in the future.[99]

What of the *partizanka*s who had young children during the war? Although most females volunteering for the Partisans were young and single, some were married and some already had children or became pregnant after the war began. Very little information exists on the rank-and-file women who gave birth. Rare cases mentioned in CPY correspondence indicate that, as in the Soviet Union, a new mother would be sent to the rear and given a leave of several months.[100] An early communiqué, for instance, referring to a person who trained Partisan girls in radiotelegraphy, reads: "This woman is a member, but of a purely antiparty type. She should be sent in a nice manner to Slovenia, and there, with some excuse, given leave of two or three months, because she gave birth now."[101] Party documents, however, provide little evidence to confirm that this

---

[98] *Zbornik sanitetske* 3, doc. 41, pp. 80–1.

[99] Scholars have found that worry about potential infertility was a widespread phenomenon during the war. For such concerns among the Soviet airwomen, see Pennington, *Wings, Women, and War*, 157. For women in the Holocaust, see Marlene Heinemann, *Gender and Destiny: Women Writers and the Holocaust* (Westport: Greenwood Press, 1986), 18.

[100] For Soviet policy, see Anne Noggle, *A Dance with Death: Soviet Airwomen in World War II* (College Station: Texas A&M University Press, 1994), 187.

[101] *Zbornik* 2. 2, doc. 14, p. 56, n. 11. In this particular case, it seems that there were other reasons for the woman's transfer, and that the birth of the baby proved convenient. The woman in question, Urska Zatler, was killed in Slovenia in 1943 as a fighter.

was the official policy on the matter, or that an official policy existed at all. But personal narratives and veteran biographies suggest that most *partizanka*s – especially if party members – had to give up motherhood until the war was won. References to women who left behind, or were separated from, their children in order to be able to continue fighting abound in participant reminiscences and postwar literature, where their stories are often told with a particular pathos. As notable as these tragic stories is the fact that the choices their heroines had made were acknowledged, even glorified, in the postwar master narrative of female courage.

Female communists, who had gained experience in underground activities during the interwar period, were accustomed to the idea that their party work took precedence over everything, including their personal and family lives. Some of them made the decision to give up mothering in the name of the future revolution even before the war began. A typical example is the Serbian professional revolutionary Cana Babović, who, on the Central Committee's recommendation in 1933, sent her three-year-old son to a children's home in the USSR so that she could fully dedicate herself to her revolutionary duties. Babović reclaimed the boy only after Serbia's liberation in 1944.[102]

If the party required that its female members be ready to suspend their roles as mothers during their prewar activism, the outbreak of the war and the launching of the revolution only reinforced that requirement. After the occupation, some underground activists (*ilegalka*s) remained in the occupied territories and took on new tasks, such as preparing sabotage actions and serving as couriers. Those among them who gave birth during the war were sometimes, for reasons of security and conspiracy, separated from their children. Such was the case of Radmila Trifunović, a brave and respected *ilegalka*, who, as a Serbian communist leader remembers, "had to be separated from her daughter Stojanka Ankica as soon as she was born."[103] The *ilegalka* Ivanka Muačević-Nikoliš shared Trifunović's predicament. Expecting a child when the war started, she worked as a courier and distributed communist propaganda even late in her pregnancy. She was arrested in the fall of 1941 and kept in a penitentiary hospice in Belgrade, where she gave birth. After a spectacular rescue mission had been organized by her comrades, she and her child were liberated but were forced to part. Her newborn was given to a woman who had a baby herself, while the party sent the mother from Serbia with

---

[102] For more on personal life and Babović's case, see Chapter 4.
[103] See Moma Marković, *Rat i Revolucija: Sećanja, 1941–1945* (Beograd: BIGZ, 1987), 29.

an assignment to Zagreb, where she was captured again and killed. The biography of the national heroine Dragica Končar is tragic in a strikingly similar way. Končar, who also worked underground, gave birth under an assumed name in a Zagreb hospital in April 1942. Upon leaving the maternity ward she left her son in the care of some relatives and resumed her clandestine duties. Only a couple of months later, in the summer of 1942, she was arrested and executed in a Ustasha prison.[104]

The necessity to choose between being a mother and being a soldier of the revolution was felt even more acutely by females in the Partisan units than it was by the *ilegalka*s. Whereas some *ilegalka*s could and did stay together with their babies while continuing their covert work, the *partizanka*s did not have that option: Combat units were simply no place for children. Most young mothers had decided to leave their babies behind with relatives or friends prior to enlisting. In his vivid description of Tito's entourage, Fitzroy Maclean tells the story of Olga, one of the marshal's personal secretaries. "Tall and well-built, in her black breeches and boots, with a pistol hanging at her belt, speaking perfect English," Olga seems to have been Maclean's favorite. A daughter of a minister in the royal Yugoslav government, she received her education in a finishing school in London. Despite her background and upbringing, she joined the illegal Communist Party upon returning to prewar Yugoslavia and spent some time in prison for her activism. "Now, for two years," writes Maclean, obviously impressed, "she had hidden in the woods and tramped the hills, had been bombed and machine-gunned, an outlaw, a rebel, a revolutionary, a Partisan." There was, however, a source of anguish in Olga's adventurous life:

Somehow one never thought of her as being married, but she had a husband who was a Bosnian Moslem and a baby that she had left behind when she joined the Partisans. Now the baby – a little girl – was in Mostar, a German garrison town down towards the coast, at the mercy of the Gestapo and of frequent R.A.F. bombings. She wondered if she would ever see her again. Once a photograph was smuggled out by an agent who had been working underground in Mostar for the Partisans, a tiny, blurred snapshot, which, as Vlatko Velebit said, made the child look like a tadpole. But Olga was delighted. At least her baby had been alive a week ago.[105]

[104] Bosa Cvetić et al., ed., *Žene Srbije u NOB* (Beograd: Nolit, 1975), 125, 137. Šoljan, *Žene Hrvatske*, vol. 1, 121–2.

[105] Fitzroy Maclean, *Eastern Approaches* (London: Cape, 1950), 328. Maclean does not provide her full name, but it is most likely that the *partizanka* in question is Olga Ninčić Humo, who served at the Supreme Staff as Tito's translator at the time of Maclean's visit.

The incompatibility between mothering and fighting was perhaps nowhere more painfully apparent than for a woman who found herself in the troops together with her young child, only to discover that she would have to give it up. When she joined a Partisan column in retreat from the village where she had worked underground, Zaga Ilić-Stjepanović took her little daughter, Dana, along. But after a lengthy march through the snow, under incessant enemy fire, she realized that the child could not survive in these conditions. She decided to send Dana to her relatives in the liberated territory. The girl died of exposure on the way. In the recollections of her Partisan friend, the mother's parting with her only child is described in terms of her admirable communist self-deprivation: "As for all communists, for Zaga the struggle had priority over the home, family, and children. This was a moment when tears poured over her cheeks.... But Zaga's human and communist consciousness was high. She endured although it was not easy." The mother herself fell sick and died shortly thereafter.[106]

Among all the tragic and heroic tales of motherhood, war, and sacrifice that permeate veteran narratives, Đina Vrbica's stands apart for its deep poignancy. Vrbica, a prewar communist, AFW leader, and party activist posthumously proclaimed a national hero, learned that she was pregnant shortly after her Partisan husband had been killed in battle. Despite the party's preference for abortion, she decided to keep the child. Her baby girl was born in unbelievably harsh conditions: Vrbica delivered in the Partisan hospital in Goransko in June 1942, literally under enemy fire. Immediately after the delivery, she and the baby had to join the units on a lengthy march through the mountains. Vrbica's comrades were surprised that she survived. A woman from the brigade remembers:

The enemy encircled us.... Under pressure, our units were retreating ... during the retreat, a love child was born. We needed to gather all strength possible in order to have our units penetrate towards Bosnia. Đina was a fighter: a rifle in one arm, and now, a newborn baby in the other. Silence was necessary, not a sound to be heard, because we needed to outflank the enemy. But the child cried.... The child in her arms, now, in the middle of the battle, on the front, was superfluous and incomprehensible to the fighters' notions. Had not several of them told her to leave it?[107]

When they reached the mountain, it was decided: The baby could not be kept alive. The *partizanka* Nada Jovović received orders to convince

---

[106] Draga Lađević, "Učiteljica iz sela Blatnice," in Hurem, *Žene Bosne*, 540–1.
[107] Lidija Jovanović, in Beoković, *Žene heroji*, 463.

Vrbica that the child had to be liquidated. The execution itself was also to be performed by Jovović, of all people: by a woman, the mother's best friend. After a painful conversation, Vrbica agreed and gave up her baby girl. Yet Jovović could not find the strength to do the assignment and soon returned the baby to the mother. Only a few days later, though, Vrbica had to leave the child with some unknown people in a village her unit was passing by, thus giving her up for the second time. That day, Mitra Mitrović noted in her journal: "Đina left her child. In a cottage at Vučevo, with some people. She will die of sorrow before the child does, I fear. Now she cries alone somewhere. None of us has the time now to cry with her."[108] Mitrović's words were prophetic. Until her death, Vrbica hoped to return and find her baby girl. In 1943, she was finally permitted to transfer to the units that were advancing to the region in Montenegro where her child had been left. But her hopes were in vain. She was killed in a battle by the river Blatnica in May 1943.[109]

The examples discussed are not isolated. In Partisan narratives and Yugoslav literature of the communist era, one can find numerous references to women who gave birth during the battles and exhausting marches; to women whose children succumbed to hunger, exposure, and disease; and to women who had to leave their babies with relatives, friends, or villagers they did not know. For most of these Partisan mothers, the necessity to leave their children behind was dictated primarily by the conditions of guerrilla warfare or underground work. Keeping a child alive and healthy through battles and marches was almost impossible. Besides, the presence of a baby was often as dangerous for everyone in the unit as it was for the child itself. But these conditions were not always the key factor in a woman's decision to part with her child. One should not disregard the party's expectations (in some cases, the party's directives). For many female communists and their peers in the CPY, abandoning revolutionary duties in order to stay together with the child was never an option. Prewar members, in particular, had to set an example and demonstrate an absolute dedication to the party. The voices of these women themselves are, however, largely missing from the sources. Many perished in the war. With rare exceptions, the surviving mothers left no written account of their experiences; their stories were mostly told by others.[110]

---

[108] Mitrović, *Ratno putovanje*, 112.

[109] Based on Nada Jovović's recollection, in Beoković, *Žene heroji*, 464–71.

[110] Among the exceptions is the Partisan doctor Saša Božović, who left a moving account of her daughter's death. See Saša Božović, *Tebi, moja Dolores* (Beograd: 4. jul, 1981). See also Eta Najfeld's narrative in Milinović and Petakov, eds., *Partizanke*, 47–50.

In view of the CPY's postwar emphasis on motherhood, one may wonder why the stories of the *partizanka*s giving up their children had such a prominent place in the master narrative of the National Liberation Struggle. Even such unflattering details as potential infanticide in Vrbica's case were not masked. The answer lies in the interpretative framework within which these stories were placed. The personal drama of each of these women was represented in participant reminiscences in terms of one's voluntary sacrifice for the higher cause, thus fitting well the official interpretation of the Partisan struggle. The essence of the official version is well captured in the following passage from the Yugoslav literature of the communist era:

Women fighters and activists of the national liberation movement understood that for all the brightness and joy that would emerge with the future victory, in the better tomorrow, one has to sacrifice today's individual wishes; that one should want only that which is in the interest of the people as a whole. The Revolution has no time for individuals, for kindness, for love, for motherhood. Fighting for all that, it [the revolution] demands asceticism and deprivation. Women of Yugoslavia learned this wartime truth and were its faithful followers … in a quiet, proud sorrow for everything that the homeland went through, their cries for their newborn babies turned into silence.[111]

It is worth stressing that cases like Vrbica's symbolize not only individual heroism and self-abnegation but also gender specific martyrdom. In the traditional patriarchal culture, the position of a mother was the most important and prestigious domain of women's authority. Motherhood was considered a woman's primary social role and the most cherished part of her life. For a woman, thus, the ultimate sacrifice was that of her giving up her child. Young Partisan mothers who had put motherhood on hold during the war were recognized – even glorified – in the postwar communist literature because their willingness to make that ultimate sacrifice served as the definitive proof of the justice of the Partisan cause.

WITHDRAWAL OF THE *PARTIZANKA*

In the final year of the war, the transformation of Partisan guerrillas into a regular army accelerated. A parallel, though less conspicuous, process entailed women's withdrawal from the front lines. In 1944 and 1945, two general trends of gender redistribution in the military were under way: First, some commands began transferring female fighters from

---

[111] Kovačević, *Borbeni put*, 26.

combat to auxiliary units and political or administrative positions in the army; second, the *sanitet* authorities increasingly reassigned female medics from medical units at the front lines to hospitals in the rear. Unlike in the Spanish Civil War, when the *milicianas* left the war fronts shortly after the republican government had ordered women's removal from combat in 1936, women's withdrawal in Yugoslavia was gradual and intermittent, and in most units females remained active until the liberation. Nevertheless, the process of women's exclusion from combat and, ultimately, from the postwar Yugoslav military was already set in motion during the war.

Officials in the Montenegrin brigades were once again the first to broach the issue. Already in early 1943, the Politodjel of the 4th Proletarian Brigade proposed that experienced female fighters should be removed from combat units and prepared for political functions in the rear.[112] This suggestion could not be put into practice for much of that year, since the brigades were almost permanently engaged and suffered great casualties during the two most lethal enemy offensives against the Partisans: the fourth and the fifth ones (Operation Weiss, famous for the Neretva battle; and Operation Schwartz also known for its decisive battle at the Sutjeska River, respectively). But beginning with the summer of 1943, the *partizanka*s were progressively withdrawn from combat and sent to political courses or transferred to work in the *sanitet*, in the kitchens, and in the administrative and agitprop sections attached to Partisan staffs; in mid-August 1943, the 4th Proletarian Brigade had no female fighters left.[113]

The decision to exclude the Montenegrin *partizanka*s from combat duty was reportedly made "in view of their already small numbers and their [great] value."[114] Their transfer to new positions was supposed to ensure that the remaining experienced and devoted female cadres would survive the war. The loss of life among the old communist cadres – male and female alike – was indeed great. Of the twelve thousand CPY members in mid-1941, only three thousand survived the war. The Weiss and Schwartz offensives decimated some of the core units of the Partisan army; the 5th Montenegrin Brigade alone lost half of its manpower at Sutjeska, and the 4th did not fare much better. After the Sutjeska carnage, the brigades' cadre politics aimed at keeping veteran communists and

---

[112] Izveštaj Politodjela IV Crnogorske brigade CKKPJ-u, 16 January 1943, as cited in Bojović, *Žene Crne Gore*, 183.
[113] *Zbornik* 9.4, doc. 26, p. 133; Bojović, *Žene Crne Gore*, 183-4.
[114] *Zbornik* 9.4, doc. 26, p. 133.

distinguished fighters of both sexes safe. But there was a gender aspect of the withdrawal that cannot be explained away as concern for the lives of the best cadres: The Montenegrin leadership resolved shortly not only to remove all *partizanka*s from combat but also to stop recruiting females as fighters altogether. "Our corps has come to the decision to accept as few women in the army as possible," announced Montenegro's party leadership in January 1944.[115] Remarkably, the CPY Central Committee disagreed with the Montenegrins at the time. In February, in a message that voiced its objections to a series of their policies, the Central Committee insisted that the withdrawal of women was "a major error," to be corrected by keeping female veterans in the units as well as by recruiting new female fighters.[116]

Yet a similar redeployment process started the following winter. It affected female medics in particular, as the *sanitet* officials began withdrawing nurses from operative units and sending them to Partisan hospitals or reassigning them to administrative and political jobs. The official explanation accompanying the transfer of female nurses was the same as that for the Montenegrin fighters a year earlier: their high casualty rate. "Our experiences thus far have taught us that female company nurses frequently perish [in battle]," read a September 1944 directive of a division staff in Croatia. "Since they are our old comrades we have to try to spare them." The directive ordered that newly recruited men from the ranks of the Croatian Home Guards, who had served as medics there, replace the Partisan women.[117] After a brief period of instruction that the *partizanka*s were required to provide for their male substitutes, they were transferred to the rear.

Although female nurses remained active in many units until the country's liberation, the preparations for their removal began almost everywhere during the war. The party in a Herzegovina division, for instance, reported in January 1945 that steps were being taken to "gradually involve men" in the *sanitet*.[118] The transition did not always go smoothly, especially if there were no trained male Partisans available to replace the

---

[115] AVII, NOR, IRP SFRJ 1/5–16, 14, PK KPJ za Crnu Goru i Boku (Blažo Jovanović) CKKPJ-u, 1 January 1944.

[116] *Zbornik* 2.12, doc. 27, p. 80.

[117] *Zbornik sanitetske* 3, doc. 276, pp. 516–17. Men from the Croatian Home Guards joined the Partisans in great numbers after Tito's offer of amnesty in the summer of 1944.

[118] AVII, NOR, IRP SFRJ 1/820–4, 826–7, Sekretar komiteta XXIX Herc. Divizije CKKPJ-u, 17 January 1945.

*partizanka*s. "Our *sanitet* is deficient" since most "female comrades left for hospitals," admitted the leadership of a Krajina brigade, adding that organizing medical courses for men had become an urgent issue.[119]

The process of women's withdrawal – incomplete, uneven, and inconspicuous as it was in the turbulent preliberation period – met with little organized resistance by *partizanka*s. There is no doubt, though, that many females would have preferred to stay on the front lines. The Montenegrins noted that the policy caused a great deal of "confusion and worry" among their female fighters: "We have been explaining to women that they should be nurses and that they should form labor units in the rear, but that is insufficient to them…. they still want that at least a percentage of them [be allowed ţo] participate in combat."[120] There were also individual acts of defiance: Some women returned to the troops on their own in order to take part in the final operations in 1945. "Female comrades were sent to us from the units, but many of them escaped back" to the front, complained the commissar of the new hospital center in Sombor (Vojvodina), "for they prefer being there to working in the hospital"[121] (Figure 9).

Female Partisans were not demobilized immediately – in the last year of the war, the party still needed women's military service. In fact, campaigns for their enlistment intensified. The Partisans now systematically recruited females for medical, administrative, and technical positions, because the enlargement of their army was accompanied by an increased need for auxiliary service personnel. Female medics were in particularly great demand once the general conscription of men took effect; as military hospitals mushroomed in the newly liberated regions so did announcements inviting women to sign up as hospital personnel.[122] In February 1945, the Lika committee launched a broad campaign enlisting women for service on "various duties outside combat squadrons" – as telephone operators, cooks, couriers, ciphers – in order to release as many men as possible for combat in the final operations for the country's liberation.[123]

---

[119] AVII, NOR, IRP BiH 12/617–18, Izveštaj VII Kr. NOU Brigada Ob. kom.-u KPJ za B. Krajinu, January 1945.

[120] AVII, NOR, IRP SFRJ 1/5–16, 14, PK KPJ za Crnu Goru i Boku (Blažo Jovanović) CKKPJ-u, 1 January 1944.

[121] AJ, SKJ 507, CKKPJ 1945/46, Polkom Somborskog bolničkog centra CKKPJ-u, 14 February 1945; also *Izvori* 22, doc. 164.

[122] AVII, NOR, IA PK SKS Vojvodine NOB 2/37, Komanda mesta Zemun Mesnom NOO Ugrinovci, 10 November 1944, is a good example.

[123] AVII, NOR, Muzej Like Gospić NOB 1/564, Okr. kom KPH za Liku Kotarskom Kom. Donji Lapac, 6 February 1945.

FIGURE 9. A Partisan nurse tending a fighter of the 6th Lika Division at the Srem/ Srijem (Syrmian) front, 1945.
Courtesy of Muzej Istorije Jugoslavije.

There is no doubt, however, that the CPY planned to oust women from the postwar military altogether. The party's decision, made during the war, to ban females from enrolling in the future military academy suggests that it saw women's presence in the army as provisional.[124]

In assessing the reasons behind the party's decisions to begin withdrawing women from the front and ultimately exclude them from military service, the international context needs to be taken into account. As Reina Pennington notes, demobilization of women once the emergency conditions of war ended was a common phenomenon in the twentieth century. Servicewomen of practically all belligerents of World War II were discharged or banned from combat duty when the crisis ended. The United States passed laws excluding women from combat in 1948, although American females did not even participate as soldiers during the war. The Soviets, who were seemingly willing to dismantle gender boundaries by employing women in military units on a much larger scale than other countries and in such nontraditional roles as combat pilots and snipers, moved to eliminate them from the service as soon as the war was won.[125]

The Soviet case is particularly relevant for our discussion here, since during the war the CPY faithfully waited for directives from Moscow and, whenever possible, modeled its policies on the Soviet example. As Pennington argues, plans to oust most women from the service in the postwar period existed in the Soviet military well before the fighting ended. The framework for their exclusion was set already in 1943, as the Soviets introduced gender segregation in the school system and banned women from the newly created cadet schools. Clearly, the Soviet elite allowed for the use of women in combat only as a temporary measure in extraordinary circumstances.[126]

A look beyond the USSR to Moscow-directed communist parties in Spain, France, Italy, and elsewhere only confirms that this was a European-wide policy. In the French resistance, for example, where female combatants were usually affiliated with the Communist Party, one can recognize the same pattern. As a part of a larger process of restructuring the partisan fighters into "real" soldiers of a single military organization (the French Forces of the Interior) and ultimately the regular French army, Paula Schwartz tells us, instructions were issued late in 1943 "to

[124] AJ, SKJ 507, CKKPJ 1944/704, Depeša CKKPJ Miladinu Popoviću, Obkom Kosmet, 19 December 1944.
[125] Pennington, *Wings, Women & War*, 174.
[126] Ibid., 158, 173.

phase women out of the *maquis* and even to replace female liaisons with men." Much as in Yugoslavia, the French preparations for the elimination of women were set in motion at the same time that propaganda campaigns exhorting them to sign up intensified.[127] As in the Spanish Civil War a couple of years before, communist factions in World War II allowed for the use of women in combat only temporarily and in irregular forces. As soon as the guerrillas and militias began turning into a regular army, women were turned away. The Yugoslavs were no exception in this respect. Egalitarianism may have played a role in Tito's decision to authorize women's recruitment as fighters, but this, again, was provisional and reserved for the contemporary war of national liberation.

"WARTIME DAYS WERE MY MOST BEAUTIFUL DAYS"

The policies and problems discussed here notwithstanding, relationships in the Partisan units should not be understood solely in terms of gender conflict. Veteran *partizanka*s describe their lives in the military as an experience of togetherness and equality with their male comrades.[128] "It is a relationship that would be difficult to achieve in civilian life," one female veteran explains. "Always head on the block." This creates extraordinary closeness among people."[129] The conditions of guerrilla warfare and constant danger in which the troops operated, coupled with communist indoctrination, forged a sense of camaraderie and solidarity between men and women. They went through the same ordeals, sharing hopes and fears, exhaustion and responsibilities, losses and victories. Perhaps most important of all, they shared a cause.

In women's narratives, the time spent among the ranks is represented not only as one of camaraderie, but also as one of idealism and grandeur.[130] Active involvement in the war led many women away from their villages, exposed them to new people and ideas, and opened new vistas to them. The struggle gave them an unprecedented sense of purpose: It was the

---

[127] Paula Schwartz, "Partisanes ...," 146.

[128] Malgorzata Fidelis finds a similar case of gender integration and solidarity, despite the persistence of discrimination, among the miners of postwar Poland. Fidelis, *Women, Communism, and Industrialization in Postwar Poland*, 168.

[129] Radojka Katić, interviewed by Barbara Wiesinger. As quoted in Wiesinger, *Partisaninnen*, p. 113, n. 111.

[130] Jancar-Webster, who interviewed 19 Partisan women, reports statements about equality, grandeur, and accomplishment similar to those in the personal narratives discussed earlier. Jancar-Webster, *Women & Revolution*, 80–1, 99.

segment in their life stories, they proudly remember, when they took an active part in and contributed to something truly grand. Even the rare women who recall the persistence of gender discrimination and hierarchy in the Partisan army find their wartime experiences fulfilling. For most female Partisans, the war – for all of its horrors – represented the defining moment and the high point of their lives. "Wartime days were my most beautiful days (*najljepši dani*)," insists one former *partizanka*, her words summing up the feelings of her many female peers. "They were marked by comradeship, modesty, love for the Party, work for the Party. And that will never happen again."[131]

In the Yugoslav case, it is certain that women's reminiscences – rosy and nostalgic as many of them are – were influenced by the state-sponsored master narrative about the Partisan movement. It is also certain that post-war censorship and women's self-censorship worked in tandem to fashion their recollections into an idealized picture of their Partisan past. Yet the phenomenon should not be dismissed as "false consciousness" and attributed solely to the impact of state propaganda. Nor is it reserved specifically for Yugoslav Partisan women. Fond memories of military participation are a common characteristic of women soldiers' testimonies across cultures and periods. They dominate the accounts of female participants in various World War II resistance groups Europe-wide, regardless of the postwar fate of the resistance or the state's stake in shaping the memory of the war. Similar assessments emerge from women's narratives from such diverse places as Greece and France.[132] In Greece, for example, where members of the communist-led resistance movement EAM suffered persecution after having lost the civil war and where the state-promoted official memory of the war looked radically different from that in Yugoslavia, women remember their time in the movement with the same nostalgia. "Strange, perhaps, that war and a triple occupation could be associated with happiness and fulfillment," writes Tassoula Vervenioti in her study of female veterans of the EAM; "yet even today women members of EAM or the KKE [Greece's Communist Party] feel that they acted as historical subjects and gained self-confidence, equality and esteem through their resistance activity."[133] Such memories of participation on equal footing

---

[131] As quoted in Bulatović, *Bila jednom*, 206–7.

[132] For France, see Schwartz, "Partisanes … ," 129. See also Margaret Collins Weitz, *Sisters in the Resistance: How Women Fought to Free France, 1940–45* (New York: J. Wiley, 1995), 145.

[133] Tassoula Vervenioti, "Left-Wing Women between Politics and Family," in *After the War Was Over: Reconstructing the Family, Nation and State in Greece, 1943–1960*, ed. Mark Mazower (Princeton, NJ: Princeton University Press, 2000), 105.

with men, sometimes in sharp contrast with the historical record, suggest that for most women the very opportunity to take an active part in the struggle represented a radical, if temporary, break from the past. Perhaps their experience did not match the ideal of gender equality, but it was the closest to that ideal they had ever been.

CONCLUSIONS

Women's entrance, en masse, into the most secluded and celebrated male domain, the army, destabilized the traditional gender order. But tradition was not to give in. Opposition to the recruitment of women and discrimination they faced in the units reveal the power and persistence of the old patterns. Judging by its proclamations and directives, the communist leadership was true to its role as the champion of gender equality. In issues concerning the *partizanka*s, however, there was a gap between party declarations and realities in the units. This was in part due to the fact that ordinary people on the ground – including local CPY officials, military commanders, and Partisan rank and file – influenced the ways that party policy was implemented. But it was also because the communist leadership lacked a genuine determination to effect a revolution in gender relations. On the party's agenda women's issues remained secondary, at best. Although the problems preventing women's integration into the units on an equal basis with men were acknowledged, the efforts invested to solve them were inconsistent. The party found it easier to accommodate established practices and traditional notions about gender than to tackle them.

In World War II, communist belligerents and communist-led resistance movements were willing to go further than their contemporaries in stretching gender barriers and employing women in nontraditional tasks, including combat. Yet they proved as eager as any of the non-communist Allies to discharge women as soon as the fighting was over. Their greater flexibility during the war may have been due in part to their ideological commitment to equality. It is clear, however, that they too considered women's participation in combat expedient in desperate conditions of total war, but opposite to presumably natural gender roles.[134] The implementation of party policies regarding female combatants reveals the prevalence, on all levels, of a widespread belief in "organic" and fixed gender features, which naturally govern the division

[134] Conze and Fiesler, "Soviet Women," 227.

of labor into men's and women's jobs. This division the CPY did not aim to abolish. Ironically, women's presence in the units challenged neither the traditional separation of the female/male spheres of work nor the hierarchy of gender roles. Still, the phenomenon of the *partizanka* – as a woman who took on the ultimate men's role at the moment critical for the nation's survival – found its place in the postwar master narrative as a testament to the readiness of the populace to recognize, and sacrifice itself for, the rightful cause.

In the final analysis, however, one must not ignore the voices and memories of the *partizankas* themselves. Their narratives suggest that the very experience of participation in the war was liberating. Idealized and nostalgic though they are, such accounts should not be attributed solely to party propaganda. Participation in the Partisan movement led women away from their secluded villages to see new places and meet new people; faith, commitment, and idealism that most had not dreamed of before the war now enriched their lives, giving them a new meaning and an unprecedented feeling of purpose and accomplishment. Thanks to their active involvement in the struggle, Partisan women began seeing themselves as political subjects and historical agents in their own right. Many of them would look back on the war as the best time of their lives.

4

The Personal as a Site of Party Intervention

Privacy and Sexuality

Under the influence of communist propaganda and practices, a considerable number of previously modest and chaste girls have become sexually unbridled, and in that sexual freedom – or, in "free love," as the communists call it – one should look for the reason why many girls have joined the Partisans.

(from a pro-Chetnik newspaper, 1942)[1]

Especially the wild lifestyle and relationships of "female comrades," who took to the woods to relieve the lives of male partisans, have disgusted everyone.... These human scumbags roam through the woods, living on plunder and pillage, and bestially gratifying themselves with a multitude of male Partisans on the principle of "free love."

(from a Ustasha newspaper, 1943)[2]

Promiscuity is nonexistent in Tito's army. This is remarkable for many reasons, but principally because the Slavs are a lusty, full-limbed, pleasure-loving people.

*(from a laudatory article on Yugoslav Partisans
in the Allied press, 1944)[3]*

For the warring factions in Yugoslavia, sex had a political dimension. Behind the ferocious struggle on the battlefront, diverse ideologies and

---

[1] *Glas Crnogorca*, no. 22, 30 May 1942. As quoted in Mihailo Stanišić, "Stavovi (Ravnogorskog) Četničkog pokreta prema ženi," in Perović, *Srbija u modernizacijskim procesima*, Vol. 2, 345.
[2] "Hrvatska žena vjerna je vjekovnim narodnim predajama," *Nova Hrvatska*, 4 July 1943, 7. AJ, AFŽ, 141-10-56.
[3] Frank Gervasi, "Tito," *Collier's Weekly*, 19 February 1944; as radioed from Cairo.

political visions vied for authority among the masses. The question of sexuality figured in that competition on a number of levels. Social anxieties regarding the wartime destabilization of the traditional gender system were projected onto the sexual arena and expressed, in part, as concerns over unregulated female sexuality. All factions engaged in redefining sexual morality, and each used these definitions to debase its political rivals by portraying them as sexually debauched. The Partisans in particular were an easy target for the accusations of dissoluteness – they were the only faction that recruited females en masse; only in their mixed units did numerous young women live together with men. That alone was enough to serve as rich propaganda material for their adversaries.

What, then, were the Partisan sexual mores? Existing historiography has little to offer in response. Yugoslav literature of the socialist era, works of Western scholarship, as well as the majority of reminiscences of former Partisans, all insist that relations between the sexes in the units were – as one Western historian put it – "elevated to a high moral standard."[4] Apart from that assertion, however, there are no studies explaining what this "high moral standard" entailed or how it was accomplished. This chapter concentrates on behavioral and sexual norms in the Partisan movement. It shows how the question of sexuality found its way into the political mêlée among the local factions and onto the party agenda. In the face of repeated charges of debauchery, sexual asceticism became one of the central pillars of the Partisan self-portrait and Partisan sexual conduct a site of party intervention. Quite in contrast to the rumors about the "free love" that the communists presumably preached, the party enforced a strict code of sexual behavior; far from bearing the banner of sexual liberation, the party became the champion of discipline and control. These norms catered to the traditional patriarchal mores of peasant Partisans, simultaneously allowing the party to enter, in a modern interventionist manner, into the most personal affairs.

The Partisan sexual code and regulations were tied to the extraordinary conditions of total war; many policies emerged in direct response to women's presence in the units. Yet despite their temporary character, these regulations helped the CPY solidify its control over its growing membership and, most important, normalize its interventionism for years to come. In this process, the party's leadership was the driving force, but it was neither the sole agent nor the only locus of power. As we shall

---

[4] Kenneth Macksey, *The Partisans of Europe in the Second World War* (New York: Stein and Day, 1975), 141.

see, ordinary people on the local level increasingly took part in the game of mutual surveillance and policing, thus helping support the nascent party state.

The first part of the chapter outlines the behavioral norms and regulatory mechanisms that the CPY had developed before the war and shows how these were introduced into the Partisan movement as a whole. The second section shifts the focus onto the policies that emerged in the course of the war to regulate relations between the sexes and examines their gendered character and implications. Although the Partisan code applied equally to both sexes, officials on the ground often identified women's presence as the destabilizing factor in the units and aimed their punitive measures primarily at females.

PERSONAL LIFE OF A REVOLUTIONARY: VALUES AND NORMS

"Whenever a revolution has been preceded by a long established underground movement," writes Richard Stites, "the structure of that movement – just as much as its leadership and its ideology – super-imposes itself on the political life of the new society."[5] The Partisans, being the nucleus of a new Yugoslav society in the making, were no exception. Much like the Bolshevik Party prior to 1917, the CPY in the interwar period had been an association of local cells and committees directed by the small group of leaders in the Central Committee, which passed its directives to its branches though correspondence, legal and underground publications, and traveling agents. Feedback from below flowed to the center by means of personal correspondence, reports, and occasional conferences and congresses.[6] The same mechanisms of political organization and communication spread over the Partisan movement. Thus, in the course of the war, the Partisans became permeated by party cells, committees, and *politodjels* (political sections). Organs of the Central Committee, *Proleter* and *Borba,* defined the party's – and therefore the Partisans' – line on all relevant issues; directives from above were radioed or dispatched via couriers down the hierarchical ladder, while CPY cells and committees in the units and the rear sent regular, mandatory reports to higher forums. Military and political hierarchies were

---

[5] Richard Stites, *The Women's Liberation Movement in Russia: Feminism, Nihilism, and Bolshevism, 1860–1930* (Princeton, NJ: Princeton University Press, 1977), 329.
[6] On the Bolshevik Party, see ibid.

intertwined, since each unit's staff included a political commissar and a deputy political commissar, as representatives of the party and – in Tito's words – the "soul" of the army.

Just as the party's organizational and communication systems were superimposed onto the Partisan institutions, so did the values and behavioral norms that the CPY had developed in the interwar period gradually extend to the Partisan movement as a whole. The Communist Party leadership had long before the war tried to forge cadres with absolute dedication to the party and their underground duties. Similarly to their Soviet patrons, the Yugoslavs cultivated a revolutionary ethos that demanded one's preparedness to sacrifice individual interests and personal life for the good of the communist cause. A lead *Proleter* article in 1929, entitled "What a Communist Should Be Like," explained that a member ought to "subordinate to the interests of the Party his whole life, work, profession, family relations, job, personal freedom, possessions and all income – in one word – everything!" The article insisted on "the most complete loyalty" and "unlimited, fanatical devotion." And it instructed each communist to resist the bourgeoisie – which could spread its influence via one's spouse, family, or friends – even if this meant "tearing down the most intimate personal relationships."[7]

Apart from the party's efforts to inculcate unquestioning allegiance, the conditions of constant fear and persecution – under which communist activists worked during the interwar Yugoslav dictatorial regime – contributed to the fact that only the most loyal and fanatically devoted members remained active. Outlawed in 1921, the party continued to operate underground, experiencing a gradual dissipation of its members and strength. As Ivo Banac writes, the most ravaging period for the CPY began in 1929, when King Aleksandar abolished the constitution, the parliament, and political parties and proclaimed a royal dictatorship, under which the party cadres were decimated even further. This period saw the party's most active members either imprisoned or killed. The headquarters of the Central Committee had to be moved outside the country. Consequently, during the 1930s, the minuscule CPY operated from two centers – one in exile, another in Yugoslav prisons. The penitentiaries, the most notable of which was in Sremska Mitrovica, allowed the gathering of political prisoners and inadvertently served as revolutionary training facilities of sorts. Sremska Mitrovica harbored a new generation of radicals who were to become the "backbone of the party" in the late

---

[7] "Kakav treba da je komunista," *Proleter*, December 1929, 3–4.

1930s. This group of youths, who had become politically active under the dictatorship, were ultraleftist, militant, and intolerant of anyone who exhibited personal weaknesses and vacillations of any kind.[8]

In addition to the Yugoslav dictatorship, which unwittingly produced some of the most fanatical cadres, internal party purges strengthened the homogeneity, centralization, and unquestionable loyalty among the CPY ranks. The Stalinist Great Purge in Moscow of 1936–8 affected the party center in exile and "made a shambles" of the CPY apparatus in the USSR. The preponderance of the topmost CPY leaders, who had already been in the USSR or had been summoned from Paris and elsewhere, perished in the Soviet gulag. The purge "created a leadership vacuum" in the party, into which Tito stepped. Following his ascension to the position of CPY head in 1937, Tito himself purged the party, removing all leaders of rival factions, all those who acted independently, and all "vacillating elements." Tito's purges of 1938–9 ended factionalism in the CPY, put leftist party fringes in power, and finished the job of creating a centralized, disciplined, "tightly knit and fully bolshevized Communist organization in Yugoslavia." On the eve of the war, the core of the CPY membership was made of those whose revolutionary zeal and dedication to the party had passed the test of long imprisonment, exile, factional struggles, and internal purges.[9]

It is small wonder then that, by 1941, members of the CPY and the communist youth organization of both sexes had been accustomed to the idea that they should have no loyalties other than those to the party leadership and to the communist cause. The communist ethos assumed that one's duty as a revolutionary had priority over everything, including one's personal life; or, to be more precise – particularly over one's personal life. It was not unusual for devoted communists to renounce their marriages or temporarily abandon their children in order to be able to dedicate themselves entirely to their underground duties.

Illustrative in this respect is the case of Spasenija Cana Babović, one of the most prominent women in the CPY before, during, and after the war. She became a party member in the late 1920s and a professional

---

[8] Among those young ultraleftist militants were the future party leaders Milovan Djilas and Aleksandar Ranković. For more on Djilas's evolution as a revolutionary, see his *Memoir of a Revolutionary* (New York: Harcourt Brace, 1973); quote on p. 181. For a concise discussion of the party's interwar history, which has informed my discussion, see Ivo Banac, *With Stalin against Tito: Cominformist Splits in Yugoslav Communism* (Ithaca, NY: Cornell University Press, 1988), 45–116; esp. 61, 67.

[9] Banac, *With Stalin against Tito*, 67, 69, 78.

revolutionary in the mid-1930s. Babović and her communist husband had initially decided not to have children, since they believed that a child would distract them from their underground work. Her husband's words concisely sum up their position: "People like us, who are always under the threat of imprisonment, exile, and turbulences in life, should not have children. Children represent an obstacle. They would limit our freedom and could separate us from the Party." When she did become pregnant, though, they decided to keep the baby boy, who was named Vladimir (after Lenin). But their focus on parenting was to be only temporary. Once her husband was imprisoned, Babović had to give up her child in order to be able to dedicate herself exclusively to her underground activities. In 1933, she sent Vladimir, then three years old, into the First International Children's Home in Ivanovo-Voznesensk, an institution established in the USSR for the children of prominent revolutionaries operating in "capitalist countries." Her biographer writes that she did so "following the recommendation of the Party's Central Committee." Babović continued her party work until the beginning of the war, when she joined the Partisan units. She took her son back from the USSR only after the liberation of Belgrade in 1944.[10]

Private life was clearly supposed to be subordinate to one's revolutionary duty, yet it was also considered inseparable from one's political work. Since the party was envisioned as a vanguard of the working class, made up of its very best sons and daughters, a member of such an elite group was supposed to be exemplary in every respect. To be worthy of party membership, one had to live up to high standards in private life as well. Under Tito, model behavior in candidates' personal lives became an important condition for their admission to the CPY. According to the way Tito explained his cadre politics, of the six qualities that each communist should possess, spotless private life was the very first on the list.[11] "Immaculacy in his *private life* is what is first required from each Party member," wrote Tito. "A Party member's political work cannot be

---

[10] The Ivanovo-Voznesensk home housed the children of prominent communist leaders and professional revolutionaries who could not take care of them – those who had perished, or had been arrested, or were working underground in harsh conditions – from all over the world. Of about 250 children in the home, most were of German, Polish, Czech, French, or Chinese origin. At various times, the institution housed the children of Dolores Ibarruri, Mao Zedong, Palmiro Togliatti, and other international communist icons. Stanko Mladenović, *Spasenija Cana Babović* (Belgrade: Rad, 1980), 26, 36.

[11] The other five were ability to connect to the masses, Bolshevik modesty, discipline, alertness, and continued dedication to the study of Marxism-Leninism.

separated from his personal life.... Nobody can be accepted into the Party without having his private life checked."[12]

In this, as in other matters, Tito adopted the Soviet model. As David Hoffmann tells us, from its early years, the Soviet system had tried to erase the line dividing private life from the public domain, and leading Soviet communists opposed the very notion that the two could be separated. In the 1920s, an internal party system of control commissions was developed to police the behavior and values of Soviet party members, in order to ensure that they merited membership in the proletarian vanguard; members' personal lives were formally declared to be the party's concern. Under Stalin, moral transgressions in the private sphere became increasingly equated with political disloyalty. Thus in the 1930s, behavior in the personal lives of individual party members became a criterion for judging their political reliability, with fatal consequences for many during the Great Purges. Tito's stress on the importance of immaculate behavior in private life was clearly in line with Moscow's practice at the time.[13]

But what did moral behavior and "immaculacy in private life" mean? Neither the Soviets nor the Yugoslavs issued written guidelines or an official code of behavior for communists. Yet relatively strict norms were nevertheless established. According to the unwritten Soviet code, proper behavior in private life meant sobriety, self-discipline, honesty, modesty, and sexual temperance. As Hoffmann writes, the Soviet leadership under Stalin held conservative, "almost Victorian," notions about sexuality. This was in sharp contrast with the conventional imagery of communists as proponents of "free love" and libertinism.

Some justification for such imagery may be found in the revolutionary zeal of the first decade following the October Revolution, when Soviet radicals called for the eradication of all "bourgeois" standards. In their rebellion against traditional morality, many communists adopted a dissolute lifestyle. The revolution indeed created openings to alter existing values and sexual norms, and some Bolsheviks began arguing for the elimination of marriage and the traditional family as a means of women's emancipation and sexual liberation. Alexandra Kollontai's work is most often cited in this context. But not all communist leaders shared – or even

---

[12] "Briga o kadrovima," *Proleter*, May 1939, 6. Emphasis in the original.

[13] For more on the communist behavioral code, morality in private life, and the Great Purges in the USSR, see David Hoffmann, *Stalinist Values*, 57–79. My discussion is based on this work, esp. 58, 62. On the private/public division see also Eric Naiman, *Sex in Public: The Incarnation of Early Soviet Ideology* (Princeton, NJ: Princeton University Press, 1997), 91–7.

understood – her ideas. Lenin himself was hostile to the contemporary preoccupation with sex and the sexual question alike. He considered sexual promiscuity to be bourgeois and particularly disdained those who tried to justify dissoluteness by Marxist principles. Concerned by the waste of Soviet youth's strength and health on libertinism, he proposed that sexual energy should be sublimated and diverted toward self-improvement and the building of socialism. Yet despite the presence of conservative notions at the very top, this was a period in which ideas about sexual liberation and sexual control continued to coexist and compete. The 1920s were, in fact, marked by lively public debates about sexuality. The first post-October decade also saw some of the most thorough and liberal reform legislation ever passed on sexual, marital, and family issues.

In the 1930s, however, official Soviet values underwent a shift. After they had debated with the advocates of sexual liberation for much of the previous decade, the proponents of conventional notions about marriage, the family, and propriety found their ideas triumphant. In part as a reaction to the excesses of the sexual revolution, in part as an attempt to boost the birth rate, an era of sexual Thermidor set in. Official culture now promoted traditional family values, celebrated motherhood, and endorsed a host of pronatalist laws. Abortion was banned, access to divorce restricted, and male homosexuality recriminalized. Kollontai's works were no longer published, and sex surveys and debates disappeared from the public arena. Sexuality was again tied with matrimony and procreation. Evaluating the extent of conservatism, some scholars even speak of Stalinist sexophobia.[14]

What the Yugoslavs advocated in the late 1930s would also fall on the conservative side of the spectrum of communist ideas about sexual morality. The closest that the CPY's Central Committee approached issuing a written statement was a 1937 *Proleter* article, "For a Proletarian Sexual Ethics."[15] The article began by explaining why attention should be given to sexual issues when so many questions stood before the party

---

[14] The preceding section on the Soviet sexual norms is pieced together from the work of other scholars: Hoffmann, *Stalinist Values*, 88–117; Stites, *Women's Liberation*, 346–91; Henry P. David and Joanna Skilogianis, "The Woman Question," in *From Abortion to Contraception: A Resource to Public Policies and Reproductive Behavior in Central and Eastern Europe from 1917 to the Present*, ed. Henry P. David (Westport, CT: Greenwood Press, 1999), 41–2. On sexophobia, Andrej Popov and Henry P. David, "Russian Federation and USSR Successor States," in David, *From Abortion*, 252–3. On public debates about sexuality in the 1920s, see Naiman, *Sex in Public*.

[15] "Za Prolletersku [*sic*] seksualnu etiku," *Proleter*, August 1937, 6. The author is Rodoljub Čolaković, one of the top party leaders.

in such turbulent times: Apparently, some ideas and practices contrary to the proletarian sexual ethics were noticed among CPY activists. Certain comrades, for example, took sexual freedom to mean the absence of any restraint. These people, *Proleter* asserted, were trying to sell bourgeois anarchism in sexual matters as something revolutionary and proletarian. Communists, the article stressed, did struggle for freedom from the bonds of bourgeois sexual morality. But the freedom in love that they envisioned had nothing to do with "free love," the latter being "merely an unhealthy reaction to bourgeois hypocrisy and often but a mask for sexual depravity."

Other negative practices were noticed as well. Male communist youths tended to label their female comrades who would not have sexual relations with them "petty bourgeois." Even worse, some older, more influential men, abusing the authority of the party and the respect that female comrades had for them, did the same. Such ugly, pseudorevolutionary behavior only served the class enemy, the article stressed. Communists were fighting against bourgeois hypocrisy that turned women into objects of men's pleasure, *Proleter* insisted. They strove to free women from the bonds of bourgeois sexual morality, in which the power of money forced them into open or hidden prostitution in a loveless marriage. This did not mean that communists opposed all norms in male-female relations. On the contrary, while battling bourgeois sexual morality, they put forward their own sexual ethics. It was based on two principles: first, to respect a woman as a human being and a comrade in life and in the struggle; second, to respect a woman's feelings and her right to make decisions about her own body. The article concluded by denouncing sexual dissoluteness and calling for a determined struggle against it and all those who preached it.

No other specifics about the proletarian sexual ethics were provided. The piece was written *against* certain practices rather than *for* a clearly defined sexual code; in specifying what it opposed, *Proleter* condemned sexual indulgence and "free love." On the whole, the article reflected Moscow's conservatism, and there are some indications that much of its content was in fact copied from Soviet texts.[16]

---

[16] Some sections in the *Proleter* piece show striking similarities with the words of Sofiya Smidovich, whom Richard Stites calls "the most articulate voice of conservatism" in the USSR, and whose articles were displayed on German bulletin boards by the German Communist Party as an example of official communist morality. See Stites, *Women's Liberation*, 383.

Judging by the Central Committee's publication, one may conclude that the Yugoslav leaders on the eve of the war adopted the Leninist position on sexuality. To be sure, they were no prudes in any sense of the term. Although they disdained promiscuity and tried to foster self-discipline and restraint, they did not necessarily advocate asceticism. For them, communist morality in the domain of intersex relations meant respect, honesty, and camaraderie. Whether they lived what they preached was another question. Some in the leadership, such as Milovan Djilas, were known as puritans. Others, including Tito, earned a different reputation. But there is little doubt that all of them adhered to the most important rule in the communist code – to the demand that one's private life and intimate affairs be secondary to one's revolutionary activism.

If the CPY expected its members to put their private lives on hold during their interwar underground work, the war – which gave the party a unique opportunity to take power and establish a communist state – only added urgency to that expectation. Revolutionary fervor and self-discipline became a modus vivendi for many a communist, as the following statement by a female veteran eloquently expresses:

At that time we tried to break away from the preoccupations of the bourgeois understanding of society. That society was not to be changed only in title and form; our life in its essence, in its foundations had to be changed, and that could not happen painlessly ... to this Marxist prism we subordinated all our wishes, all our desires, all of our youth. That transformed us into proud fighters, ready to sincerely and without second thoughts sacrifice ourselves and all we held dear in our lives, in order to win this great tomorrow for all of our people.... We ... wanted to subordinate all of our personal lives to this unique, great goal of ours – to the struggle![17]

This attitude was superimposed onto the Partisan movement as a whole. "Our fighters subordinate all their personal interests, desires, and pleasures to the interests of the National Liberation Struggle" reads a 1943 directive of the Main Staff for Vojvodina, insisting that relationships between men and women in the Partisan army should be "comradely and correct."[18] Personal narratives indicate that from the onset of the uprising on, sexual abstinence and noninvolvement in the units were the prescribed norms for all fighters. Even Milovan Djilas, who is known for his candor and uncompromising austerity, insists that among "the troops the strictest puritanism was practiced in every respect."[19]

---

[17] Beoković, *Žene heroji*, 466–7.
[18] *Zbornik* 1.6. doc. 177, Naredjenje GŠ Vojvodine, 27 December 1943, p. 532
[19] Djilas, *Wartime*, 93.

The CPY's notions about discipline, loyalty, and self-control proved ideal for its military organization. Ever since the formation of the first Partisan detachments, the party had insisted that discipline in the Partisan units differed from that among the enemy ranks. While the latter was "rigid and forced"[20] and based on "violence and humiliation,"[21] the Partisan one rested on the "self-consciousness" of those who fought for "the freedom of the peoples." This view was incorporated in the statute of proletarian brigades, which insisted on "comradely relations" among all fighters and underscored that "iron discipline" in Partisan units was radically different from that in capitalist armies. This special Partisan discipline was conceived as "self-discipline (*samodisciplina*), based on the consciousness and political conviction of every individual fighter."[22] To be sure, the statute made it clear that the staff would not rely exclusively on the expected self-disciplining vigor of individual fighters: Those who transgressed would have to face the "most severe" penalties. Yet it was the notion of the self-controlled, "politically conscious" fighter that became the benchmark for Partisan behavior, which was supposed to distinguish the Partisans from their local opponents and occupiers alike.

"The Communist Way of Looking into the Soul": To facilitate the transformation of guerrillas into self-disciplined soldiers, the party had recourse to some well-established communist regulatory devices. One of the most potent control mechanisms for CPY members was the practice of "criticism and self-criticism." Throughout the war, "criticism and self-criticism" was a regular item on the agenda of the meetings of CPY members in the army.[23] During such discussions, individuals were expected to engage in introspective analysis, openly admit and publicly deliberate about their weaknesses, and promise to rectify their behavior subsequently. Early on in the war, the Party organ *Borba* published an article that instructed all CPY members to take the practice of self-criticism seriously; the article was also made into a leaflet and distributed among the units. Party members were informed that

[only] through a relentless and uncompromising struggle against one's own weaknesses and by exposing one's own errors in practical work is it possible to overcome difficulties.... Personal responsibility facilitates both the exposure of one's own mistakes and their correction, and every communist knows that precisely

---

[20] *Zbornik* 5. 1, doc. 81, p. 242.
[21] *Zbornik* 5. 1, doc. 22, p. 74.
[22] *Bilten Vrhovnog Štaba*, no. 14–15, February/March 1942, in *Zbornik* 2.1, p. 135.
[23] See, for example, *Zbornik* 9. 1, doc. 52, p. 181; *Zbornik* 9.1, doc. 47, 164; *Zbornik* 9. 1, doc. 108, 388; also *Zbornik* 9. 2, doc. 88, 447, and others.

self-criticism is the weapon that best solidifies our Party. So, "PERSONAL RESPONSIBILITY and BOLSHEVIK SELF-CRITICISM" – this needs to be the password of a communist on the front and in the rear alike.[24]

Some, like Vladimir Dedijer, who considered this practice to be "the communist way of looking into the soul," embraced it earnestly. From his descriptions it appears that at "criticism and self-criticism" sessions he underwent a purifying, cathartic experience of almost religious quality.[25] The way that the devoted communists viewed and engaged in "self-criticism" indeed bears striking similarities with the Christian practice of confessing one's sins, except that in the communist ritual the party assumed the role that the church – or even the divinity itself – played in Christian traditions. Much like the phrase "the communist way of looking into the soul," the language that party officials used to describe self-criticism to communist novices was often imbued with religious references. In personal narratives and the CPY's directives alike, the party appears as an independent, supernatural entity that – once one completely opened up and surrendered to it – would help one conquer one's weaknesses and would heal, shepherd, and keep one on the right path. Consider how the district committee for Slavonia instructed its lower forums on what a member was supposed to do:

He should bring out before his Party everything that he accidentally did and that he considers unworthy of a Party member, [he has] to be honest here and rid himself of everything that bothers him, to feel his Party as the one who will heal him and help him get on the right path. Only in this manner would a member avoid making one mistake after another.[26]

Besides confessing their own doubts and weaknesses, activists at "criticism and self-criticism" sessions were expected to expose and condemn the mistakes of others. Throughout the war, the party instructions reminded the commanders and commissars that not only the work but also the *personal life* of those in the units should be subjected to criticism and self-criticism.[27]

---

[24] "Lična odgovornost i samokritika," *Borba*, 20 November 1941; also made into a leaflet and distributed in the units, for example, AJ, SKJ 507, Hrvatska II/150, Ok. Kom KPH Lika in February 1942.

[25] See Dedijer, *The War Diaries*, vol. 1, 81, 121, 123. Quote from p. 121.

[26] AJ, SKJ 507, Hrvatska II/150, "Obl. komitet KPH za Slavoniju, okruznom kom. KPH Brod," 3 February 1944, p. 1.

[27] A 1943 directive, for example, emphasized that "it is obligatory to conduct in the units criticism and self-criticism, not only of the work of individuals but also of their personal behavior and personal life, of their personal features and weaknesses, for this is

It was often during such séances that one's improper behavior in private life, including the domain of sexual activity, was exposed and criticized. Dedijer recounts the "touching case" of old Čiča Ćosić, whose habit of visiting a certain Dara, the wife of an imprisoned baker in Foča (Bosnia), was raised in a "criticism" discussion early in 1942:

> Old red Ćosić suffered a thousand deaths when he had to speak of this at the party meeting. He stiffened and said nothing. But ... others attacked him like wasps. And then as self-criticism, Ćosić began to speak through clenched teeth, "But this old man still wishes to taste life."[28]

It is difficult to estimate whether other Partisans shared Dedijer's enthusiasm for such exercises in the building of revolutionary cadres. Old man Ćosić did not seem to find much enjoyment in being forced to admit, ruminate upon, and ultimately relinquish his affair. It is certain, however, that party leaders considered "criticism and self-criticism" such "a powerful weapon" of control that they decided to extend it to "all Partisan meetings."[29] Thus, besides serving as an instrument for regularizing behavior of its members and, by extension, of everyone in the units, "criticism and self-criticism" facilitated the party's intrusion into the lives of individual Partisans.

Keeping Tabs on the Personal: Apart from criticism and self-criticism, the party solidified its practice of keeping track of individual members in the course of the war. Under the strong hand of Aleksandar Ranković,

---

how the full responsibility of a Party members develops." AJ, SKJ 507, BiH II/28, Zamjenik političkog "100N" Bataljonskom birou 1, 14 November 1943, p. 4.

[28] Dedijer, *The War Diaries*, vol. 1, 123.

[29] See, for example, *Zbornik* 9.1, doc. 108, p. 388. One of the reasons for extending criticism and self-criticism to the units was the improvement of Partisan military skills. Since critical evaluation of combat actions was considered crucial for the development of military expertise, the practice of criticism and self-criticism extended from the meetings of party members in the units to conferences at which all Partisan fighters participated. At meetings that followed combat actions, the floor was open for political commissars and all other Partisans to criticize the action, the individual and group conduct in the battle, and the way the action was led. It was assumed that through criticism the units would learn from their own frontline experiences. Thus regular critical analyses of actions – as Ranković directed the staff of the 13th Brigade – were to become an obligatory part of military instruction. In Ranković's words: "To militarily strengthen the brigade, alongside exercises and combat training, one should regularly analyze actions ... through criticism one should learn from one's own experiences." The introduction of criticism and self-criticism into the units was not unique to Yugoslav Partisans who, in fact, followed the Soviet model in this respect. In 1937, Stalin instituted the policy of criticism and self-criticism in the Red Army. The Ranković quote is from AVII, NOR, IRP BIH 5/92–3, CKKPJ (Ranković) Zameniku politkomisara XIII brigade X Divizije, 10 November 1943.

the Central Committee's Commission for Cadres sought to establish a card file – a database in today's terms – with detailed information about each party member. Early in 1942, Ranković initiated the collection of data, asking individual communists to submit their autobiographies in writing. The communist honor code assumed that nothing should be kept from the party's eye, and that included one's intimate affairs and personal thoughts. The very idea of hiding something from the party was alien to dedicated communists. And for true believers, like Dedijer, any insinuation that they might have wanted to do so was offensive. Insulted by such an insinuation, Dedijer noted in his diary: "Marko [Ranković's alias] ordered each of us today to write our biographies. When he looked through mine he asked whether I had written everything about my life. This affected me terribly; I cried."[30]

Later that year, the Central Committee sent a directive to party leaders in the army and the rear instructing them to assign to all committees a so-called *kadrovik* – a person in charge of collecting information about communist cadres.[31] The Commission for Cadres designed special questionnaires that each member was to answer. They were distributed among various party forums and, upon completion, sent back to the Central Committee. The questionnaires consisted of five sections: 1) general data (name, date and place of birth, profession, etc.); 2) party biography (date the person became a member, name of the supervisor who accepted him/her, duties performed in the party); 3) participation in the Partisan struggle (enlistment date, rank/capacity, military tasks); 4) level of political consciousness (familiarity with the Marxist-Leninist theory, completed courses, professional skills); 5) general evaluation (personal and family life, character, dedication to the party, military performance, and special comments).[32] Each member was to fill out the first four sections personally; the fifth section, general evaluation, which asked about one's personal life, was to be completed by another party member – one's peer or superior in the party hierarchy. Providing information on one's private life was mandatory.

In addition to the database of the Central Committee, the party kept track of individual members through the so-called *karakteristike*

---

[30] Dedijer, *The War Diaries*, vol. 1, 173.

[31] AVII, NOR, IA PK SKS Vojvodine NOB 2/115–16, CK KPJ, Komisija za kadrove, direktiva svim partijskim rukovodiocima u vojsci i na terenu, 25 September 1942.

[32] AVII, NOR, CK SK HRV 51/480–1, 482, 483, "Obrasci upitnika za kadrove;" also AVII, NOR, IRP BIH 6/305; AVII, NOR, IA PK SKS Vojvodine NOR 2/122.

(personnel file; literally, "characteristics"). Whenever party members completed a political course and advanced in the hierarchy, moved to another unit or terrain, or accepted a new duty, their sealed *karakteristike* accompanied the transfer. Much like section five of the questionnaire for cadres, one's personnel file was written by one's superiors or peers and similarly evaluated one's level of political consciousness, military prowess, dedication to the party, and performance on previous duties. Upon listing one's party credentials and personal strengths and weaknesses, the *karakteristike* writers often suggested the kind of work that would best suit the person named. Simply put, one's personnel file was a statement about one's qualifications and character, akin to references that one submits to potential employers today, but with some distinctly communist concerns. It ordinarily included an evaluation of one's personal and family life. Occasionally, one's private life could be the primary focus, as in the case of comrade Dušanka, who apparently made some grave mistakes in that domain:

She was assigned to work at a county committee as a secretary. However, she has not performed satisfactorily at work. She proved to be a poor organizer. Besides, we are under the impression that she is not honest. Her private life was not on a level appropriate for a Party activist. We have been informed that she had a male comrade in the 6th brigade with whom she had not broken up, and here she got attached and got into relations with [another] male comrade ... She claimed that she had informed a member of the district committee in advance about her decision to get into these relations, but it later turned out that she had simply presented this comrade [of the district committee] with a fait accompli.[33]

As the writers of a personnel file were supposed to note any potential weaknesses and problematic predilections in one's intimate life, it is not uncommon to find in cadre records such characterizations as "tendency to womanizing," "inclination to adventurism in love and to jealousy," "prone to sexual transgressions," or "brags about his successes with women."[34]

---

[33] AVII, NOR, IRP BiH 3/848, Oblasni komitet KPJ za Srem, pismo Obl. Kom.-u KPJ Istočna Bosna, 23 June 1943; same document in AVII, NOR, IA PK SKS Vojvodine NOB 2/504.

[34] AVII, NOR, IRP BIH 12/166–8, 167, Izveštaj o radu Part. org. VII KNOU Brigade X Divizije NOVJ Oblasnom kom. za B. Krajinu, 6 January 1945; AVII, NOR, IRP BIH 9/16 "Karakteristike 3 druga," 4 August 1944; AVII, NOR, IRP BiH 10/86–7, 86, Karakteristike drugova koji se nalaze na partijskom kursu, Okr. KPJ za Kozaru Oblasnom kom. za B. Krajinu, 3 October 1944; AVII, NOR, IRP BiH 9/328, Karakteristike Remze Duranovića, Od Pom. Komesara XVII brigade (Šemso Šabanović) Oblasnom kom. KPJ za B. Krajinu, 29 August 1944.

The "privilege" of having their personnel files passed up or down the hierarchical ladder was not reserved solely for party members. In fact, it happened to anyone holding any position in the Partisan movement, irrespective of rank and political affiliation. That included even older female peasants who worked as laundrywomen or assisted in Partisan kitchens. For instance, the characteristics of a female assistant to the cook at a Partisan headquarters, Dragica Banjeglav (neither a party nor an AFW member), written by the municipal AFW committee in her village, noted that she was of "good behavior, very good in personal life, and attached to our national liberation struggle."[35]

None of the communist practices described was invented by the CPY. Criticism and self-criticism rituals, cadre questionnaires, and *karakteristike* had all been well-established tools in the Soviet party. The Yugoslavs also followed the Soviet model when they extended "criticism and self-criticism" to the units and introduced "iron discipline" into the army. But during the war, they encountered specific problems for which Moscow's solutions could not work. They also had to deal with situations for which there were no customary procedures in Moscow, or at least none that the Yugoslavs knew of at the time. Many regulations of sexual behavior emerged in direct response to unforeseen issues caused by women's presence in the units. Policies on romantic relations, marriage, pregnancy, abortion, and immoral behavior in the units thus had a particular Yugoslav imprint. But before turning to those policies, we will look at yet another unforeseen issue resulting from women's prominence in the units – the propaganda fuel that the *partizanka* provided to Partisan enemies.

Combating Enemy Propaganda: Apart from the communist value system, Partisan leaders had other reasons to insist on sexual discipline in the units. Among the most pressing ones was enemy propaganda. Much of it focused on spreading rumors about "debauchery" in the Partisan units in general, and about "sexual depravity" of Partisan women in particular. Such allegations often issued from the most prominent political figures. General Nedić, prime minister of the Serbian puppet government, for instance, reportedly described female Partisans as "perverse,

---

[35] AVII, NOR, k. 422, f. 1, dok. 23, Karakteristike Dragice Banjeglav, pomoćne kuvarice, od Zamj. Sekretara Opć. AFŽ za općinu Bunić, 24 June 1943. For other examples of personnel files for people who were not party members, see AVII, NOR, IA PK SKS Vojvodine NOB 2/285, Ok. Za Severni Banat, 19 March 1944; AVII, NOR, IA PK SKS Vojvodine NOB 2/37, Komanda mesta Zemun Mesnom NOO Ugrinovci, 10 November 1944, and others.

homeless, unreasonable women and world-wide prostitutes."[36] Similarly, the Chetnik leader Draža Mihajlović claimed that "women in the Communist ranks were either prostitutes before they joined or became such during their stay in the Communist forces."[37]

Degrading statements about the *partizanka*s were not limited to Serbian leaders, but became a staple of anti-Partisan rhetoric shared by practically all local warring factions in the region. Their common repertoire included charges against Partisan women of sexual promiscuity and perversity. "These human scumbags," as a Ustasha article describes them, "bestially" gratify themselves "with a multitude of male partisans on the principle of 'free love.'"[38] Ustasha propaganda also focused on female Partisans' alleged brutality;[39] the Ustashas' Department of Public Security represented the *partizanka*s as particularly "bloodthirsty."[40] In some instances, Partisan men were depicted as rapists while women were more favorably seen as victims "forcibly taken from their homes," doubtless for male pleasure.[41] The Chetniks in particular made the Partisan women – to use Jozo Tomasevich's words – "a favored butt of their propaganda." The Chetniks' speeches, pamphlets, leaflets, and journals portray the *partizanka*s as courtesans, debauched and dangerous women. They also spread stories about the practice of "free love" in the Partisan units. A Chetnik appeal to the Serbs, for instance, blames the Partisans for "propagating free love among the youth; saying that brother and sister, son and mother, father and daughter can live together as husband and wife; bringing with them many fallen women from the towns ... to serve the Communist bosses for the purpose of physical pleasure."[42] Such stories were further spiced up with details about "brothels" and "harems" that the Partisans presumably organized in territories under their control.[43] In Chetnik-held territories in Montenegro, women known

---

[36] Petar Martinović-Bajica, *Milan Nedić* (Chicago: First American Serbian Corporation, 1956), 321. This statement is also mentioned, in a slightly different translation, in Tomasevich, *The Chetniks*, 189.

[37] Tomasevich, *The Chetniks*, 189.

[38] "Hrvatska žena vjerna je vjekovnim narodnim predajama," *Nova Hrvatska*, 4 July 1943, 7. AJ, AFŽ, 141-10-56.

[39] For an example of Ustasha propaganda, which emphasizes the brutality of a Partisan woman, see Hoover Institution Archives (hereafter HIA), Wayne Vucinich Collection, box 2, Introduction to the "Grey Book" of the Independent Croatian State, p. C3.

[40] Hoare, *Genocide and Resistance*, 288.

[41] HIA, Trivun Jeftic papers, letter to M. Nedić, 13 March 1942.

[42] As quoted in Hoare, *Genocide and Resistance*, 161.

[43] For a detailed discussion of Chetnik views of women, including their propaganda against Partisan women, see Mihajlo Stanišić, "Stavovi (Ravnogorskog) Četničkog pokreta

for their sympathies for the Partisans were scolded in public and labeled as "whores."[44]

Given the persistence and power of such propaganda, it is small wonder that the party found it necessary to respond. *Naša borba* (Our Struggle), the organ of the Partisan movement in Srem, featured in August 1942 an article entitled "Our Morality," which purported to affirm the high moral standards to which the Partisans subscribed. The article criticizes the enemy who "fabricates the most banal lies, imputing that the Partisans lead dissolute lives" and maintains that all fighters – married and unmarried – abstain from any sexual activity:

The men's attitude to women in our detachments is on a respectable level. In the interest of strengthening and solidifying morality and discipline in the detachments, the Partisans who are married and whose wives are with them have renounced certain natural needs and satisfactions. And all of our other Partisans obey the following rule: to see in a woman only a good comrade, a friend and a fighter, and to relate to her in a comradely fashion, to respect and appreciate her. And vice-versa – all our *partizanka*s relate to men in a way that befits people's fighters.[45]

At the same time, an article reportedly written by young *partizanka*s, in which they themselves speak out against the enemy's "disgusting lies," appeared in the communist youth journal, *Glas omladine* (Voice of the Youth). To repudiate the enemy allegation that women enlisted in the Partisans in order to practice "free love," the *partizanka*s decided to explain why they joined and what they did in the detachments. The article emphasized that they traveled to the woods to become fighters, and thus to contribute in the most noble way to the national liberation.[46] In addition to such declarations, in which they presented sanitized self-portraits as morally impeccable sons and daughters of the people, the Partisans were all too happy to provide counterallegations about the "lewdness and immorality" of enemy soldiers. This wartime Partisan self-image of camaraderie and sexual puritanism was to become one of the centerpieces of the postwar master-narrative about the National Liberation War.

---

prema ženi," in Perović, *Srbija u modernizacijskim procesima*, vol. 2, 342–52; for a fine analysis of women's position in the Chetnik-controlled territory in Serbia, see Bojan Dimitrijević, "Žene ravnogorskog sela 1943–1944," in ibid., 353–66.

[44] *Zbornik* 3.4, doc. 144, p. 386.
[45] "Naš moral," *Naša borba*, August–September 1942, 4–5.
[46] "Zašto smo došle u odred," *Glas omladine* 4, August 1942, 3.

PROTECTING THE HONOR OF THE PARTY: REGULATIONS

According to the CPY elite, the personal lives of individual party members were directly related to the party's authority and reputation. The same logic extended to the Partisan movement as a whole. The CPY and its army were thought to be the revolutionary vanguard introducing a new, superior morality, and each Partisan was responsible for upholding the party's honor by living up to its high standards. This is how a typical party declaration explains the matter:

> Our Party is the bearer of new ethical principles, of the new morality of the working class.... It fights for the moral purity of relationships in our army, for proper and sound relations between male and female comrades ... every Party member needs to fight for the strengthening of the honor of our Party and our army ... [in the army] there is no room for dissolute elements and moral crooks.[47]

In other words, the honor of the party and its army depended on the moral behavior of Partisan soldiers, and that included their personal lives. In this respect, the party came to encompass some of the functions attributed to the traditional Balkan patriarchal family – just as the behavior of individual family members could uphold or undermine the honor of the family as a whole, so did the party's reputation rest on the shoulders of its rank and file.[48] This was particularly so for female Partisans, who made the most radical breach with the traditional gender system and were singled out in enemy propaganda. Their sexual propriety, upon which the honor of their families had depended before the war, now similarly came to represent the honor of the Partisan movement. The discipline and sexual puritanism that the CPY introduced into the army indeed catered to the patriarchal morality of the Balkan mountain folk who filled the units.[49] And just as in traditional peasant culture the *zadruga* patriarchs could intervene to punish a disreputable member – and thus protect the

---

[47] AVII, NOR, IRP BiH 5/454–455, Divizijski komitet XI NOU Divizije, Zaključci sa sastanka divizijskog komiteta, December 1943.

[48] Tassoula Vervenioti notes a similar tendency of the Communist Party in Greece (the KKE) to assume some of the functions of the traditional family during the war and the Civil War in Greece. See Tassoula Vervenioti, "Left-Wing Women between Politics and Family," in *After the War Was Over: Reconstructing the Family, Nation, and State in Greece, 1943–1960*, ed. Mark Mazower (Princeton, NJ: Princeton University Press, 2000), 109.

[49] Some Partisan officials equally credited the party influence and the traditional ethos for the high standards of intersex relations in their units. See report from the 4th Proletarian Brigade (Montenegrin), *Zbornik* 9.1, doc. 131, pp. 503–4.

honor of the family as a whole – so did the party take it upon itself to intervene in the intimate affairs of its members in order to protect its honor. These similarities should not be overstated, however. Party interventionism – in its goals, scope, and execution – had a distinctly modern character.

Internal party documents provide ample information about the ways that the CPY regulated sexual behavior in the Partisan movement. To keep the higher forums informed about the situation in the ranks, each party organization in the units and the rear was expected to send regular reports up the hierarchical ladder. Significantly, in these documents issues pertaining to the relationship between the sexes were often subsumed under the rubric "work with women." Issues involving both sexes were thus identified as specifically women's. In early party documents this rubric appeared rarely and erratically. In the second half of 1941, however, the regional CPY committee for Valjevo sent a directive to party organizations in the region, demanding that all party secretaries in the units submit regular written reports including a section describing their work with women, as well as other issues related to women's participation in the struggle.[50] It seems that a similar diktat reached party forums in other areas, for, already at the beginning of 1942, an increasing number of reports from various regions introduced such a section. The rubric also figured in directives passed down to brigades and companies from higher levels in the party and military hierarchy. Most directives simply called for the initiation or intensification of the political work with women and stressed that the relations between the sexes in the units had to be "proper."[51] Yet the latter term remained underdefined, leaving it to the judgment of officials in the field to identify, record, and penalize "improper" behavior.

In the reports from below, the most frequently repeated phrase – "relations between women and men comrades are correct" – indicated both that the men's attitude to women was satisfactory (i.e., that men accepted

---

[50] *Zbornik*, 9. 1, doc. 19, p. 55.

[51] Occasionally, they would also give specific suggestions on sleeping arrangements in the units, asking that men and women be separated. For instance, a letter of the secretary from the 3rd Battalion of the Krimski detachment (Slovenia) read: "The attitude of male comrades towards female comrades should be comradely and in no way different [*nikako drukčiji*]. Women comrades must sleep alone in their own tents." *Zbornik* 9. 1, doc. 125, p. 467; in a similar manner, a Bosnian party commissar insisted that in his detachment it was "underlined that female comrades should not sleep near the [rest of the] army." AVII, NOB, IRP BiH 10/475–9, 477, Pom. Politkomesaru Grahovsko-P. odreda NOV, Okr. kom-u za Drvar, 26 October 1944.

women as fighters and as their equals) and that fighters of both sexes did not engage in improper relations. This favorable state of affairs was typically attributed to the authority of the party and the accordant high level of "political consciousness" in the units. If, conversely, the relations were not "correct," party representatives in the units tried to find a remedy through additional "political work" to raise the consciousness of the fighters of both sexes.

More often than not, though, the party tried to solve the problem by prescribing additional political work exclusively with women. The Politodjel of the 4th Proletarian Brigade, for instance, convened special group meetings (*aktivi*) of women to address the question of male-female relationships.[52] And when the problem emerged in the 6th Bosnian Brigade, the party intensified "political work with *female comrades*" and organized "transfer of certain *female comrades* out of the brigade."[53]

This tendency to ascribe problems involving both sexes to women alone was perhaps never more obvious than in early 1944, when the party launched a campaign against "disreputable" females among the ranks. To be sure, individual misogynist Partisan military commanders and party officials used accusations of sexual impropriety to discredit women in their units throughout the war, but in 1944 such accusations led to the involvement of the highest party echelons and to a general move against women in the Partisan army.[54]

The immediate reason for the campaign was the rapid increase in the number of female recruits in the winter of 1943–44. The year 1943, as we have seen earlier, proved decisive as a result of a series of political and military developments that altered the situation on the ground in favor of the Partisans. First, thanks to the fall of Mussolini and the surrender of Italy in September 1943, the Partisans were able to rearm and greatly extend the areas under their control, which spread over the formerly Italian-held zones in the Ustasha state. Later that year, the Western Allies decided to withdraw their support of the Chetniks and turned to the Partisans, raising the Partisans' morale and drawing new recruits into their ranks. Having succeeded in consolidating the civil administration in

---

[52] *Zbornik* 9. 1, doc. 129, 493, my italics. The work of women's *aktivi* was, however, shortly abandoned. Bojović, *Žene Crne Gore*, 176.

[53] AJ, SKJ 507, CKKPJ-1944/116, Zam. Politkomesara VI Bos. NOU Brigade CKKPJ-u, 28 March 1944. Also *Izvori* 16, 418–28. My emphasis.

[54] For typical individual misogynist accusations see AVII, NOR, CK HRV 18/26–7, Pismo druga Čanice CK-u KPH, 24 March 1943; AVII, NOR, IRP BiH 5/317–20, 319, Partijska jedinica bolnice br. 1 Korpusa NOVJ Okr. Komitetu za Vlasenicu, 1 December 1943.

the liberated zones, Tito now felt confident enough to extend his political claims – in November 1943, his AVNOJ proclaimed itself to be the Provisional Government of Yugoslavia. In Partisan-held territories, general conscription of all men between eighteen and forty-five years of age was ordered. Consequently, the Partisan ranks swelled. Women's recruitment, unlike men's, remained voluntary, but young women in the newly liberated zones seemed eager to sign up and did so in thousands.

Amid these events, in the fall and winter of 1943–44, internal reports increasingly began to complain about the quality of new recruits, noting among them the presence of women with suspicious pasts and problematic reputations.[55] This development in Dalmatia and the islands, where many of the core units now operated, particularly alarmed the party. The Central Committee sent a directive to the main committees of Dalmatia, Croatia, and the Partisan corps active in the area, informing them that females of "dubious morality and unchecked behavior in the occupied cities" should "not be permitted" to enter the army.[56] Some party officials in the field asked for the expulsion of city women who had already entered the units. "There are considerable numbers of girls who have come to our ranks after Italy's capitulation, and who are of dubious past so they have passed their habits onto our fighters," wrote the Politodjel of the 26th Division to the Central Committee, adding that the party would "have to find the opportunity of removing them, as disreputable, from the army ranks."[57] Orders to expel such women from the units were promptly issued, subjecting the past of all new female recruits to scrutiny.[58]

It is worth stressing that the policy specifically targeted women. There was no mention of men with questionable sexual reputation. It is symptomatic that the party saw the newly recruited females as the source of immorality in the military. Although they obviously had to have played their part in the spread of immoral behavior in the units, men were seen as naïve victims who had fallen under the influence of sexually liberal girls from the formerly occupied cities. Such views reflect the power and persistence of traditional gender ideology and the accordant double

[55] AVII, NOR, IA PK SKS Vojvodine NOB 4/569–570, Izveštaj o radu NOO Okrug Zap. Srem, 20 October 1943.

[56] AVII, NOR, IRPJ 1/173–7, 177, CKKPJ direktiva Oblasnom KPH za Dalmaciju, CK KPH-u, i Pol. Komesaru VIII Korpusa NOV, 8 February 1944.

[57] AVII, NOR, IRPJ 1/313–16, 315, Politodjel XXVI divizije VIII korpusa NOVJ CKKPJ-u, March 1944.

[58] AVII, NOR, Muzej NR Split NOB 7/14–20, 19, Oblasni Kom. KHP za Dalmaciju, svima okr. Odb. KPH I Divizijskim komitetima VIII Korpusa, 16 March 1944.

standards of sexual morality. Although the party's sexual code nominally did not differentiate between the two sexes, in practice women were held to different sexual standards than men.

Policing: Customary procedures for punishing sexual transgressions differed depending on the transgressor's party status. For immorality among the Partisan rank and file, officials generally prescribed additional political courses, meetings, and lectures and occasionally transferred or expelled women from the units. Party members were generally subject to stricter measures. When they were suspected of immorality, the CPY committee in charge would form a three-member commission to investigate the case, question the suspect and witnesses, and recommend the appropriate penalty. The committee would then confirm or change the penalty and inform the higher party forums of the case.[59] The illicit behavior for which such commissions were responsible included incidents of sexual misconduct, such as cheating on one's spouse, initiating a new relationship or marrying without the party's permission, and engaging in promiscuity. Recommended penalties for sexual transgressions typically ranged from mild reprimands to the revoking of one's party membership.

Thus in a theatrical case that captured the attention of the highest party forums, including the Central Committee, the promiscuity of a midranking party official, Vera C., was raised. Comrade Vera, a member of the Politodjel of the 39th Division, although "diligent and dedicated to her political work," made mistakes of an intimate nature that discredited both her and the Politodjel as a whole. "In her everyday conduct, her every move and gesture, she tried to make the woman in her visible, forgetting her advisory and tutoring functions," wrote the Politodjel to the Bosnian party leadership. When she worked in the 13th Brigade, she had relations with a staff member. Then she moved to the 16th Brigade, "where she began to live with comrade Dragan D., commander of the 1st battalion." Dragan D. reportedly confirmed the affair, "mentioning that comrade Vera had offered herself to him." The Politodjel asserted that Vera's was the "case of open immorality bordering on prostitution." It not only discredited her work in the eyes of the fighters, but also "disarmed the *Politodjel* as a whole in its fight against daily occurrences of such nature in the brigades." The letter recommended that comrade Vera be not only dismissed but also "most severely punished." Upon receiving the report, the provincial committee for Bosnia invited Vera C. – as well

---

[59] For detailed instructions on the process, see, for example, AVII, NOR, IRP BiH 3/480, Oblasni kom. za Bosansku Krajinu Okr. Kom-u za Ključ-Mrkonjić, 17 January 1943.

as her two lovers – for questioning. The division's political leadership considered the case important enough to report it not only to the Bosnian Provincial Committee but also to the Central Committee itself. Bosnia's Party leaders seemed equally alarmed, and they themselves passed a note about the case to Ranković. The latter confirmed the Bosnian committee's decision, whereupon comrade Vera was dismissed from the Politodjel, expelled from the party, and sent to a remote unit as an ordinary company nurse. Documents do not mention any penalty for her lovers.[60]

In the struggle against immorality, the lowest party officials proved by far the most zealous. Their readiness to monitor, report incidents, and penalize those involved often exceeded both the established procedures and expectations of the leadership. Reports from local party forums tend to provide the most detailed accounts of the intimate lives of those under their supervision, and, at times, rather explicit descriptions of episodes of "improper behavior."

This enthusiasm for total control from below can in part be explained by the dramatic enlargement of the party during the war, which gave these new cadres – who were for the most part poorly educated peasants from some of the most underdeveloped regions – a unique opportunity for social mobility. The war, which ravaged their villages, uprooted these hitherto "apathetic, alienated, or 'pre-political' sectors" of the Yugoslav population, whereupon the party mobilized them, politicized them, and gave them positions of authority.[61] The CPY's enlargement in the course of the war was indeed massive: from 6,600 members in 1940 to 140,000 in 1945. The new cadres were often fanatically devoted to the party in general and to Tito and his inner circle in particular, to whom they owed their transformation from the hitherto lowest strata to the new elite. In addition, many among those new cadres were mountain folk from regions such as Montenegro, Herzegovina, and Krajina, who were known for their strong and persistent patriarchal mores. For peasants from these regions, communist notions of collectivism, discipline, and sexual propriety were appealing as they resonated well with their traditional values.

Eager to please the party yet facing ambiguous directives about what exactly – and how – to report, some ardent local officials on the ground

---

[60] AJ, SKJ 507, CKKPJ 1944/279, Politodjel 39. Divizije PK-u KPJ BiH o Veri Crvenčanin, 6 August 1944, uz Izv. o XVI brigadi, Politodjel 39. Divizije CK KPJ-u, 3 September 1944; also *Izvori* 19, 256–89. AJ, SKJ 507, CKKPJ 1944/292, Djuro Pucar, PK KPJ BiH Ranković-u, 9 September 1944; *Izvori* 19, 366–8.

[61] I borrow the phrase "apathetic, alienated, or 'pre-political' sectors" from Joseph Rothschild, *Return to Diversity*, 3rd ed. (New York: Oxford University Press, 2000), 55.

developed extraordinary monitoring skills. Their reports to higher party forums show surprising attention to detail and include more or less graphic descriptions of incidents. Thus a party cell in Drvar (Bosnia) found it pertinent to note that, in the village of Smoljane, a certain Smiljana R. "winked at Dmitar M.," her married neighbor, after which the two "went to Smiljana's house and spent 4 hours together." Or that, on the occasion of a village dance, male and female youths tended to go outside "into the darkness, whispering, in couples."[62] Another report informed on a local committee member, who, although married, was "one evening with a female youth, in a place where he should not have been."[63] Few documents, however, could better illustrate all the main features of such low-level records on immorality – the zeal of local officials, attention to detail, explicitness of description, and poor literacy – than the following report, which is therefore reproduced here almost in its entirety:

We are sending you data about an incident that took place between comrade Lenka I., a SKOJ [Communist Youth League] member, and comrade Osme I., a CPY member, who is employed in the Agitprop [agitation and propaganda section] of the Regional Committee for Bosnian Krajina.

On the day of the 7th this month, this detachment ... presented a performance in the evening. During the same performance comrade Lenka and Osme got together, continued to talk, and when she decided to leave for home, Osme asked to accompany her, and they went. When they left the building, Osme asked Lenka to take a shady street while the female comrade rejected that and after some debating they agreed to take the main street to the house of comrade Mijatović Mažena where they stood next to a veranda and continued to talk. According to the statement of the female comrade, comrade Osme was drunk and they had started dating earlier, i.e., during the offensive....

Upon their arrival at the veranda of the said house they stopped and Osme continued to tell the female comrade about what he was and where he worked in order to win her over more easily. The male comrade talked to her and after a while he proceeded to kiss her and to try to reach her body, i.e., her breasts. The said [male comrade] managed to kiss her, i.e., several times and to reach her bare breasts and when he succeeded in this the female comrade said: what would you want now, you've reached the breasts and kissed me all over. Then Osme said: this is not all, I am not leaving until I do all I intended to. The same female comrade resisted but it was all in vain and Osme continued to prove to her that he was a member of the CPY and that she was just a kid, why she resisted, and he told her that he would marry her, tomorrow if she wanted, or to wait for their Bairam [Muslim holiday].

---

[62] AVII, NOR, IRP BiH 3/507–8, Part. Jed. komande područja u Drvaru, Okr. kom-u KPJ Drvar, 23 January 1943.

[63] AVII, NOR, IRP BiH 10/623–4, Sreski kom. za Konjic Oblasnom k. za Hercegovinu, 3 November 1944.

At the same time, comrade Bosiljka Jovanić, a SKOJ member, eavesdropped on the veranda of the same house and the said [female comrade] could not bear to listen to their lewdness and she threw some garments (rugs) at them over the veranda. Comrade Osme and the female comrade were surprised, but it did not bother them much and they continued to kiss and make out. While they kissed, the male comrade said: put your leg over there, Lenka, and a commotion developed, it seems that the female comrade resisted but the male comrade said: it is in vain, I'm taking you and you'll be mine. The female comrade who eavesdropped could not take it anymore and she left the veranda and entered the room of her aunt Milanović Savka, and she hit the pot that was in the hallway, and the female comrade asked: what is it, Osme? and he answered: this is a cat, it is nothing, and so they continued to kiss and make out. Comrade Jovanić could not stand this, so she went to the room adjacent to the road and started calling out for the guard who was 10 to 15 meters away and the same guard was on duty in front of this staff.

The female comrade managed to get the guard and to the same she said: call comrade Momčilo Bosnić, a member of the CPY and make him come here immediately. The guard called the said comrade and the same left but in the meantime the said [couple] parted and the female comrade went to sleep over at comrade Mijatović Mažena's, and Osme took the main road and the guard stopped him and asked him: who is it? And he said he was a Partisan and the guard let him pass. By that time, comrade Bosnić arrived at the place where Lenka and Osme had stood, and comrade Jovanić [dressed] only in a nightgown told, i.e., said to comrade Momčilo Bosnić what she had heard and all that she had seen. The same comrade can tell you how the matter proceeded.

This incident was discussed at a company meeting, the report stresses, where the matter was "correctly explained" to the fighters. It is worth noting that the fighters then opined that Lenka – the woman who was almost a rape victim in the story – was the culprit and needed to be "removed from their environs."[64]

In addition to the enthusiasm of local officials and the ambiguity of party expectations, the growing bureaucratization of Partisan institutions contributed to the presence of stories about sexual mischief in party reports from below. In the later stages of the war, liberated areas expanded, the units swelled, and so did the number of local party organizations. In addition, the frequency of mandatory reports increased. In 1943–4, local party forums were expected to submit reports bimonthly or even every ten days. In some remote villages of the liberated areas, very little seems to have happened in military and political affairs, and it is not entirely uncommon that the ten-day reports focused largely on personal affairs.[65]

[64] AVII, NOR, IRP BiH 5/82–3, Zamj. Politkomesara D. Karašević Okr. kom-u KPJ za Drvar, 10 November 1943.

[65] See, for example, the reports from the municipal party committee at Medan, Croatia. A typical example is its report in AVII, NOR, Muzej Like Gospić 1/728–30, Desetodnevni izveštaj, Opć. Komitet KPJ Medar Kotarskom Komitetu KPH za Gospić, 1 August 1944.

Given the power of enemy propaganda and the zeal of some local officials, it is easy to find examples of extremism on the ground. Party documents and personal narratives record instances in which Partisan women faced capital punishment for allegedly licentious behavior. The period of the so-called left deviationism in early 1942 – when party activists launched revolutionary terror to purge the Partisan ranks and the population from the "fifth column" – was notorious for such extreme measures. At the height of the red terror in Herzegovina, for example, two *partizanka*s of the Mostar Battalion were executed for allegedly practicing "free love." When it came to sexual norms, party extremists apparently had different standards for women and men – the women's male consorts, Partisan officers, were not punished.[66] According to Dobrica Ćosić, a similar fate befell the *partizanka* Boginja Mihailović of the Rasin detachment. While being treated for tuberculosis in a village, she reportedly had "intimate relations" with a local teacher and thus "morally compromised the Partisan movement." She was shot.[67]

Cases of extremism in the field could be found even after the party had abandoned and condemned the radicalism of its left errors. In one such instance, the promiscuous behavior of Mira S. caught the eye of some members of the district committee in southern Herzegovina. The committee promptly formed a commission with the task of investigating the case. "We have questioned Mira S.," wrote the commission in its statement, "and we have concluded that she had relations with many men." Mira S. reportedly admitted to having been drunk and to have slept with a deserter from the Partisan army. In addition, noted the commission, "when Omer P. was her comrade, she made out with comrade Bata in a stable." And in the same period, she apparently wrote love letters to another male comrade. To make matters worse, she was not humble during the questioning. The commission decided to expel her from the party and to send her to a higher party forum – to the regional committee for Herzegovina – for the final decision about her fate, with a warning that she "looked pregnant" and "should be medically examined." The commission's recommendation was that she be shot.[68] Whether she was actually executed is unknown.

[66] Marko A. Hoare, *Genocide and Resistance in Hitler's Bosnia: The Partisans and the Chetniks, 1941–1943* (Oxford, New York: Published for the British Academy by Oxford University Press, 2006), 229.

[67] Dobrica Ćosić, *Lična istorija jednog doba: Vreme otpora 1969–1980* (Beograd 2009), 31. As quoted in Pantelić, *Partizanke kao građanke*, 67–8.

[68] AVII, NOR, IRP BiH 6/725–6, Okr. kom za Južnu Hercegovinu, Oblasnom kom. KPJ za Hercegovinu, 14 April 1944.

The customary procedure involving the three-member commission for investigating the behavior of CPY members was, like most other party institutions, imported from the USSR. Whenever possible, CPY leaders attempted to model their policies on the Soviet example. But in unscripted wartime situations – when both their contact with Moscow and their familiarity with the current Soviet line on a particular issue were limited – the leadership had to improvise. As we shall see, many regulations were, in fact, unplanned and made in response to immediate circumstances.

Homosexuality: I have not seen any reference to homosexuality in Partisan documents or veteran reminiscences. It is perhaps not surprising to find the sole exception in the work of the Yugoslav communist dissident par excellence – Milovan Djilas. In his memoir Djilas describes how, in the fall of 1941, Rifat Burdžović, secretary of the Sandžak party committee at the time, informed him "in amazement" that the fighters of a Serbian battalion had exposed one of their Muslim comrades as a homosexual. Burdžović consulted Djilas about the situation, wondering whether this "freak" should be executed. Lamenting the fact that Marx and Lenin had never written about such matters, and that he knew of no standard party policy on the issue, Djilas had to decide the man's fate on the spot.[69] It was particularly hard since the man was "a good soldier" and "a zealous Communist." "While my common sense led me to conclude that not only bourgeois decadents but proletarians too were subject to such vices," Djilas writes, "I decided that no perverts could hold positions or be party members." The man was forced to resign from the party. He remained in the unit, though; proved "exceptionally courageous"; and ultimately "fell bravely."[70] While one should be cautious not to read too much into this one case, it is reasonable to assume that, despite the lack of standard policy, Partisan commands showed little tolerance for homosexual relations.

Prostitution and Venereal Disease: In the party's eyes, prostitution was a capitalist evil, reigning in reactionary and fascist armies. In the initial stages of the war, prostitution seems to have been of little concern to the leadership. But if the party in the first couple of wartime years could rely on the "political consciousness" of its most devoted members, the developments in 1943–4 made it necessary to establish a policy. Because of the rapid influx of recruits, new men, unfamiliar with the strict communist behavioral code,

[69] In fact, there was a policy of which Djilas seemed unaware – in the USSR, male homosexuality was outlawed in 1934.
[70] Djilas, *Wartime*, 127.

became a majority among the Partisan rank and file. Additionally, the liberation of many towns and cities – to which the Partisans had had little access previously, since their guerrillas had operated in rural peripheries and made very few incursions into urban centers – introduced unprecedented opportunities to find and hire women for sex. Male Partisans in such circumstances apparently proved not much different from the soldiers of any other army, and the party found it necessary to intervene. The committee of the 11th Division, for example, issued a proclamation explaining why prostitution was alien to the Partisans:

To every fighter it must become clear that we are the soldiers of a liberation war and the pioneers of a happier future and to us, as such, prostitution is alien. Prostitution is born and flourishes in reactionary, fascist armies. One of the goals of these armies is the rape of our wives, mothers, and sisters. We are fighting against them and against everything they stand for. The struggle against prostitution is part and parcel of our struggle for freedom.[71]

In 1944, the Supreme Staff issued an order that prohibited all fighters and officers from meeting with "problematic women." As usual, the order was passed down the hierarchical ladder, reminding male fighters that frequenting prostitutes would undermine the reputation of the National Liberation Army.[72] After the ban, the measures against prostitution – and against prostitutes – became increasingly coercive, particularly in the areas where the army had been stationed for longer periods. If caught, women suspected of prostitution near military barracks could expect to be incarcerated or sent to forced labor.[73]

Prostitution was closely linked with what Partisan leaders viewed as another, perhaps even more dangerous menace – venereal disease. Documents suggest that venereal disease caused the leadership a great deal of worry, perhaps second only to typhus, which periodically ravaged the units. This concern was not baseless as the Partisans faced what appeared to be an epidemic of venereal disease in two waves, first in winter 1943–44, and second in the latter half of 1944 and early 1945.

---

[71] AVII, NOR, IRP BiH 5/454–5, XI NOU Divizija, Sastanak divizijskog komiteta, December 1943. Emphasis in the original.

[72] AVII, NOR, IRP BiH 9/691–2, Naredba, Štab III korpusa NOVJ Oblasnom kom. za Ist. Bosnu, 23 November 1944.

[73] For example, the staff of the 6th Corps ordered "sanitary police measures," including "mandatory examinations and eventual incarceration of prostitutes and others suspected of spreading venereal disease." *Zbornik sanitetske*, vol. 3, doc. 297. Also, when the island of Vis was transformed into a military camp, the district committee there sentenced several prostitutes to forced labor. AVII, NOR, Muzej NR Split NOB 7/749–52, 752, Kotarski kom. KPH Vis-Lastovo Okr. Kom.-u KPH Dalmacije, 8 July 1944.

Internal party documents primarily blamed new recruits for the epidemic. "In the first years, the number of venereal patients in the ranks of the National Liberation Army was very small, almost infinitesimal," states a directive from the Croatian Main Staff, "but it has increased in the course of the war." This change was caused, the staff asserts, by the arrival of large numbers of "new fighters from the regions that had been under the occupiers for prolonged periods," as well as the entry of Partisan units into the formerly occupied villages and cities.[74] Indeed, the epidemic waves do correspond with the increased influx of new fighters, the first after the fall of Italy and the second following the beginning of mass conscriptions and Tito's amnesty to Partisans' local adversaries who switched sides. Very little documentation regarding venereal disease in the units exists on earlier periods.

The leadership responded with a broad educational and propagandistic campaign against the spread of venereal disease, organizing lectures and meetings both in the units and in the rear to inform the people about the dangers of infection. The campaign aimed to make it clear that venereal disease was a danger not only to infected individuals but also to the Partisan cause. "Such illnesses dishonor the people among whom they are being spread" – reads one proclamation – "and especially the army which has to be the best and most noble part of that people"[75] Lecturers stressed the political and military consequences of venereal disease. Militarily, it harmed the units by incapacitating the fighters. Politically and morally, it hurt the Partisan reputation and fueled enemy propaganda. "A high incidence of venereal disease does not speak of a high moral standard," warned the staff of the 6th Corps. "Our enemy counts on that."[76] Party propaganda made sure to identify the source of epidemics outside its ranks and to tie immorality, of both a political and a sexual nature, to the fascist enemy. The staff of the 6th Corps informed its ranks that it was, in fact, the enemy who was responsible for the spread of venereal disease in the first place by infiltrating the Partisan units with infected individuals.[77] In the same vein, party members elsewhere were instructed to explain to the masses that venereal disease had been "inserted by the enemy."[78]

---

[74] *Zbornik sanitetske* 5, doc. 77, p. 326; see also doc. 137, p. 448, which assigns the blame specifically to former Domobrans (Home Guard); see also AVII, NOR, IRP BiH 10/673–7, Pol. kom. XXVII Divizije NOVJ Oblasnom kom. KPJ za Ist. Bosnu, Izveštaj, 7 November 1944.

[75] *Zbornik sanitetske* 3, doc. 314, p. 580.

[76] *Zbornik sanitetske* 3, doc. 316, pp. 583–4.

[77] Ibid.

[78] AVII, NOR, IRP BiH 5/445–7, Zapisnik sa konferencije KPJ Opštine Srpska Jasenica, 3 December 1943.

Besides education, Partisan authorities increasingly used interventionist and policing measures. Among the first such measures was the introduction of questionnaires collected by the medical personnel about each patient. The patients were asked to provide information about the source of their infection – to identify the individuals with whom they had sexual encounters. The Area Command was authorized to find and send the named persons – be they Partisans or civilians – to the hospital to be medically examined and treated.[79] Local party committees in liberated zones had instructions to "watch closely" for cases of venereal disease. In the county of Jasenica (Bosnia), the committee reminded all party members that it was their duty to find and invite the sick to register and get medical treatment.[80]

Policing measures became even more drastic with the second wave, beginning in the latter half of 1944. In this period the National Liberation Army again swelled dramatically as a result of the liberation of large territories and general conscription there, as well as Tito's offer of amnesty to former Chetniks, Domobrans (Home Guard), and others should they join the Partisans. To suppress the spread of infection, the Croatian Main Staff ordered mandatory bimonthly examinations of all ranks in the operative units and in the military institutions in the rear alike.[81] In regions that were most severely affected, special medical teams led by venereologists formed to instruct medical personnel and provide specialist examinations.[82] (Women in the units were examined separately, usually by a female physician. The staff of the 10th Corps even ordered the formation of a separate medical team to examine female Partisans.)[83] In the operational zone of the 6th Corps, which was among the most gravely affected areas, the staff ordered medical personnel to provide a list of all venereal disease patients, which would include for each individual – besides the usual identifying information (name, age, birthplace, marital status, date of recruitment, military unit) – the date and place of infection and name of the person responsible for infecting the patient.[84]

In other words, lists of patients stating when, where, and with whom they had sex were compiled; concealing or failing to report an infected

---

[79] *Zbornik sanitetske 3*, doc. 125, p. 233; doc. 127, p. 236; doc. 132, p. 244.

[80] AVII, NOR, IRP BiH 5/445–7, Zapisnik sa konferencije KPJ Opštine Srpska Jasenica, 3 December 1943.

[81] *Zbornik sanitetske 5*, doc. 77, p. 326.

[82] *Zbornik sanitetske 3*, doc. 263, p. 474; *Zbornik sanitetske 5*, doc. 141, p. 466.

[83] *Zbornik sanitetske 3*, doc. 314, p. 580; *Zbornik sanitetske 5*, doc. 144, p. 474.

[84] *Zbornik sanitetske 3*, doc. 314, p. 580.

person became punishable. Moreover, the fighters were informed that becoming infected could get them into trouble. Anyone who knowingly became infected or infected another person – that is, anyone who had a sexual encounter while infected or with an infected person with the knowledge that that person had an infection – was to be "most severely punished."[85] Even those who contracted or spread the disease unwittingly would be held responsible, the staff noted, making sure that carelessness would not be an acceptable excuse. Most drastically, the staff of the 10th (Zagreb area) Corps decided that concealing one's condition or knowingly infecting someone else would be considered "an act of sabotage" and punished accordingly.[86] To be sure, most of these directives also noted that it would be counterproductive to reproach, mock, or penalize infected individuals publicly and called for a comradely attitude toward them. But they also made it clear that one's sexual activity and sexual health were *not* personal issues. If anything, the campaign against venereal disease normalized institutional intrusion into one's personal life.

Marriage and Separation of the Couples: No uniform, consistently implemented policy on marriage between fighters existed in the early stages of the war, but it seems that the Partisan soldiers were generally allowed to wed. Dedijer – as did other devout communists – considered wartime weddings, especially if accompanied by a feast, inappropriate. When Rade Stefanović, the commander of the Foča Battalion in February 1942, married, Dedijer noted in his diary:

Rade ... was married today.... Five other couples were also married. Rade asked Arso to be his best man and invited some ten people to a lunch with ten courses. The guests fired off 30 rounds ... Stefanović's guests were warned not to do this. Each bullet is dear now. The wedding is a stupidity.[87]

Although marriage for the Partisan rank and file and for officials in the Partisan institutions in the rear was not officially prohibited, it was strongly discouraged from the early stages of the war. The CPY emphasized that for everyone in the Partisan movement the first and foremost concern should be the struggle; love, marriage, and other personal matters were secondary and should be postponed until the war was won. The leadership was especially careful to explain its position to the young people associated with the Communist Youth League, who – much like young people anywhere – were most likely to be interested in these matters. In

---

[85] *Zbornik sanitetske* 3, doc. 316, pp. 583–4, and doc. 318, pp. 586–7.
[86] *Zbornik sanitetske* 5, doc. 144, p. 474.
[87] See Dedijer, *The War Diaries*, vol. 1, 85.

Bosnia, for example, the Communist Youth League took it upon itself to clarify the party line on wartime marriages. "Marrying," wrote the League of Drvar in a directive to its lower forums, "is wrong and damaging to our organization.... . For young people, today, at this hour, the struggle is the main and most pressing task, the struggle alone should be the primary item on one's agenda, and not love and marriage." To be sure, marrying did not have to be completely banned, but its harmful effect on the Partisan cause was to be made known to everyone.[88] Similarly, local party committees instructed activists to organize conferences and meetings at which they would denounce marrying and try to suppress the practice.[89] A party secretary in a liberated zone of Bosnia found it necessary to systematize various kinds of marriages, dividing them into useful and harmful ones, and directed his peers to "explain to the people the differences, to advise the people, and to ban the harmful practices via the organs of civil administration." According to him, marrying for any reason other than for the purpose of signing up for the army (which was a peasant tradition – it was customary that a young man marry prior to his military service) was an undesirable act and should be postponed.[90]

In their efforts to prevent the peasant youth from marrying, the communists met with mixed results. In some of the liberated zones, their successes were limited at best. "The occurrence of female and male marrying [*udaje i ženidbe*] is not as widespread as it used to be, but there are still many cases, even among the Communist Youth League members," wrote a member of the league's district committee in Bosanska Krajina. Female youths led the way in this respect, the report complained, assessing that the reason behind their eagerness to marry was "simple hunger for men, fear that they would stay unmarried."[91] Not only were the females more eager to wed, but also they reportedly seemed more likely to neglect or abandon their political duties afterward.[92]

Party members needed special permission to marry or divorce; to get it, they had to provide compelling reasons. Needless to say, this often led

[88] AVII, NOR, IRP BiH 5/500–3, Okr. kom. SKOJa Drvar, svim sreskim i op. komitetima SKOJa, 12 December 1943.

[89] AVII, NOR, IRP BiH 5/445–7, Zapisnik sa konferencije KPJ Opštine Srpska Jasenica, 3 December 1943.

[90] AVII, NOR, IRP BiH 5/414–17, Zapisnik, Partijska opštinska konferencija op. Srednji Dubovik, 7 December 1943.

[91] AVII, NOR, IRP BiH 5/720–3, Okr. kom SKOJ za Podgrmeč Oblasnom kom. SKOJ za B. Krajinu, 2 January 1944.

[92] AVII, NOR, IRP BiH 5/712–15, 713, Okr. kom SKOJ za Podgrmeč Oblasnom kom. SKOJ za B. Krajinu, 1 January 1944; AVII, NOR, IRP BiH 13/23–6, 24, Sreski SKOJ Bos. Novi Okr. kom-u SKOJ za Podgrmeč, 26 February 1945.

to misinterpretations and abuses on the local level.[93] As for the Partisan units, the first directive to spell out an official policy on marriage was issued in the spring of 1943. It prohibited marriage only for Partisan staff members; those who had already been married could not stay together in the same staff – one spouse had to be reassigned elsewhere. Other Partisan fighters were allowed to wed. Yet the directive reiterated that spouses, whether in the staff or not, must be appointed to the duties for which they were best qualified and that their potential wish to stay together should have no weight in the assignment process.[94]

Officials in the units interpreted the policy liberally, and it seems that in most cases it was taken to mean that all couples, irrespective of their marital status or position in the military hierarchy, should be subjected to such a regulation. Later directives upheld this interpretation; a 1944 instruction of a Serbian staff, for example, specifies that a "male comrade and female comrade, who come to the detachment [together]," must be assigned to two different companies. "They could live together only outside the military unit if circumstances allow."[95] In other words, whenever there were indications of romantic involvement, the couple in question was separated. Rava Janković and Mitar Minić, both Partisan fighters and both national heroes (she posthumously), were married in 1943. Almost immediately after the wedding, she was transferred to another unit. Minić described his disappointment with the party's decision:

It was the first marriage in our brigade.... After a day or two, they separated us. Rava was transferred from the First to the Third battalion ... we could not understand why they separated us, It looked as an attack on our marriage. Ultimately, we had to learn to accept that we could not be together. Separation was hard for

---

[93] For various reasons that party members provided and local committees reported, asking for directives from above, see AVII, NOR. IRP BiH 10/667, Okr. kom. SKOJ za Banja Luku Obl.komu SKOJa, 7 November 1944; AVII, NOR, Muzej Like Gospić 1/728–30, Opć. Komitet KPJ Medar Kotarskom Komitetu KPH za Gospić, 1 August 1944. For poor party records of those who married or started new relationships without permission, see AVII, NOR, IRP BiH 3/848, Oblasni komitet KPJ za Srem, pismo Obl. Kom.-u KPJ Istočna Bosna, 23 June 1943 (same document in AVII, NOR, IA PK SKS Vojvodine NOB 2/504); AVII, NOR, IRP BiH 12/767, Okr. kom. KPJ za Srednju Bosnu, Obl. Kom-u za B. Krajinu, 18 February 1945. For party reactions to cases of married members' separation in order for one of them to remarry see AVII, NOR, IA PK SKS Vojvodine NOB, 2/289–90, 290, PK KPJ za Vojvodinu Okr. kom-u za Severni Banat, 18 April 1944; AVII, NOR, IRP BiH 10/38–41, Sreski kom. Novi Okr. kom-u za Podgrmeč, 1 October 1944; AVII, NOR, IRP BiH 12/277, Sreski kom. za Bihać Okr. kom-u za Drvar, 17 January 1945; AVII, NOR, IRP BiH 12/277, Okr. kom Drvar Sreskom kom. za Bihać, 29 January 1945, and others.

[94] *Zbornik* 9.3, doc. 167, p. 706.

[95] *Zbornik* 1.7. doc. 154, p. 361.

us. We even blamed ourselves for not hiding our love, for, otherwise, we would have stayed together.[96]

Similar expressions of disappointment and anxiety could be found even in the recollections of the party elite. Despite the privileges that the top echelons of the CPY tended to reserve for themselves, they were not entirely exempted from this rule. Milovan Djilas and his wife, Mitra Mitrović, spent long intervals on duty, separated; so did Aleksandar Ranković and his wife Andja before she perished, and Vladimir and Olga Dedijer, just to name a few.[97] Mitra Mitrović left a touching account of her love for Djilas and the torment of separation in a letter:

I feel foolish and wretched when I think that I wish, at this moment, in such times, to speak to you about us and about our love. A *petite-bourgeoise*? ... I have not seen you for months ... my mother, our mothers and sisters in previous wars were free to think aloud, to pray that their beloved ones should be saved from death. But I, being a fighter myself, am not allowed to.... Please don't be killed.... . How much I wish to be in the column with you, especially when the road is dangerous.[98]

The way that the separation policy was implemented had an important gender aspect. It was almost always the woman of the couple suspected of romantic involvement who was transferred to another unit. A former *partizanka* remembers, not without exasperation:

One needs to understand that we were young folks.... Thus there existed some more or less public manifestations and expressions of special affections for a certain comrade. Such things happened. When they were noticed, when they became conspicuous, certain measures were taken, they were singled out, and sometimes people were transferred. The fact that a female comrade had a boyfriend was the reason to separate the two. I understand why that was done. *But to this very day it has remained unclear to me why it was only the women and not the men comrades who were transferred.*[99]

The punitive aspect of the policy, the separation itself, obviously affected both partners. But the way it was implemented through transfer often specifically targeted women. This should not be surprising, since individual party leaders, and to some extent the leadership in general,

---

[96] Mitar Minić, in Beoković, *Žene heroji*, 82.
[97] Both Andja Ranković and Olga Dedijer were killed in the war.
[98] Mitrović, *Ratno putovanje*, pp. 182–5. The letter is also quoted in Vladimir Dedijer, *The Beloved Land* (London: MacGibbon & Kee, 1961), 318–21, from which the preceding translation is taken.
[99] Draginja Višekruna-Lukač, "Ženska omladina u IV krajiškoj udarnoj brigadi," in Hurem, *Žene Bosne i Hercegovine*, 474. My italics.

deemed women the source of sexual tensions and accordant problems in the units. Party officials were not hesitant to single out the *partizanka*s overtly as a destabilizing factor. According to the party secretary of the 13th Proletarian Brigade, women's presence appeared to have had a debilitating effect on men's fighting spirit and military prowess. He complained that it was typical for the fighters of his brigade to "fall in love," whereupon "the female comrade, with the words 'be careful,' reduce[d] the fighting ability of the male comrade."[100] If romantic involvement not only was an aberration that fell short of the desired ascetic ideal but also proved detrimental to men's combat skills, and if female fighters were the cause of the problem, then the practice of transferring women appeared only logical.

Pregnancy and Abortion: Another reason behind the couple-separation policy may have been the leadership's attempt to prevent pregnancies, which would render women fighters temporarily incapable of fighting. An official of the Serbian gendarmerie noted in his report that "according to the seized acts of the Communist archive, it was strictly forbidden for [Partisan] women to get pregnant, in order to have as many of them as possible participating in combat."[101] While this statement should be viewed with caution, and while extant Partisan documents do not include such an explicit ban on pregnancy, it is certain that the leadership tried to minimize the occurrence among the *partizanka*s.

In some units, the general atmosphere was hostile to the possibility of a woman fighter's becoming pregnant. Within the ideological scheme that insisted on one's absolute dedication to the struggle, it was considered a serious mistake for a fighter to allow herself to conceive. As the former *partizanka* Nada Jovović remembers, in the eyes of Partisan hard-liners, it was an "attack on [their] often superhuman efforts to resist the superior enemy force," which was almost tantamount to treason. Jovović recounts the bitterness she herself felt toward a friend who became pregnant: "I thought that we, prewar Communists, could not behave [irresponsibly] like this, for we were more rigorous when judging our own mistakes, and this was a mistake in my view." It was also a mistake for which only women were held responsible. In Jovović's words,

[100] *Zbornik*, 9. 3, doc. 216, p. 903. For a similar complaint about a woman's fear for a man's life and its detrimental effects, see AVII, NOR, IRP BiH 13/252–7, 255, SKKPJ Visoko, Okr. kom-u Sarajevo, 10 March 1945.

[101] Report on the battle of 18 October 1943, between the Partisans and the SDS (Srpska Državna Straža – Serbian State's Guard, gendarmerie of the Serbian puppet government under Milan Nedić). Document reproduced in Cvetić, *Žene Srbije,* 686.

only females were blamed and reprimanded by their comrades, "as if only they [the women] would be the culprits for the birth of a child in such horrendous circumstances."[102]

But despite all the measures that the leadership undertook, pregnancies were not easy to prevent, even among some of the most prominent female Partisans and most devout communists. Given the extreme hardships of guerrilla warfare, there was but one solution for many pregnant *partizanka*s – abortion. There is no doubt that female fighters and activists could opt to terminate pregnancy with medical assistance both in the units and in the rear. From the onset of the war, abortions were performed by Partisan physicians, initially wherever circumstances allowed and later on in gynecological or surgical sections of Partisan hospitals.[103] As early as March 1942, the Supreme Staff's Central Hospital had a doctor assigned for gynecological practice in its civilian ambulance, located at the time in Foča, Bosnia.[104] Gynecological sections also existed elsewhere in the liberated areas where longer periods of tranquility allowed for the development of relatively advanced hospital networks. Although it is not possible to establish exact figures, evidence suggests that the practice was routine and approved by the leadership. Yet the party's position on abortion remained ambiguous. It vacillated to encompass contradictory issues: a dire wartime need for free access to abortion for Partisan women, an uneasy awareness of the Stalinist abhorrence and prohibition of abortion, and an increasing tendency for party intervention in the private lives of its members and followers.

In order to understand the party's wartime position, one needs to pause and look at how the communist line on this matter evolved prior to the war. As on any other question, the CPY's stance on abortion in the interwar period followed – and was often frustrated by – the Moscow line. Marxist thinkers in general had long been divided on the issue, with one group arguing for the annulment of all laws prohibiting abortion and another seeing childbearing as a woman's obligation and any fertility regulation as antisocialist. Lenin himself deemed free access to abortion

---

[102] Nada Jovović, in Beoković, *Žene heroji*, 467.

[103] For accounts of Partisan physicians (Julka Mešterović, Bela Hohšteter, and Saša Božović) who performed or were asked by their superiors to perform abortions for Partisan women during the war, see Mešterović, *Lekarev dnevnik* (Beograd: Vojnoizdavački zavod, 1968), 38; Saša Božović, *Tebi, moja Dolores* (Beograd: 4. jul, 1981), pp. 302–4; Bela Hohšteter's account in Beoković, *Žene heroji*, p. 96, and others.

[104] *Zbornik* 2.3, doc. 31, p. 92. The physician whose duties included gynecological services was Julka Pantić (Mešterović).

an elementary workers' right but also feared that a high incidence of abortion would be a barrier to constructing a new socialist society.[105] In 1920, three years after the revolution, the Soviet Union legalized abortion on a woman's request; pregnancy termination was to be provided free of charge in state hospitals by licensed physicians.[106] The 1920 decree was made in response to the growing number of illegal abortions due to economic privations in the wake of the Civil War and in the interest of women's health. Many Bolsheviks, including such women's rights activists as Alexandra Kollontai, who thought motherhood to be a natural and preeminent woman's duty, supported the law as a matter of principle, but "saw it as a necessary and temporary evil."[107] The Bolsheviks believed that social conditions would improve with the building of socialism, thus eventually solving the problem of unwanted pregnancy. Whether a transitory concession or genuine expression of Bolshevik values at the time, the USSR's legislation was the most liberal the world had seen.

In Yugoslavia of the 1920s, in contrast, abortion was considered homicide and was severely punished. Minimal revisions occurred with the new Penal Code, introduced in 1929, which allowed abortion for certain strictly defined medical reasons (only for cases in which pregnancy or childbirth endangered the woman's life).[108] In accordance with Moscow's policy, the CPY in the 1920s and early 1930s incorporated into its revolutionary program a demand for legalized abortion with free medical assistance.[109]

When, in the mid-1930s, the official Soviet cultural values underwent a profound shift, and a 1936 decree outlawed abortion and introduced a number of pronatalist incentives, the CPY found itself in an awkward position. Long known as the agitator for the legalization of abortion on the Soviet model, the party now had to defend the Stalinist antiabortion policy. *Proleter* promptly featured an article to explain the shift. The article began by noting that socialists had always opposed the bourgeois ban on abortion. This was the case, however, because of their concern for workers in capitalist societies who could barely provide sustenance for their children. Reiterating Stalin's claim about the purported realization

---

[105] David and Skilogianis, "The Woman Question," in David, *From Abortion*, 42.
[106] For more on abortion legislation in Russia and the USSR see Popov and David, "Russian Federation," in ibid., 223–77.
[107] Stites, *Women's Liberation*, 355.
[108] For more on abortion legislation in both Yugoslav states and in their successors, see Nila Kapor-Stanulovic and Henry P. David, "Former Yugoslavia and Successor States," in David, *From Abortion to Contraception*, pp. 279–316.
[109] See *Proleter*, January 1930, 6.

of socialism, *Proleter* concluded that, since capitalist conditions had been erased in the Soviet Union, abortion there became unnecessary.[110] The unsaid but clear implication was that the CPY would continue to agitate for legal abortion in the still bourgeois Yugoslav lands. Indeed, at the 5th Conference of CPY in October 1940, Vida Tomšič's report on women's issues placed on the revolutionary agenda a demand for abortion rights "until all conditions for carefree motherhood have been reached."[111] The party remained faithful to this principle when the country disintegrated in 1941, launching a propaganda campaign against the ban on abortion in the newly established Ustasha state. Party activists were instructed to discredit the new state's program, including its antiabortion legislation, by emphasizing that the latter was a measure against the poor, since those who were better off would find ways to have abortions illegally.[112] And, as noted, the principle was put into practice immediately in the newly formed Partisan units and on Partisan-held territories, where, if circumstances permitted, *partizanka*s had access to free physician-assisted abortions.

It is worth emphasizing that neither the Soviet nor Yugoslav communist elites officially proclaimed that abortion was a matter of individual choice or right. This was so even at the times of their most liberal policies – the Soviet 1920 decree, for example, did not recognize abortion as a woman's right.[113] Parroting Stalinist proclamations, the *Proleter* article discussed previously insisted that socialists in bourgeois countries agitated for abortion rights because of social conditions and "*not* for some faulty [idea of] a woman's freedom over her own body."[114] Similarly, the 1940 Tomšić report demanding legal abortion avoided declaring it a matter of women's elementary rights and instead underlined that it would be needed until social conditions have improved.

The Yugoslavs adopted the Soviet view of reproduction as a social rather than individual concern, in which party-state regulation was not only legitimate but also necessary. In the course of the war, the CPY

---

[110] "Zakon o zaštiti materinstva i zabrani pobačaja," *Proleter*, July–August 1936, 11.

[111] AJ, AFŽ, 141-10-47, Vida Tomšić's report, V zemaljska konferencija, October 1940; also published in *Izvori za istoriju KPJ, Peta zemaljska konferencija KPJ*, 128.

[112] For the campaign against the Ustasha ban on abortion, see AJ, SKJ 507, Hrvatska II/1, Cirkular KPH sa direktivom za stav po raznim pitanjima, 15 June 1941.

[113] Indeed, Soviet health officials in the 1920s insisted that abortion was *not* an individual right, that it could damage the state's interests, and that it should be reserved for extraordinary situations. Wendy Goldman, *Women, the State, and Revolution*, 255–6; Hoffmann, *Stalinist Values*, 100.

[114] "Zakon o zaštiti materinstva i zabrani pobačaja," *Proleter*, July–August 1936, 11.

assumed an increasingly interventionist role, trying to place the practice of abortion in the Partisan units firmly under its control. Initially free, abortion became less a matter of Partisan women's choice and more party controlled as the war progressed. Free access apparently led to a high incidence of abortions in Partisan hospitals. Reacting to the growing number of pregnancy terminations, the leadership decided to restrict the practice among the rank-and-file *partizanka*s. The year 1943 saw the introduction of abortion permission documents: Partisan physicians were now prohibited from performing the surgery without a document specially issued by the staff. According to the directive of the 6th Corps' staff (Croatia), military hospitals needed to submit an application to the staff for every pregnancy termination and "especially for those with social [rather than medical] indications"; the application had to provide information about the pregnant woman, including her marital status, military rank, and medical condition. This measure was taken, the directive stated, in order to place the practice under control and ensure that this surgery would be performed "only in truly necessary cases."[115]

Besides attempting to control the pregnancy termination practice through requiring permission, the party's intervention could go in another direction – toward suggesting abortion to a reluctant woman. This is most dramatically obvious in the biography of a prominent Montenegrin female communist, Đina Vrbica. The facts that she was married and, perhaps more importantly, that she died courageously and was posthumously proclaimed a national hero explain in part the openness of the sources in her case. Her story indicates that in situations involving female leaders, whose actions were supposed to be exemplary and who were thus not supposed to let themselves become pregnant, abortion could have been ordered from above. Vrbica discovered that she was pregnant soon after her Partisan husband had perished in a battle. According to her friend's recollection, she wanted to keep the baby. Knowing that Dr. Saša Božović could perform an abortion in the nearby Partisan hospital, she decided to conceal her pregnancy until it was too late for the surgery.[116] In her own memoir, the doctor in question, Saša Božović, provides a different story. She writes that Vrbica actually visited her, claiming that the "comrades" had sent her to do what was necessary, but that she wanted the baby more than anything. In an admirable act of women's solidarity, Dr. Božović, a mother herself, went to the Montenegrin Main Staff and

---

[115] *Zbornik sanitetske*, 3, doc. 164, p. 293.
[116] Nada Jovović, in Beoković, *Žene heroji*, 467.

used her medical authority in Vrbica's favor. After having maintained that an abortion would be too great a risk for the mother's life, she returned with permission not to perform the surgery.[117]

Some details in these contradictory recollections – Vrbica's reluctance to reveal her pregnancy, her claim to the doctor that the "comrades" had sent her, and, most important, the fact that the doctor needed permission *not* to perform the surgery – suggest that abortion was not always a matter of a woman's free choice. In Vrbica's case, it seems to have been the choice that the party made for her. Deserting the units and retreating to civilian life or to the rear was obviously not considered an option, at least not for some women in top positions, whose behavior was supposed to set an example for others.

Ideals and Realities: In their values and their wartime rhetoric, the Yugoslav revolutionaries differed from their predecessors, the early Bolsheviks. Although they too disdained bourgeois morality, sexual revolution was nowhere to be found on their agenda. Timing was one of the reasons behind this – by the time the Yugoslavs entered the historical stage, cultural values in the communist center, the USSR, had changed. The norms that they advocated were not those of the Bolshevik proponents of sexual liberation. Nor had the local history of female communist activism produced a character of the stature and influence of Alexandra Kollontai to bear the Yugoslav banner of women's sexual emancipation. Surely, among the CPY members one could find many erudite communists who had read Kollontai alongside Nikolai Chernyshevsky, August Bebel, and the classics of Marxism-Leninism, but very few still valued her ideas once the party elite had officially adopted Stalinist notions of sexual temperance. And hardly any among them deemed these ideas important during the perils of war. In an exceptional case, an overly enthusiastic party cell in Vojvodina included lectures on "free love" and the "sexual question" on the curriculum of its wartime political courses.[118] The cell members were immediately reprimanded from above for "distancing themselves from the current struggle," in which there was no room for such issues.[119]

It is difficult to evaluate the degree to which the actual sexual behavior in the units corresponded to the official ideal. Still more challenging

---

[117] Saša Božović, *Tebi, moja Dolores*, 302–7.
[118] AVII, NOR, IA PK SKS Vojvodine NOB 2/609–12, 609, Part. ćelija Sremska Mitrovica Okr. kom.-u za Ist. Srem, spisak predavanja, n.d.
[119] AVII, NOR, IA PK SKS Vojvodine NOB 2/616–17, Rukovodećoj part. ćeliji Sremska Mitrovica, od OK KPJ Ist. SREM, 29 September 1944.

is gauging the extent to which the Partisan rank and file internalized the prescribed value system and behavioral code. The official rhetoric's stress on discipline, propriety, and heroism did cater to the patriarchal moral code of traditional peasant communities, and it is reasonable to assume that many peasant Partisans accepted these values as their own. Most participant reminiscences either remain silent about the issue of sexuality or simply replicate the idealized official image emphasizing restraint and celibacy. These statements should not be taken at face value, though, since most of these accounts were subjected to censorship or self-censorship in order to conform to the official master narrative about the National Liberation Movement. But even sympathetic outsiders, such as Brigadier Maclean, appraise the Partisan lifestyle in similar terms:

The life of every one of them was ruled by rigid self-discipline, complete auster-ity: no drinking, no looting, no love-making. It was as though each one of them were bound by a vow, a vow part ideological and part military, for, in the condi-tions under which they were fighting, any relaxation of discipline would have been disastrous; nor could private desires and feelings be allowed to count for anything.[120]

Documentary evidence, however, seems to contradict such statements. A high incidence of abortion, a fair amount of reports mentioning inci-dents of a sexual nature, and the rapid spread of venereal disease in the units, all suggest that this idealized picture of abstinence needs some revi-sion, official rules notwithstanding. And it surely needs to be revised for the party leadership, as Milovan Djilas reminds us.

In the mass of Partisan recollections, Djilas's memoir stands apart for exposing the emergence of a new "hierarchical and official decorum" in the units and the accordant set of privileges that the party leadership reserved for itself. Precisely because of the high expectations regarding the behavior of the Partisan rank and file, he is critical of the top echelons of the CPY – including Tito, Sreten Žujović, and Moša Pijade – who failed to live up to such standards. As early as the fall of 1941 in Užice, he writes, the leading men of the Central Committee "were followed about by pretty little secretaries who were obviously more intimate with them than their duties required." Puritan that he was, Djilas found the matter "shocking."[121]

In politics, sexual license is often a symbol of power and privilege, and in that the party's leadership was not exceptional. Djilas's wife, Mitra

[120] Fitzroy Maclean, *Eastern Approaches*, 325.
[121] Djilas, *Wartime*, 93.

Mitrović, was perceptive when she remarked in Užice that such behavior "goes with power," adding that "a minister without a mistress" was "unthinkable" in the region.[122] Tito's affair with his secretary was known among the members of his entourage. Anecdotal evidence suggests that the behavior of the top was no secret among the troops, either.[123] Internal party documents confirm that the link between sexual license and status in the Partisan movement persisted down the hierarchical ladder: When it came to sexual mischief, high- and midranking party officials and military commanders – the so-called leaders (*rukovodioci*) – were disproportionally involved. Reports noticing immoral behavior in the units often identified the *rukovodioci* as primary culprits. The Politodjel of the 12th Krajina Brigade, for example, found the leading men of the battalion staffs responsible for spreading "unsound relations towards female comrades," which had almost "assumed the character of prostitution."[124] *Rukovodioci* also figured prominently among those who carelessly spread venereal disease.[125]

A double standard of sexual behavior clearly reflected the hierarchy and separated the party elite from the rest in the movement. Whereas Tito and his inner circle were off limits, party regulations did apply to those below them. The case of Vlado Dapčević, who tried to justify his own promiscuous habits by pointing to the leadership's behavior, is telling in this respect. According to a report sent to the Central Committee, Dapčević had "lost authority" in his staff "by living with many women and girls." But instead of responding self-critically during interrogation, he insisted that his conduct was not different from that of the highest party echelons. His superiors in Bosnia's provincial committee showed

---

[122] Ibid., 93.

[123] A humorous song, reportedly popular at the war's end, openly referred to Tito's penchant for women. In the song, a male narrator asks, "Comrade Tito, I'd like to ask you / whether one may make love to two," and Tito responds: "If you're diligent, you may to seven / But careful, comrade, not to be seen!" [Druže Tito, ja bih te upito / da l' se smije ljubiti po dvije / Smije sedam, samo da si vredan / Pazi, druže, da te ne utuže!]. As quoted in Darko Hudelist, "Anna Kőnig: Titova Tajna Žena," *Globus*, 10 November 2006.

[124] AJ, SKJ 507, CKKPJ 1943/283, Politodjel XII KNOU Brigade CKKPJ-u, 8 September 1943. Another report mentions a large number of "immoral relations," mostly among the leaders [*rukovodioci*]. AVII, NOR, IRPJ 1/790, Branko Petričević Kadja CKKPJ-u, 5 January 1945. Still another notes staff members' "grave mistakes in personal life" in relation to female comrades, AVII, NOR, IRPJ 1/197–201, Zam. Polkoma V Vojvodjanske brigade CKKPJ-u, 15 February 1944, and others.

[125] On leaders' carelessness and the spreading of venereal diseases, see *Zbornik sanitetske* 3, doc. 316, pp. 583–4; also AVII, NOR, IRPJ 1/828–30, Politkomesar 42. vazduhoplovne divizije CKKPJ-u, 30 January 1945, and others.

little understanding for this argument; it is hard to tell what appalled them more: his libertinism or his defense. They recommended that he be dismissed from his position and reprimanded by the Central Committee.[126]

CONCLUSIONS

In the final analysis, in assessing both the party's sexual politics and actual behavior in the movement, the picture seems far more complex than the official imagery suggests. In its proclamations, the party promoted communist self-discipline and sexual propriety as the values of all Partisans. For the noble cause of national liberation, both Partisan men and women were expected to sacrifice their private lives, and that included the realm of intimacy. They were supposed to suppress their sexuality and refrain from romantic involvement in the units. The sexual discipline that the party promoted accommodated the traditional patriarchal mores of peasant Partisans, and many accepted the CPY's norms as their own. The leadership, however, did not simply rely on the self-restraint of individual soldiers to uphold these standards, but established a modern system of regulatory mechanisms that allowed for the party's intrusion into and control of Partisans' intimate lives. The practice of monitoring and policing the personal lives of CPY members – through criticism and self-criticism, cadre questionnaires, *karakteristike*, and party commissions – was perfected during the war. And with the steady influx of new cadres, tens of thousands of people were introduced to the idea that their privacy was the domain of the party. Besides CPY members, the personal lives of everyone else in the movement could be subject to regulation. Romantic relationships were discouraged, couples separated, and illicit sexual behavior was sometimes penalized. In the extraordinary conditions of total war, campaigns against immorality, prostitution, marriage, and venereal disease further extended and normalized party interventionism. But regulations did not apply equally to all, and a double standard, mirroring the newly established political hierarchy, developed early on in the war. The behavior of many leaders never matched the official model of restraint.

---

[126] AJ, SKJ 507, CKKPJ 1944/591, Avdo Humo, pismo Marku (A. Ranković-u), 18 November 1944. Also *Izvori* 21, 132. Vlado Dapčević, brother of the famous Partisan commander Peko Dapčević, was a devout and unruly communist. He was several times expelled from and readmitted to the party. In 1948, he sided with Stalin against Tito. The following four decades until the collapse of communism he spent part in exile, part in and out of Yugoslavia's prisons, remaining a true believer in the communist cause.

In addition to the double standard that distinguished the party elite from everyone else in the movement, another double standard separated the two genders. The CPY's sexual politics affected women differently than men. Although party officials tried to police the sexuality of both female and male Partisans, they regarded women's sexuality as particularly dangerous and often directed their tutoring or punitive measures solely at women. Officials on the ground ordinarily identified women as culprits in incidents of a sexual nature, and some blamed them even for thwarting men's commitment to combat. The campaign against immorality in 1943–4 solely targeted the newly recruited women from the formerly occupied areas. The manner in which the separation policy was implemented simply affirmed this view: It was primarily women who were transferred to other units. Despite the party's genuine commitment to egalitarianism, sexual double standards and traditional notions about gender persisted. They would outlive the war and revolution, as we shall see in the following chapter.

5

After the War Was Over

Legacy

In the fall of 2005, the Serbian provincial town of Požarevac hosted an unusual event: a pageant electing "the most beautiful *partizanka*." Several girls from various parts of Serbia, together with one representative from Croatia, gathered to compete for the title. Runners-up could hope for one of the consolation prizes such as "the most photogenic *partizanka*," "the most charming *partizanka*," and "the *partizanka* with the firmest military step [*najčvršći korak*]." Among the program's many attractions were the contestants' march in Partisan uniforms with rifles and in (not-so-Partisan) high-heeled boots, and, as the high point of the evening, their parading in camouflage-painted bikinis. This odd beauty contest was held on 29 November to mark the major state holiday of Tito's Yugoslavia, the Day of the Republic – a date no longer celebrated in the region. High profile guests included Stevan Mirković, general of the former Yugoslav People's Army, and Josip Broz Joška, grandson of the late Josip Broz Tito. The pageant's organizer, Slavko Adamović, explained that his intention was to remind the people of a recent past that they seemed to have all but forgotten. And General Mirković saw this program as "an indicator of the fact that the people realized how superior the time before the disintegration" of Yugoslavia had been to the present. The Serbian media covered the event as an entertaining curiosity; some featured footage or photos of almost naked "Partisan" beauties in provocative poses.[1]

---

[1] "Lepo stoji partizanski bikini," *Glas javnosti*, 1 December 2005; "Na Dan Republike SFRJ održan izbor za naj pionire i partizanke," *Danas*, 1 December 2005; "Dnevnik," Radio Televizija Srbije, 29 November 2005.

Thus sixty years after the socialist Yugoslavia was founded in the wake of one war, and fourteen after it began falling apart in another, the *partizanka* was invoked to represent the regime and the nation that were no more. The manner in which she returned to Požarevac might have been a matter of parody, tasteless entertainment, simple ignorance, or all of the above. Still, she was no less a symbol of Tito's Yugoslavia than she had been in 1944, when the poet Vladimir Nazor named her the "new type of woman" and a unique Yugoslav contribution to the world. But what had happened to her in the meantime? How was she so forgotten that the Požarevac crowd felt the need to rescue her from obscurity? Equally puzzling, how did she turn – how could she have turned – from Nazor's *partizanka*, the heiress of the noblest South Slavic epic heroines, into a sex object in the camouflage bikini?

This chapter explores the legacy of women's mass mobilization and the Partisans' victory in World War II. The first section discusses women's position in the new socialist state. The second shifts the focus to the history of memory; it examines the ways that the *partizanka* was represented in postwar Yugoslav culture, following her evolution from the revolutionary icon in the early postwar years, over the first cracks in her heroic image, to the oblivion of the present. I look both at the officially sanctioned memory of the female Partisan – as promoted by state-sponsored commemorations, historiography, and memorials – and the emergence of alternative images in cinematography and literature. At the war's end, as we shall see, the *partizanka* became the preeminent symbol of Tito's Yugoslavia. The waning of her star in the following decades, through progressive sexualization, marginalization, and trivialization, reflected the decline of Tito's regime and, with it, of the Yugoslav nation itself.

WOMEN'S POSITION IN TITO'S YUGOSLAVIA

In turbulent Yugoslav history, few peacetime periods were as dramatic as the first decade after World War II. These were the years when communist revolutionaries, having succeeded in winning the war and seizing power, launched a series of programs in socioeconomic and cultural realms that aimed to transform society and build a new socialist nation out of the region's ethnoreligious mosaic. Their job was not easy, yet they lacked neither ambition nor drive. Much as their Soviet patrons, the Yugoslavs sought to restructure the economy through centralized planning, large-scale industrialization, and the collectivization of peasant land. In a country freshly emerging from a conflict that saw extreme interethnic violence, they offered a federal solution to the national question and dedicated themselves to the promotion of "brotherhood and unity" among its divided peoples. They also introduced sweeping legal reforms, aiming to solve the woman question and institute equality between the sexes.

In that same decade, while they were trying to establish a Soviet-style system within the country's borders, the CPY leaders suffered a tremendous blow from abroad – they were expelled from the Soviet bloc. The Tito-Stalin rift in 1948 forced the Yugoslavs to search for their own path to socialism. Among the first steps in that direction was the passing, in 1950, of the law on workers' self-management, which introduced a system of participatory workers' councils to replace centralized state control in the economy. The country's development thereafter would be characterized by gradual democratization and decentralization in the economic and political spheres. In 1953, the party abandoned Soviet-style collectivization of agriculture and approved the restoration of land parcels to private peasant ownership. In the international arena, the Yugoslavs increasingly took a neutral stance in the Cold War, orienting themselves primarily toward the Third World, while the country began opening to cultural trends from the West. By the mid-1950s, Yugoslavia had been well set on an independent reformist course it would retain for the duration of communist rule. That course rested on the triple principle of "self-management" in the economy, "nonalignment" in foreign policy, and "brotherhood and unity" in nationality policy. On this course, much as in the Stalinist era that preceded it, the promotion of gender equality remained one of the party's professed goals.[2]

Judging by the range of new legal and political rights they bestowed on women in the 1940s and 1950s, Yugoslav communists were true to their wartime promise. Already during the war, as we have seen earlier, the party had accorded to women the right to vote and be elected in the so-called national liberation councils. This right was confirmed in the 1946 Constitution. Article 24 established the basic framework for legal equality between the sexes, stating that "women have equal rights to men in all areas of state, economic, and socio-political life." The same article guaranteed equal pay for equal work and "special protection" for females who were employed. Women became primary beneficiaries of a

---

[2] In 1952, the CPY changed its name to the League of Communists of Yugoslavia. For simplicity, I will continue to use "the party" to refer to this organization throughout the chapter.

comprehensive social welfare program. An emphasis was placed on the protection of mothers and children; the new state took it upon itself to establish nurseries, children's homes, and day care centers, as well as to guarantee the mother's right to paid leave before and after giving birth. Maternity leave was at first set at ninety days, but in the ensuing years it was extended to the child's first birthday. In a huge step away from the prewar civil law, the 1946 Constitution instituted civil marriage, while a series of laws further elaborated regulations of matrimonial and family relations that made the rights and duties of marital partners equal. Divorce was made accessible to both partners. Discrimination against children born out of wedlock was also abolished, their rights becoming equal to those of children born to married mothers. In the following decades, a number of legislative measures built on this constitutional framework to improve women's legal position further. The prewar discrimination against women in inheritance laws, for instance, was annulled by new legislation in 1955 that guaranteed inheritance rights regardless of sex.[3]

Abortion was a more controversial issue for the new regime and its full legalization would take longer. The old prewar Penal Code, which permitted pregnancy termination only for strictly defined medical reasons, remained in effect until 1951. For illegal abortions, the old code stipulated harsh penalties: imprisonment of up to five years for the pregnant woman and ten years for the person who assisted her.[4] This was in sharp contrast to the Partisan practice during the war, when abortions were routinely performed by Partisan physicians. Once in power, the communist leadership could have been reluctant to decriminalize pregnancy termination on request in part because it initially modeled its policies on those of the Stalinist Soviet Union, where abortion was prohibited at the time; the Yugoslavs moved toward a more liberal policy only after the Tito-Stalin break. A decree promulgated in 1952 made "sociomedical" reasons acceptable grounds for pregnancy termination. Further liberalization ensued in the following years, with a 1960 decree authorizing abortion on demand if birth could place the pregnant woman "in serious personal, family, or material" circumstances. Thereafter, Yugoslavia would have one of the most tolerant abortion policies in the world. Abortion on demand was reaffirmed in a 1969 law, which also

---

[3] Dr. Vera Gudac-Dodić, "Položaj žene u Srbiji (1945–2000)," *Srbija u Modernizacijskim procesima XIX i XX veka, Vol. 4: Žene i deca*, ed. Latinka Perović (Beograd: Helsinški odbor za ljudska prava, 2006), 34–8. See also idem, *Žena u socijalizmu: polozaj žene u Srbiji u drugoj polovini 20. Veka* (Beograd: INIS, 2006).

[4] Neda Božinović, *Žensko pitanje u Srbiji u 19. i 20. veku* (Beograd: 94, 1996), 158.

established that families have the right to decide on the number of children they wish to have. In 1974, it became the first country to proclaim the right to choose about the birth of children to be a human right. Article 191 of the 1974 Federal Constitution declared, "It is a human right to decide freely on childbirth. This right can be restricted only for the purpose of health protection."[5]

The Partisan women's organization, the AFW, remained in charge of "work with women" in the initial postwar years. Why did the party pay attention to women's issues in its socialist nation-building efforts? Most obvious, gender equality was an integral part of the communist ideological script, and the early postwar era was one of ideological hyperorthodoxy in Yugoslavia. In addition, the country's reconstruction and the creation of an industrialized socialist nation depended upon the development of a large industrial proletariat – female as much as male. Drawing females into the labor force now became as important as drawing them into the Partisan movement had been during the war. On the other hand, in communist eyes, women remained a generic category, presumably more backward, narrow-minded, and passive than the male half of the population, and thus in need of special guidance and control. After the war, the party began worrying that females, backward as they were perceived to be, were easy prey for counterrevolutionary propaganda and a potential threat to the new order. "The enemy spreads its propaganda mainly through women, using their ignorance [*neukost*] and cultural backwardness," reported Bosnian officials, with alarm, in 1947.[6] At the same time, as mothers and primary educators of future generations, women were considered indispensable to the success of the communist project. The CPY thought it necessary that they be educated in the spirit of socialism and "brotherhood and unity" in order to transfer these

[5] Nila Kapor-Stanulovic and Henry P. David, "Former Yugoslavia and Successor States," in *From Abortion to Contraception: A Resource to Public Policies and Reproductive Behavior in Central and Eastern Europe from 1917 to the Present*, ed. by Henry P. David (Westport, CT: Greenwood Press, 1999), 296–7. Gudac-Dodić, "Položaj žene," 43–4; Sabrina Ramet, "In Tito's Time," in *Gender Politics in the Western Balkans: Women and Society in Yugoslavia and the Yugoslav Successor States*, ed. Sabrina P. Ramet (University Park: Pennsylvania State University Press, 1999), 96. (Ramet provides a slightly different translation of the Constitution.)

[6] AJ, AFŽ, 141-2-4, "Zemaljski odbor AFŽ za BiH, Centralnom odboru AFŽa: Izveštaj o radu organizacije od prvog kongresa AFŽa," 24 March 1947. Their comrades from Croatia noted that the enemy, particularly the reactionary clergy, had influence on the female masses due to "women's low cultural level and lack of orientation." AJ, AFŽ, 141-2-4, "Predkongresni Izveštaj NR Hrvatske, od GO AFŽ Hrvatske za CO AFŽ Jugoslavije," 29 December 1947.

values to their children.[7] For all these reasons, special work with women was considered necessary, and the existing women's organization, which had already proven its usefulness to the party during the war, seemed the best medium. The AFW in the revolutionary postwar years thus played multiple roles as women's organizer, political educator, lobbyist for women's rights, and transethnic mediator. It was particularly active in the cultural and educational work among women as well as in organizing help and services for working mothers.

The party, however, had never given up the notion that a separate, centralized political organization for women in a socialist polity could only have a provisional character. As soon as the major battles with "reactionary forces" and then with Stalin seemed to have been won, the necessity of the AFW was called into question. In 1950, the AFW lost its status as an autonomous organization; it officially became a part of the main mass organization, the Popular Front, women's councils turning into the front's sections.[8] Three years later, after its organizational form had been pronounced "outdated and superseded" in view of the general trend toward decentralization, the AFW self-dissolved.[9] According to the official explanation, the basic sources of women's legal and political subjugation had by then been removed. The still existing forms of inequality and "retrograde views" about women were due to the fact that Yugoslavia's socioeconomic basis was not yet fully developed; the solution, party ideologues insisted, lay in the further "socialist building of our country."[10] In such circumstances, special political work with females and a separate women's organization were no longer needed.[11] The AFW's dismantling ended a unique era in the history of the Yugoslav women's movement – one

---

[7] On the AFW as "the educator of mothers as primary educators," AJ, AFŽ, 141-2-5, Referat Cane Babović, II kongres AFŽ, 25–27 January 1948; AJ, AFŽ, 141-7-6, Referat Vide Tomšič "O ulozi AFŽ u vaspitanju socijalističkog čoveka," IV Plenum AFŽ, 14–15 February 1950; AJ, AFŽ, 141-3-8, Referat Mare Radić; also Rezolucija po referatu Mare Radić, III kongres AFŽ, 28–9 October 1950. For similar concerns of the Bolshevik leadership about women's potential to sabotage the new order and their importance as mothers in the Soviet Union, see Elizabeth Wood, *The Baba and the Comrade: Gender and Politics in Revolutionary Russia* (Bloomington: Indiana University Press, 2000).

[8] AJ, AFŽ, 141-3-7, Pregled statuta AFŽ, 1953.

[9] AJ, AFŽ, 141-4-10, Pripremni materijal za Četvrti kongres AFŽ, Pismo sekretarijata CO AFŽ, 1953.

[10] AJ, SŽDJ, 354-10, Edvard Kardelj, "O položaju žena;" Dobrivoje Radosavljević, "Dalji rad na poboljšanju društvenog položaja žena," referat na 5. plenumu SSRNJ, 1956, quote from pp. 14–15; AJ, SŽDJ, 354-2, Marija Šoljan, "Pred konferenciju žena Jugoslavije," *Vjesnik* 16 April 1961; "Riješeni su osnovni problemi žena kod nas [interview with Veljko Vlahović]," *Vjesnik*, 20 April 1961.

[11] AJ, SŽDJ, 354-10 "Materijal o borbi žene za socijalizam," 1962, p. 33.

of women's unprecedented politicization and mobilization en masse. Its successors, decentralized associations, the League of Women's Societies of Yugoslavia (Savez Ženskih društava Jugoslavije, 1953–61) and the Conference for the Social Activity of Women (Konferencija za društvenu aktivnost žena, after 1961) had only marginal organizational powers.

It is worth mentioning that, around the same time that the wartime women's organization disbanded, precommunist ideas about femininity started creeping back into public discourse. In the first postwar years, party propaganda, the media, and culture in general adopted the Soviet socialist-realist imagery, which favored strong females, activists, and shock workers who exceeded all work quotas *and* were exemplary mothers as well. The image of the "muscular" female shock worker with her "monumental femininity," as one Yugoslav scholar characterized it, glorified "strength and fertility that were necessary for socio-economic and demographic renewal" after the war.[12] That model, however, soon started to give way to different ideals. In the early 1950s, the cult of beauty and the culture of female fashion, which had been rejected immediately after the war, began to return.[13] Major Yugoslav newspapers started featuring a section entitled the "Women's Page" (*ženska strana*), which was dedicated primarily to fashion, cosmetics, and recipes. Such topics also assumed a prominent place in the official women's press. Party officials and AFW activists disapproved of the trend but did little besides voicing mild criticisms.[14] Looking back at the 1950s, it seems ironic that a relaxation in the political and economic spheres coincided with a backlash in gender values and with the beginning of a stagnant episode in the history of women's organizational activity.

As far as women's status in Tito's Yugoslavia is concerned, the regime's formal commitment to gender equality indeed led to many striking advances. Take education, for instance. Although illiteracy was not entirely eliminated, illiteracy rates for females older than ten years of age were reduced from the appalling 56.4 percent in 1931, to 35.8 percent in 1953, to 28.8 percent in 1961; almost three-quarters of illiterate women in 1961 were older than thirty-five. Gradually, women's representation

---

[12] Neda Todorović-Uzelac, *Ženska štampa i kultura ženstvenosti* (Beograd, 1987), 113, as quoted in Gudac-Dodić, "Položaj žene," 65–6.

[13] Gudac-Dodić, "Položaj žene," 66.

[14] AJ, AFŽ, 141-4-10, Pretkongresni izveštaj iz BiH, Četvrti kongres AFŽ, 1953; AJ, AFŽ, 141-5-11, Vida Tomšič, govor na četvrtom kongresu AFŽ, 1953; Josip Broz Tito, "Odgovori na pitanja glavnog urednika časopisa Žena danas," *Govori i članci*, vol. 14 (Zagreb: Naprijed, 1962), 252.

in the school system began approaching men's, starting with elementary schools all the way up to universities. In the period between 1945 and 1977, women constituted 36.5 percent of all graduates of Yugoslav institutions of higher education, in comparison to 19 percent in 1939.[15]

Similar advances could be reported in the labor force. The First Five Year Plan was launched in 1947, opening the process of the country's rapid industrialization. The number of employed women, as well as their percentage in the workforce, increased dramatically in the first years of industrialization and continued growing throughout the communist era. Already in 1949 the number of working women was four times higher than in 1945, while the number of working men tripled in the same period. The rate of growth in the employment of women would remain consistently higher than that of men until the late 1980s.[16]

Despite the remarkable progress in the economic and educational spheres, feminist scholars argue, several problems pertaining to women's position remained unresolved. First, women's political participation was consistently low in socialist Yugoslavia. From the early revolutionary days on, females were underrepresented in government institutions and within the party itself. This was particularly visible in leadership bodies. Their participation in the Federal Assembly, for example, never exceeded 20 percent.[17] In 1948, women constituted 19.9 percent of party members, and their representation dropped dramatically at the upper levels of party hierarchy – that year, only three women (4.8 percent) were included on the list of candidates for the Central Committee.[18] No significant changes to that pattern would occur in the future.

Second, the traditional division of labor within the family persisted, as household duties and care for children and the elderly continued to rest on women's shoulders. Although the communist regime put some effort into including females in the "men's sphere" of work and politics, it did little to promote men's engagement in the household, leaving women with the triple burden of job, domestic responsibilities, and child rearing. Importantly, women's organizations and the regime itself

[15] Ramet, "In Tito's Times," 96.
[16] Neda Božinović, "Žene u modernizacijiskim procesima u Jugoslaviji i Srbiji," in *Srbija u modernizacijskim procesima 19. I 20. veka*, ed. by Latinka Perović, vol. 2, 525.
[17] By the end of the 1950s, women's representation had been less than 7 percent; after the high of 19.6 percent in 1963, it varied: 13.3 percent in 1967, 8.1 percent in 1969, 13.6 percent in 1974, 17.5 percent in 1978, 17.5 percent in 1982, and 16.2 percent in 1986. Gudac-Dodić, "Položaj žene," 114.
[18] Ramet, "In Tito's Time," 99.

recognized the conflict between women's domestic and social roles as a major obstacle to gender equality. Political elites believed that the problem would be solved, first, by a general rise in the standard of living, and, second, through the socialization of domestic work: through the development of state-subsidized services – such as day care centers, workers' canteens, laundry facilities, and the like – that would relieve women of some domestic chores. But improvement in both areas proved insufficient; inadequate availability of day care centers in particular remained a chronic issue.[19] Third, and related to that, the sex-based division of labor transcended the confines of the family and was, to a degree, mirrored in the workforce. Women continued to be concentrated in traditional female occupations (social services, textiles, sales, health care, elementary education) and underrepresented in, or excluded from, others (judges, university professors, state administrators, journalists, lawyers).[20]

The last and most important problem was also possibly the root cause of all these listed. It concerned the system of values and attitudes about gender, as promoted in public discourse, the media, education, and culture in the broadest sense. Here traditional notions proved stubbornly resistant and the party did not bother to launch a sustained attack on them. This was the case in part because the communists, following Marx, believed that gender values would eventually change with the structural transformation of the material base and did little to enforce that change. But it was also because the leadership, though advocating equality and believing in social engineering, abandoned neither the notion of "organic" gender differences and "natural" roles nor the propensity to value those roles differently. A study of elementary school textbooks, published in 1979, provides a good illustration of the gender values that, despite the party's mantra of equality, prevailed in Tito's Yugoslavia. According to the study, 73 percent of all persons mentioned in the schoolbooks were male. What is more, the books portrayed men and women in radically different terms. Male characters were strong, brave, soldierlike, and creative; boys were encouraged to become so themselves. There was, on the other hand, little incentive for boys to become good parents or care about their looks. The schoolbooks offered another set of values to girls: The women depicted in them were as a rule "maternal, beautiful, and indecisive."[21] Gender, in brief, remained one of the key mechanisms to separate human

---

[19] Božinović, "Žene u modernizacijiskim procesima," 526–9.
[20] Ramet, "In Tito's times," 97–8.
[21] Rajka and Milan Polić, "Dječji udžbenici o neravnopravnosti medju spolovima," *Žena* 36.1 (1979), as described and cited in ibid., 104.

characteristics and delineate social roles, as well as one of the principal axes of their hierarchical ordering in the new system. Yet in the final analysis one must note that, for all of the failures of communist gender politics, the rights accorded to women in the communist era remain one of its most positive legacies in the region.

What happened to the women of Yugoslavia who had been recruited into the wartime Partisan movement when the war ended? Like women everywhere after World War II, most *partizanka*s were demobilized. The process of women's withdrawal from the regular army forces, which had already begun during the war, was finalized in the early postwar years. According to the 1946 Military Service Law, female citizens could be drafted into the professional and technical services in the preparatory stages for war or in wartime conditions; however, they were *not* to serve as permanent military cadre. The few female Partisans who did remain in the military after World War II were serving as reserve and petty officers, most of them physicians in the medical corps. Other women were typically employed in clerical positions. In 1953, for example, not a single woman could be found among the rank and file in the regular units of the Yugoslav military (infantry, artillery, navy). Altogether there were only 1,676 females in the army. The vast majority of them, 1,086, were in administrative positions; 14 were noncommissioned officers; 576 women, former *partizanka*s, were officers, but only 20 of them were among the higher-ranking ones (2 colonels, 5 lieutenant colonels, and 13 majors), all serving in the medical corps as doctors.[22]

By the 1950s, communist authorities had started excluding women not only from the military but also from all professions that demanded the use of arms. In the initial postwar era, women could at first serve in the police force (at that time known under the name of "People's Militia"). Female militias were primarily to be found among the security guards of women's penitentiaries. But after 1951, when Aleksandar Ranković launched a reform of the legal system and the police, new, all-male prison guards were introduced, driving out females even from this service. The belief in organic gender characteristics, which naturally organize the division of labor into men's and women's jobs, continued to shape communist policy despite the party's obvious attempts to expand women's roles. Some careers were simply to remain off limits for Yugoslav females. According to a 1953 AFW report, "There is no tendency to include women in the

---

[22] AJ, AFŽ, 141-12-62, "Žene u Jugoslovenskoj Narodnoj Armiji," 1953; *Službeni list* 28/46 (April 1946).

People's Militia, because this is a *difficult and inappropriate [neprimeren]
job for women today.*"[23]

Yet unlike their counterparts in the West, who were also largely
removed from the workforce in order to make room for returning soldiers, Yugoslav women did not return to the home after the war. Instead,
the majority of former female Partisans moved to towns and cities, find-
ing employment or assuming administrative positions in the new state.
The AFW often helped the demobilized women find accommodations
and jobs. In Croatia, for example, the front of women organized a special commission in charge of providing aid to discharged female soldiers.
The city AFW of Zagreb ran two homes for former *partizanka*s that
could host ninety women at a time; the organization also facilitated the
accommodation of Partisan women in the homes of local female workers until they found appropriate employment and housing.[24] In the new
regime, lower-ranking female Partisans could hope for clerical posts in
the state and party bureaucracy. The more prominent *partizanka*s, usually those with prewar party membership and important functions during
the war, were assigned to higher party committees, government ministries, and various other offices in the growing administrative apparatus
of the new regime. Those with medical training tended to remain in the
profession, with the select few working for the army. Many party women
who had fought in the war retained or assumed important positions in
the postwar AFW.

Although removed from daily reality, the figure of the female Partisan
soldier did not disappear from the public eye. The *partizanka* instead
moved to the realm of cultural representation and memory. In the first
postwar decades, she was a ubiquitous symbol of the new state – a revolutionary icon par excellence.

REMEMBERING THE *PARTIZANKA*

For Tito's Yugoslavia, the memory of the victorious Partisan struggle was
of enormous importance. It was the state's foundational myth, whose
powers could perhaps be grasped if one recalls the merging of the memory of the 1917 Revolution and the Great Patriotic War in the Soviet
context. Remembering the war in Yugoslavia was therefore, as Wolfgang
Hoepken writes, "a matter of a wide-ranging and sophisticated 'policy of

---

[23] AJ, AFŽ, 141-12-62, "Žene u Jugoslovenskoj Narodnoj Armiji," 1953; my italics.
[24] AJ, AFŽ, 141-2-4, "Rad AFŽ Hrvatske 1945–47," 1947, p. 26.

memory.'" "Offending" the memory of the National Liberation Struggle was considered a "political crime" and could lead to legal persecution.[25] The war was by far the most favored topic of historical scholarship; thanks to the state's practice of commissioning research and writing on the Partisan struggle, today we have a colossal body of publications on the topic. Works of professional historians, however, constitute only a small segment of what seems a hyperproduction of texts, both visual and verbal, on the war and revolution. One can find an astonishing number of memoirs, poems, diaries, reminiscences, fictionalized accounts, children's books, films, documentaries, comic books, works of art, plays, songs – Partisan-themed narratives in practically every existing type of cultural production. And almost all official holidays of the second Yugoslavia and all memorials built during Tito's era were dedicated to the war.

As is always the case with official versions of historical memory, the function of the memory of World War II in Tito's Yugoslavia was to legitimate the regime and forge a common national feeling, if not a collective identity.[26] The master narrative of the national liberation struggle portrayed the war in rather black-and-white colors. The narrative centered on the CPY and the Partisans and served to demonstrate their ideological and moral superiority over all other warring factions and political options in Yugoslavia.[27] It recounted the struggle of the Partisans, the working class, and even more broadly "the people as a whole" (*narod*) led by the party, against "the people's enemies" (the term that delineated a network of foreign invaders, prewar bourgeoisie, the Ustashas, the Chetniks, and various other local factions). In its less sophisticated renderings, the master narrative transformed the war into one between absolute good and absolute evil, ultimately naturalizing the hyperproduction of texts about it. A typical, if simplistic, illustration appears in a children's book on the National Liberation Struggle. In one of the stories, the main character is a Partisan girl chased by an undefined "enemy." She runs through a forest, and, as the enemy approaches, various creatures from the forest, including the bushes, birds, and trees, which supposedly

---

[25] Wolfgang Hoepken, "War, Memory, and Education in a Fragmented Society: The Case of Yugoslavia," *East European Politics and Societies* 13.1 (Winter 1999): 196, 197.

[26] Ibid. On the "phenomena of memory" and the role of official memory see Pierre Nora, *Realms of Memory: Rethinking the French Past* (New York: Columbia University Press, 1996–8); Henry Rousso, *The Vichy Syndrome: History and Memory in France since 1944* (Cambridge: Harvard University Press, 1991); Jay Winter, *Sites of Memory, Sites of Mourning: The Great War in European Cultural History* (New York: Cambridge University Press, 1995).

[27] Hoepken, "War, Memory, and Education," 197.

"hate the black fascists," warn her and help her hide, thus saving her life. The narrator frames her story with the assertion that "then, when we were in the Partisans, everything was with us [on our side]: the people, forests, animals."[28] Nature itself thus became an active participant in the struggle and placed itself on the side of the Partisans. During much of the party's reign, the master narrative had no public rivals; its omnipresence simultaneously dehistoricized the struggle and turned the Partisan epos into the supreme historical metatext of the communist era.

A prominent place in the master narrative was reserved for the *partizanka*. She, in fact, emerged as one of the most eminent symbols of Tito's Yugoslavia and a major source of legitimacy for the regime. The AFW and its successors, the League of Women's Societies and the Conference for the Social Activity of Women, alongside the Partisan veterans' association, served as official promoters and guardians of her memory. After the war, the female Partisan was remembered on such occasions as official holidays and celebrations of March 8, International Women's Day. In 1946, for instance, when the new regime organized a ceremonial gathering and performance in observance of March 8, disabled women veterans and mothers of fallen Partisan fighters were invited together with some of the country's highest officials. The ceremony opened with a minute of silence in honor of "fallen female comrades," while the principal speaker, Cana Babović, reminded the audience of the heroic deeds of Yugoslav women during the war.[29] That year, and many years thereafter in Tito's Yugoslavia, on March 8, the press kept recalling women's participation in the struggle.

Commemorations for the anniversaries of major wartime events did the same. On the tenth anniversary of the uprising in 1951, the house that had hosted the first AFW conference in Bosanski Petrovac was decorated with a memorial plaque.[30] Next year, ten years after the founding conference, another commemoration was organized in Bosanski Petrovac.[31] The AFW's founding event was memorialized even after the organization

---

[28] Vida Brest, "Ptice i grm," in *Priče iz Narodnooslobodilačke Borbe* (Zagreb: "Naša djeca," 1979), 252.

[29] "Svečana akademija u Kolarčevoj zadužbini povodom proslave 8. marta," *Politika*, 9. mart 1946.

[30] AJ, AFŽ, 141-7-18, Stenografske beleške, VI plenum CO AFŽ, izlaganje Maje Koš, 25–6 November 1952; AJ, AFŽ, 141-14-74, Pozivno pismo Titu, Materijali II konferencije AFŽ u Bosanskom Petrovcu povodom održavanja proslave 10-god. Ustanka i priprema za 10 godina I konf. AFŽ, 1951.

[31] AJ, AFŽ, 141-14-74, Materijali II konferencije AFŽ u Bosanskom Petrovcu povodom održavanja proslave 10-god. Ustanka i priprema za 10 godina I konf. AFŽ, 1951.

itself ceased to exist, and each anniversary honored the *partizanka*, with commemorations becoming ever more elaborate. For the twentieth anniversary in 1962, for example, the League of Women's Societies formed a federal committee to prepare the celebration. The committee created a detailed plan that involved the press and several commemorative events. It first gave the media a "special task" for the occasion – they were not only to feature interviews with prominent individual women, but also to "revive the remembrance" of all female participants in the struggle and, using the documentary material that the committee supplied, highlight the diversity of their wartime roles. It also planned two commemorative galas, one in Bosanski Petrovac, another in Belgrade, the latter to be held in the largest auditorium of the city, the Syndicates' Home (Dom Sindikata), featuring speeches and a musical performance by the Belgrade Philharmonic.[32]

In addition to commemorations and holidays, many other symbolic forms of historical memory kept the image of the *partizanka* alive. The most prominent women of the National Liberation Movement had schools, streets, and various institutions named after them. The anonymous rank-and-file *partizanka* was remembered through Partisan songs, photographs such as the legendary *Kozarčanka* (see Figure 10), and Partisan-themed literature taught in Yugoslavia's schools, as well as through memorial complexes honoring war heroes and victims of fascism. And she had memorial sites of her own: monuments to the Partisan mother and to the woman fighter, and a museum dedicated to the first female Partisan unit, among others.

Yugoslav historical literature on women's participation in the struggle is itself a series of memorials to the *partizanka* – and not only in a metaphorical sense. The preponderance of that literature is not the work of professional historians; rather it is the product of meticulous research and documentation that were initiated and sponsored by the AFW and its successors and conducted by the organizations' various committees. In Tito's time, the country's six federal units each had a volume published on the wartime exploits of women from their respective regions; in addition, one volume was dedicated to all women of Yugoslavia.[33] These books are

---

[32] AJ, SŽDJ, 354-10, Informacija o proslavi dvadesetogodišnjice AFŽa, Jubilarne proslave AFŽa, 1962.

[33] See Rasim Hurem, ed., *Žene Bosne i Hercegovine u narodnooslobodilačkoj borbi 1941–1945. godine: sjećanja učesnika* (Sarajevo: Svjetlost, 1977); Marija Šoljan, ed., *Žene Hrvatske u narodnooslobodilačkoj borbi* (Zagreb: Izdanje glavnog odbora, Savez Ženskih Društava Hrvatske, 1955); Vera Veskovik-Vangeli, and Marija Jovanovik, ed., *Ženite na Makedonija vo NOV: Zbornik na dokumenti za učestvoto na ženite od Makedonija vo narodnoosloboditelnata vojna i revolucijata 1941–1945*. (Skopje: Institut

FIGURE 10. A Partisan girl from the mountain of Kozara (*Kozarčanka*). Photographed in the winter of 1943/44 by the renowned photographer and filmmaker Žorž Skrigin, *Kozarčanka* became one of the most famous wartime portraits in Tito's Yugoslavia and an icon of postwar party propaganda. Long anonymous, the woman in the photograph was decades after the war identified as Milja Marin (née Toroman), who had served as a nurse in the 11th Krajina Brigade.

Courtesy of Jugoslovenska Kinoteka and Muzej Istorije Jugoslavije.

truly monumental, not only in the extensiveness of the documentary and biographical material that they bring to light but also in their size and presentation. Their origins can be traced back to the AFW's intention to mark the tenth anniversary of its first conference by presenting a memorial compilation (*spomenica*) of documents about women and the war to the museum in Bosanski Petrovac. The AFW's central council entrusted the republican councils to gather sources. Since collecting these materials took longer than expected, the idea of the *spomenica* was abandoned. Instead, the republics began publishing their collections once they were completed, with Croatia leading the way.[34] Most of these volumes represent a mixture of documentary records, articles from the wartime press, photographs, reminiscences, biographies, and historical commentary, and each is a *spomenica* in its own right.

The sheer quantity of these *lieux de memoire* testifies that keeping the memory of the *partizanka* alive was important to the regime. But what kind of imagery did these memorial sites promote? What was the female Partisan of the official version supposed to represent? How was she to do the work of legitimizing the system and fostering a common national feeling? Perhaps it is best to take answers directly from the makers and guardians of her official memory. Documents surrounding the building of the first memorial site dedicated to the *partizanka* have been well preserved and they tell us explicitly why it was built and what meanings the officials wanted it to express.

The initiative for the first monument was that of the committee for the celebration of the twentieth AFW anniversary. In 1962 the committee decided that "for the extraordinarily important role that women ... played in the revolutionary struggle of the peoples of Yugoslavia," a monument to "the woman-fighter" be erected. Its design and location were to be determined jointly by the League of Women's Societies and the war veteran association.[35] The league's proposals for the memorial are particularly

za nacionalna istorija, 1976); Jovan Bojović, et al., *Žene Crne Gore u Revolucionarnom pokretu 1918–1945* (Titograd: Istorijski Institut u Titogradu, 1969); Bosa Cvetić, et al., ed. *Žene Srbije u NOB* (Beograd: Nolit, 1975); Stana Gerk, Ivka Križnar, and Štefanija Ravnikar-Podvebšek, ed., *Slovenke v Narodnoosvobodilnem boju: Zbornik dokumentov, člankov in spominov*, Vols. 1–2 (Ljubljana: Zavod 'Borec', 1970); Dušanka Kovačević, ed, *Borbeni put žena Jugoslavije*, foreword by Josip Broz Tito (Beograd: Leksikografski zavod "Sveznanje," 1972).

34 AJ, AFŽ, 141-14-75, Zapisnik sa sastanka grupe drugarica iz NR Srbije koje pripremaju materijal za spomenicu o učešću žena u NOB, 1952; AJ, AFŽ, 141-7-18, Stenografske beleške, VI plenum CO AFŽ, izlaganje Maje Koš, 25–6 November 1952.

35 AJ, SŽDJ, 354-10, Odluka o podizanju spomenika ženi-borcu, Jubilarne proslave AFŽa, 22 October 1962.

useful sources because they literally spell out how the female Partisan was supposed to be remembered. The monument, the league members resolved, needed to represent the range and variety of women's participation in the national revolution, and it should take the form of a relief composition, accompanied with excerpts from Tito's speeches and other quotations. "The composition should evoke the self-abnegation, dedication, heroism and valiancy of the woman fighter," they suggested; "it should symbolize women-fighters from all regions of our republic [and] show women's militancy and endurance."[36] But the most important aspect of the *partizanka*, in their view, was the heroic *sacrifice* that she had made for the Partisan victory. "Distinct in our struggle," the league's proposal draft reads,

are the images of the female fighter with a rifle in hand [and] the woman courier, and *above all, the image of the Partisan mother*. Women's participation is characterized by courage, endurance, self-abnegation, giving everything up [*lišavanje svega*]: husbands, brothers, and, *above all, children*.[37]

Here, in a nutshell, are the basic premises of the official imagery. What the officials intended the monument to convey, in other words, was the enormity of the sacrifice that ordinary women from all Yugoslav lands willingly made for the struggle and the heroic manner in which they did so. The commonality of the phenomenon – underscored by the recognition of women from all regions – was to help foster a supraethnic all-Yugoslav feeling, rooted in the perception of shared wartime suffering and heroism. Women's voluntary martyrdom on a mass scale was to stand as the superior justification of the communist cause and a significant source of legitimacy for the regime. Since a mother giving up her children was considered the embodiment of one of the highest sacrifices imaginable, the image of the Partisan mother received a particular emphasis. The same set of messages, it is worth recalling, was promoted in the government sponsored literature. In her comprehensive volume on women of Yugoslavia, Dušanka Kovačević insists that women fighters of the National-Liberation Movement understood "the wartime truth" that they had to sacrifice their individual wishes and that the revolution had "no time for motherhood." In a "proud sorrow for everything that the homeland went through," she writes, "their cries for their newborn babies turned into silence."[38] The

[36] AJ, AFŽ, 141-11-57, Spomenik ženi-borcu u Bosanskom Petrovcu, n.d. Materijali iz istorije Ženskog pokreta.

[37] AJ, AFŽ, 141-14-75, Spomenik ženi-borcu Jugoslavije, n.d. Materijali o proslavi godišnjice I konf. AFŽ u Bosanskom Petrovcu; my italics.

[38] Kovačević, *Borbeni put*, 26. See also Chapter 3 of the present study.

many participant recollections published after the war also glorified the heroism of young Partisan mothers who lost their children or put aside motherhood and old mothers of Partisan soldiers who proudly sent their sons and daughters off to the battlefield. The two pillars of the wartime representation of women – the female warrior and the patriotic mother – thus survived the war and often merged in Tito's Yugoslavia.

This official imagery, centering on transethnic yet gender-specific heroism, self-deprivation, and sacrifice, would remain unchanged throughout the communist era. In 1963, a monument that was a fairly faithful embodiment of the league's idea was built in Bosanski Novi. The work of the well-known Yugoslav sculptor Dušan Džamonja, the *Partisan Mother* consists of a relief sculpture on a marble base inscribed with quotations from wartime poetry about women, such as Skender Kulenović's "Stojanka, Mother from Knežopolje." The relief provides a vivid portrayal of fascist terror, of the many sacrifices that women made during the war, and of their heroism. Other memorials to the female Partisan followed, including the museum to the First Female Company of Lika, which opened in 1977 in the village of Trnovac,[39] and the monument to the woman fighter within the Vraca memorial park near Sarajevo, erected in 1981.

Official commemorations of the war, memorials and monuments, communist historiography and popular historical texts, the venerable flood of published participant reminiscences, and celebrations of 8 March, all played a role in the canonizing of the *partizanka* as an emblem of the national-liberation struggle. Yet these state-sponsored mnemonic practices and sites were not fated to become the only – or even the primary – shapers of the memory of the female Partisan. It was instead the increasingly independent postwar cultural production, mostly in the domains of literature and cinematography, that was responsible for the creation (and subsequent dismantling) of her stardom. Unlike the official vision, which remained homogeneous and frozen throughout the communist era, the imagery in Yugoslav culture was subject to change. Here the *partizanka*, as we shall see in the following, progressively departed from the official heroic icon toward a more sexualized character and more conventional women's roles, sliding in the process from the center to the margins of the war story. Her slide reflected the country's political troubles and a general disintegration of the belief in the Titoist Yugoslav

[39] Desanka Stojić, *Prva ženska partizanska četa* (Karlovac: Historijski Arhiv u Karlovcu, 1987), 99–100.

project. It is perhaps not surprising that a prominent symbol of a regime crumbles together with the regime itself. What set the *partizanka* apart from any other Titoist emblem, however, was the manner in which she was dethroned – her fall was distinctly gender specific and marked by an ever-increasing dose of misogyny and sexism.

Four phases are recognizable in the *partizanka*'s descent from the venerable icon of the early postwar years to the obscurity and trivialization of the last two decades. These phases correspond to the changing patterns of political organization and party control over culture and mirror the gradual erosion of the elites' support for Tito's Yugoslavism. In the first phase, roughly between 1945 and 1962, the *partizanka* was a revolutionary icon in Yugoslavia. Her representation in Yugoslav culture of the time largely coincided with the official version. It was an image that stressed heroism and sacrifice and, in the very first years, conformed to the aesthetic principles of socialist realism. This concurrence with the official representation is understandable in view of the political context of the time. The beginning of this early postwar period was characterized by a tight party grip on cultural life, a rigid centralized cultural policy, and joint efforts of political and cultural elites to create a unified Yugoslav socialist culture. In such a political climate, there was little room for alternative images. Though the party's control of culture began to loosen in the 1950s, the icon of the female Partisan remained unchanged.

During the second phase (1963–1980), the *partizanka*'s heroic image suffered its first fissures in cinematographic and literary representations of the war. These fissures could be traced to contemporary changes in the political context. Thanks to the new constitution of 1963, the systemic reform toward administrative decentralization gained momentum, and so did the transfer of state power from the center to the country's federal units. At the same time, the party abandoned its goal of integrating Yugoslavia culturally. The political and cultural fragmentation created an opportunity for Yugoslav writers and filmmakers to challenge the dominant vision of the past. These developments had immediate repercussions for the eminent Titoist emblem, the *partizanka*, whose stability depended on the regime's unity and the party's ability to monopolize public discourse. The first to signal the change was the Yugoslav feature film. From the moment that her heroic cinematographic portrait suffered its first, relatively innocent cracks in the 1960s, the *partizanka* began to move gradually toward the sidelines of the revolutionary story and toward traditional women's roles, her image assuming increasingly sexual overtones along the way.

The third phase began in 1980, when, with Tito's death, the Yugoslav family lost the father figure that held it together and the party started losing its monopoly on the interpretation of the revolutionary past. As challenges to the old Manichean portrait of the war intensified, the *partizanka* was pushed further to the margins. At the same time, a new element emerged in her, even more sexualized, representation: She was now unfavorably juxtaposed to the bourgeois model of womanhood, which rendered her the bearer of lesser culture and inferior femininity.

The final phase started in the late 1980s, with the rise of nationalist elites in Yugoslavia's federal units and the beginning of their dismantling of Yugoslavia. Amid the verbal and then real nationalist wars that tore the country apart, the *partizanka* fell into oblivion, in which she remains to this day. If recalled at all from this obscurity, she has appeared mostly in humiliating or trivial representations. Each of the four phases will be discussed through an analysis of exemplary literary and cinematographic texts in the following.

The Revolutionary Icon (1945–1962): Indicative both of the *partizanka*'s significance as a symbol in the new state and of the role that films and novels had in her mythologization is the fact that the very first feature film of the socialist Yugoslavia, *Slavica*, focused on a young female Partisan who fought heroically until her death at the hands of the occupiers. The film encapsulates the revolutionary vision of the *partizanka* and therefore deserves a somewhat lengthier consideration. Directed by the Croatian Vjekoslav Afrić, who had experienced the Partisan struggle firsthand working in the Partisan National Liberation Theater, *Slavica* was released in 1947 to become an instant hit (see Figure 11). Set in a Dalmatian village in the vicinity of Split on the Adriatic coast, the story begins by depicting the gloomy life of local fishermen in the class-stratified prewar society. Many villagers, having no boats of their own, fish for a rich boat owner, Baron, who exploits their labor. Others, like young Slavica, the only daughter of a poverty-stricken couple, work in a sardine factory owned by a local bourgeois family. In dire circumstances and under pressure, Slavica's parents demand that she marry the much older Baron. However, the despondent girl meets a poor young fisherman, Marin, who refuses to labor for her intended husband-exploiter and instead joins a group of locals who dream of building their own fishing boat and founding a fishermen's cooperative. Delighted with the idea of the cooperative, Slavica joins the group. The two youths fall in love, their relationship shaped by their common ideals. (There is little romance or passion between the two. Throughout the film, they barely venture

FIGURE 11. Creating the icon: Slavica with Marin. *Slavica,* directed by Vjekoslav Afrić, 1947.
Courtesy of Jugoslovenska Kinoteka.

innocent, friendly hugs.) By collecting donations from workers in the factory, the girl manages to procure enough funds to help her friends build their boat, which they name *Slavica* after her. But this idyllic respite is not to last. Slavica and Marin's wedding and the christening of *Slavica*, scheduled to occur on the same day, are interrupted by the outbreak of the war.

When the Italians occupy Dalmatia, they order that all ships be requisitioned in order to supply provisions for their army. The young couple, together with their friends in the cooperative, decide to hide their newly built fishing boat. The Italians discover and arrest Slavica, Marin, and their friends, who are then liberated by a local Partisan band. The couple joins the Partisans and Slavica becomes a fierce *partizanka* who takes part in a series of actions against the occupiers. Striving to cover every major event in the wartime history of the Dalmatian Partisan movement, the movie follows its protagonists as they fight against the Italians; as some of them, including Slavica, take Dalmatian volunteers to Bosnia and Herzegovina to help the surrounded Partisan Supreme Staff during the Neretva offensive; as the couple and their band celebrate the fall of Italy and the arrival of the proletarian brigades in Split; as the Germans take over much of the region and the Partisans find refuge on the island of Vis; to the final struggles and the liberation day. In this event-packed crash course of the war's history, combat on land is followed by combat at sea, with Slavica and Marin at times fighting side by side, at others being separated by their commander and assigned to different duties. As the fighting moves to the sea, their fishing boat, *Slavica*, becomes a Partisan warship – one of the first vessels of the minuscule Partisan fleet – with Marin as its commander.

In the course of the final sea battle, the film's heroine, Slavica, is killed as she tries to save her precious vessel – the foundation of the future Yugoslav navy – from sinking. The melodramatic scene depicting Slavica's death so that *Slavica* can survive is replete with meanings easily detectable by the moviegoers of the time, representing the tragic yet necessary sacrifice of Partisan heroes for the greater good. It is literally with their blood that the new Yugoslav state was founded. That it is the blood of a young, lovely, and innocent woman – a true "daughter of the people" – who chooses to give up everything, including her own life, for the struggle adds yet another dimension to the message. Her voluntary sacrifice serves as the ultimate proof of both the righteousness of the Partisan cause and the popular support behind it, thus giving legitimacy to the postwar regime. The film closes with a depiction of celebrations in Split, now liberated, where Marin meets Slavica's parents. The family joins in the celebratory parade, looking proudly into the revolutionary triumph represented by the large portrait of Tito and Yugoslav flags that the marching masses carry.

As a work of cinematographic art, *Slavica* has little to offer. The film follows the aesthetic principles of Soviet socialist realism, with naive melodramatic scenes and exaggerated pathos dominating its representation of wartime realities. Most characters are stereotyped, all the Partisans being brave, strong-minded, and good; all their enemies evil.[40] The local bourgeoisie, which in the film consists of factory and ship owners, police agents, and clergy, is portrayed in a particularly simplistic manner as a band of exploiters who eagerly put themselves in the service of the occupiers. The film's artistic failings are so obvious that even well-meaning critics of the time could not ignore them. They pointed to the prevalence of the one-dimensional and naive in *Slavica* and declared that this was not the direction they wanted the Yugoslav film to take.[41]

[40] Daniel J. Goulding, *Liberated Cinema: The Yugoslav Experience, 1945–2001* (Bloomington: Indiana University Press, 2002), 17.

[41] Petar Volk, *Savremeni jugoslovenski film* (Beograd: Univerzitet Umetnosti i Institut za film, 1983), 131–2. Also Goulding, *Liberated Cinema*, 20.

Yet the audiences were delighted. In the forty-three days the movie was shown in Belgrade, it was seen by some 173,000 viewers, in Zagreb it attracted 68,000, while by the end of its first year in theaters, *Slavica* had been seen by nearly two million viewers from all over Yugoslavia.[42] To be sure, this strong showing could be due to the fact that this was the very first indigenous movie that dealt with Yugoslav viewers' own recent past and experiences. It is certainly one of the reasons that *Slavica* remains an inevitable subject in all Yugoslav film anthologies and studies. But besides being the opening cinematographic achievement of the new socialist polity, scholars argue, *Slavica*'s importance lay in its setting the structural formula that was to be followed by most of the early Partisan films and their literary counterparts, Partisan epic novels.

The war epic was a genre that was dear both to the cultural authorities and to the reading and cinema audiences for much of the communist era. It was not only immensely popular in the postwar era, but also became, as Andrew Wachtel writes, "the primary vehicle" for "a description or interpretation of the meaning of the partisan struggle." In the late 1940s and 1950s, the minuscule Yugoslav film industry was dominated by features thematically dedicated to the war of liberation and its heroes. So was Yugoslav literature; numerous pieces, including several of high quality, appeared on the topic in the immediate postwar epoch. Among the best known literary works of this genre in its early stages were those written by the Serbian authors Dobrica Ćosić and Oskar Davičo, the Bosnian writer Branko Ćopić, the Montenegrin Mihailo Lalić, the Slovene Miško Kranjec, and others. The plots of these early epic films and novels vary to a great degree, but, as Wachtel argues, *Slavica*'s structural model could be recognized in all of them: They typically depict a small, locally based, and ethnically homogeneous group of Partisans fighting against a much more powerful enemy and great odds; the story follows a set of actions in which the Partisans face immense difficulties; as the plot unfolds, several most attractive characters – sometimes including the main protagonist him/herself – lose their lives, yet their sacrifice is not in vain, for the group reaches its aim.[43]

Scholars who have studied cultural politics in Tito's Yugoslavia, including Andrew Wachtel and Daniel Goulding, argue that these works reflected the authorities' striving to construct a unified Yugoslav socialist culture, one based on the supranational Partisan myth and characterized

---

[42] Peter Volk, *Svedočenje*, as cited in Goulding, 20.
[43] Andrew Wachtel, *Making a Nation*, 151–2.

by the postulates of "brotherhood and unity" among the country's many nationalities. Although the early epics typically depict a Partisan band of one particular nationality, their structural formula presupposes the existence of a "metonymic connection" linking that band to all other groups of Partisans in Yugoslavia.[44] And every local Partisan story is represented as part of a larger collective history. Daniel Goulding describes this structural model:

> It is a pattern which begins by affirming Partisan-led local initiatives in specific locales, involving the distinctive nationalities of the region, and builds organically to an affirmation of the epic all-Yugoslav character of its leadership and heroes – with Tito presented as the preeminent heroic unifying symbol – and of the all-Yugoslav character of the Partisan fighting forces, which becomes the essential guarantor of the ultimate victory in war, as well as the basis upon which to build a completely new Yugoslavia.[45]

Dalmatian Partisans, in other words, are connected to all other Partisans, and Slavica stands for all Yugoslavia's *partizanka*s, regardless of what their particular ethnic origin may be.

Besides encapsulating supranational Yugoslavism, the film sets a specific mold for the representation of Partisan women. The *partizanka*s of early war epics are depicted as major war protagonists and action heroes in their own right. *Slavica* in fact makes an explicit point of the Partisan women's active participation in combat. In this respect, the scene in which the villagers liberated from the Italian prison join the Partisans and Slavica becomes a *partizanka* is particularly telling. As the Partisan commander distributes weapons to the village volunteers, there are only three pieces available, two rifles and a revolver. Marin and another volunteer are given rifles, and Slavica asks for the revolver. To her mother's protests that weaponry is "not for a woman," the commander responds, "No, mother, she has both of her hands and a head, and she has the right to fight." The camera then closes up on Slavica's face glowing with delight and pride. Slavica is not only a fighter, though. As a representative of all *partizanka*s, she appears in a multiplicity of roles that women could play in the Partisan movement – at times we see her with Marin behind a machine gun, at others she serves as a nurse in Bosnia, still at others she is an agitator who spreads the word about the Partisans and mobilizes volunteers into the units. In all of these roles she acts either as

---

[44] Ibid., 153.
[45] Goulding, *The Liberated Cinema*, 19–20. Also discussed in Wachtel, *Making a Nation*, 154.

an independent, ideologically motivated agent or as a disciplined Partisan soldier, and *not* as a support character for male protagonists. She thus emerges as a symbol not only of Partisan sacrifice but also of women's emancipation and gender equality.

For all of its propagandizing and simplicity, *Slavica* should be credited with the creation of the *partizanka* icon and its symbolic positioning at the center of the revolutionary epos in the early postwar years. That the image of the *partizanka* in Yugoslav films and literature of the late 1940s coincided with the one propagated by CPY and AFW officials is not surprising – Yugoslav cultural production at the time was under strict party direction and censorship. Following the Soviet model of centralized organization, both literary and cinematographic outputs were controlled on the local level by agitprop committees subordinated to the central propaganda department. Small wonder, then, that both the newly established national cinema and the country's literature were governed by party orthodoxy, treading both ideologically and aesthetically in the steps of Soviet socialist realism.

It is perhaps more surprising that the *partizanka* icon, as shaped by *Slavica*, remained unchanged even as the Yugoslavs abandoned the Stalinist model and the party's control relaxed. After the dramatic break with the Soviets and a short period of heightened ideological orthodoxy, we have seen, the country entered a new epoch of comparative freedom in the 1950s. In the realm of cultural politics, scholars generally view the Union of Yugoslav Writers' Third Congress, held in Ljubljana in 1952, as a milestone in this direction. More specifically, they point to the famous speech "On Cultural Freedom," by the influential Croatian writer Miroslav Krleža. Krleža criticized the domination of dogmatism and socialist realism on the literary scene, calling for an open dialogue among the authors and critics as well as for diversity and independence of artistic expression. Krleža's speech ended a debate among the leftist literati about the ideological and aesthetic merits of socialist realism, opening the door to considerable liberalization in Yugoslav culture.

Consequently, the works of the war epic genre that emerged in the 1950s departed from naïve propaganda and the dogma of Soviet-style socialist realism toward a more nuanced portrayal of the war. Yet their narrative structures, plots, and interpretations of the Partisan struggle remained largely within *Slavica*'s mold – as did their *partizanka*s: young, beautiful, and pure maidens who consciously join the units for ideological reasons, serve simultaneously as fighters and nurses (and sometimes in other roles as well), act as independent heroic agents, and sacrifice their youth or lives for the higher cause, their sacrifice represented as higher and nobler than that of Partisan men.

A good example is provided in what was probably the most popular and most widely read of the early war epics, Dobrica Ćosić's *Far Away Is the Sun*. Ćosić's book was required reading in the school curricula of all Yugoslav republics for much of the communist era. In 1953 the novel was adapted into a movie, directed by Radoš Novaković. It was, in brief, the work with which most postwar generations were familiar and, as Wachtel writes, "one canonized by the educational authorities as telling the story 'in the proper way.' "[46]

Both the novel and its cinematographic version, critics agree, moved beyond the common stereotypes and simplifications that had by then dominated works on the National Liberation War. "Far Away Is the Sun is one of the key moments," as one Yugoslav film expert put it, "at which our war film rose above conventionalism and turned towards more liberal, more active, and more original forms."[47] Ćosić's work tells the story of a Serbian Partisan detachment, which, outnumbered and encircled by enemy troops, finds itself in a nearly hopeless situation. Much like the Dalmatian Partisan band in *Slavica*, the Serbian Partisan group is mostly made up of villagers from the region where their unit operates; it faces superior enemy forces and in the process loses some key protagonists but manages to triumph in the end. Yet, unlike the unwavering, courageous, and grinning superheroes of *Slavica*, Ćosić's characters are visibly human – they make decisions only after long inner debates, they fear for their lives, they are torn between their loyalties to the cause and to their families and homes.

The *partizanka* Bojana, the sole female in the Serbian Partisan band, though not the novel's lead protagonist, is a character important for the description of the group's dynamic and symbolically stands for all female Partisans. Although Ćosić's *partizanka* is more complex and believable than Slavica, she still retains some of the latter's major features. Bojana is both the detachment's nurse (*sanitarka*) and a fighter who takes an active part in a series of battles. She and the unit's commander, Uča, are in love, their relationship as idealistic and platonic as Slavica and Marin's. In one passage, the wounded Uča reflects upon their love and Bojana's role in the unit: "A girl warrior … that is surely why he loves her. He is no hero; she is the hero in this detachment. For freedom, he is giving his strength

---

[46] Wachtel, *Making a Nation*, 152.
[47] Volk, *Savremeni jugoslovenski film*, 44.

and his life, and she her beauty and the most precious thing that life possesses: motherhood."[48]

The passage reveals the crux of the *partizanka*'s icon. Whether a mother or not, she is the symbol of a gender-specific sacrifice: a woman fighter inevitably gives up either her child or her childbearing potential. The *partizanka*'s significance, in brief, lies in her conscious decision to cross gender boundaries and give up (at least temporarily) her natural, sacred role of childbearing for the good of the community. This sacrifice, viewed as greater than any other, is the ultimate confirmation of the validity of the Partisan cause, turning the *partizanka* into a major emblem of supranational Yugoslavism and a source of legitimacy for Tito's Yugoslavia.

In sum, in the early postwar period, the *partizanka* emerged as one of the preeminent symbols of the new state. Her official image – one sponsored by the party and the AFW and promoted in commemorations, memorials, historiography, and published participant reminiscences – was also largely adopted by Yugoslav authors and filmmakers of the time. This image centered on heroism and sacrifice. A female character typically functions not as a universal but rather as a gender-specific symbol, and the *partizanka* too stood for gender-specific martyrdom. As a woman temporarily abandoning her natural role of child rearing for the greater cause, the *partizanka* came to represent what was envisioned as the ultimate women's sacrifice – that of motherhood. This willing sacrifice, thought to be higher and nobler than any other, served to confirm the justice of the Partisan cause and validate the regime and its vision of the Yugoslav nation. This heroic image would remain unaltered until the early 1960s, in spite of some loosening of party control after 1952. In the 1960s, however, a new political climate made it possible for Yugoslav artists and intellectuals to revisit the war with a critical eye. In their works, the *partizanka* departed from the official icon, which marked the beginning of her downfall in the following decades.

The Fissures (1963–1980): In the 1960s and 1970s, Yugoslavia made further headway on its own road to socialism. Thanks to the new constitutional framework in 1963, the experiment in socialist self-management that had started modestly in the early 1950s gained new momentum. So did administrative decentralization. With the fall of the security police chief, Aleksandar Ranković, in 1966, the last major bastion of opposition to the country's political decentralization and liberalization was gone. The transfer of centralized state power to the country's six republics

[48] Dobrica Ćosić, *Daleko je sunce*, 12th ed. (Beograd: Prosveta, 1966), 105.

established a "quasi-confederal" system of relatively independent republican oligarchies, thus creating the institutional fractures along which Yugoslavia would tear apart in the future.[49] The newly empowered republican elites at times openly flirted with nationalism, and Tito, in turn, used repressive measures, as was the case with the "Croatian Spring" in 1971. In the first half of the 1970s, such measures extended beyond Croatia to Serbia and elsewhere, targeting leftist liberals and reformists in general. This phase of ideological rigidity and relative political repression notwithstanding, the general trends of the last two decades of Tito's rule were a gradual relaxation of central control and strengthening of the power and independence of Yugoslavia's federal units and autonomous provinces. Parallel to the country's political reorganization, cultural policy was modified to accommodate the new concept of a federalist and decentralized country. The party and the cultural elites alike abandoned their previous goal of integrating Yugoslavia culturally. Instead of failed cultural unitarism, the emphasis now shifted to separate developments of individual ethnonational cultures within the larger Yugoslav framework. Trying to explain the Yugoslav collapse, several scholars have pointed to these changing patterns of official ideology and statesmanship in the 1960s as containing the seeds of future discord and facilitating the process of the country's disintegration.[50] More important for our discussion, the fragmentation and relative liberalization of the cultural domain created openings for novel and challenging readings of the revolutionary past. These developments had immediate repercussions for the *partizanka*, whose heroic image experienced its very first fissures at the time.

The sixties represented a singularly creative period in Yugoslav art and literature. Nowhere was this more obvious than in cinematography, which, as Daniel Goulding writes, "advanced to the forefront of artistic experimentation and was often a lightning rod which attracted heated polemic exchanges on the proper role of artistic expression in a socialist state."[51] In this period a number of filmmakers, critics, and theorists

---

[49] Sabrina Ramet, *Balkan Babel: The Disintegration of Yugoslavia from the Death of Tito to the Fall of Milosevic*, 4th ed. (Boulder, CO: Westview Press, 2002), 6.

[50] Ibid.; Ivo Banac, "Foreword" in Ramet, *Balkan Babel*, xiv; Wachtel, *Making a Nation*, 174; also Ramet, *Nationalism and Federalism in Yugoslavia, 1962–1991* (Bloomington: Indiana University Press, 1992), 51–4, and others.

[51] Goulding, *Liberated Cinema*, 66. The following section on New Film and representative features draws on the work of other scholars, film experts, Daniel Goulding, Pavle Levi, and Petar Volk. See ibid.; see also Pavle Levi, *Disintegration in Frames: Aesthetics and Ideology in the Yugoslav and Post-Yugoslav Cinema* (Stanford, CA: Stanford University Press, 2007), 11–56; and Petar Volk, *Savremeni jugoslovenski film*. The analysis of the image of the *partizanka*, however, is entirely mine.

became associated with what has been known as Yugoslav New Film (Novi Film). Among the best-known directors of New Film features were Dušan Makavejev, Aleksandar Petrović, Puriša Djordjević, Vatroslav Mimica, Živojin Pavlović, Ante Babaja, Boštjan Hladnik, Želimir Žilnik, and Matjaž Klopčić; some of their works have attained international fame and acclaim.

New Film creators confronted many established party myths and introduced new stylistic and thematic paradigms to Yugoslav cinema. Ideologically, they openly challenged communist mythologies, seeing it as their job to expose problems and contradictions in contemporary society. They did so primarily from a leftist position, situating themselves within a Marxist framework or reference, but advocating a democratic and humanistic version of socialism as opposed to statism and ideological dogmatism. Even in the relatively liberal political climate of the sixties, their ideas found little understanding in party circles. Some authors provoked the wrath of bureaucrats, their works being banned for years or subjected to a series of reedits before being shown to larger audiences.

The war and revolution were among the thematic preoccupations of New Film authors. Several directors revisited the established myths surrounding the National Liberation War with a critical eye, often upsetting the powers that be. Although they did not openly attack the revolution per se (after all, theirs was a Marxist perspective and a belief in the possibility of humanistic socialism), they did not shy away from exposing its gloomier sides. They made a qualitative break with the Manichean picture of the liberation struggle and its agents, leading their characters through more complex and nuanced wartime realities. They were less interested in discovering the glorious, beautiful, or heroic face of the war; rather, they often portrayed it as a senseless and dehumanizing force that could degrade the winners as much as the losers. Likewise, their Partisans could be vacillating characters significantly different from the heroes of the immediate postwar revolutionary period.

In such an atmosphere, the early static portrayal of the *partizanka* could not survive unscathed. It was, indeed, in New Film works that her heroic image suffered some of its first cracks. The greatest offense to her memory, in the eyes of party officials, the war veterans' association, and other watchdogs of the revolutionary legacy, lay in her fallibility and sexualization. Such concerns were not entirely baseless – some New Film works indeed introduced new and, at the time, shocking descriptions of the female (and male) Partisans as imperfect and sexual beings.

One of the most innovative, poetic, and controversial takes on the war and its aftermath was provided by Puriša Đorđević's film *Morning* (*Jutro*), 1967, the third part of his wartime tetralogy; the remaining three were *Girl* (*Devojka*), 1965; *Dream* (*San*), 1966; and *Noon* (*Podne*), 1968. Like the director of *Slavica*, Vjekoslav Afrić, Đorđević had experienced the war in person, having joined the Partisans as a teenager. *Morning*, film experts agree, is his "most complete and most powerful creation," which won the highest awards at domestic and international festivals in Pula and Venice that year.[52] It is also one that sparked vivid debates and serious polemics in Yugoslavia. The plot focuses on the last day of war and the first day of peace in a provincial town, where the desire for tranquility among the local populace, expressions of carnal joie de vivre by the victors, and a succession of reprisal killings exist side by side.

One of the central stories of the film is that of a lovely young Partisan *illegalka*, Aleksandra. Captured by the Nazis during the war, she divulged, under torture, the names of some of her comrades, Partisan activists. Now, on the last day of the war, Aleksandra is no longer in German captivity. Her former lover, a person in a high position in liberated Belgrade, finds her nonheroic conduct before the enemy unacceptable and demands that she be executed, although the comrades whom she betrayed had already been dead. Her execution is to be performed immediately; what is more, it is her friend, the Partisan officer Mali, who is given the task of carrying out the execution. Aleksandra does not seem to fear death but dreads the thought of perishing at the hands of her own comrades. She asks to be killed instead by a German so that she can at least have the illusion that an enemy bullet did her in. The Partisans accept, turning her execution into a dramatic play reenacting the war. They find a German POW and dress him in a uniform. Aleksandra is taken to a field by a river and released, and the German officer is sent to chase her. He shoots and kills her only then to be killed himself by Aleksandra's Partisan friend, Mali.

Aleksandra's death closes the film in a manner much different from the one in which Slavica's death closes *Slavica* – there are no parades, no symbols of hope and new beginnings, only a sense of loss and sorrow. Aleksandra herself is a *partizanka* noticeably different from Slavica. She, for one, is a frail and fallible person who betrays the names of her comrades – a deed unthinkable in the context of *Slavica*, even if those betrayed were already dead. Nor could she stand for the cause the way Slavica did. She is an appealing, believable, complex character whose

---

[52] Volk, *Savremeni jugoslovenski film*, 272.

execution may leave the audiences deeply moved, but her victimhood is not of the kind that can symbolize the righteousness of the Partisan war or the justness of the regime; if anything, it can symbolize the opposite.

Đorđević's portrayal of victorious Partisans met with much criticism in Yugoslavia. Critics disapproved of the coldblooded, rushed, and unlawful fashion in which reprisals and executions were performed in the film; they also disliked the lack of restraint of some Partisan characters, particularly their libertine behavior.[53] *Morning*'s Partisans, especially men, were indeed far from the puritans of the early postwar depictions. As far as the sexuality of Partisan women is concerned, however, Đorđević's work was relatively understated. It was another, earlier film from the 1960s, Mića Popović's *The Man from the Oak Forest* (*Čovek iz hrastove šume*, 1964), that announced the trend toward the *partizanka*'s growing sexualization in Yugoslav culture.

Popović's film tells the story of the peasant Maksim, a rogue Chetnik executioner with a deep, mystical connection to the local ancient oak forest and the region's traditions, who starts a murderous campaign in the environs of a Serbian village at the beginning of the war. He attacks lone travelers on their way to the village and takes them to the forest to kill them. Maksim is attracted to a young city woman who often passes through the village on her bike. The woman appears to be a black marketer. As his attraction develops into passion, he discovers that the woman tricked him – she is in fact a communist activist who has the task of organizing Partisan resistance in the region. After a series of events, in which the audiences see Maksim going to town in the pursuit of the young woman and killing several people along the way, he himself is shot and killed by the female Partisan, the object of his desire.

In comparison to Đorđević's film, Popović's provoked considerably harsher criticism, much of it being voiced in the highest circles of the Serbian party. The concerns from above led to the banning of the movie; it was released only after significant changes had been made to the original version. As Goulding writes, official critics reacted with alarm to the fact that the author chose a Chetnik as his main protagonist and decided to paint him as a psychologically complex character. But the source of their particular rage was the character of the *partizanka*, who, in the film's original version, apparently reciprocated Maksim's feelings of sexual attraction. Not only was she portrayed as a sexual being, but also as one with erotic passions for a primitive murderer and

[53] Goulding, *Liberated Cinema*, 93.

an ideological enemy at that. This was an utterly unacceptable offense
to the revolutionary icon. What is more, the first version of the film
makes it obvious that she killed Maksim in order to purge herself from
guilt. In the film's reedited rendering, which was released to the public, both her desire and her motivation for killing Maksim are largely
obscured.[54]

Although the original version of Popović's movie did not reach general
audiences, it did signal the direction that cinematographic and literary
representations of the *partizanka* would increasingly take from then on;
it was the direction toward her dethroning, primarily through sexualization. This trend was noticeable even in the officially sanctioned, "tra-
ditionalist" Partisan epic movies and novels that continued to coexist
with New Film experiments throughout the 1960s and 1970s, and in
some forms survived well into the 1980s. The *partizanka* of these conventional Partisan stories began turning from an independent heroine
into a sexualized love object or, rarely, subject. Her transformation here
may have been more subtle and gradual than in the works that aimed
to challenge the dominant values and interpretations, but the result was
similar. She was at the same time increasingly marginalized as a protagonist, assuming more traditional female support roles of a girlfriend, lover,
sister, mother, or relative of male heroes.

It is worth emphasizing that the works of New Film authors, with
their innovative approaches, represented only a tiny minority of the
films produced in the 1960s; the vast majority tended to reaffirm the
established values and imagery. Within that majority, the conventional
Partisan epic remained the most authentic and popular Yugoslav genre.
In the late 1960s and 1970s the genre actually reached its apogee, as
Partisan movies evolved from naïve, technically primitive works into
majestic spectacles with an international cast, innumerable extras,
impressive pyrotechnic effects, and expensive – even by Hollywood standards – production. Unlike the early Partisan films, which were made
solely for domestic audiences and served to legitimize the regime in the
eyes of the masses, these newer, spectacular projects were also meant for
international distribution. Feeling secure on its unique path to socialism
and enjoying a respectable position on the international scene, the regime
could now showcase its glory abroad, and it spared no money for the
show. By acceding to such gigantic and costly projects and by allowing
the Yugoslav army to participate, Tito himself served as their executive

[54] Ibid., 94–6.

producer of sorts.[55] The best known among such projects were Veljko Bulajić's *The Battle of Neretva* (*Bitka na Neretvi*, 1969), Stipe Delić's *Sutjeska* (1973), and Stole Janković's *The Partisans* (*Partizani*, 1975). They featured such names as Richard Burton starring as Marshal Tito – with Tito's blessing – in *Sutjeska*; Orson Welles in a bizarre episode as a Chetnik, together with Yul Brynner and Sergei Bondarchuk as Partisan leaders in *The Battle of Neretva*. As their titles suggest, these movies did not focus on small, regionally based, and isolated Partisan bands engaged in local struggles, as the early Partisan epic had, but rather on the core Partisan forces, including the Supreme Staff, during major enemy offensives or large-scale operations.

Bulajić's *The Battle of Neretva* was arguably the genre's greatest success. It was dubbed in at least four languages, distributed globally, and selected as one of the 1969 foreign language nominees for the U.S. Academy Award. Based on historical events, the film tells the story of one of the most dramatic and lethal enemy offensives – Operation Weiss, also known as the fourth offensive in Yugoslav historiography – against the Partisans. Early in 1943, fearing the Allied intervention in the Balkans, the film reminds us, the Germans launched the offensive that aimed to eradicate the Partisans. As the Partisan Supreme Staff with the Central Hospital and countless refugees faced the combined forces of the German, Italian, and Ustasha units, it seemed that the only exit for them would be to cross the bridge on the Neretva River and break through the Chetnik bands on the other bank. By blowing up the bridge and building a small makeshift viaduct in its place, the Partisans managed to deceive their enemies and transport the wounded and civilians to safety.

Bulajić's colorful cast includes quite a few major protagonists, yet women appear in episodic and relatively marginal roles. The film retains many elements of the *Slavica*-style revolutionary imagery of women in traditionally men's jobs, showing them as active participants and fighters, but also introduces new elements of sexuality and a new degree of conformity with old ideas about femininity. One *partizanka*, for example, a demolition woman, is shown as she bathes in the river with a Partisan commander at her side, with explicit hints at a sexual relationship between the two. The most visible female character is the *partizanka* Danica, who finds herself in the group of fighters assigned to cross the river before all others and provide cover while the wounded are being

---

[55] Dejan Kosanović and Dinko Tucaković, *Stranci u raju* (Beograd: Biblioteka Vek, 1998), 145.

transported. In the middle of the fighting with the Chetniks, the camera focuses on her while she interchangeably shoots, and, as the sole female in the group, serves as a nurse tending her male comrades – a familiar representation seen many times in old Partisan movies. Danica's role is, however, primarily defined through her relationship with male protagonists; she is the sweetheart of one important male character and the sister of another. In one of the most emotional scenes of the movie, she is killed together with her brother, their deaths representing the Partisan struggle as the heroic sacrifice of a whole family.

Later projects of the same kind did not match the success of *The Battle of Neretva* with the audiences, signaling the twilight of the grandiose Partisan epic movies. By the late 1970s, the Partisan narrative had become a dated cliché that had lost much of its appeal. War stories, however, did not disappear entirely from the visual media. An interesting phenomenon of the time was the emergence of popular TV series on the Partisan struggle. Some, like the series *Kapelski Kresovi*, which described the resistance against the Italians in the Gorski Kotar region of Croatia, retained the iconography of the classical Partisan film. Others departed from it to make the old topic more appealing to the new generations of viewers.

In the latter category, probably the most important was the Belgrade television series *Otpisani* (*The Written Off*). First aired in 1974, *Otpisani* became a sensation with no rivals in popularity, achieving over the years the cult status that persists to this day in the region. Its opening episodes were made into a film of the same title, followed by a sequel, *Povratak Otpisanih* (*The Return of the Written Off*), in 1976, and another TV series two years later. Set in occupied Belgrade, *Otpisani* depicts a group of youths who join the resistance and wage their own war against the Gestapo. Commentators have noted that the series owed much of its popularity to the novelty of its approach to the struggle. An unpretentious and entertaining mixture of action and suspense with virtually no sloganeering, ideological content, or pathos, it stood in sharp contrast with the increasingly outmoded Partisan epics. The series introduced youthful urban characters and stories that were much closer to the experiences and interests of contemporary viewers born after the war.

What makes *Otpisani* particularly important for our discussion, in addition to its popularity, is its striking reversion to traditional gender roles. The cast of main protagonists and resistance heroes in the original series is entirely male. The only prominent female character, Marija, is introduced only in the spin-off, *Povratak Otpisanih*. As important, Marija never openly crosses traditional gender boundaries. Although she becomes a member of the gang of Belgrade resisters, she does not participate in street fighting, sabotage, or other actions undertaken by her male comrades. She is a beautiful, classy, and extremely feminine blonde who works as a secretary of the Gestapo chief. Her underground activity consists of leaking information from the Gestapo office to the resistance. As the girlfriend of the series' leading male hero, Tihi, she figures as a support character rather than an autonomous protagonist.

In sum, with the emergence of the first challenges to the Manichean portrayal of the revolution in the 1960s, the *partizanka*'s heroic icon also began to crumble. By the late 1970s, as the preceding examples suggest, the female Partisan had progressively moved from the center of the war narrative to its margins, assuming in the process conventional women's support roles as love objects or relatives of male protagonists. Simultaneously, sexuality became an increasingly pronounced and important component of her image. To be sure, the growing sexualization of the *partizanka* was in line with a general trend in the representations of women in Yugoslav culture (as well as Western culture), and perhaps did not seem extraordinary in the eyes of the contemporary audiences. But in her case, sexualization had a definite, if implicit, political connotation.

A Lesser Woman (1980–1987): While Tito was alive, most of the challenges to the official vision of the war in the cultural sphere remained within the dominant interpretive framework, even if they provided a more shaded and complex picture of the Yugoslav past. But in the years after Tito's death, as the Party began to lose its monopoly on public discourse, opposition to the regime and its version of history broke out of that framework, contributing significantly to the demythologization of the Partisan war and the delegitimation of the communist system as a whole. In the 1980s, writers, filmmakers, journalists, and historians started to address issues in the revolutionary past that had hitherto been off limits, creating an increasingly vocal chorus of dissident voices. Communist use of violence and repression, long a taboo topic excluded from official memory, was the revisionists' first target.[56] Their repertoire soon expanded to include, among other things, attempts to rehabilitate the Partisans' political opponents and class enemies.

While some authors and screenwriters tackled forbidden subjects explicitly, others used stories about intersex relations for less overt but

[56] Robert M. Hayden, "Recounting the Dead: The Rediscovery and Redefinition of Wartime Massacres in Late- and Post-Communist Yugoslavia," in *Memory, History, and Opposition under State Socialism*, ed. by Rubie S. Watson (Santa Fe, NM: School of American Research Press, 1994), 168–9.

equally powerful social commentary and political messages. In that context, one narrative trope that gained increasing prominence in literary and cinematographic representations of the revolution in the 1980s is of interest for our present discussion. Its central motif is a romantic relationship between a coarse Partisan man and a cultured upper-class woman. The story is usually situated in the liberation days or the immediate postwar period and revolves around the dichotomy between the supposedly "lower" rural culture of the Partisans and the "higher" bourgeois culture that they are about to destroy. In this type of narrative the typical Partisan hero lacks manners and education, has little understanding of city ways, and despises the cultured lifestyle that, in his view, represents bourgeois decadence. He may also have a pure peasant heart and childish faith in revolutionary slogans. The woman to whom the Partisan protagonist is drawn is on the opposite side of the ideological spectrum and thus officially his political enemy. She is, in fact, his opposite in every conceivable manner; well-bred, educated, and refined, often a family member or former lover of a wartime collaborator, she has nothing in common with the Partisan brethren of half-literate mountaineers turned Marxists who conquer her world. Yet loathing between the two polar opposites soon turns into attraction, which, in the postwar climate of ideological superorthodoxy, inevitably ends in tragedy.

The trope appears in a series of influential literary and cinematographic pieces dealing with the war and its aftermath. One of the probably best-known renderings is the film *Samo jednom se ljubi* (1981) by the Zagreb director Rajko Grlić (released in the United States under the title *The Melody Haunts My Reverie*). Grlić's film tells the story of the country's thorny transition from war to peace by focusing on a small Croatian town where Tomislav, a raw Partisan veteran, discovers beauty while falling in love with a ballerina of bourgeois descent, Beba, and simultaneously finds his revolutionary ideals and postwar realities difficult to reconcile. Several novels written by the renowned Serbian writer Slobodan Selenić, including *Heads/Tails* (*Pismo/Glava*, 1982) and *Premeditated Murder* (*Ubistvo s predumišljajem*, 1993), touch upon the same motif, albeit from a different, Serbian-centered perspective. Selenić's *Premeditated Murder* was also adapted into a critically acclaimed and popular film, directed by Gorčin Stojanović, in 1995. Another variation of the theme frames the Croatian director Dejan Šorak's 1987 movie *The Officer with a Rose* (*Oficir s ružom*), which will be discussed in the following. Although it first gained popularity in the 1980s, the motif does not seem to lose its appeal even today. It figures as one of the subthemes in the play *Velika Drama* (*The Great Drama*) by the Serbian playwright Siniša Kovačević, the most popular play in Belgrade throughout the first decade of the new millennium.[57]

Although the works described vary in artistic value as well as the authors' point of view, they all attest to the existence of a particular vision of the revolutionary past – the vision that, from 1980 on, became increasingly present on the cultural scene in the region. In its many fictional adaptations, the story of the Partisan hero and the bourgeois lady became the artistic vehicle for exposing the corruption of revolutionary ideals once the revolutionaries gained power, as well as their secret fascination with the (presumably better and more beautiful) civilization they had slated for destruction.

The topic was in fact neither new nor entirely a product of artistic imagination. It had a relatively long history and a politically charged one at that. The subject was first broached to the Yugoslav public during the affair that led to Milovan Djilas's fall from power. In 1953, Djilas started publishing a sensational series of articles in which he demanded more democracy in the country. He also openly criticized the higher echelons of party bureaucracy for distancing themselves from the masses and assuming positions of wealth and privilege. The article that ultimately spelled his doom was entitled "Anatomy of a Moral" and it targeted the personal ethics of the party's uppermost circle, in particular the wives of the highest party functionaries. What angered Djilas was the treatment that the new wife of Peko Dapčević – the famous Partisan commander, and at the time, chief of the Yugoslav General Staff – received from other elite wives. With Djilas as his best man (*kum*), Dapčević had recently married a young opera singer and actress, who had no Partisan past or party credentials. The wives of other party leaders, most of them former *partizanka*s and senior party activists from a social stratum different than Dapčević's wife's, approached the newcomer to their circle with contempt. In the article, Djilas was particularly eager to expose their hypocrisy. While ostracizing Dapčević's wife because of her social origin, some of "those exalted women [who] came from semi-peasant backgrounds and were semi-educated," he wrote, "grab and hoard deluxe furniture and works of art ... with all the pretentious omniscience of the ignorant."[58] Djilas provided no names in the text, but contemporary

---

[57] "Najgledanije predstave na scenama beogradskih pozorišta: *Velika Drama* bez konkurencije," *Glas javnosti*, 20 May 2009.

[58] Milovan Djilas, *Anatomy of a Moral: The Political Essays of Milovan Djilas*, ed. Abrahan Rothberg (New York: Praeger, 1959), 165.

domestic readers would have had no problems recognizing the characters in his piece. Those whom the article targeted were quick to react. In 1954 Djilas was expelled from the Central Committee and stripped of all government duties. He resigned from the party and resumed writing about communists in power, becoming one of the world's most famous communist dissidents.

Much as Djilas used the case of the Partisan commander and the young actress to expose the moral failings of the "new class" of the privileged in the 1950s, Yugoslav artists later used variations of the story to make their own comments about the revolution. In the fictional versions of the story, however, the *partizanka* either is absent or remains on the margins, appearing primarily as a support character. In the latter case, we see her in juxtaposition with the bourgeois woman, where she is defined primarily as the bearer of "lower" culture and, as important, *inferior femininity*.

Probably the best example of this juxtaposition is provided in *The Officer with a Rose* (*Oficir s ružom*, 1987), a film by the Croatian director Dejan Šorak. Set in liberation-era Zagreb, the film focuses on a twenty-nine-year-old upper class woman – the elegant widow Matilda Ivančić – and her romance with a Partisan lieutenant. Since Matilda lost her husband in the war and lives alone in a large Zagreb apartment, the new communist authorities assign her a tenant. She reluctantly welcomes the eighteen-year-old *partizanka* Ljiljana to her home. Ljiljana is a stereotypical peasant Partisan girl – young, simple, uneducated, and full of revolutionary élan. The sophisticated Matilda, though admittedly a class enemy, seems to fascinate Ljiljana, who tries to befriend her host and become more refined herself. Ljiljana's friendship with Matilda is not to the liking of Ljiljana's fiancé, the handsome Partisan officer Petar. Petar initially seems to despise everything about Matilda and angrily reproaches Ljiljana when, for instance, she tries Matilda's perfume but soon becomes attracted to the bourgeois lady himself. When Ljiljana leaves on a party assignment, the relationship between Matilda and Petar evolves into a passionate love affair that takes up most of the film's course. As Petar plans to wed Matilda, his communist superiors intervene, ordering an end to the affair. Petar ultimately yields, leaves Zagreb to go fight the remaining anti-Partisan bands in the countryside, and is killed. It is Ljiljana, now in late pregnancy, who breaks the news of his death to Matilda at the movie's conclusion. She also reveals that Petar married her before perishing. For all of his heroism on the battlefield, one may conclude, Petar was a coward who escaped when matters became complicated in his private life.

Similar to other works that share this motif, *The Officer with a Rose* makes bourgeois femininity the marker of refinement and higher culture. Bourgeois femininity also appears as the object of revolutionary desire, enthralling all Partisans, male and female. It is clear in the movie that not only Petar but also Ljiljana is seduced by Matilda's sophistication. Ljiljana, in addition, attempts to "better" herself and become more like Matilda. In this, *The Officer with a Rose* goes beyond other works to naturalize the bourgeois ideal of womanhood. The film makes a point of contrasting the skinny, uncouth, dark-haired Partisan tomboy, Ljiljana, dressed in uniform and boots, to the fair, soft, and classy Matilda, and the comparison is not in Ljiljana's favor – it certainly is not so in the eyes of their common lover. The *partizanka*, in short, emerges in the Partisan man/bourgeois woman trope not only as the representative of lesser culture but also as a *lesser woman*. From there, the step toward the ignominious representations of the 1990s would be easy to take. This step would be further facilitated by a sea change in the political arena – the country's disintegration – in which memory of the war played a significant role.

Into Obscurity and Ignominy (1987 to the Present): The 1980s in Yugoslavia were marked by a resurfacing of memories that had been suppressed during Tito's era. As historians, artists, and politicians began to address taboo topics, the party lost its monopoly on the interpretation of the revolutionary past. These initial revisionist attempts, we have seen, were not necessarily inspired by nationalism; they were rather directed at exposing the party's repressive policy and use of violence. But once unleashed, the process of uncovering "hidden" histories took on a life of its own. Increasingly adopting nationalist overtones, it fueled the currents of what ultimately culminated in the nationalist frenzy of the 1990s. Of all the memories that the revisionists tried to revive, the most perilous for the fragile interethnic ties among the Yugoslavs were those of World War II.[59] And it is precisely the war that emerged as the primary focus of revisionist attention and one of the major subjects of public discussion in the late 1980s. In hindsight, it appears that one of the key problems with the communist master narrative of the war, besides its Manichean nature, lay in its attempt to "deethnicize" the conflict in Yugoslavia.[60] The official version viewed the war as one of antifascist resistance and class struggle, while its other crucial dimensions as an ethnic conflict and a civil war were downplayed. This oversimplification of the nature of the conflict created

[59] Ramet, *Balkan Babel*, 53.
[60] Hoepken, "War, Memory, and Education," 200.

a gap between what was officially remembered and what certain social and ethnic groups remembered in private. In the 1980s, the terminology began to change. What had by then been termed the "national-liberation struggle and socialist revolution" now was increasingly viewed in an ethnic light and dominated by the term "genocide." Nationalists on all sides began revisiting wartime violence and giving ethnic faces to its agents and victims. The communist version of history appeared to them as one concocted specifically to suppress the truth about their nationality's wartime suffering. In the late 1980s and 1990s, historians and politicians – as Sabrina Ramet writes – "raked at the open wounds by engaging in one-sided and largely undocumented revisions of the figures of war dead," with all sides providing greatly inflated estimates.[61] The most vicious exchanges in this "war of words" were those between the Serb and Croat nationalists. On the Serbian side, the repressed memory of the Ustasha atrocities against Serbs in the Independent State of Croatia – especially in the Jasenovac concentration camp – came to dominate both historiographical and public discussions about the war.[62] In Croatia, meanwhile, public attention focused on Croat victims of Chetnik, and more importantly, Partisan atrocities. The Bleiburg massacre – referring to the Partisan execution of Croatian troops at the end of the war – became the central symbol of Croat wartime suffering.

The aspiring elites in each of the Yugoslav republics were quick to manipulate the resurfacing of the memories of war traumas for their own political goals. Similarly to the way that the Titoist official memory was used to legitimize his regime and socialist Yugoslavia, the new, diverging memories now served to discredit the common state and legitimize new political projects. Memories of war massacres thus turned into means of political promotion and confrontation and shortly became part and parcel of nationalist mobilization for new military conflicts. In the period from 1991 to 1999, as Yugoslavia disintegrated in bloodshed, the

---

[61] Ramet, *Balkan Babel*, 53.

[62] Some revisionists argued that, for the sake of promoting "brotherhood and unity" among the South Slavs, the communist regime had deliberately covered up the Ustasha genocide of Serbs. While the Ustasha atrocities had hardly been ignored in official memory, their ethnic aspect had indeed been largely downplayed, as Jasenovac had been treated as a supraethnic symbol of fascist terror. For Serbs, Jasenovac now turned into *the* symbol of their suffering at the hands of Croats. See Hoepken, "War, Memory, and Education," 210–11; Robert M. Hayden, "Recounting the Dead," 184. For a discussion of how genocide became the focus of the debate, see also Bette Denich, "Dismembering Yugoslavia: Nationalist Ideologies and Symbolic Revival of Genocide," *American Ethnologist* vol. 21, no. 2 (May 1994): 367–90.

"verbal civil war" – reinforced by the control that the repressive regimes of Slobodan Milošević in Serbia and Franjo Tudjman in Croatia had over the media – was "reenacted by the militia on the ground."[63]

While nationalism-driven wars, both verbal and real, dominated the cultural and political scenes in the former Yugoslav republics, the memory of the female Partisan was pushed further to the sidelines. Much as the ethnic dimension of the Second World War had been neglected in official memory during the communist era, the war's important gender aspects were now overlooked and the *partizanka* disappeared from the public eye and discussion. In the context of World War II polemics, historiographical and popular alike, women figured primarily as casualties, rape victims, and concentration camp inmates. In 1998, the Belgrade scholar Anđelka Milić lamented that women's participation in the Partisan struggle and the revolution lingered in "historical oblivion":

In this case we can notice that there is no great effort to get to the facts, there are no polemics, no historical falsifications, no debates among the participants themselves or between the participants and those who would perhaps try to belittle their contribution and accomplishments. We are witnessing the silence [*muk*] of a generation of women, who, as girls, empty-handed and barefoot, carried "brotherhood and unity" from "Triglav [in Slovenia] to the Vardar" [in Macedonia; meaning "throughout the country"] and then quietly exited history. We do not know who they were or what they wanted, what they did, whether they are still alive, what happened to them and what their postwar fate was. Darkness and silence![64]

To be sure, occasional communist-style works on women from particular localities and their role in the National Liberation War did appear, through inertia, in the 1990s.[65] A few of those were authored by professional historians; others were collections of articles, stories, reminiscences, and commentary collected by individual Partisan veterans in honor of their comrades. They were typically published by small private presses or sponsored by dinosaur organizations that survived unreformed

[63] Norman Naimark, *Fires of Hatred: Ethnic Cleansing in Twentieth-Century Europe* (Cambridge, MA: Harvard University Press, 2001), 158.

[64] Anđelka Milić, "Patrijarhalni poredak, revolucija, i saznanje o položaju žene," in Perović, ed., *Srbija u modernizacijskim procesima*, vol. 2, 551–9, 554.

[65] Stana Džakula-Nidžović, *Žene borci NOR-a Sedme Banijske Udarne Divizije: 1941–1945* (Čačak: Bajić, 1999); Ruža Gligović-Zeković, *San i vidici: žene nikšićkog kraja u NOB* (Nikšić: Organizacija žena i SUBNOR, 2000); Petar Avramoski, "Ženite od Struga i struško vo NOB i revolucijata," in *Ohridsko-struško vo Narodnoosloboditelnata vojna 1941–1945* (Ohrid: Opštinski odbor na SZBNOV, 1990), 121–34; Nikola P. Ilić, "Žene Jablanice i Puste Reke u NOB 1941–1942. god," *Leskovački zbornik* 38 (1998): 221–33, and others.

from Tito's times, such as the War Veterans' Association (SUBNOR). Such works held on to the old official interpretation and outdated narrative; they had limited audiences and were generally unnoticed. They certainly sparked no academic or popular debates.

As if to ensure the *partizanka*'s removal from historical memory, monuments of the Partisan heroes and victims of fascism were plundered and destroyed in the conflicts of the 1990s. For instance, the Vraca memorial complex, which included the monument to the woman fighter, was used for sniper and artillery fire on Sarajevo during the 1992–5 war. The complex was badly damaged.[66] Many other memorials were either completely demolished or neglected. The latter fate befell the *Partisan Mother,* which received no care.[67] Milić's comment about "historical oblivion" was indeed pertinent – as the end of the millennium approached, the *partizanka* seemed all but forgotten.

In the rare instances when she was pulled out of obscurity, it was in a sexualized imagery reminiscent of anti-Partisan propaganda spread by the Ustashas and Chetniks during World War II. Probably the best example of this revival of the 1940s rhetoric is provided in *Četverored* (variously translated as *Four by Four, In Four Rows,* or *By Four Rows*), a novel written by Ivan Aralica, the standard bearer of nationalism among Croatian writers and a devotee of Franjo Tudjman's ideology. In the 1990s, following Tudjman's rise to power in Croatia, Aralica launched a fairly successful political career in the ruling party. He was also elected a member of the Croatian Academy of Arts and Sciences. Parallel to his promotion into a luminary of contemporary Croatian literature, Aralica moved into the spotlight for his endorsement of hatred toward Bosnian Muslims at the height of the Croat-Muslim conflict in Bosnia. His *Četverored* was heralded as the first work of fiction about the Bleiburg tragedy and, despite the novel's poor reception among the critics, soon adapted as a film. It is primarily in this cinematographic version that Aralica's story reached the broadest audiences and caused controversy in Croatia and the region.

This state-sponsored spectacle released in 1999 remains one of the most expensive productions of the Croatian film industry. It was obvious that the film had been made with a political agenda in mind; it aimed to stir nationalist passions and boost the election campaign of Tudjman's

---

[66] *Službeni glasnik BiH,* 12/06. Available at: http://www.kons.gov.ba/main.php?id_struct=6&lang=1&action=view&id=2559 (accessed 22 June 2013).

[67] Opština Novi Grad, *Vijesti,* 22 April 2009.

party at a time when its popularity was in palpable decline. *Četverored* was scheduled to be aired on national television only two weeks after its release in theaters and a day before parliamentary elections, provoking sharp criticism and negative reactions from many sides. But it also found a grateful audience, especially among lowbrow viewers at home and in the émigré communities of Australia and the Americas.

The movie, directed by Jakov Sedlar, is a faithful adaptation of the novel (Aralica himself wrote the script), which chronicles the sufferings of the Croats at Bleiburg from the perspective of the survivors. The history of the massacre is represented through the ordeal of a young couple, Ivan and Mirta, employees of the Croatian National Theater in Zagreb. The lives of the two lovers become intertwined with those of many Croat soldiers on the road to Bleiburg and back, when they, together with the masses of civilian refugees, decide to join the troops of the defeated Independent State of Croatia withdrawing before the arriving Partisan victors.

The film opens in Zagreb, depicting the atmosphere of panic and anarchy in the city on the eve of the Partisans' arrival. It then follows the column of refugees, subjected to Allied bombings and the outbursts of the defeated and bitter Ustasha leaders, until its arrival at Bleiburg. There the refugees surrender to the British, only to be extradited back to the dreaded Partisans. Although he is a civilian, the Partisans treat the main protagonist, Ivan, as an enemy officer and send him, without a trial, to reeducation. "Reeducation," however, is only a cynical euphemism for liquidation, and Ivan ends up before a firing squad. He miraculously survives the attempted execution and, together with a small group of acquaintances, joins another group of refugees, who are led back home by the Partisans in what turns out to be a death march. Ivan is ultimately saved with the help of a Jewish Partisan and reunited with Mirta. He is released from captivity, however, only after he pledges never to reveal what he saw and experienced. This vow, given in exchange for his life, represents – as the audiences are explicitly told – "the Croatian silence."

Despite the extravagant production and cast of leading Croatian actors, the movie, as with the novel itself, rarely rises above the level of a propaganda pamphlet with crude ethnic stereotyping. The Partisans as a rule are depicted as primitive and deranged murderers; almost all are Serbs. Their prisoners, on the other hand, are invariably innocent Croat civilians, most of them artists and intellectuals infinitely superior to their captors.

Female Partisans appear in four memorable episodes. In a manner similar to Ustasha propaganda half a century earlier, the film's *partizankas* are characterized either by extreme brutality or perverse sexuality, or by both. One of them is a girl executioner, member of the firing squad in charge of liquidating Croatian officers. Her pale face with its empty stare returns to haunt Ivan long after he evades death at her hands. Another is a brain-washed communist sister of one of the prisoners. Blinded by ideologically driven hatred, she goes to the prisoner camp in order to execute her "bandit" brother personally. She does so with robotic calmness, devoid of any feelings and incapable of empathy.

The two remaining *partizanka*s are portrayed in still more ignominious terms as sexually depraved brutes. The first, as one critic aptly characterizes her, is "supposed to be a typical Jane Partisan, a Croat[ian] Serb woman who is jealous because Partisans are mass raping refined Zagreb women," whom she then "kills with a machine gun."[68] The second is Spiridona Atanacković, a *partizanka* who visits the camp in search of Petar, Ivan's fellow prisoner. She accuses Petar of being the Ustasha butcher who tried to slay her during the war, leaving a deep scar on her neck. He, of course, did nothing of the sort. It ultimately turns out that she is a debauched woman who hunts Petar down to kill him for having rejected her sexual advances before the war. "She pushed me to become her lover," explains Petar in a conversation with Ivan; "'I will not!' That's what I said to her face in front of everybody. 'I will not, even if that means I shall not lie down with a woman for the rest of my life.'"

Echoing the familiar World War II rhetoric, *Četverored* aims to discredit the *partizanka* by focusing on her base sexuality. Men in the camp use the term "whore" consistently in reference to Spiridona. Petar's words debase her first and foremost as a *woman,* presenting her femininity as so defunct that a proper Croat man would rather give up all women than have anything to do with her. In addition, the film also makes a point of emphasizing the two *partizanka*s' names to make their ethnic background obvious, simultaneously disqualifying the Partisans as a movement and the Serbs as a nation of deviants. With *Četverored,* the long process of the *partizanka*'s dethroning reached its climax.

CONCLUSION

The function of official, state-sponsored historical memory, especially that of a past war, has often been to legitimize the regime in power and forge national identity. But probably nowhere has the memory of a war

---

[68] Miljenko Jergovic, "Naked in Saddlear," *Feral Tribune,* 27 December 1999; available at http://www.ex-yupress.com/feral/feral99.html, accessed 23 June 2013.

played as important a role for a state's existence as did the memory of World War II for socialist Yugoslavia. There it was literally a key component of the glue that held the country together, only eventually to turn into a major instrument of its disintegration.

A special place in the memory of the war was reserved for the female Partisan. In the early postwar years, the *partizanka* emerged as an eminent source of legitimacy for Tito's Yugoslavia and a symbol of supranational Yugoslavism. Her official image, which was shared by Yugoslav literature and cinematography in the 1940s and 1950s, was based on the notions of heroism and sacrifice for a greater cause. She was not a gender-neutral emblem – her heroism and sacrifice were envisioned as different from, and nobler than, those of Partisan men. According to the official vision, what the *partizanka* gave up for the cause was her sacred role of motherhood, and that sacrifice, thought to be superior to any other, served as a confirmation of the righteousness of the Partisan struggle.

In the 1960s and 1970s, however, portrayals of the *partizanka* in Yugoslav culture began to depart from the static official version. As she was a gender-specific symbol of the Partisan movement and of the nation, her downfall too took on a gender-specific form and was shaped by an ever-growing dose of misogyny and sexism. The primary target of the attacks on the *partizanka* was neither her ideology, nor her political affiliation, nor any particular deed, nor even the gender equality that she came to represent; it was instead her sexuality and womanhood. At the same time that her sexuality became visible, she was progressively removed from the center of the revolutionary story to its margins, from being a major protagonist to assuming support roles. This process of her marginalization and sexualization culminated in the late 1980s and 1990s, when, amid the verbal and real wars that tore the country apart, the *partizanka* virtually disappeared from the public eye; if recalled, it was in humiliating representations that stressed her sexual depravity. She was, in short, pushed to reassuming conventional women's roles – a lover or sister at best, or a debauched female at worst – and the conventional women's position on the margins of society. Her downfall encapsulates the corrosion of the regime and, more broadly, the breakdown of the belief in the Yugoslav national project.

Conclusion

The Axis attack of April 1941 ushered in a cataclysmic four-year period for Yugoslavia's peoples. In practically all occupied Yugoslav lands, the new rulers instituted policies of racial classification, economic exploitation, and political persecution, which were accompanied by mass deportations and killings. The conquest, coupled with the brutality of the occupation and collaborationist regimes, engendered resistance that soon took the form of guerrilla warfare against the invaders and their local allies. The occupation also polarized the populace along ideological and ethnonational lines, pitting communist Partisans, fascist Ustashas, royalist Chetniks, and other, smaller factions against one another. It was a war of "each against everybody,"[1] which annihilated the interwar political system and called into question all existing lines of social order and authority.

This profound destabilization of social arrangements created openings for change in the gender system. A major challenge to established norms was indeed launched by one of the warring factions. Championing equality between the sexes, Tito's Partisans promised to abolish all traces of women's subjugation and create a new socialist polity of equals. They were eager to mobilize and employ women, en masse, in their support network in the rear. Defying old social conventions, they decided to enlist large numbers of females as combatants in their guerrilla units. For the first time in Yugoslav history, women gained the right to vote and hold

---

[1] Slobodan Inić, "Jedan ili više ratova," *Tokovi istorije* 1–2 (1993), as quoted in Wolfgang Hoepken, "War, Memory, and Education in a Fragmented Society: The Case of Yugoslavia," *East European Politics and Societies* 13.1 (Winter 1999): 202.

office in civil administrations that the Partisans set up in territories under their control. The Communist Party's propaganda celebrated the female fighter and acknowledged the contribution of noncombatant females who supported the Partisan units. After the war, the communists instituted sweeping reforms that marked a dramatic improvement in women's legal position. These policies underscored the contrast between the revolutionary egalitarian ideal and the traditional gender order. Yet a closer look reveals that the Partisans' gender politics accommodated traditional values and culture in unexpected ways.

This study has tried to show that in the Partisan institutional setup, mobilizing rhetoric, and daily practice, the party often handled differences between the revolutionary and the traditional by active adaptation rather than confrontation. To attract women and legitimize their participation in the struggle, the CPY invoked the heroic imagery from Balkan folklore and combined it skillfully with a revolutionary language stressing women's emancipation. In the process, party leaders shifted the argument for gender equality from a modern one based on rights to one encompassing traditional notions of duty and sacrifice. The CPY consciously appealed to women's traditional concerns and directed, in a remarkably structured way, their age-old tasks and labor skills toward the Partisan effort, thus facilitating their mass participation in modern warfare. Rather than advocating a sexual revolution, communist leaders instituted a behavioral code that catered to the time-honored patriarchal mores and enforced it in an interventionist manner through modern regulatory devices. Much like peasant custom, Partisan sexual puritanism was gendered, with women figuring disproportionally at the receiving end of the party's policing and punitive measures. In the Partisan units and movement as a whole, women were greeted as equals and granted access to the battlefield, yet the customary sexual division of labor persisted and gender remained a chief delineator of hierarchy.

The case of the Yugoslav *partizanka* reveals the extent to which mass mobilization for a modern and revolutionary cause could rest on the appropriation of traditional culture. The story that this book tells is not only about Partisan women and the war in the Balkans, but more broadly about the modern state and its continuing reliance on invocation and reinvention of local traditions. It is also a story about modernization and the building of communism in a specific social and cultural context. That context involved a revolutionary urban-based party; its Marxist ideology and modernizing, egalitarian agenda; and its largely rural and patriarchal constituency. The Yugoslav case illuminates the complexities that accompanied the consolidation of communist power in a primarily rural society, exemplifying at the same time some working – and perhaps original – solutions devised by the modernizing elites.

The success of the Partisans' mobilizing campaigns could not be fully understood without taking into consideration their deft weaving of the ideological and the traditional. And this success was indeed remarkable; the official communist-era figure for the participation of Yugoslavia's females in the National Liberation Movement is two million, of whom 100,000 were soldiers of the National Liberation Army.[2] While these estimates seem high and are difficult to confirm, there is little doubt that in many regions peasant women participated en masse in the Partisan support system, and extant documents do suggest that it is safe to talk about several tens of thousands females who joined the units. Some 2,000 women acquired officer's rank during the war, and 92 were proclaimed National Heroes.[3]

The extraordinary features of the Yugoslav phenomenon are perhaps best appreciated within a larger international comparative framework. Among World War II resistance organizations, Tito's Partisans stand out for the extent of women's active involvement, especially in the military. No other antifascist movement in occupied Europe managed to mobilize so many women and deploy so many female combatants. In the best-known European resistance network, in France, women seldom took part in paramilitary or combat activities. "Full-time, gun-toting *partisanes*," as Paula Schwartz writes, did exist, but they were exceptions to the rule.[4] The French postwar government recognized about 220,000 participants of both sexes in the Resistance, among whom only "an infinitesimal number of women fought with weapons" and very few joined the *maquisards*.[5] A larger number of females assumed nontraditional roles in the Italian case, although resistance in Italy gained momentum much later than in France (after the capitulation and German invasion in 1943) and was concentrated in the occupied central and northern portions of the country. After the war, about 200,000 Italians, including 55,000 women, were recognized as having been resistance members. An

[2] Kovačević, *Women of Yugoslavia*, 51; idem, *Borbeni put*, 25; Jancar-Webster, 92.

[3] Ibid.; Lagator and Ćukić, *Partizanke Prve Proleterske*, 9.

[4] Paula Schwartz, "*Partisanes* and Gender Politics in Vichy France," *French Historical Studies* 16.1 (Spring 1989): 129.

[5] According to a report at the 1975 conference on women in the French Resistance, as quoted in Margaret Collins Weitz, *Sisters in the Resistance: How Women Fought to Free France, 1940–1945* (New York: John Wiley & Sons, 1995), 148.

estimated 35,000 of these women were *partigiane combattente* (literally, Partisan combatants).[6]

In Poland, where resistance began early and developed into one of the most effective forces in occupied Europe, some 40,000 females became sworn-in members of the Home Army.[7] Women played multiple roles in the Polish underground, their contribution ranging from liaison work to sabotage, intelligence, and diversionary activities. Although most of them were not soldiers in the customary sense, during the Warsaw uprising many took part in the arduous street fighting. Besides the underground, women served in two Polish militaries formed in the USSR. Some 5,850 females joined the Women's Auxiliary Service of the Polish force known as the Anders Army, which was raised in 1941 under General Anders, gathering the Polish units that had been held in Soviet captivity since Stalin's 1939 occupation of eastern Poland; the army left Soviet territory in 1942 and fought ultimately under British command. After its evacuation, Stalin raised another Polish army in the USSR. Composed mostly of Polish and Soviet communists and the remaining Polish deportees from eastern Poland, the Polish People's Army was modeled on the Soviet military. An all-female battalion was attached to it. Though most of its women played noncombat roles, a small group rose through the ranks and some even commanded all-male platoons. At the end of the war, the Polish People's Army could boast more than 8,000 service women. Taken together, there were some 14,000 Polish women in military service at the war's conclusion in May 1945.[8]

By far the largest number of women was involved in the Soviet war effort, which is the only case that, at first glance, seems to overshadow the Yugoslav one. According to rough estimates, 800,000 women served in the Red Army. Some 500,000 of them saw duty at the front in combat or support services and carried weapons.[9] According to official data,

[6] Jane Slaughter, *Women and the Italian Resistance, 1943–1945* (Denver, CO: Arden Press, 1997), 33, 58.

[7] Shelley Saywell, "Uprising: Poland, 1939–1945," *Women in War* (Markham, Ontario: Viking, 1985), 103, 107. For an excellent description of women's roles in the Polish resistance, see Jan Karski, *Story of a Secret State* (Boston: Houghton Mifflin, 1944), 280–6.

[8] Section on women in the Polish People's Army and the Anders army is based on Malgorzata Fidelis, *Women, Communism, and Industrialization in Postwar Poland* (New York: Cambridge University Press, 2010), 38.

[9] Anne E. Griesse and Richard Stites, "Russia: Revolution and War," in *Female Soldiers – Combatants or Non-Combatants? Historical and Contemporary Perspectives*, ed. by Nancy L. Goldman (Westport, CT: Greenwood Press, 1982), 71, 73. Anna Krylova provides a higher estimate of more than 900,000 women in the armed forces, and more than

about 28,500 took part in Partisan activities, constituting 9.8 percent of Soviet Partisan forces.[10] Barbara Jancar-Webster has noted that in proportion to the total population these figures do not match the Yugoslav ones.[11] Any comparisons with the Soviet Union, however, have to be qualified. The mobilization campaign that drew women into the Soviet military ranks took place in a dramatically different milieu from those of the European resistance movements; as Gordon Wright reminds us, it involved the functioning apparatus of a totalitarian state, the prewar government stationed in the nation's capital, and the regular army actively defending the country. The Partisans of the occupied regions of the USSR operated under different conditions than guerrillas elsewhere in occupied Europe, where armies were defeated, decimated, and disbanded, and governments forced into exile. The Soviet Partisans functioned as an integral part of the USSR's military effort, in concert with the Red Army. They were not only supplied by Moscow and placed under orders from the Soviet High Command, but were also often organized by people who had been trained in special Soviet camps for guerrilla fighters and dispatched into the occupied borderlands.[12] Given the power of the Soviet government, the control it exerted over the populace, and the mobilizing tools at its disposal, the figure of 800,000, though impressive, becomes easier to understand. In addition, Soviet volunteers belonged to the first postrevolutionary generation who had lived all their lives under a regime advocating gender equality. In a recent study, Anna Krylova suggests that prewar Soviet popular culture, the educational system, and paramilitary training helped raise a generation of women who had nontraditional perceptions of their position in society and considered their proper wartime place to be in combat.[13] None of this was true for women in Yugoslavia, or for that matter anywhere else.

520,000 in the field army. See Krylova, *Soviet Women in Combat: A History of Violence on the Eastern Front* (New York: Cambridge University Press, 2010), 145. For a fine social history of Soviet female soldiers, see Roger D. Markwick and Euridice Charon Cardona, *Soviet Women on the Frontline in the Second World War* (New York: Palgrave Macmillan, 2012).

[10] Julianne Fürst, "Heroes, Lovers, Victims – Partisan Girls during the Great Fatherland War," *Minerva* 18.3–4 (Fall–Winter 2000): 38–74.

[11] Jancar-Webster, *Women & Revolution*, 215 n. 9.

[12] Gordon Wright, *The Ordeal of Total War*, 159–60.

[13] Anna Krylova, "Stalinist Identity from the Viewpoint of Gender: Rearing a Generation of Professionally Violent Women Soldiers in 1930s Stalinist Russia," *Gender and History* 16.3 (November, 2004): 626–53. The same argument is made in Krylova, *Soviet Women in Combat.*

For a better comparison with Yugoslavia, it may be necessary to look beyond Europe to the Chinese revolution and War of Resistance against Japan. To be sure, there were significant cultural differences between the Balkans and China in the 1930s and 1940s. Yet the social contexts in which the two revolutions took place bear striking parallels. In both cases, the communists gained power independently of the Soviet Union, by successfully garnering the allegiance of a considerable portion of the local population. The peasantry constituted the main support base for both communist parties. This alliance between the party – a radical, elite organization – and the patriarchal peasant masses was in fact the defining feature of both revolutions, and in both cases the alliance was forged and the party transformed into a mass movement during the war of resistance against a foreign invader. Each party also fought a series of civil wars against its local nationalist rivals, eventually emerging victorious. Yugoslav leaders during the war were themselves aware of the similarities and apparently inspired by what they knew about the Chinese revolutionary struggle. In honor of the Chinese, they named their own transfer from eastern to western Bosnia in 1942 "the Long March," after the legendary retreat of the Chinese Red Army from the southern to the northern provinces of China in 1934–5. These analogies between wartime China and Yugoslavia have not escaped scholarly attention. Already in the early 1960s, in his seminal book on the Chinese revolution, Chalmers A. Johnson drew parallels between the two. His work emphasizes the mass popular following that the two communist parties – each with a limited support base in the 1920s and 1930s – acquired during the war. Johnson argues that the Communist Party's rise to power in both countries should be understood as "a species of nationalist movement," whereby the peasant masses were awakened and politicized in response to the dramatic disruption of daily life brought about by the foreign invasion.[14]

Given the analogous social contexts, it is small wonder that the Chinese and Yugoslav communists faced similar dilemmas in their gender politics. They had to balance their egalitarianism with the patriarchal mores of their constituents, and both parties often found concessions in this area opportune to preclude alienating the peasantry. As Kay Ann Johnson eloquently puts it, the contradictions that "arose from the successful revolutionary coalition of radical intellectuals and peasants that came together

---

[14] Chalmers A. Johnson, *Peasant Nationalism and Communist Power: The Emergence of Revolutionary China, 1937–1945* (Stanford, CA: Stanford University Press, 1962), viii–ix, 7–30.

in the 1930s and 40s" were "reflected, in part, by an enduring tension between ideological goals and practice on women's issues."[15] A result of these tensions was the persistence of many patriarchal practices and hierarchies in both revolutionary movements. But in the Yugoslav case the party did more than simply allow prerevolutionary practices to coexist with revolutionary ones. As this study has tried to show, Yugoslav communists actively invoked and adapted local traditions to their agenda in order to facilitate women's mass mobilization in their movement. It remains to be seen whether the same held true for the Chinese.[16]

Similarly to women in Yugoslavia and the Soviet Union, women in China contributed both directly and indirectly to the communist war effort, though a much smaller percentage saw combat duty. Scholars have generally avoided providing cumulative estimates of women's military participation, perhaps because the Chinese revolution passed through several distinct phases and the party's gender policy varied. In the period of the Kiangsi (Jiangxi) Soviet, 1929–34, when the party was involved in a civil war against the nationalist Kuomintang forces, women took on a range of support and military roles. The majority of organized women joined the Red Guards and Youth Volunteers. They received some military training, but engaged primarily in rear-area services, nursing soldiers, carrying supplies, guarding villages, and helping run laundries, sewing groups, and kitchens.[17] Though military service was not off limits to females, there were few women in the Red Army, still fewer participated in combat, and their importance was primarily symbolic.[18] According to Judith Stacey, party propaganda and official revolutionary histories added to the symbolic significance of female warriors, publicizing their exploits

[15] Kay Ann Johnson, *Women, the Family, and Peasant Revolution in China* (Berkeley: University of California Press, 1983), 39.

[16] As a suggestion for further research, it may be interesting to examine whether and how the CCP made use of prerevolutionary culture, including the imagery of female warriors, to mobilize women. The image of Hua Mulan – the legendary heroine who, much like the Balkan epic heroines, dresses as a man and enlists in the army to replace her father – comes to mind. It is well known that the "Ballad of Mulan" inspired several party women, and one of them, Huang Dinghui, even changed her name to Mulan once she joined the revolution. See Wang Zheng, *Women in the Chinese Enlightenment: Oral and Textual Histories* (Berkeley: University of California Press, 1999), 297, 347–51; Christina Kelley Gilmartin, *Engendering the Chinese Revolution: Radical Women, Communist Politics, and Mass Movements in the 1920s* (Berkeley: University of California Press, 1995), 74, 100, 189. The sources do not elaborate on whether the party actually used this imagery for mobilization purposes.

[17] Based on Johnson, *Women, the Family, and Peasant Revolution*, 52–3; Elizabeth Croll, *Feminism and Socialism in China* (Boston: Routledge & Kegan Paul, 1978), 193.

[18] Johnson, *Women, the Family, and Peasant Revolution*, 52–3.

out of proportion to their real numbers.[19] The highest scholarly estimate mentions some three thousand women taking part in the Long March, including a two-thousand-strong all-female logistical unit, the Women's Independence Brigade, and the five-hundred-member Women's Engineer Battalion, both of the Fourth Front Red Army; most of these women did not survive the march.[20] When, in 1937, the communists united forces with the Kuomintang to fight the invading Japanese, their gender policy turned more conservative, relegating women entirely to support roles. Thus though the War of Resistance against Japan (1937–45) saw thousands of new female recruits, they were assigned to noncombat and auxiliary functions – a practice that would continue after the Japanese defeat in the final round of the civil war against the Kuomintang, 1945–9.[21]

Back in the European context, probably the closest and most similar to Tito's Partisans were two other communist-led Balkan guerrillas: the Greek EAM/ELAS and the lesser-known Albanian National Liberation Movement. These two resemble the Yugoslav resistance with regard not only to women's participation but also to the movements' characters, strategies, and involvement in civil wars alongside antiinvader resistance. Both were in close contact with the Yugoslavs, the latter being actually founded under Yugoslav tutelage and on the Yugoslav model. Sources on Albania mention that women contributed more than six thousand soldiers, constituting approximately one-tenth of the Albanian partisan troops.[22] The exact number of women in the Greek resistance is unknown; existing literature provides only estimates for the total participation, involving both sexes. These estimates mention between 1.5 and 2 million EAM supporters, of whom about 120,000 men and women served as fighters.[23]

Despite the variations in scale and form of women's participation, the female soldier was, to use Anna Krylova's words, "a shared transnational

---

[19] Judith Stacey, *Patriarchy and Socialist Revolution in China* (Berkeley: University of California Press, 1983), 152.

[20] Mady Wechsler Segal, Xiaolin Li, and David R. Segal, "The Role of Women in the Chinese People's Liberation Army," *Minerva* 10. 1 (March 1992): 48–55. For personal narratives of female Long March survivors, see Helen Praeger Young, *Choosing Revolution: Chinese Women Soldiers on the Long March* (Urbana: University of Illinois Press, 2001). About 100,000 soldiers participated in the Long March.

[21] Segal, Li, and Segal, "The Role of Women."

[22] John Kolsti, "From Courtyard to Cabinet: The Political Emergence of Albanian Women," in *Women, State, and Party in Eastern Europe*, ed. by Sharon L. Wolchik and Alfred Meyer (Durham, NC: Duke University Press, 1985), 144.

[23] Janet Hart, *New Voices in the Nation: Women and the Greek Resistance, 1941–1964* (Ithaca, NY: Cornell University Press, 1996), 30, n. 1.

problem of the mid-twentieth century," and certain characteristics of the Yugoslav experience seem common to many other resistance movements and World War II belligerents.[24] For one, women were nowhere readily accepted in the military, especially as combatants. Europe's antifascist leaders who decided to recruit women for armed combat did so reluctantly, usually under severe military pressure. The Soviet government began mobilizing female volunteers into the regular army only in spring 1942, as a result of manpower shortages caused by the heavy losses of the previous winter. Tito authorized women's recruitment in Yugoslavia at approximately the same time, also after a difficult winter for the Partisans. Communist parties elsewhere in Europe apparently waited for the Soviets to take the first step; the French party, for example, extended its call to women in the summer of 1942.[25] The noncommunist French Resistance leaders never even tried to enlist females as fighters; de Gaulle had rather conservative ideas about the army, and the Women's Auxiliary that his provisional government established in January 1944 was created to release men for the front by assigning support functions to females.[26]

In part because of their egalitarian ideology, the Yugoslav Partisans together with some other communist movements and belligerents of World War II went further than others in their willingness to employ females in nonconventional roles. Yet they too considered women better suited to serve in traditional capacities on the home front or in the rear. Their policies suggest that they saw women's soldiering as a matter of temporary expediency in turbulent times that was not to be extended to "normal" conditions. Not only were they hesitant to enlist women initially, but they also proved keen to discharge them as soon as possible. In Spain, females were removed from the front lines already during the first year of the conflict. In the Soviet Union and Yugoslavia, the stage for women's withdrawal from the army was also set before the war ended. For all of their egalitarianism, the communists' policy in this regard was not much different from that of the Western Allies. In what seems a universal trend, women of practically all World War II belligerents were either excluded from combat duty or released from service shortly after the war.

The existence of a gender division of labor within the resistance is another issue common to all antifascist movements. Unlike men, who

---

[24] Krylova, *Soviet Women in Combat*, 295.
[25] Schwartz, "*Partisanes*," 143.
[26] Ibid., 147. Also Weitz, *Sisters in the Resistance*, 147–70.

were present in combat and leadership positions, women did most of the unglamorous support work. The lion's share of women's contribution consisted of countless repetitive and mundane yet indispensable tasks that have largely remained unacknowledged by contemporaries and historians alike.[27] The sexual division of labor could be noticed even on the front. The Yugoslav *partizanka* may have been one of the most daring European heroines in battle, but when the fighting stopped she turned to domestic chores, such as cooking, sewing, laundering, and cleaning. In this, she was not unique; from Spain to the Soviet Union to China, the women at the front often remained in charge of traditional women's duties.[28]

The story of the Yugoslav *partizanka* exposes with particular force one of the key mechanisms by which societies resist change in the gender system. Social anxieties regarding gender rearrangements are typically expressed as concerns over unrestrained female sexuality. Accusations of sexual impropriety almost always accompany women who dare to challenge the established social order and cross the gender divide. Such accusations reveal much more about the values of the society in which the transgression takes place than about the actual behavior of the women. Nowhere was this more obvious than in the *partizanka*'s case. From the moment of her appearance on the battlefield, she had been accompanied by the charge of promiscuity and sexual debauchery. During the war, her sexual behavior became both the favorite target of enemy propaganda and the focus of the party's discipline. The Chetniks portrayed her as the "fallen woman" without morals, the antipode of the chaste and venerable Serb girls and mothers. The Ustashas similarly insisted on her alleged sexual depravity, further adding spice to their propaganda with rumors about her bloodthirstiness and brutality. The large dose of misogyny associated with the charge of impropriety is an indicator of how deeply embedded traditional gender values were in society. An equally important indicator is the fact that the attitude toward the female fighters within the Partisan movement itself was often negative. Party officials and Partisan

---

[27] Weitz, *Sisters in the Resistance*, 80. Paula Schwartz, "Redefining Resistance: Women's Activism in Wartime France," in *Behind the Lines: Gender and the Two World Wars*, ed. Margaret Higonnet et al. (New Haven: Yale University Press, 1987), 141–53.

[28] For Spain, Mary Nash, *Defying Male Civilization: Women in the Spanish Civil War* (Denver, CO: Arden Press, 1995), 108–9; for Italy, Slaughter, *Women and the Italian Resistance*, ch. 3; for Soviet Partisan women, Julianne Fürst, "Heroes, Lovers, Victims." On the hard work of Soviet laundresses, see Barbara Engel, "Soviet Women Remember World War II," in *Women and War in the Twentieth Century: Enlisted with or without Consent*, ed. Nicole Ann Dombrowski (New York: Garland, 1999), 138–61.

commanders of various ranks often saw women as the source of potential and real sexual problems in the movement and directed a greater share of their tutorial and policing measures at them. At the level of implementation, the party's policies were frequently marked by misogyny and double standards.

Although perhaps not as powerful as in Yugoslavia, the same mechanism of debasing the female fighter by focusing on her sexuality was at work in other countries at war in the 1930s and 1940s. In the Spanish Civil War, Mary Nash tells us, allegations linking women combatants with prostitution and venereal disease surfaced shortly after the initial outpouring of revolutionary enthusiasm in 1936. Such accusations received significant coverage not only in fascist propaganda but also in the republican press. That coverage was decisive in dishonoring the *milicianas* and "resulted in the popular demand" that women "be dismissed from the war fronts."[29] In the Soviet context during the war, when women's presence in the army was necessary, communist propaganda insisted on female fighters' sexual purity. But after the war, as Anna Krylova notes, a backlash ensued and the meanings assigned to female fighting underwent a radical reinterpretation. "In rumors and folk stories," she writes, "the front women's effort was reduced to prostitution and husband-hunting."[30]

The final commonality concerns the experiences and memories of the women resisters themselves. Yugoslav female veterans portray the time spent in the struggle as one of idealism, fulfillment, and grandeur. Similar appraisals emerge from personal narratives of women participants throughout Europe, regardless of their country of origin, their respective movement's wartime fate, or the ways that official memory of the war was constructed in the postwar period. Female activists of the antifascist movements that lost their wars – those who fought on the side of republican Spain, the Greek EAM/ELAS, or the Polish Home Army – describe their participation in the war in the same terms as their victorious counterparts in Yugoslavia, France, Italy, or the Soviet Union. Despite the many hardships and horrors of the war, many female veterans remember it as an exhilarating and liberating experience. Through their resistance activity, they developed their potential to a degree unheard of

---

[29] Mary Nash, *Defying Male Civilization*, 112.

[30] Krylova, "Stalinist Identity," 650. In postwar Soviet popular opinion, confirms Barbara Engel, all women combatants were stereotyped in negative terms as the so-called mobile front wives, who had relations with higher-ranking men in exchange for privileges. See Engel, "Soviet Women Remember World War II," 138–61.

before the war, gaining in the process self-esteem, confidence, and respect. Commitment to the higher cause aroused an unprecedented feeling of purpose and accomplishment, while active participation allowed women to see themselves as political subjects and historical agents. Judging by their reminiscences, it appears that for women the very opportunity to be involved in the struggle represented a welcome break from the past. Wartime experiences became the highlight of their lives, which many recall with nostalgia as their "most beautiful days."

Selected Bibliography

Archives

Arhiv Jugoslavije (AJ)
Vojni Arhiv (formerly known as Arhiv Vojnoistorijskog Instituta (AVII))
Hoover Institution Archives (HIA)
Muzej Istorije Jugoslavije (MIJ)
Jugoslovenska Kinoteka

Periodicals and Newspapers

Antifašistkinja
Borba
Dalmatinka u borbi
Drugarica
Glas omladine
Goranka
Istranka
Lička žena u borbi
Naša žena
Nova žena
Primorka
Proleter
Rijec žene
Rodoljupka
Udarnica
Vojvodjanka u borbi
Žena danas
Žena kroz borbu
Žena u borbi
Žena zbjega
Zora

Published Primary Sources

Božović, Saša. *Tebi, moja Dolores.* Beograd: 4.jul, 1981.

Bynum, David E. *Serbo-Croatian Heroic Poems: Epics from Bihać, Cazin and Kulen Vakuf.* Translated by David E. Bynum. New York: Garland, 1993.

Ćosić, Dobrica. *Daleko je sunce,* 12th ed. Beograd: Prosveta, 1966.

Dedijer, Vladimir. *The Beloved Land.* London: MacGibbon & Kee, 1961.

The War Diaries of Vladimir Dedijer. Vols. 1–3. Ann Arbor: University of Michigan Press, 1990.

With Tito through the War. London: A. Hamilton, 1951.

Djilas, Milovan. *Anatomy of a Moral: The Political Essays of Milovan Djilas.* Edited by Abraham Rothberg. New York: Praeger, 1959.

Memoir of a Revolutionary. New York: Harcourt Brace Jovanovich 1973.

Wartime. New York: Harcourt Brace Jovanovich, 1977.

Đurović, Milinko et al., eds. *Peta Proleterska Crnogorska Brigada: Knjiga Sjećanja* Belgrade: Vojnoizdavački zavod, 1972.

Džakula Nidžović, Stana. *Žene borci NOR-a Sedme banijske udarne divizije.* Čačak: Bajić, 1999.

Frndić, Nasko, ed. *Muslimanske Junačke Pjesme.* Zagreb: Stvarnost, 1969.

Gerk, Stana, Ivka Križnar, and Štefanija Ravnikar-Podvebšek, eds. *Slovenke v Narodnoosvobodilnem boju: Zbornik dokumentov, člankov in spominov.* Vols. 1–2. Ljubljana: Zavod 'Borec', 1970.

Giron, Anton, and Mihael Sobolevski, eds. *Goranke, Istranke, Primorke u NOB: Izbor iz Glasila AFŽ.* Rijeka: Muzej Narodne Revolucije, 1978.

Građa za historiju Narodnoslobodilačkog Pokreta u Slavoniji. 6 vols. Slavonski Brod: Historijski Institut Slavonije, 1966.

Hrvatske Narodne Pjesme. Odio Prvi. Junačke Pjesme. Vols. 1–3. Zagreb: Matica Hrvatska, 1896–8.

Hurem, Rasim, ed. *Žene Bosne i Hercegovine u narodnooslobodilačkoj borbi 1941–1945. godine: Sjećanja učesnika.* Sarajevo: Svjetlost, 1977.

Izvori za istoriju SKJ, Series A: Dokumenti centralnih organa KPJ: NOR i revolucija (1941–1945). 23 vols. Beograd: Izdavacki centar Komunist, 1985–1996.

Jones, William. *Twelve Months with Tito's Partisans.* Bedford, England: Bedford Books, 1946.

Karadžić, Vuk. *Srpske Narodne Pjesme.* Edited by Vladan Nedić. Belgrade: Prosveta, 1969.

Songs of the Serbian People: From the Collection of Vuk Karadžić. Translated and edited by Milne Holton and Vasa D. Mihailovich. Pittsburgh: University of Pittsburgh Press, 1997.

Komnenić-Džaković, Jelisavka. *Staza jedne partizanke.* Beograd: Narodna knjiga, 1980.

Maclean, Fitzroy. *Eastern Approaches.* London: Cape, 1950.

Marković, Moma. *Rat i Revolucija: Sećanja, 1941–1945.* Beograd: BIGZ, 1987.

Martinović-Bajica, Petar. *Milan Nedić.* Chicago: First American Serbian Corporation, 1956.

Mešterović, Julka. *Lekarev dnevnik.* Beograd: Vojnoizdavački zavod, 1968.

Miladinovci. *Zbornik 1861–1961.* Skopje: Kočo Racin, 1962.

Milinović, Daško and Zoran Petakov, eds. *Partizanke – Žene u Narodnooslobodilačkoj borbi*. Novi Sad: CENZURA, 2010.

Mitrović, Mitra. *Ratno putovanje*. Beograd: Prosveta, 1962.

Nazor, Vladimir. *Partizanska knjiga*. Zagreb: Nakladni zavod Hrvatske, 1949.

Patković, Milenko, ed. *Izbor iz štampe Narodnooslobodilačkog Pokreta u Slavoniji 1941–1945*. Slavonski Brod: Historijski Institut Slavonije, 1968.

Purović, Milinko, ed. *Ustanak naroda Jugoslavije, 1941: Zbornik. Pišu učesnici*. Beograd: Vojno delo, 1962. Vols. 1–6.

Sandes, Flora. *The Autobiography of a Woman Soldier: A Brief Record of Adventure with the Serbian Army, 1916–1919*. New York: F. A. Stokes, 1927.

Skrigin, Žorž. *Rat i pozornica*. Beograd: Turistička štampa, 1968.

Šoljan, Marija, ed., *Žene Hrvatske u narodnooslobodilackoj borbi*. 2 vols. Zagreb: Izdanje glavnog odbora Saveza Ženskih Društava Hrvatske, 1955.

Žene Hrvatske u radničkom pokretu do aprila hiljadu devetsto četrdeset prve. Zagreb: Konferencija za društvenu aktivnost žena Hrvatske, 1967.

Tito (Josip Broz). "Govor na Prvoj Zemaljskoj Konferenciji Antifašističkog Fronta Žena." In *Tito-Ženama Jugoslavije*. Edited by CO AFŽ, 3–13. Beograd: Centralni odbor Antifašističkog Fronta Žena Jugoslavije, 1945.

Govori i Članci. Zagreb: Naprijed, 1962.

Veskovik-Vangeli, Vera, and Marija Jovanovik, eds. *Ženite na Makedonija vo NOV: Zbornik na dokumenti za učestvoto na ženite od Makedonija vo narodnoosloboditelnata vojna i revolucijata 1941–1945*. Skopje: Institut za nacionalna istorija, 1976.

Zbornik dokumenata i podataka o narodnooslobodilackom ratu jugoslovenskih naroda. 15 vols., 173 books. Beograd: Vojnoistorijski institut, 1949–86.

Zbornik dokumenata i podataka sanitetske sluzbe u narodnooslobodilačkom ratu jugoslovenskih naroda. 12 vols. Beograd: Vojnoistorijski institut, 1952–78.

Secondary Sources

Ačanski, Radivoj. *Žene kulske opštine u radničkom pokretu, NOR-u i socijalističkoj revoluciji*. Kula: Konferencija za društveni položaj i aktivnost žena, 1985.

Alexander, Ronelle. "The Poetics of Vuk Karadžić's songs: An Analysis of "Kosovka Devojka." In *Kosovo: Legacy of a Medieval Battle*. Edited by Wayne S. Vucinich and Thomas S. Emmert, 189–202. Minneapolis: University of Minnesota Press, 1991.

Anagnostopoulou, Margaret P. "From Heroines to Hyenas: Women Partisans during the Greek Civil War." *Contemporary European History* 10.3 (November 2001): 481–501.

Attwood, Lynne. *Creating the New Soviet Woman: Women's Magazines as Engineers of Female Identity, 1922–53*. New York: St. Martin's Press, 1999.

Auty, Phyllis and Richard Clogg, eds. *British Policy towards Wartime Resistance in Yugoslavia and Greece*. New York: Barnes & Noble Books, 1975.

Avramoski, Petar. "Ženite od Struga i struško vo NOB i revolucijata." In *Ohridsko-struško vo Narodnoosloboditelnata vojna 1941–1945*, 121–34. Ohrid: Opštinski odbor na SZBNOV, 1990.

Banac, Ivo. *The National Question in Yugoslavia: Origins, History, Politics.* Ithaca, NY: Cornell University Press, 1984.
——. *With Stalin against Tito: Cominformist Splits in Yugoslav Communism.* Ithaca, NY: Cornell University Press, 1988.
Barker, Thomas M. *Social Revolutionaries and Secret Agents: The Carinthian Slovene Partisans and Britain's Special Operations Executive.* Boulder, CO: East European Monographs, 1990.
Beissinger, Margaret. "Epic, Gender, and Nationalism: The Development of Nineteenth-Century Balkan Literature." In *Epic Traditions in the Contemporary World: The Poetics of Community.* Edited by Margaret Beissinger, Jane Tylus, and Susanne Wofford, 69–86. Berkeley: University of California Press, 1999.
Beoković, Mila. *Žene heroji.* Sarajevo: Svjetlost, 1967.
Bulatović, Ljiljana. *Bila jednom četa devojačka.* Beograd: Nova knjiga, 1985.
Bojović, Jovan R. et al. *Žene Crne Gore u revolucionarnom pokretu, 1918–1945.* Titograd: Istorijski institut, 1969.
Bokovoy, Melissa K. *Peasants and Communists: Politics and Ideology in the Yugoslav Countryside, 1941–1953.* Pittsburgh: University of Pittsburgh Press, 1998.
Bokovoy, Melissa K., Jill A. Irvine, and Carol S. Lilly, eds. *State-Society Relations in Yugoslavia, 1945–1992.* New York: St. Martin's Press, 1997.
Bonnell, Victoria. *Iconography of Power: Soviet Political Posters under Lenin and Stalin.* Berkeley: University of California Press, 1997.
Bošković-Stulli, Maja. "Narodna poezija naše oslobodilačke borbe kao problem suvremenog folklornog stvaralaštva." In *Usmena književnost: Izbor studija i ogleda.* Edited by Maja Bošković-Stulli, 317–55. Zagreb: Školska knjiga, 1971.
——. "Pjesma o prerušenoj djevojci." In *Usmena književnost: Izbor studija i ogleda.* Edited by Maja Bošković-Stulli, 107–12. Zagreb: Školska knjiga, 1971.
Božinović, Neda. *Žensko pitanje u Srbiji u XIX i XX veku.* Beograd: 94, 1996.
Bracewell, Wendy. "'The Proud Name of Hajduks': Bandits as Ambiguous Heroes in Balkan Politics and Culture." In *Yugoslavia and Its Historians: Understanding the Balkan Wars of the 1990s.* Edited by Norman Naimark and Holly Case, 22–36. Stanford, CA: Stanford University Press, 2003.
Brozičević-Rikica, Anka, ed., *Žene Vinodola u NOB-u: Zbornik radova.* Rijeka: Koordinacioni odbor za njegovanje i razvoj tradicije NOB-a, 1986.
Conze, Susanne and Fieseler, Beate. "Soviet Women as Comrades-in-Arms: A Blind Spot in the History of the War." *The People's War: Responses to World War II in the Soviet Union.* Edited by Robert W. Thurston and Bernd Bonwetsch. Urbana and Chicago: University of Illinois Press, 2000.
Corrin, Chris, ed. *Superwomen and the Double Burden: Women's Experience of Change in Central and Eastern Europe and the Former Soviet Union.* London: Scarlet Press, 1992.
Crampton, R. J. *Eastern Europe in the Twentieth Century – and After.* 2nd ed. New York: Routledge, 1997.
Croll, Elizabeth. *Feminism and Socialism in China.* Boston: Routledge & Kegan Paul, 1978.

Cvetić, Bosa, et al., eds. *Žene Srbije u NOB*. Beograd: Nolit, 1975.

David, Henry P. and Joanna Skilogianis. "The Woman Question." In *From Abortion to Contraception: A Resource to Public Policies and Reproductive Behavior in Central and Eastern Europe from 1917 to the Present*. Edited by Henry P. David, 39–47. Westport, CT: Greenwood Press, 1999.

David-Fox, Michael. "Multiple Modernities vs. Neo-Traditionalism: On Recent Debates in Russian and Soviet History." *Jahrbücher für Geschichtes Osteuropas* 54 (2006): 535–55.

Denich, Bette. "Dismembering Yugoslavia: Nationalist Ideologies and Symbolic Revival of Genocide." *American Ethnologist* 21, no.2 (May 1994): 367–90.

Djilas, Aleksa. *The Contested Country: Yugoslav Unity and Communist Revolution, 1919–1953*. Cambridge: Harvard University Press, 1991.

Dombrowski, Nicole Ann, ed. *Women and War in the Twentieth century: Enlisted with or without Consent*. New York: Garland, 1999.

Duchen, Claire and Irene Bandhauer-Schoffman, eds. *When the War Was Over: Women, War and Peace in Europe, 1940–1956*. New York: Leicester University Press, 2000.

Edwards, Louise. *Gender, Politics, and Democracy: Women's Suffrage in China*. Stanford, CA: Stanford University Press, 2008.

Egić, Obrad. *Žene borci Druge Proleterske Dalmatinske narodnooslobodilačke udarne brigade*. Zadar: "Narodni List," 1983.

Einhorn, Barbara. *Cinderella Goes to Market: Citizenship, Gender, and Women's Movements in East Central Europe*. New York: Verso, 1993.

Emmert, Thomas. "Ženski Pokret: The Feminist Movement in Serbia in the 1920s." In *Gender Politics in the Western Balkans: Women and Society in Yugoslavia and the Yugoslav Successor States*. Edited by Sabrina P. Ramet, 33–50. University Park: Pennsylvania State University Press, 1999.

Engel, Barbara. "Soviet Women Remember World War II." In *Women and War in the Twentieth century: Enlisted with or without Consent*. Edited by Nicole Ann Dombrowski, 138–61. New York: Garland, 1999.

Erlich, Vera St. *Family in Transition: A Study of 300 Yugoslav Villages*. Princeton, NJ: Princeton University Press, 1966.

Fidelis, Malgorzata. *Women, Communism, and Industrialization in Postwar Poland*. New York: Cambridge University Press, 2010.

Ford, Kirk. *OSS and the Yugoslav Resistance, 1943–1945*. College Station: Texas A&M University Press, 1992.

Fürst, Julianne. "Heroes, Lovers, Victims – Partisan Girls during the Great Fatherland War." *Minerva* 18.3–4: (Fall–Winter 2000): 38–74.

Gavrilović, Vera S. *Žene lekari u ratovima 1876–1945. Na tlu Jugoslavije*. Belgrade: Naučno društvo za istoriju zdravstvene kulture Jugoslavije, 1976.

Gilmartin, Christina Kelley. *Engendering the Chinese Revolution: Radical Women, Communist Politics, and Mass Movements in the 1920s*. Berkeley: University of California Press, 1995.

Gligović-Zeković, Ruža. *San i vidici: žene nikšićkog kraja u NOB*. Nikšić: Organizacija žena i SUBNOR, 2000.

Goldman, Wendy. *Women at the Gates: Gender and Industry in Stalin's Russia*. New York: Cambridge University Press, 2002

Women, the State, and Revolution: Soviet Family Policy and Social Life. New York: Cambridge University Press, 1993.

Gordiejew, Paul Benjamin. *Voices of Yugoslav Jewry.* Albany: State University of New York Press, 1999.

Goulding, Daniel J. *Liberated Cinema: The Yugoslav Experience, 1945–2001.* Bloomington: Indiana University Press, 2002.

Grayzel, Susan. *Women's Identities at War: Gender, Motherhood, and Politics in Britain and France during the First World War.* Chapel Hill: University of North Carolina Press, 1999.

Greble, Emily. *Sarajevo 1941–1945: Muslims, Christians, and Jews in Hitler's Europe.* Ithaca, NY: Cornell University Press, 2011.

Grémaux, René. "Woman Becomes Man in the Balkans." *Third Sex, Third Gender: Beyond Sexual Dimorphism in Culture and History.* Edited by Gilbert Herdt, 241–81. New York: Zone Books, 1994.

Griesse, Anne E. and Richard Stites. "Russia: Revolution and War." *Female Soldiers – Combatants or Non-Combatants? Historical and Contemporary Perspectives.* Edited by Nancy L. Goldman. Westport, CT: Greenwood Press, 1982.

Gudac-Dodič, Vera. "Položaj žene u Srbiji (1945–2000)." In *Srbija u Modernizacijskim procesima XIX i XX veka,* vol. 4: *Žene i deca.* Edited by Latinka Perović, 33–130. Beograd: Helsinški odbor za ljudska prava, 2006.

Žena u Socijalizmu: Položaj žene u Srbiji u drugoj polovini 20. veka. Beograd: INIS, 2006.

Hart, Janet. *New Voices in the Nation: Women and the Greek Resistance, 1941–1964.* Ithaca, NY: Cornell University Press, 1996.

Hawkesworth, Celia. *Voices in the Shadows: Women and Verbal Art in Serbia and Bosnia.* Budapest: Central European University Press, 2000.

Hayden, Robert M. "Recounting the Dead: The Rediscovery and Redefinition of Wartime Massacres in Late- and Post-Communist Yugoslavia." In *Memory, History, and Opposition Under State Socialism.* Edited by Rubie S. Watson, 167–84. Santa Fe, NM: School of American Research Press, 1994.

Heinemann, Marlene. *Gender and Destiny: Women Writers and the Holocaust.* Westport, CT: Greenwood Press, 1986.

Higonnet, Margaret R. et al., eds. *Behind the Lines: Gender and the Two World Wars.* New Haven, CT: Yale University Press, 1987.

Hoare, Marko A. *Genocide and Resistance in Hitler's Bosnia: The Partisans and the Chetniks, 1941–1943.* Oxford, New York: Published for the British Academy by Oxford University Press, 2006.

"The People's Liberation Movement in Bosnia and Herzegovina, 1941–1945: What Did It Mean to Fight for a Multi-National State?" *Nationalism and Ethnic Politics* 2 (1996): 415–45.

Hobsbawm, Eric and Terence Ranger, ed. *The Invention of Traditions.* New York: Cambridge University Press, 1992.

Hoepken, Wolfgang. "War, Memory, and Education in a Fragmented Society: The Case of Yugoslavia." *East European Politics and Societies* 13.1 (Winter 1999): 190–227.

Hoffmann, David. *Stalinist Values: The Cultural Norms of Soviet Modernity, 1917–1941.* Ithaca, NY: Cornell University Press, 2003.

Ilić, Nikola P. "Žene Jablanice i Puste Reke u NOB 1941–1942. god," *Leskovački zbornik* 38 (1998): 221–33.

Irvine, Jill A. *The Croat Question: Partisan Politics in the Formation of the Yugoslav Socialist State.* With a foreword by Ivo Banac. Boulder, CO: Westview Press, 1993.

Jalušič, Vlasta. "Women in Interwar Slovenia." In *Gender Politics in the Western Balkans: Women and Society in Yugoslavia and the Yugoslav Successor States.* Edited by Sabrina P. Ramet, 51–66. University Park: Pennsylvania State University Press, 1999.

Jambrešić, Renata. "Testimonial Discourse between National Narrative and Ethnography as Socio-Cultural Analysis." *Collegium Anthropologicum* 19 (1995): 17–27.

"Verbalno nasilje i (raz)gradnja kolektivnih identiteta u iskazima ratnih zarobljenika i političkih zatvorenika." *Narodna Umjetnost* 37.2 (2000): 181–98.

Jancar, Barbara. "Women in the Yugoslav National Liberation Movement: An Overview," *Studies in Comparative Communism* 14.2 (1981): 143–64.

Jancar-Webster, Barbara. *Women and Revolution in Yugoslavia, 1941–1945.* Denver, CO: Arden Press, 1990.

"Women in the Yugoslav National Liberation Movement." In *Gender Politics in the Western Balkans: Women and Society in Yugoslavia and the Yugoslav Successor States.* Edited by Sabrina P. Ramet, 67–88. University Park: Pennsylvania State University Press, 1998.

Jelinek, Yeshayahu. "On the Condition of Women in Wartime Slovakia and Croatia." In *Labyrinth of Nationalism, Complexities of Diplomacy.* Edited by Richard Frucht, 190–213. Columbus, OH: Slavica, 1992.

Johnson, Chalmers A. *Peasant Nationalism and Communist Power: The Emergence of Revolutionary China, 1937–1945.* Stanford, CA: Stanford University Press, 1962.

Johnson, Kay Ann. *Women, the Family, and Peasant Revolution in China.* Chicago: University of Chicago Press, 1983.

Jolluck, Katherine. *Exile & Identity: Polish Women in the Soviet Union during World War II.* Pittsburgh: University of Pittsburgh Press, 2002.

Kapor-Stanulovic, Nila and Henry P. David, "Former Yugoslavia and Successor States." In *From Abortion to Contraception: A Resource to Public Policies and Reproductive Behavior in Central and Eastern Europe from 1917 to the Present.* Edited by Henry P. David, 279–316. Westport, CT: Greenwood Press, 1999.

Kecić, Danilo, ed. *Žene Vojvodine u ratu i revoluciji, 1941–1945.* Novi Sad: Institut za istoriju, 1984.

Kecman, Jovanka. *Žene Jugoslavije u radničkom pokretu i ženskim organizacijama.* Beograd: Narodna knjiga, 1978.

Kenez, Peter. "Black and White: The War on Film." In *Culture and Entertainment in Wartime Russia.* Edited by Richard Stites, 157–75. Bloomington: Indiana University Press, 1995.

Krippner, Monica. *The Quality of Mercy: Women at War, Serbia 1915–1918.* Newton Abbot: David & Charles, 1980.

Koljević, Svetozar. *The Epic in the Making.* New York: Oxford University Press, 1980.

Kolsti, John. "From Courtyard to Cabinet: The Political Emergence of Albanian Women." In *Women, State, and Party in Eastern Europe.* Edited by Sharon L. Wolchik and Alfred Meyer, 138–51. Durham, NC: Duke University Press, 1985.

Kosanović, Dejan and Dinko Tucaković. *Stranci u raju.* Beograd: Biblioteka Vek, 1998.

Kovačević, Dušanka, ed. *Borbeni put žena Jugoslavije.* Beograd: Leksikografski zavod "Sveznanje," 1972.

Women of Yugoslavia in the National Liberation War. Belgrade: Jugoslovenski Pregled, 1977.

Kovačević, Srbislava-Marija. "Antifašistički front žena u Vojvodini, 1941–1945." In *Žene Vojvodine u ratu i revoluciji, 1941–1945.* Edited by Danilo Kecić, 93–125. Novi Sad: Institut za istoriju, 1984.

Krylova, Anna. *Soviet Women in Combat: A History of Violence on the Eastern Front.* New York: Cambridge University Press, 2010.

"Stalinist Identity from the Viewpoint of Gender: Rearing a Generation of Professionally Violent Women Soldiers in 1930s Stalinist Russia." *Gender and History* 16.3 (November 2004): 626–53.

Kučan, Viktor. "Sutjeska – Dolina Heroja – Žene Borci." *Vojnoistorijski Glasnik* 39, no. 3 (1988): 183–247; 40 no. 1 (1989): 101–60; 40, no. 2 (1989): 49–126; 40, no. 3 (1989): 139–89; 41, no. 1 (1990): 127–89.

Lagator, Špiro and Milorad Čukić. *Partizanke Prve Proleterske.* Beograd: "Eksport-pres" i Konferencija za pitanja društvenog položaja žena u Jugoslaviji, 1978.

Lapidus, Gail. *Women in Soviet Society: Equality, Development, and Social Change.* Berkeley: University of California Press, 1978.

Lees, Michael. *The Rape of Serbia: The British Role in Tito's Grab for power, 1943–1944.* San Diego: Harcourt Brace Jovanovich, 1990.

Leček, Suzana. "'Ženske su sve radile': Seljačka žena između tradicije i modernizacije u sjeverozapadnoj Hrvatskoj između dva svjetska rata." In *Žene u Hrvatskoj: Ženska i kulturna povijest.* Edited by Andrea Feldman, 211–34. Zagreb: Ženska infoteka, 2004.

Levi, Pavle. *Disintegration in Frames: Aesthetics and Ideology in the Yugoslav and Post-Yugoslav Cinema.* Stanford, CA: Stanford University Press, 2007.

Lilly, Carol S. *Power and Persuasion: Ideology and Rhetoric in Communist Yugoslavia, 1944–1953.* Boulder, CO: Westview Press, 2001.

Lines, Lisa. *Milicianas: Women in Combat in the Spanish Civil War.* Lanham, MD: Lexington Books, 2012.

Lord, Albert Bates. *The Singer of Tales.* Cambridge: Harvard University Press, 1960.

ed. *The Multinational Literature of Yugoslavia.* Jamaica, NY: St. John's University, 1974.

Maksey, Kenneth. *The Partisans of Europe in the Second World War.* New York: Stein and Day, 1975.

Markwick, Roger D. and Euridice Charon Cardona. "'Our Brigade Will Not Be Sent to the Front': Soviet Women under Arms in the Great Fatherland War, 1941–45." *Russian Review* 68.2 (2009): 242.

Soviet Women on the Frontline in the Second World War. New York: Palgrave Macmillan, 2012.

Martin, Terry. "Modernization or Neo-Traditionalism: Ascribed Nationality and Soviet Primordialism." In *Russian Modernity: Politics, Knowledge, Practices.* Edited by David Hoffmann and Yanni Kotsonis, 161–82. New York: St. Martin's Press, 2000.

Milinović, Daško and Zoran Petakov, eds. *Partizanke – Žene u Narodnooslobodilačkoj borbi.* Novi Sad: CENZURA, 2010.

Mladenović, Stanko. *Spasenija Cana Babović.* Belgrade: Rad 1980.

Mosely, Philip E. *Communal Families in the Balkans: The Zadruga.* Edited by Robert F. Byrnes. Introduction by Margaret Mead. Notre Dame, IN: University of Notre Dame Press, 1976.

Naiman, Eric. *Sex in Public: The Incarnation of Early Soviet Ideology.* Princeton, NJ: Princeton University Press, 1997.

Naimark, Norman. *Fires of Hatred: Ethnic Cleansing in Twentieth-Century Europe.* Cambridge, MA: Harvard University Press, 2001.

Nash, Mary. *Defying Male Civilization: Women in the Spanish Civil War.* Denver, CO: Arden Press, 1998.

Noggle, Anne. *A Dance with Death: Soviet Airwomen in World War II.* College Station: Texas A&M University Press, 1994.

Nora, Pierre. *Realms of Memory: Rethinking the French Past.* Vols. 1–3. New York: Columbia University Press, 1996–8.

Pantelić, Ivana. "Dejanović Draga." In *Biographical Dictionary of Women's Movements and Feminisms in Central, Eastern, and South Eastern Europe: 19th and 20th Centuri.* Edited by Francisca de Haan, Krasimira Daskalova, Anna Loutfi, 106–7. Budapest: Central European University Press, 2006.

Partizanke kao građanke: društvena emancipacija partizanki u Srbiji, 1945–1953. Beograd: Institut za savremenu istoriju, 2011.

Passmore, Kevin, ed. *Women, Gender, and Fascism in Europe, 1919–45.* New Brunswick, NJ: Manchester University Press, 2003.

Pavlowitch, Stevan. *Hitler's New Disorder: The Second World War in Yugoslavia.* New York: Columbia University Press, 2008.

Penn, Shana, and Jill Massino, eds. *Gender Politics and Everyday Life in State Socialist Eastern and Central Europe.* New York: Palgrave Macmillan, 2009.

The Improbable Survivor: Yugoslavia and Its Problems, 1918–1988, Columbus: Ohio State University Press, 1988.

Pennington, Reina. *Wings, Women and War: Soviet Airwomen in World War II Combat.* Lawrence: University Press of Kansas, 2001.

Perović, Latinka. "Kako žena vidi sebe u vreme otvaranja 'ženskog pitanja' u srpskom društvu." *Tokovi istorije* 1–2 (2000): 9–18.

ed. *Srbija u modernizacijskim procesima XX veka (Naučni skup)*. Beograd: Institut za noviju istoriju Srbije, 1994.

ed. *Srbija u modernizacijskim procesima 19. i 20. veka. Vol 2: Položaj žene kao merilo modernizacije*. Beograd: Institut za noviju istoriju Srbije, 1998.

ed. *Srbija u modernizacijskim procesima 19. i 20. veka. Vol 4: Žene i Deca*. Beograd: Helsinški odbor za ljudska prava u Srbiji, 2006.

Pittaway, Mark. *The Workers' State: Industrial Labor and the Making of Socialist Hungary, 1944–1958*. Pittsburgh: University of Pittsburgh Press, 2012.

Pollard, Miranda. *Reign of Virtue: Mobilizing Gender in Vichy France*. Chicago: University of Chicago Press, 1998.

Predragović, Milenko. *Kata Pejnović: Životni put i revolucionarno delo*. Gornji Milanovac: Dečje novine, 1978.

Ramet, Sabrina. *Balkan Babel: The Disintegration of Yugoslavia from the Death of Tito to the Fall of Milosevic*. 4th ed. Boulder, CO: Westview Press, 2002.

"In Tito's Time." In *Gender Politics in the Western Balkans: Women and Society in Yugoslavia and the Yugoslav Successor States*. Edited by Sabrina P. Ramet, 89–105. University Park: Pennsylvania State University Press, 1999.

Nationalism and Federalism in Yugoslavia, 1962–1991. Bloomington: Indiana University Press, 1992.

Reed, Mary E. "The Anti-Fascist Front of Women and the Communist Party in Croatia: Conflicts Within the Resistance." In *Women in Eastern Europe and the Soviet Union*. Edited by Tova Yedlin, 129–39. New York: Praeger, 1980.

Roberts, Walter R. *Tito, Mihailovic, and the Allies, 1941–1945*. New Brunswick, NJ: Rutgers University Press, 1973.

Romano, Jaša. *Jevreji Jugoslavije, 1941–1945: Žrtve genocida i učesnici narodnooslobodilačkog rata*. Beograd: Savez Jevrejskih opština Jugoslavije, 1980.

Rossiter, Margaret L. *Women in the Resistance*. New York: Praeger, 1986.

Rothschild, Joseph. *Return to Diversity: A Political History of East Central Europe Since World War II*. 3rd ed. New York, Oxford: Oxford University Press, 2000.

Rousso, Henry. *The Vichy Syndrome: History and Memory in France since 1944*. Cambridge, MA: Harvard University Press, 1991.

Rupp, Leila. *Mobilizing Women for War: German and American Propaganda, 1939–1945*. Princeton, NJ: Princeton University Press, 1978.

Šarčević, Predrag. "'Tobelija': A Female-To-Male Cross-Gender Role in the 19th and 20th Century Balkans," *Studies on South Eastern Europe, Vol. 1: Between the Archives and the Field: A Dialogue on Historical Anthropology in the Balkans*. Edited by Miroslav Jovanović, Karl Kaser, Slobodan Naumović, 35–46. Münster: Lit, 2004.

"Sworn Virgins." In *Studies on South Eastern Europe, Vol. 3: Gender Relations in South Eastern Europe: Historical Perspectives on Womanhood and Manhood in 19th and 20th Century*. Edited by Miroslav Jovanović and Slobodan Naumović. Münster: Lit, 2004.

Sartorti, Rosalinde. "On the Making of Heroes, Heroines, and Saints." In *Culture and Entertainment in Wartime Russia*. Edited by Richard Stites, 176–93. Bloomington: Indiana University Press, 1995.

Saywell, Shelley. "Uprising: Poland, 1939–1945." *Women in War*. Markham, Ontario: Viking, 1985.

Schwartz, Paula. "'Partisanes' and Gender Politics in Vichy France." *French Historical Studies* 16.1 (1989): 126–51.

"Redefining Resistance: Women's Activism in Wartime France." In *Behind the Lines: Gender and the Two World Wars*. Edited by Margaret Higonnet et al., 141–53. New Haven, CT: Yale University Press, 1987.

Shepherd, Ben. *Terror in the Balkans: German Armies and Partisan Warfare*. Cambridge, MA: Harvard University Press, 2012.

Sklevicky, Lydia. "Emancipated Integration or Integrated Emancipation: The Case of Post-Revolutionary Yugoslavia." In *Current Issues in Women's History*. Edited by Arina Angerman with Judy de Ville, 93–108. London: Routledge, 1989.

"Karakteristike organiziranog djelovanja žena u Jugoslaviji u razdoblju do drugog svjetskog rata." Parts I and II. *Polja* 308 (October 1984): 415–16, and *Polja* 309 (November 1984): 454–6.

Konji, Žene, Ratovi. Zagreb: Ženska infoteka, 1996.

Organizirana djelatnost žena Hrvatske za vrijeme Narodnooslobodilačke borbe 1941–1945. Special publication *Povijesni Prilozi*. Zagreb: Institut za historiju radničkog pokreta Hrvatske, 1984.

"Der Utopie entgegen: Das Bild der 'Neuen Frau' im Befreiungskrieg Jugoslawiens 1941–1945." In *Frauenmacht in der Geschichte: Beiträge des Historikerinnentreffens 1985 zur Frauengeschichtsforschung*. Edited by Jutta Dalhoff, Uschi Frey, and Ingrid Schöll, 229–36. Dusseldorf: Schwann, 1986.

Slaughter, Jane. *Women and the Italian Resistance, 1943–1945*. Denver, CO: Arden Press, 1997.

Stacey, Judith. *Patriarchy and Socialist Revolution in China*. Berkeley: University of California Press, 1983.

Stites, Richard. *Russian Popular Culture: Entertainment and Society Since 1900*. New York: Cambridge University Press, 1992.

The Women's Liberation Movement in Russia: Feminism, Nihilism, and Bolshevism, 1860–1930. Princeton, NJ: Princeton University Press, 1977.

Stojaković, Gordana. "Skica za portret: Antifašistički Front Žena Vojvodine, 1942–1953," in *Partizanke – Žene u Narodnooslobodilačkoj borbi*. Edited by Daško Milinović and Zoran Petakov, 13–39. Novi Sad: CENZURA, 2010.

Stojić, Desanka. *Prva ženska partizanska četa*. Karlovac: Historijski Arhiv u Karlovcu, 1987.

Summerfield, Penny. "British Women in Transition from War to Peace," in *When the War Was Over: Women, War and Peace in Europe, 1940–1956*. Edited by Claire Duchen and Irene Bandhauer-Schoffman, 13–27. New York: Leicester University Press, 2000.

Todorova, Maria. *Balkan Family Structure and the European Pattern*. Washington, DC: American University Press, 1992.

Tomasevich, Jozo. *War and Revolution in Yugoslavia, 1941–1945: The Chetniks*. Stanford, CA: Stanford University Press, 1975.

War and Revolution in Yugoslavia, 1941–1945: Occupation and Collaboration. Stanford, CA: Stanford University Press, 2001.

"Yugoslavia during the Second World War," in *Contemporary Yugoslavia.* Edited by Wayne S. Vucinich, 59–118. Berkeley: University of California Press, 1969.

Vervenioti, Tassoula. "Left-Wing Women between Politics and Family." In *After the War Was Over: Reconstructing the Family, Nation, and State in Greece, 1943–1960.* Edited by Mark Mazower, 105–21. Princeton, NJ: Princeton University Press, 2000.

Veskovik-Vangeli, Vera. *Ženata vo osloboditelnite borbi na Makedonija 1893–1945.* Skopje: Kultura, 1990.

Ženata vo revolucijata na Makedonija 1941–1945. Skopje: Institut za nacionalna istorija, 1982.

Volk, Petar. *Savremeni Jugoslovenski Film.* Beograd: Univerzitet Umetnosti i Institut za film, 1983.

Wachtel, Andrew. *Making a Nation, Breaking a Nation: Literature and Cultural Politics in Yugoslavia.* Stanford, CA: Stanford University Press, 1998.

Wang, Zheng. *Women in the Chinese Enlightenment: Oral and Textual Histories.* Berkeley: University of California Press, 1999.

Weitz, Margaret Collins. *Sisters in the Resistance: How Women Fought to Free France, 1940–1945.* New York: John Wiley & Sons, 1995.

Wheeler, Mark. *Britain and the War for Yugoslavia.* Boulder, CO: East European Monographs, 1980.

Wheelwright, Julie. *Amazons and Military Maids: Women Who Dressed as Men in the Pursuit of Life, Liberty and Happiness.* London: Pandora Press, 1989.

Wiesinger, Barbara. *Partisaninnen: Widerstand in Jugoslawien (1941–1945).* Köln: Böhlau Verlag Köln, 2008.

Williams, Heather. *Parachutes, Patriots, and Partisans: The Special Operations Executive and Yugoslavia, 1941–1945.* London: C. Hurst, 2003.

Wingfield, Nancy M. and Maria Bucur, eds. *Gender and War in 20th Century Eastern Europe.* Bloomington: Indiana University Press, 2006.

Winter, Jay. *Sites of Memory, Sites of Mourning: The Great War in European Cultural History.* New York: Cambridge University Press, 1995.

Wood, Elizabeth. *The Baba and the Comrade: Gender and Politics in Revolutionary Russia.* Bloomington: Indiana University Press, 2000.

Wright, Gordon. *The Ordeal of Total War, 1939–1945.* New York: Harper & Row, 1968.

Young, Helen Praeger. *Choosing Revolution: Chinese Women Soldiers on the Long March.* Urbana: University of Illinois Press, 2001.

Žanić, Ivo. *Prevarena Povijest: Guslarska Estrada, Kult Hajduka i Rat u Hrvatskoj i Bosni i Hercegovini, 1990–1995. Godine.* Zagreb: Durieux, 1998.

Index

abortion, 156, 175, 183, 203–8,
    209, 216–17
Adriatic, 18, 23, 109, 232
Afrić, Vjekoslav, 232, 233f11, 242
AFW. *See* Antifascist Front of Women
agitprop, 48–50, 51, 159, 192, 237
Albania, 18, 62, 265
Alliance of Women's Movements,
    82–83, 87
Allies, 9, 21, 22, 23–24, 138, 166, 188,
    261, 266
Antifascist Council of National Liberation
    of Yugoslavia. *See* AVNOJ
Antifascist Front of Women, 4, 13, 15,
    28–29, 55, 76–77, 122–23
  charged with feminism, 116–20
  first conference of, 29, 55, 69,
    93–94, 225
  function and responsibilities of, 97–102
  organizational problems of, 102–5
  political neglect of, 108–11
  in postwar Yugoslavia, 217–19, 223,
    225, 226–28
  profile of women organized by, 94–97
  reorganization of, 120–22
  successes of, 105–7
AVNOJ, 23, 70, 93, 112, 130n16, 189
Axis forces, 17, 18, 20, 22, 24, 74, 89, 258

Babović, Spasenija Cana, 97, 154,
    172, 225
Bačka, 20, 135, 135n28
Banat, 18, 135, 151

Banija, 45, 108, 134, 135
Battle of Neretva, The (Bitka na Neretvi),
    1969 (film), 245–46
Bay of Kotor, 18, 38
Bebel, August, 208
Belgrade, 13, 18, 24, 81, 82, 84, 85, 87, 97,
    154, 226, 235, 246, 249, 253
Berus, Anka, 69
Big Three, 23, 24
Bihać, 23, 93
Bleiburg, 252, 254, 255
Bolsheviks, 68, 85, 170, 174, 179, 205, 208
Borba, 170, 178
Bosanski Petrovac, 93, 225, 228
Bosnia, 29, 33, 34, 42, 49, 85, 107,
    190, 200, 263. *See also* Bosnia and
    Herzegovina
Bosnia and Herzegovina, 20, 34, 42, 61,
    62, 83, 92, 102, 104, 233
Božović, Saša, 157n110, 204n103, 207
Bulajić, Veljko, 245
Bulgaria, 18, 60n109
Bursać, Marija, 124–25, 151
Bursać, Savka, 145f8

censorship, 49, 49n80, 165, 209, 237
Chernyshevsky, Nikolai, 79, 208
Chetniks, 8, 21, 22, 24, 33, 42, 47, 53, 89,
    104, 129, 132n19, 136, 137, 198, 224,
    246, 258
  propaganda of, 27, 184–85, 254, 267
  and Western Allies, 24, 188
  women's organizations of, 105–6

China, 129, 263–65
class struggle, 33, 36, 251
collectivization, 214, 215
Comintern, 86, 128
Communist International. *See* Comintern
communist orthodoxy, 33, 36, 85, 129,
    217, 237, 248
Communist Youth League, 29, 77, 87, 115,
    127, 135, 139, 192, 199, 200
Ćopić, Branko, 47, 48, 125n3, 235
Ćosić, Dobrica, 194, 235, 238–39
criticism and self-criticism, 178–80,
    183, 211
Croatia, 27, 29, 44, 80, 91, 98, 102, 104,
    116, 144, 153, 228, 240, 253, 254.
    See also Independent State of Croatia
Croatian army. *See* Home Guard

Dalmatia, 20, 21, 23, 38, 95, 104, 112,
    114, 135, 138, 189, 232, 233,
    236, 238
Dapčević, Peko, 211n126, 249
Dapčević, Vlado, 210, 211n126
de Gaulle, Charles, 266
Dedijer, Olga, 202
Dedijer, Vladimir, 33, 34, 48, 92, 94, 114,
    136, 179, 180, 181, 199, 202
divorce, 175, 200, 216
Djilas, Milovan, 34, 43, 45, 49, 177, 195,
    202, 209, 249–50
Domobrans. *See* Home Guard
Đorđević, Puriša, 242, 243
double standard, 16, 189, 211, 212, 268
double/triple burden, 150, 220
Drvar, 24, 28, 90, 103, 200

education, 35, 43, 49, 101, 106, 107, 197
    postwar, 220, 221–22, 238
    prewar, 79, 82, 84
employment, 82, 220, 223
epic poetry. *See* folklore

family, 175
    legislation/policy, 32, 175, 216
    traditional structure. *See* zadruga
female soldiers
    and conscription, 130
    military experience and training
        of, 138–40
    and motherhood, 153–58
    motivation of, 135–38

neglect of, 143–48
official memory of, 225–30
opposition to, 140–43
and party policy, 126–30
profile of, 133–35
remember the war, 164–66, 167, 268–69
withdrawal of, 158–63
and women's work, 148–51, 266–67
feminism
    communist views of, 78, 84–85, 116–18,
        119, 123. *See also* Antifascist Front of
        Women, charged with feminism
    feminist organizations. *See* women's
        organizations, interwar, feminist
First Female Company, 127, 134, 230
Five Year Plan
    and female employment, 220
Foča, 31, 92, 180, 199, 204
folklore
    Balkan heritage, 41, 57–59
    Partisan, 47–50
    in party rhetoric, 4, 14–15, 41–47,
        50–51, 64–67, 70, 73, 74–75, 259
Four by four (Četverored), 1999
    (film), 254–56
France, 163, 165, 260, 266, 268
"free love," 168, 169, 174, 176, 184, 185,
    194, 208

German military. *See* Wehrmacht
Germany, 12n25, 17, 18, 21, 91, 135n28
Gestapo, 155, 246, 247
Gorski Kotar, 104, 135, 246
Goulding, Daniel, 235, 240
Greece, 17, 49, 73, 74, 165, 265, 268
Gubec, Matija, 44

hajduks, 41, 42, 43, 44, 45, 58, 63
Herzegovina, 33, 35, 38, 60, 115, 142,
    160, 194. *See also* Bosnia and
    Herzegovina
Hitler, Adolf, 17
Hočevar Mali, Albina, 146
Hoffmann, David, 74, 174
Home Guard, 21, 24, 132n19, 160,
    160n117, 197n74, 198
homosexuality, 175, 195
hospitals, 132, 144, 156, 159, 160, 161,
    198, 204, 205, 207
    Central Hospital, 204, 245
Hungary, 20

Ibarruri, Dolores, 93, 173n10
Independent State of Croatia, 18, 20, 21,
    23, 104, 134, 136, 252, 255
Internal Macedonian Revolutionary
    Organization (IMRO), 63
International Women's Day, 50, 84, 225
Istria, 53, 58n106, 135
Italy, 18, 21, 23, 79, 116, 135, 138, 163,
    188, 189, 197, 233, 260, 268

Jajce, 23, 50, 103
Jancar-Webster, Barbara, 10, 29, 36
Janković, Rava, 71, 149, 201
Jasenovac, 252, 252n62
Jews, 20, 135, 136
Jones, William, 2, 149–50
Jugović Mother, 26, 30, 50, 51, 51n85, 52

Karadžić, Vuk, 38–40, 41, 58n106
Kardelj, Edvard, 92, 129
Kollontai, Alexandra, 174, 175, 205, 208
Komnenić-Džaković, Jelisavka, 138
Končar, Dragica, 155
Kordun, 95, 98, 102, 108, 135
Kosmodem'ianskaia, Ljubov, 54–55
Kosmodem'ianskaia, Zoia, 54–55
Kosovo, 18, 34, 63, 135
Kosovo, Battle of, 41, 42, 43, 44, 51, 52
Kosovo Maiden, 30, 51, 51n85, 67, 67n128
Kovačić, Ivan Goran, 47, 47n66
Kovačić, Olga, 97
Kozara, 51, 227f10
Kozarčanka, 227f10
Krleža, Miroslav, 237
Kulenović, Skender, 46, 51–52, 55, 230
Kveder, Zofka, 80

left deviationism, 32–33, 36, 43, 194
Lenin, Vladimir, 173, 175, 195, 204
Lika, 29, 38, 48, 55, 89, 90, 91, 95, 96, 97,
    98, 104, 109, 127, 134, 135, 139, 141,
    161, 162f9, 230
literacy, 34, 35, 82, 84, 88, 97, 101, 114,
    192, 219
Ljubljana, 18, 82, 97, 237

Macedonia, 18, 61, 63, 135, 253
Maclean, Fitzroy, 155, 209
Mao Zedong, 173n10
Marić-Vujanović, Duja, 149
Marković, Svetozar, 79

marriage
    legislation, 32, 216
    Partisan policy, 199–202
Materić, Danica, 72
Mažuranić, Ivan, 38
medics. *See sanitet*
Mešterović, Julka, 204n103, 204n104
Mihailović, Draža, 8, 21, 22, 106
Milosavljević, Danica (Dana), 138, 146
Milošević, Sima, 93
Milošević, Slobodan, 253
Mitrović, Mitra, 97, 110, 128, 149, 157,
    202, 209
Montenegro, 18, 21, 23, 31, 33, 37, 38, 42,
    43, 61, 97, 114, 128, 131, 134, 139,
    157, 160, 184, 191
Morača, Mira, 89, 97, 103
Morning (Jutro), 1967 (film),
    242–43
Moscow, 5, 34, 52, 54, 77, 97, 128, 129,
    163, 172, 174, 176, 183, 195, 204,
    205, 262
Mostar, 155, 194
Mother Margarita, 26, 51n85
Mother of the Jugovićs, the. *See*
    Jugović Mother
motherhood, 30, 175, 205, 206
    imagery of, 50–57, 229–30,
        239, 257
    and Partisan women. *See* female soldiers
        and motherhood
Mountain Wreath, The, 38, 42, 43
Mussolini, Benito, 188

Nazor, Vladimir, 27, 50, 214
Nedić, Milan, 18, 183
Neretva, Battle of, 159, 233, 245
Njegoš, Petar II Petrović (see also
    Mountain Wreath, The), 37, 43
Novosel, Vanda, 97
nurses. *See sanitet*

Officer with a Rose (Oficir s ružom), 1987
    (film), 248, 250–51
Operation Schwartz. *See* Sutjeska,
    Battle of
Operation Weiss. *See* Neretva,
    Battle of
orphanages, 82, 98
Ottoman Empire, 41, 42, 43, 44,
    63, 80

Partisan units
  5th Montenegrin Proletarian Brigade,
    130, 159
  1st Dalmatian Proletarian Shock
    Brigade, 147
  1st Proletarian Brigade, 23, 134,
    134n26, 146
  4th Montenegrin Proletarian Brigade,
    130, 131f6, 139, 159, 188
  2nd Proletarian Brigade, 93, 146
  7th Banija Shock Division, 134, 135
  6th Bosnian Shock Brigade, 140, 188
  6th Krajina Division, 145f8
  6th Lika Division, 162f9
  16th Slavonian brigade 4th Divsion, 35
  3rd Sandžak Proletarian Brigade, 141f7
  13th Proletarian Brigade "Rade
    Končar," 203
  12th Herzegovinian Shock Brigade, 132
  12th Krajina Shock Brigade, 143, 210
  21st Shock Brigade, 148
partizankas. *See* female soldiers
Pavelić, Ante, 20, 21, 104
peasant women
  preponderance in Partisan units,
    29, 133–34
  preponderance in the AFW, 29, 95
  and the "promise of gender equality,"
    31–32, 35–37
peasantry. *See also* left deviationism
  communist views of, 33–35
  support for Partisans, 13, 36–37, 263–64
Pejnović, Kata, 55–56, 96, 97, 112
Pijade, Moša, 209
Poland, 261
Popović, Mića, 243, 244
private life
  norms, 171–78
  regulations, 186–95
Proleter, 110, 142, 170, 171, 175–76,
    205, 206
prostitution, 176, 190, 195–96, 210,
    211, 268
purges, 25, 172, 174. *See also* left
  deviationism

Ranković, Aleksandar, 180, 181, 191, 202,
    222, 239
Ranković, Andja, 202n97
rape, 136–37, 193, 196, 253
Red Army (Chinese), 263–65

Red Army (Soviet), 13, 24, 128,
    129, 261–62
red terror. *See* left deviationism
Ribar, Ivan, 70
Ribar, Ivo Lola, 92, 129
Rittig, Svetozar, 27n3, 51n85

Sandes, Flora, 64
Sandžak, 34, 195
sanitet, 127, 139–40, 152, 153
  neglect of, 144–47
  training, 139–40
  withdrawal of female nurses,
    159, 160–61
Sarajevo, 230, 254
Savić, Milunka, 63
Sedlar, Jakov, 255
Serbia, 18, 21, 32, 33, 34, 42, 70, 83, 84,
    85, 97, 106, 134, 138, 154, 240, 253
Slavica, 1947 (film), 232–35, 236–37, 238,
    242, 245
Slavonia, 20, 65, 83, 85, 113, 140, 179
Slovenia, 18, 20, 21, 23, 44, 60, 80, 83, 85,
    90, 135, 149, 153, 253
Šorak, Dejan, 248, 250
Soviet Union, 21, 36, 50, 119, 153,
    205, 206, 216, 262, 263, 264, 266,
    267, 268
Spain, 128, 129, 163, 266, 267, 268
Spanish Civil War, 25, 68, 89, 93, 128, 159,
    164, 268. *See also* Spain
Split, 87, 95, 232, 233, 234
Srem/Srijem, 20, 38, 66, 70, 96, 104, 105,
    107, 109, 113, 146, 147, 185. *See also*
    Srem/Srijem (Syrmian) front
Srem/Srijem (Syrmian) front, 24, 162f9
Stalin, Joseph, 23, 47, 93, 174, 205, 215,
    216, 218, 261
Stalinism, 15n30, 73, 172, 175, 204, 205,
    206, 208, 215, 216, 237
"Stojanka, Mother from Knežopolje"
  ("Stojanka Majka Knežopoljka"),
    1942 (poem), 51–52, 230
SUBNOR. *See* veterans' association
Sutjeska, Battle of, 133, 135, 159, 245

Tehran Conference, 23, 24
Tito, Josip Broz, 3, 6, 15, 22, 23, 24, 25,
    33, 47, 50, 69, 74, 92, 93, 112, 129,
    130, 146, 148, 155, 164, 171, 172,
    173, 174, 177, 189, 191, 197, 198,

209, 210, 213, 215, 216, 232, 234, 236, 240, 244, 245, 247, 266
Titoism, 17, 230, 231, 252
Tomšič, Vida, 97, 206
Tripartite Pact, 17
Tudjman, Franjo, 253, 254
typhus, 144, 153, 196

Udarnica, 70
uskoks, 41, 42, 43
Ustasha atrocities, 21, 90, 96, 128, 135, 136, 252
Ustasha propaganda, 168, 184, 255
Ustasha regime, 20–21, 90, 104, 188, 206. *See also* Independent State of Croatia
Ustashas, 20, 22, 27, 45, 47, 55, 65, 89, 136, 184, 224, 254, 258, 267
Užice, 22, 32, 33, 209, 210

venereal disease, 199, 209, 210, 211, 268
veterans' association, 225, 241, 254
village guard, 100
Vojvodina, 18, 20, 79, 85, 96, 100, 103, 105, 109, 134, 135, 138, 146, 151, 161, 177, 208
Volksdeutsche, 18
Vranješević, Rada, 45
Vrbica, Đina, 97, 156–57, 158, 207–8

Wachtel, Andrew, 46, 235, 238
Wehrmacht, 1, 21, 23
women soldiers. *See* female soldiers
women's organizations
   before World War I, 78–81, 83–85
   interwar, feminist, 77–78, 83, 87–89
   interwar, socialist, 77–78, 85–89
   postwar, 217–19
   wartime. *See* Antifascist Front of Women; Chetniks, women's organizations of
"women's work," 114, 148–51, 266–67

Yugoslav government in exile, 21, 23, 24
Yugoslav Women's League, 81–82
Yugoslavia
   wartime partition of, 18–20

zadruga, 32, 60–61, 186
Zagreb, 82, 87, 88, 97, 155, 199, 223, 235, 248, 250, 255, 256
ZAVNOBiH, 50n84
ZAVNOH, 50n84
Žena danas, 53, 88, 97
Žena u borbi, 91
Zetkin, Clara, 84
Zhenotdel, 118–19, 122
Žujović, Sreten, 209

CPSIA information can be obtained
at www.ICGtesting.com
Printed in the USA
LVHW100959160522
718889LV00004B/62